Instructor's Manual to Accompany

A History of Narrative Film
Second Edition

Instructor's Manual to Accompany

A History of Narrative Film
Second Edition

David A. Cook
Emory University

W. W. Norton & Company
New York   London

Copyright © 1991 by W.W. Norton & Company, Inc.

Printed in the United States of America.

Composition by Special Projects Group
Manufacturing by Capital City Press

First Edition.
Library of Congress Cataloging in Publication Data

ISBN 0-393-95725-X

W.W. Norton & Company, Inc., 500 Fifth Avenue, New York, N.Y. 10110
W.W. Norton & Company, Ltd., 10 Coptic Street, London WC1A 1PU

1 2 3 4 5 6 7 8 9 0

Table of Contents

Introduction

This manual is divided into four unequal parts. Part I is a chapter-by-chapter guide to the text itself; Part II contains the endnotes to the text, many of which are substantive and carry their own bibliographical/filmographical appendices; Part III is a collection of sample syllabi, screening schedules, tests, and exams for a year-long survey course in film history of the sort that I teach at Emory University; and Part IV provides a brief listing of useful film and video sources. While the contents of Parts II, III, and IV are quite specific, the chapter-by-chapter guide contains three different kinds of information: a summary and rationalization of the text, suggestions for practical classroom teaching strategies and use of media, and additions and corrections to the text.

All of this material assumes the regular use of film and/or video excerpts in class, as well as the weekly out-of-class screening of features. At Emory, we have been able to set up all of our film courses on Tuesday/Thursday schedules with 80-minute classes. I usually break this time into three parts—lecture, audio-visual presentation, and discussion—whose length varies depending on the subject. I also sometimes integrate taped excerpts with lecture/discussion for an entire period. In both cases, I talk while the images are on-screen, which is especially appropriate for silent films but works perfectly well with low-volume sound. Of course, video has the advantages of freeze-frame and instant replay (and, if you are fortunate enough to have laserdisc technology, random access), and I resort to these features frequently in class. For the out-of-class screenings, on the other hand, I generally use projected 16mm film, and try to approximate the original experience of seeing it in a theater—including the use of recorded scores and restored tints for silent films whenever possible (which, for reasons of budget, sometimes brings me back to video).

Part I

Chapter-by-Chapter Guide

Chapter 1

Origins

The age of video has produced many wonders, among them a generation of undergraduate students who have never held a strip of motion-picture film in their hands. To counter this, I circulate strips of 16mm and 35mm film at the beginning of the course while I explain persistence of vision and the other optical phenomena involved in motion perception. I also use a model of a Zoetrope containing several strips of phase drawings, which I fabricated myself, and a variety of riffle books containing phase photographs, which can be found today in novelty stores and in many children's cereal boxes (e.g., Post Sugar Crisp). These toys help to concentrate attention on the nuts and bolts of motion-picture technology, since the illusions they create are the same, but the basic principles of camera and projection engineering should be diagrammed on the board for complete comprehension.

By the time I've reached this stage, I usually also put a timeline on the board (explaining that all such schema are necessarily simplistic), which begins with Roget's paper on of persistence of vision in 1824, proceeds through its application in phase drawing and—after the period 1839–45 (Daguerre through Fox Talbot)—phase photograph machines, the development of series photography in the 1870s (Muybridge) and 1880s (Marey), and finally the invention of the Kinetograph (Dickson) in 1889. The period from 1889 to 1895 witnessed the perfection of camera and projection technology, culminating in the Lumière Cinématographe, a machine combining both functions.

This timeline can now be extended to include the rest of the material in Chapter 1—the development of continuity editing and the rise of the exhibition sector—as follows. The period 1896–1900 was dominated by single-shot films (e.g., Edison Kinetograph shorts, Lumière *actualités*), usually less than one minute in length, which were perceived by their multi-class audiences as "animated photographs" within a frame. Exhibition was irregular and took place in temporary sites, most projectionists being itinerant showmen who bought their prints outright from the producer. The period 1901–5 saw the development of short multi-scene narratives (e.g., *A trip to the Moon* [Méliès, 1902], *The Life of an American Fireman* [Méliès, 1903]), usually less than ten minutes in length, that employed sequentially overlapping continuities. Exhibition became regular but its sites were still temporary (i.e., not specifically dedicated to the showing of films), and the audience had become distinctly working class. The period 1906–13 was dominated by the development of classical-style Hollywood continuity editing (e.g., Griffith's Biograph films, 1908–13), the standardization of film length at one reel (1,000 feet, or 10–12 minutes), and the spread of the first permanent exhibition sites in the nickelodeons, some 10,000 of which had appeared in the United States by 1908. Whereas itinerant exhibitors had been able to travel from one temporary site to the next with only a single (or no more than several) program(s), permanent theaters meant permanent audiences, and exhibitors now had to vary their programs regularly to attract them. The advent of the nickelodeons thus caused a shift from the practice of buying prints outright to leasing them, which both stimulated a demand for new product and gave rise to the distribution sector of the industry. Film length was standardized at one reel as a unit of trade to facilitate exchange among producers, distributors, and exhibitors.

I usually teach the development of film narrative concurrently with the industrial history of film, since the two are so completely intertwined. I move from a discussion of the unprecedented impact of the moving photographic image on early audiences to Méliès' and Porter's construction of overlapping continuities which enabled their audiences to infer meaning from one scene or shot to the next. On the history and dynamics of these overlapping continuities, there is simply no better source than Charles Musser's *Before the Nickelodeon: The Early Cinema of Edwin S. Porter* (1982), available for classroom use in both 16mm and video (see Part IV for details). This 53-minute film contains much of Porter's early work, including *The Execution of Czolgosz* (1901), *Jack and the Beanstalk* (1902), *How They Do Things on the Bowery* (1902), and both the Cross-Cut and Copyright versions of *Life of an American Fireman*, and it very effectively demonstrates some of the spatial, temporal, and narrative problems that early continuity editing attempted to resolve. Other fine sources are *Film before Griffith* (Berkeley: University of California Press, 1983), edited by John L. Fell, which contains 29 separate essays on early industrial practices and film form: *Early Cinema: Space-Frame-Narrative* (London: British Film Institute Publishing, 1990), edited by Thomas Elsaesser: Musser's own critical book on Porter, *Before the Nickelodeon* (Berkeley: University of California Press, 1990), and his *The Emergence of Cinema: The American Screen to 1907* (New York: Charles Scribner's Sons, 1990), Volume 1 of the ten-volume *A History of American Cinema* project.

Major endnotes for Chapter 1 deal with the psychophysiology of motion perception in motion pictures; Muybridge's later work; the "Edison motion picture myth"; the firm of Raff and Gammon; Louis Le Prince; the structure of Lumière actualités, the relationship between professional magic and early cinema; a bibliography of scholarship on early filmic representation; the influence of the "Brighton school" on Porter; the relationship between parallel editing and other forms of serial representation; the controversy over the Cross-Cut and Copyright versions of *Life of an American Fireman*; the relationship between film and vaudeville; and a bibliography on the nickelodeon boom and various controversies about it.

Chapter 2

International Expansion, 1907–1918

Students should understand that the film industry has always been heavily capital-intensive and that its operations are fundamentally wed to business cycles. Furthermore, the patterns that emerged in the period 1907–18 are still very much intact—the industry is still highly concentrated, centered in Hollywood, and geared to the production of features. In general, students resist thinking about film history in economic terms only to the extent that those terms are abstract; but when business configurations can be shown to have a direct impact on film style and content (as they inevitably do), interest warms.

The Motion Picture Patents Company (MPPC), or Edison "Trust," it should be emphasized, was only the first of several monopoly configurations that have dominated the American film industry in its brief history. A tendency toward monopoly is inherent in any business that depends on technical patents and machines, but when the product is entertainment that tendency

is even more pronounced (consider, e.g., the monopolization of vaudeville and of radio broadcasting in the periods just before and after 1907–18). At first, the MPPC focused on controlling production and exhibition through a patents' pool, but in 1910 it moved to control distribution as well by forming the General Film Company. This shift was conditioned by the fact that distribution had become the most lucrative sector of the industry in the wake of the nickelodeon boom (see Chapter 1, pp. 30–31)—and it has remained so ever since. Contrary to popular opinion, the independent distributors and exhibitors who stood against the Trust were quite well organized, and they formed protective trade associations of their own in imitation of the MPPC and General Film. Initially, the Trust and the independents competed for control of the same product—the one-reel short—but between 1911–12 later independents like William Fox and Adolph Zukor adopted the multiple-reel film as their basic product and stimulated public demand for features.

The industry's conversion to the production of features (defined at the time as any film of four or more reels) in and around the watershed year 1914 can be used to organize the rest of the material in the American section of Chapter 2. Because of their length, features were able to credibly adapt such popular bourgeois forms as novels and plays, and this appeal to the middle class was heightened by the spread of a new kind of theater—the urban "dream palaces"—whose luxurious accommodations would soon replace the cramped, converted storefronts of the nickelodeons, as the motion picture audience became increasingly multi-class and massified. The rise of the star system and the move to Hollywood were also related to the feature boom, since product differentiation and year-round shooting were both necessary to meet rising production costs. So too was the national system of distribution forged by Zukor and the other new studio chiefs (all former independents) through the practice of "block booking" and their aggressive acquisition of theater chains. By 1914, the American motion picture business was headed for vertical integration, and in the decade that followed, the demand for features would force its wholesale industrialization through the application of mass production techniques, division of labor, and a standardization of both manufacturing technology and product. Concurrently, the historical accident that was World War I enabled Hollywood to dominate the international film market by default, as well as by design. (A good source here is Kristin Thompson, *Exporting Entertainment: America and the World Film Market*, 1907–1934 [London: British Film Institute Publishing, 1985]; on the entire era, see Eileen Bowser, *The Transformation of the Cinema: 1908–1915* [New York: Charles Scribner's Sons, 1990], Volume 2 of the ten-volume *A History of the American Cinema* project.)

The Continental section of Chapter 2, can be related to the American section in several ways. First, the formation of both the French and Italian industries around powerful studios, and the brief periods of international dominance enjoyed by each (France, c. 1910; Italy, c. 1913), suggest the inherent tendency of cinema in capitalist economies toward monopoly control. Second, the filmed plays of the French *film d'art* movement (pp. 54–57) can be used to discuss the development of early narrative form by negative example. Third, the Italian superspectacle (pp. 57–60) provides an excellent way of moving toward the Griffith's epic ambitions, since he was decisively influenced by it. And, finally, the *films d'art* and superspectacles were directly responsible for increasing standard film length both in Europe and the United States, where they were imported by independents like Zukor and distributed as features to compete against the MPPC's one-reelers (see pp. 39–40).

Major endnotes for Chapter 2 concern "dream palace" proliferation in the twenties; the early-American industry in New Jersey; early French and Italian film comedians; Alice Guy-Blaché; and Segundo de Chomón as a pioneer of stop-motion animation.

Chapter 3

D. W. Griffith and the Consummation of Narrative Form

There has been a recent tendency to denigrate the work of D. W. Griffith and, with it, the so-called "great man" and/or "masterpiece" concept of film history. While this is no doubt a necessary corrective to what Janet Staiger has called the "Romantic auteurism" of decades past ("The Politics of Film Canons," *Cinema Journal*, 24, 3 [Spring 1985], 4–23), it can create some distortions of its own. Staiger herself, for example, suggests that Griffith's films should be thrown out of the canon because of "their racist, misogynist, and reactionary vision"—as if political correctness were somehow a criterion for artistic achievement. (An equivalent might be tossing Richard Wagner out of the history of Western music because he was a notorious anti-Semite—which has, of course, been suggested from time to time.) Rather than simply dismissing Griffith (or Wagner), it is better to acknowledge the distastefulness his world view and its particular inappropriateness to our own times, but then to accept and appreciate his unique role in the development of his century's most important art.

Griffith was a tireless self-promoter, and many of the techniques he claimed to have "invented" or "discovered" he simply learned how to use more effectively than his contemporaries. Furthermore, like that of any other filmmaker, Griffith's work was shaped by the material circumstances of its production—the availability of financing, the current state of motion-picture technology—much of which was beyond his control. But there was not a single one of his contemporaries, collaborators and critics alike, who did not finally attribute to Griffith the personal authorship of his films. And even today, when the assertion that Griffith invented nothing is as commonplace as the idea (in Joyce E. Jesionowski's phrase) "that he discovered all of cinema," it is impossible to deny his personal contributions to the medium. Because there actually were so many, and because so many more were claimed, Griffith's work becomes an excellent vehicle for teaching the fundamental principles of editing and camera-style which I categorize as "interframe" (pp. 64–69) and "intraframe" narrative (pp. 69–73) respectively.

Nearly all of these techniques evolved in the one- and two-reelers Griffith made for American Biograph, 1908–13, about which there was much misinformation until recently, because only a handful of these films were available in their original form. Since 1975, however, thanks to the efforts of Kemp Niver, Eileen Bowser, and others, most of these 450 films have become available in the archives of the Library of Congress and MoMA, and there is a new understanding about the importance and positioning of Griffith's work, as reflected in such critical books as Joyce E. Jesionowski's *Thinking in Pictures: Dramatic Structures in D. W. Griffith's Biograph Films* (Berkeley: University of California Press, 1987); and Tom Gunning's *D. W. Griffith and the Narrator System: Narrative Structure and Industry Organization in Biograph Films, 1908–1909* (Champaign, Illinois: University of Illinois Press, forthcoming), as well as in scholarly essays like Charlie Keil's "Transition through Tension: Stylistic Diversity in the Late Griffith Biographs" (*Cinema Journal* 28, 3 [Spring 1989], pp. 22–40). Many of these films are now available for instructional use in inexpensive 16mm and video formats, and I usually spend at least a week with the Biograph films before moving on to the mini-feature *Judith of Bethulia* (1913) as a bridge to *The Birth of a Nation* (1915).

In teaching *The Birth of a Nation*, it is helpful to remind students (as the text does on p. 82) that the American Civil War was a living memory for Griffith's audiences, standing in the same relationship to them as World War II and the Holocaust stand to us—that is, only one (and no more than two) generations removed. It is also useful to point out that the film's racial attitudes were not nearly so radical in 1915 as they are today, and that its version of Reconstruction was a commonly accepted one (pp. 80–82). All this said, *The Birth of a Nation* remains in many ways a shocking and repugnant film, difficult to teach and impossible to defend on political or moral grounds. It demands explanation, if not apology, in the same terms as Riefenstahl's *Triumph of the Will* (1935), which are those of formal and historical significance. And like the German film, it raises questions central to the liberal humanist tradition—can art be detached from moral judg-

ment? and can art and ideology (or propaganda for that matter) coexist?—questions which ultimately relate to issues of censorship and free speech. In fact, it was a 1915 Supreme Court decision (*Mutual v. Ohio*), upholding the right of the State of Ohio to ban *The Birth of a Nation*, that became the precedent for denying First Amendment protection to motion pictures in America for the next 40 years—a matter well worth discussing in class while reaction to the film runs high. So too is the film's social impact, which was basically to alarm every major institutional force in the country. As the first feature to achieve something close to national distribution, *The Birth of a Nation* was seen concurrently by a large number of people all over America, producing a mass reaction and backlash. In effect, the film had imposed an eccentric regional interpretation of American political reality on the entire nation with the credibility of an illustrated history lesson, creating a fearful new respect for motion pictures as an instrument of mass communication, persuasion, and social control.

Twenty years ago, *Intolerance* (1916) was the Griffith epic of choice for the classroom as the "liberal" alternative to its reactionary predecessor. But today *Intolerance* is almost universally recognized as the lesser work, "liberal" only in its substitution of ponderousness for radical unpleasantness. But it is still an extraordinary film, awesome in its narrative ambitions, even when they fail. Like *The Birth of a Nation*, *Intolerance* is currently available in several restored versions, with orchestral sound tracks and tints. While they vary in textual authenticity (a very difficult matter with Griffith in any case, because his major films were constantly recut by both himself and others), any of these scored and tinted prints will provide an instructive approximation of the era's theatrical experience, and several of his films are available on video. Of Griffith's later work, *Broken Blossoms* (1919) and *Way Down East* (1920) are the most accessible, and both are available in newly restored versions, as is *America* (1924). It is also useful to compare Griffith's first sound film, *Abraham Lincoln* (1930), with *The Birth of a Nation* since they contain many analogous scenes and the latter was re-released with a recorded orchestral score in the same year. (A fascinating eight-minute promotional interview with the director by Walter Huston on the re-release of *The Birth of a Nation* is available from Tamerelle's Film House, and is a good coda for the Griffith unit, as is an excerpt from Hal Roach Jr.'s *One Million B.C.* [1940] for whom Griffith reputedly directed the special effects.)

After briefly examining Griffith's precipitous decline and some of the reasons for it, such as the rapidly changing industry and audience standards wrought by World War I, I recapitulate his importance through several points. First, through a combination of circumstance and design, Griffith forged the narrative language of film as it is still practiced today, and he influenced everyone and everything that followed him. His approach to film form was largely intuitive—there was, for example, no written screenplay for *The Birth of a Nation*: Griffith carried its 1,544–shot continuity around *in his head* while he was shooting it. Second, he was in many ways the founder of "serious" cinema, for example, he made films of complex narrative form with subtleties of characterization and theme formerly thought possible only in theater and fiction. And third, through

The Birth of a Nation, its popularity, critical success, and scandal, Griffith helped to establish the American motion picture industry as big business; and he gave the twentieth century its first important lesson in the power of motion pictures as a mass medium, not just of entertainment, but of persuasion and propaganda—a lesson not lost on Vladimir Ilyich Lenin, who would offer Griffith the directorship of the Soviet film industry shortly after the Bolshevik Revolution.

Major endnotes for Chapter 3 deal with Griffith's acting career; the restoration of the Biograph films from Library of Congress paper prints; the nature of the 180-degree system; narrative structure in the early Biograph work; the origins of intercutting; material excised by Griffith from *The Birth of a Nation* after its New York première; the contents of the Griffith Papers; the *Hampton Epilogue* (1915) and the *Birth of a Race* (1918); the reception of *Intolerance*; and the anti-German marketing campaign for *Hearts of the World* (Griffith, 1918).

Chapter 4

German Cinema of the Weimar Period, 1919–1929

The cinema of German Expression and the Weimar Republic are fascinating to teach because they were produced by a people in the midst of convulsive social change—the most radical of the century outside of the Soviet Union. The catastrophic loss of World War I and the dissolution of Imperial Germany was compounded by a peace, embodied in the Treaty of Versailles, that defamed the country as the war's sole aggressor, imposing punitive and ultimately ruinous financial reparations. In a cycle of inflation without precedent in modern times, the accumulated wealth of the German middle class was rendered worthless; the interim military dictatorship of General Erich *Ludendorff* was replaced by the ultra-liberal Weimar Republic that governed for fifteen years without consensus while paramilitary organizations of the Left and Right turned the streets of Europe's most orderly society into a battleground.

Universum Film Aktiengesellschaft (UFA), the cartel which consolidated and energized the German film industry in December 1917, was founded out of a desperate need to rehabilitate the national image. From the outset of the war, the country had been the object of a vicious propaganda campaign mounted by the Allies, particularly Britain and the United States, which portrayed the Germans as a race apart. As Kevin Brownlow puts it, "The Germans lost their status as Europeans; embodying the most terrifying traits of ancient savagery, they became Huns," (*The War, the West, and the Wilderness* [New York; Alfred A. Knopf, 1979; p. 6]). Faked photographs and newsreel footage showing German soldiers committing atrocities in Belgium and France created myths perpetuated in popular "Hate-the-Hun" features like Griffith's *Hearts of the World* (1918), Raoul Walsh's *The Prussian Cur* (1918), and Universal's *The Kaiser—The Beast of Berlin* (1918), which the Germans, having no organized film industry, were hard pressed to refute. UFA was created at the executive order of General Ludendorff himself to counter this situation, its original charge to produce high-quality films to enhance Germany's image at home and abroad (pp. 114–16).

In the absence of a strong native tradition of film entertainment, circumstances conspired to make the postwar German cinema a self-consciously artistic one. During the war itself, Germany had been cut off from its normally large supply of British, French, and American films, and instead imported large numbers of films from neutral Sweden and Denmark. Innocent of American-style narrative montage, these productions were beautifully photographed by such world-class directors as Victor Sjöström and Mauritz Stiller (pp. 112–14), and their static, gloomy *mise-en-scène* was deeply influential on German film. Another formative influence was the *Aufbruch* (p. 115)—a revolutionary cultural break with the past to embrace the experimental and avant-garde—in the traditional arts, a rejection of naturalism in favor of Expressionism (p. 115), which blended over into Weimar cinema as well. UFA's first successful productions were the *Kostümefilme* of Ernst Lubitsch (pp. 115–16), but the prototype for German Expressionist film was Decla-Bioskop's *Das Kabinett des Dr. Caligari* (1919).

Caligari (pp. 117–21) is readily available in both 16mm and video, and it provides an excellent laboratory for Expressionism in both its generic and specific sense. I illustrate other films of the movement in class through a series of slides taken from Lotte H. Eisner's *The Haunted Screen* (Berkeley: University of California Press, 1969) and John Kobal's *Great Film Stills of the German Silent Era: 125 Stills from the Stiftung Deutsche Kinemathek* (Mineola, N.Y.: Dover Publications, 1981). These help to demonstrate the homogeneous texture of Expressionist decor and suggest the brooding psychological introspection that underwrites the films' relatively simple tales of horror and fantasy. The two major figures to emerge from Expressionism were Fritz Lang (pp. 121–24) and F. W. Murnau (pp. 124–31). For Lang, I invariably show *Metropolis* (1926) in a print scored with the original soundtrack available from a number of distributors (e.g., Filmic Archives, Golden Era); I also show taped excerpts from Giorgio Moroder's color-tinted 1984 restoration, which, despite its irritatingly inappropriate rock score, is based on a recently authenticated version of the original

script. The section on Murnau and *Der letzte Mann* (1924) introduces some fundamental concepts in camera movement and subjective camera styles, for which I distinguish both inner and outer modes.

The "Parufamet" Agreement of 1926 (pp. 131–32) is important for two reasons. First, by leading UFA four million dollars in exchange for collaborative rights, there was a mass migration of German talent to Hollywood, which by the mid-thirties (when a second wave of emigration was stimulated by the Nazis) had become known as "the new Weimar" (see endnotes for this section). Second, the Parufamet agreement made the UFA dependent on external subsidies, setting it up for Alfred Hugenberg's bailout of 1927; this maneuver led to his becoming chairman of the UFA board and enabled him to deliver the company to the Nazis in 1933. Meanwhile, in a course that paralleled that of German society itself, German cinema had moved from Expression through *Kammerspiel* to "street realism" in response to *die neue Sachlichkeit*— "the new objectivity"—that attempted to confront the increasingly grim consequences of hyper-inflation. (For a sophisticated analysis of how the Weimar cinema experimented with gender roles and gendered spectating "in a concerted effort to address a highly profitable female audience," see Patrice Petro, *Joyless Streets: Women and Melodramatic Representation in Weimar Germany* [Princeton: Princeton University Press, 1989].)

G. W. Pabst (pp. 132–36) is worth studying both as the major figure of this movement and as the innovator of "cutting on movement" in classical-style *continuity editing*, which is discussed at some length here. (See Eric Rentschler, ed. *The Films of G. W. Pabst: An Extraterritorial Cinema* [New Brunswick, N.J.: Rutgers University Press, 1990].) Pabst is also used to describe how motivated point-of-view can be maintained through the eyeline match and shot-reverse-shot figure (p. 135). I illustrate these techniques with excerpts from *Die Liebe der Jeanne Ney* (The Love of Jeanne Ney, 1927) and several *films noir* that regularly cut on movement in their dialogue sequences—specifically *Gilda* (Charles Vidor, 1946), *Where Danger Lives* (John Farrow, 1950), and *Human Desire* (Fritz Lang, 1954), all of which have clear Expressionist roots. Chapter 4 concludes with a section on "montage documentaries" and some speculations on the decline of

Weimar cinema focusing on arguments of Lotte Eisner in *The Haunted Screen* (Berkeley, 1969) and Siegfried Kracauaer in *From Caligari to Hitler: A Psychological History of the German Film* (Princeton: Princeton University Press, 1947), which are continued in the section on Nazi cinema in Chapter 9.

Major endnotes for Chapter 4 are devoted to a bibliography on Scandinavian cinema; a bibliography on *Caligari*'s reception; precedents for the "unchained camera" and subjective camera styles of *Der letzte Mann*; the two waves of German emigration to Hollywood; Murnau's late American work; and a bibliography on point-of-view.

Chapter 5

Soviet Silent Cinema
and the Theory of Montage, 1917–1931

By way of transition at this point, I find it useful to compare and contrast the German and Soviet cinemas of the twenties. Both began as state-sponsored cinemas of propaganda (or, in the German case, counter-propaganda), but only in the Soviet Union did the original purpose hold. In Germany, Universum Film Aktiengesellschaft (UFA) was privatized less than a year after its creation, and the political impulse quickly gave way to a high-art cinema, which both Marxists and Fascists considered culturally decadent. Even after the Nazis came to power in 1933, German films did not become overtly political—Josef Goebbels, in fact, mandated a cinema of Hollywood-style popular entertainment to divert public attention from radical political change and, later, the consequences of waging war. In the Soviet Union, on the other hand, the political motive was dominant from beginning to end, and every film made in that country was supposed to have an overriding ideological purpose—which, for much of Soviet history, was to represent the Communist Party's general line. As part of this distinction, Weimar cinema was one of subjectivity and introspection grounded in *mise-en-scène*, while the Soviets established a public cinema of mass persuasion (if hardly ever mass appeal) based on the manipulations of montage. Metaphorically speaking, the Soviets put their faith in Pavlov, the Germans in Freud.

In the wake of the 1917 Revolution, Lenin and his Bolsheviks clearly saw the cinema as a means of unifying the country and consolidating their own power. As in postwar Germany, however, there was very little in the way of a native film tradition for them to draw upon. The pre-Revolutionary cinema had been dominated by Europeans and was associated with bourgeois capitalism, because the vast majority of Russians were serfs, having neither disposable income nor leisure time. (See *Silent Witnesses: Russian Films, 1908–1919*, ed. Paolo Cherchi, et al. [London: BFI Publishing, 1989], a catalogue of nearly 300 fiction films produced during the tsarist period that have been preserved and restored by Gosfalmofond, Moscow; see also David Robinson, "Evgeni Bauer and the Cinema of Nikolai II," *Sight and Sound*, 59, 1 [Winter 1989–90], 51–55.) During the Revolution, this industry disappeared together with the capitalists who owned it, leaving the Soviets without equipment or film stock—and (temporarily) without the industrial capacity to produce their own. In this situation, a state film school was established, the VGIK ("All-Union State Institute of Cinematography), where aspiring film-makers made films without celluloid giving the fledgling Soviet cinema a decidedly theoretical bent. This dovetailed nicely with the revolutionary idea that cinema was the quintessential art form of the new age, since both were predicated on machines. (See Richard Taylor and Ian Christie, eds., *The Film Factory: Russian and Soviet Cinema in Documents, 1896–1939* [London: Routledge & Kegan Paul, 1988].)

The industry's first films were *agitki*—compilation documentaries made from existing newsreel footage of the Revolution and the civil war, because no new footage could be shot. This agitational/documentary impulse was deeply formative, and the first major figure of the Soviet cinema, Dziga Vertov (pp. 142–44), was also the first modern documentarist and the pioneer of *cinéma-vérité* (*Kino-pravda*) form. The second major figure, Lev Kuleshov (pp. 144–49), founded an experimental workshop at the VGIK devoted to discovering the general laws by which film communicates meaning—a goal totally in keeping with the Bolshevik's plan to establish film as the most effective means of political communication. In the famous "Kuleshov effect" (p. 146) and other experiments, the director demonstrated that the shot in film has two distinct values: first, that which it possesses as a photographic image, and second, that which it acquires when juxtaposed with another shot. It is this second meaning that provides the basis for the theory of editing known as montage.

Montage is central to a discussion of Soviet silent cinema, and it can also be used to talk about other editing styles. I generally define montage in relation to both Hollywood-style continuity, or "invisible," editing and *mise-en-scène* construction, with several examples from each mode. For classical montage pieces, I tend to use the tried and true—the "Odessa steps" sequence from

Battleship Potemkin (Sergei Eisenstein, 1925), the conclusion of *Mother* (Vsevolod Pudovkin, 1926), the shooting party sequence in *Rules of the Game* (Jean Renoir, 1939), the shower murder sequence from *Psycho* (Alfred Hitchcock, 1960), the opening and closing massacres in *The Wild Bunch* (Robert Aldrich, 1969)—all of which yoke dramatic and optical violence. Continuity editing can be found at random in nearly any studio-era film, but I tend to prefer screwball comedies—such as *Bringing Up Baby* (Howard Hawks, 1938)—because their pace can be understood as a function of the cutting's "invisibility." For *mise-en-scène*, of course, any sequence shot from *Der letzte Mann* (F. W. Murnau, 1924) or a deep-focus take from *Citizen Kane* (Orson Welles, 1941) will do, but for variety let me recommend the extraordinary and generally unremarked two-minute tracking shot that opens Andrzej Wajda's *Kanal* (1956). At this point, Eisenstein's notion of dia-lectical montage (pp. 179–83) can be introduced and diagrammed on the board, as well as the five separate types or "methods" of montage (pp. 183–89)—with reference to *Potemkin* (pp. 158–78) for the metric, rhythmic, and tonal (the "overtonal" not being so much a category as a synthesis of the first three), and to *October* (1928) (pp. 186–89) for the intellectual or ideological.

Regarding Eisenstein, Pudovkin, and Dovzhenko themselves, I really have very little in class to say. It is important, though, that students understand how real a threat the charge of "formalist error" became to them and other filmmakers after the succession of Stalin to the Party secretariat in 1927, and worth knowing, too, that Eisenstein was the only one of them who didn't finally knuckle under, although it wreaked his health and negatively effected his career (whose latter course is charted in detail in Chapter 9). Pudovkin's concept of "montage as linkage" (pp. 195–96) makes a nice contrast with Eisenstein's, as does *Mother* (Vsevolod Pudovkin, 1926) with *Potemkin* and *The End of St. Petersburg* (Pudovkin, 1927) with *October* for the same reasons. Let me also recommend Pudovkin's *Heir to Genghis Khan* (1928), a beautiful but infrequently shown film, which was produced by the Soviets to propagandize the Central Asian republics. For Dovzhenko, there is now a definitive account of his life and work— Vance Kepley, Jr.'s *In the Service of the State: The Cinema of*

Alexander Dovzhenko (Wisconsin: University of Wisconsin Press, 1986)—but beware of a surfeit of badly cut American prints of his films. Finally, it is important that students understand what is meant by "socialist realism"—that it has nothing to do with "social realism" of the sort practiced by the Italian neorealists (Chapter 11) or the British "New Cinema" in the early sixties (Chapter 14), but was rather an official doctrine demanding that all the Soviet arts (and, after World War II, those of the other Warsaw Pact nations as well) portray reality according to the the socialist ideal: in other words, reality as mandated by the Communist Party's general line.

Major endnotes for Chapter 5 concern the polemical writings of Dziga Vertov; the early industrial development of Soviet cinema; Vertov's work in the sound film; the relationship between Eisenstein and Lev Kuleshov; alternative readings of *Potemkin*; the Soviet collectivization program (1928–31); the work of Esther Shub; and the "Stalinization" of Soviet cinema.

Chapter 6

Hollywood in the Twenties

Hollywood in the twenties was the great age of the silent feature film. It was also the crucible of much popular mythology about the American film industry—a time when million-dollar movies, fantastically glamorous superstars, and lurid scandals vied for public attention as weekly theater admissions rose from 40 million in 1922, to 90 million by the decade's end. For the studios, it was a time of aggressive theater acquisition and maximal expansion in the distribution sector. By 1926 three large companies, known collectively as the "Big Three," dominated the industry. The most powerful was Adolph Zukor's Famous-Players-Lasky Corporation, which had acquired the thriving Paramount Pictures distribution exchange in 1916 (and was commonly known as "Paramount") and, by 1921, 303 first-run theaters. Loew's Incorporated, had begun life as a theater chain, expanding into production with the acquisition of Metro Pictures in 1920 and Louis B. Mayer Productions in 1924, to become the parent company of Metro-Goldwyn-Mayer and owner of over 1,500 theaters nationwide. First National (Associated First National, after 1921) had been founded in 1917 by twenty-six of the nation's largest independent exhibition chains to combat Paramount's practice of blockbooking by financing their own films—becoming Charlie Chaplin's first producer, for example—and by 1921 controlled 639 first-run theaters. Thus, wherever they had started, each of the "Big Three" had by mid-decade become a vertically integrated company competing fiercely with its counterparts in three sectors of the industry. The "Little Five" studios—Fox Film Corporation, Producers Distributing Corporation (PDC), Film Booking Office (FBO), Carl Laemmle's Universal Pictures, and Warner Bros. Pictures—owned production facilities, but during the twenties were largely dependent upon the "Big Three" for distribution and exhibition. Below these were about 30 smaller production companies, of which only Columbia, Republic, and Monogram survived into the next decade. United Artists was a unique entity, formed in 1919 by D. W. Griffith, Charlie Chaplin, Mary Pickford, and Douglas Fairbanks, to distribute their own independently produced motion pictures and thus was not a studio at all, but it would become first a minor and then a major player after the coming of sound.

These various studio histories I diagram on the board and continue through the formation of the five majors and three minors in the thirties, below a line marking the 18-month (mid-1927 through 1929) transition to sound; this is a bit premature but works to ensure continuity. (Later in the course—or in the second semester—in the unit corresponding to Chapter 18, I extend these histories into the nineties.) Then I discuss the central producer system originated by Thomas Ince, Mack Sennett, and others, and the rise of the studio system (pp. 208–11). The work of Chaplin (pp. 211–16) and Buster Keaton (pp. 217–24) I discuss comparatively, and have found Kevin Brownlow and David Gill's recent Thames Television documentaries *The Unknown Chaplin* (1985) and *The Unknown Keaton* (1989), both available on video, invaluable in this respect. Harold Lloyd and "others" (pp. 224–27) I generally leave to the students, although there is now an excellent critical biography of Lloyd in Tom Dardis' *Harold Lloyd: The Man on the Clock* (New York: Viking, 1983).

After the formation of the studios, the most important institutional force shaping the American film industry in the twenties was public reaction to "the Hollywood scandals" and the creation of Motion Picture Producers and Distributors of America (MPPDA) (pp. 227–30). Many persons in business and government had become aware of film's power to shape mass opinion as early as 1915, but concern over its influence on social behavior spread nationwide in the wake of the Fatty Arbuckle manslaughter trial and William Desmond Taylor murder case (1921–23). The creation of the Hays Office to oversee the film industry's morals in 1922 was a public relations' gimmick, that would become a boilerplate nightmare twelve years later, when Hays became the administrator of the Draconian "Production Code" (see Chapter 8). Even during the twenties, a "Purity Code" required producers to submit summaries of their screenplays to the Hays Office for prior approval, creating both the "compensating values" formula worked so successfully by Cecil B. DeMille (pp. 230–31), and

the cinema of sexual innuendo practiced so elegantly by Ernst Lubitsch and other European directors (pp. 231–33) working in Hollywood at the time. (On these latter, see Graham Petrie's excellent *Hollywood Destinies: European Directors in America, 1922–1931* [London: Routledge & Kegan Paul, 1985].) Of the era's other directors, new attention is given in the present edition to Robert Flaherty (pp. 235–37) because his later career so markedly integrated narrative and documentary tendencies; but the major figure of the decade was unquestionably Erich von Stroheim (pp. 238–52), whose ambitions and achievements marked the outer limits of what Hollywood could ever be.

Von Stroheim, however, is difficult to teach as a unit because only two of his films—*Blind Husbands* (1918) and *Foolish Wives* (1922)—are available for 16mm rental at competitive rates, and neither is complete (missing 19 and 92 minutes, at best, respectively). *The Devil's Passkey* (1919) hasn't survived and *The Wedding March* (1928) is currently out of distribution. The fragmentary *Greed* (1924) and *The Merry Widow* (1925) are available exclusively from MGM, while *Merry-Go-Round* (1922; begun by von Stroheim but completed by Rupert Julian) and an excellent reconstruction of *Queen Kelly* (1929–85) are available from Kino International (the latter with the full orchestral score originally commissioned by Gloria Swanson). That the American silent cinema's second most important director can only be taught today by reconstructions and half-measures—for example to illustrate the magnificence of the production context within which von Stroheim worked, I show excerpts from the 1987 restoration of *The Thief of Bagdad* (Raoul Walsh, 1924), with its beautiful tints and tones—underscores the tragedy of von Stroheim's career, as well as its demarcation of a major crux in the history of the American film industry.

When von Stroheim's career began (with *Blind Husbands* in 1918), the American industry had emerged clearly from its artisanal phase but was still a wildcat business mainly run by filmmakers themselves. By the time von Stroheim's career effectively ended in the *Queen Kelly* debacle of 1928, the industry had become one of the nation's largest, and it was controlled by corporate managers like Irving Thalberg at MGM who carefully monitored every aspect of the business in an effort to standardize production and maximize profits. Eccentricity bred of genius was anathema to these men, just as artistic excess was antagonistic to their goals. They weeded out the Griffiths, Chaplins, Keatons, and von Stroheim's to replace them with a system of executive producers and salaried directors who made films under contract and on demand. The dream of a director's cinema evaporated before the reality of a cinema of mass consumption based on mass retailing principles such as product differentiation and market segmentation, monopoly-structured from top to bottom and, increasingly, from side to side. (For an authoritative history of the era covered by Chapter 6, see Richard Koszarski, *An Evening's Entertainment: The Age of the Silent Feature Picture, 1915–1928* [New York: Charles Scribner's Sons, 1990], Volume 3 of the ten-volume *A History of the American Cinema* project.)

Major endnotes for Chapter 6 concern Ince's career and that of other director-producers who trained at Inceville; the Sennett Collection at the Margaret Herrick Library of the American Academy of Motion Picture Arts and Sciences (AMPAS); Film historians Kevin Brownlow and David Gill's Chaplin and Keaton documentaries; the work of Laurel and Hardy, and Harry Langdon; the solution to the William Desmond Taylor case; European directors in Hollywood in the twenties; the 1987 restoration of *The Thief of Bagdad*; the various versions of *Nanook of the North* (Robert Flaherty, 1922) and the Ackeley cameras used in shooting it; von Stroheim's payment for directing *The Merry Widow*; the influential 1927 Hayden, Stone report on containing feature film production costs.

Chapter 7

The Coming of Sound, 1926–1932

At the beginning of this unit, it's well worth reminding students that pre-sound audiences hardly ever saw "silent" films, because from the earliest Lumière projections of 1895, exhibitors almost always provided some form of musical accompaniment. Beyond that, in the "dream palace" era, features were regularly accompanied by full orchestral scores and sound effects. The same applies with somewhat less regularity to color, which was initially provided by hand-tinting and then later by mechanized chemical tinting and toning. The main point is that by 1927 audiences had come to expect both sound and color from feature films in non-naturalistic form. Missing from the experience was human speech (widely available since 1926 through network radio broadcasts) in the form of lip-synchronized dialogue and color which could credibly represent the entire spectrum. Both of these components were added to the cinema during the introduction and diffusion of sound recording technology (1927–35).

The distinction between sound-on-disk (pp. 253–55) and sound-on-film (pp. 255–57) systems is important and a little confusing. This is because sound-on-disk in the form of Western Electric's Vitaphone (pp. 257–61) was the catalyst for the conversion in 1927, while sound-on-film, or optical sound, in the form of both Fox Movietone (pp. 261–62) and RCA's Photophone (pp. 262–63) proved technologically superior and had become the industry standard by 1930. (Further complications arise because Movietone was a variable density system, and Photophone a variable area system, which competed with each other until 1945 when the latter won out.) The key to optical sound's success was literally its *photographic* nature—that it was light-encoded on the film stock in the same way as the image track—automatically resolving the problem of synchronization inherent in all disk systems.

Regarding the process of conversion (pp. 262–66), I find it useful to sketch the role of AT&T and RCA in the development of network radio broadcasting (Erik Barnouw's *Tube of Plenty* [Oxford: Oxford University Press, 1982] is a good source here). I explain the motive force of the conversion to sound as an attempt on the part of these two telecommunication giants—partially successful—to gain a controlling interest in the film industry. Whatever the case in terms of outright ownership, the corporate interdependence of film, telecommunications, and finance capital after the conversion is amply demonstrated by the charts on p. 265, and though its configuration has changed several times, this interdependence has grown in magnitude ever since.

The introduction of the so-called "natural" or photographic color processes (pp. 267–75)— initially, and for the next two decades, exclusively, Technicolor—took place concurrently with the coming of sound, although full-scale industry conversion to color would not occur until the 1950s. Sound was, in fact, a catalyst for photographic color, because non-photographic tinting and toning, so popular during the twenties, caused distortion in optical soundtracks. Technicolor offered first a two-color (1928) and then a three-color (1932) subtractive process which was both technically sound and aesthetically pleasing, but quite expensive because it involved the simultaneous exposure of three separate negatives in the same three-strip camera. Furthermore, the Technicolor Corporation monopolized its use from shooting through processing to eliminate price competition. For these reasons, Technicolor was used by the studios mainly for films of spectacle (e.g., *Gone with the Wind* [Victor Fleming, 1939]), or fantasy (*The Wizard of Oz* [Fleming, 1939]), and black-and-white became the standard medium for the sound film through the fifties (see Chapter 12, pp. 480–82). It's interesting to talk at this point about conventions of film realism relative to color, since in our own time they have been reversed: whereas audiences conditioned during the Depression and World War II associated color with fantasy and black-and-white with representation of "the real," we associate color with documentary realism and black-and-white with abstraction, nostalgia, and the kind of dream/fantasy states evoked by certain advertisements and rock videos.

Revisionist historians have recently argued that the introduction of sound did not constitute a major disruption of the silent film production process, as originally thought, and it's true that the transition was remarkably swift, taking place in less than 15 months from late 1927 through the end of 1929. But with three competing sound systems, each in a continuous state of modification, there was confusion within the studios that bordered on chaos. The point is worth making again and again that what the public wanted from sound films—lip-synchronized dialogue and what Hollywood was suddenly faced with providing *en masse*—was not what Warner Bros. had originally conceived when it showcased Vitaphone in *Don Juan* (Alan Crosland, 1926) and *The Jazz Singer* (Crosland, 1927). Lacking the first-run theater alliances of the majors, Warners intended to court second-and-third-run exhibitors—those who could not afford house orchestras—by offering them films with synchronized, pre-recorded orchestral scores. The response to this marketing campaign was indifferent until audiences heard actors speak from the screen in *The Jazz Singer* and went wild for lip-synchronized dialogue, whose affinities with radio were clear and increasingly familiar. And it was the recording and reproduction of synchronized dialogue that made the conversion so unexpectedly torturous.

The statement that "the movies ceased to move when they began to talk" is nonetheless true for being a cliché. The main points for students to remember are that both editing and camera movement became briefly problematic because of specific technical deficiencies in early recording systems (pp. 278–79). Microphones had a very limited range and required stationary placement, but they were omnidirectional within that range, so cameras—hastily motorized during the conversion to prevent soundtrack distortion—had to be crudely soundproofed through boxing and baffling. Editing in dialogue sequences became difficult, if not impossible, and there was a tendency to shoot such scenes as long, extended takes. These and other problems were resolved over a period of several years both by ingenious technological fixes and the industrial standardization of such practices as postsynchronization and rerecording (pp. 284–89). But the regression in film form produced by the conversion to sound is visible in mainstream features as late as 1932–33, and most historians agree that the inertia was not completely overcome until the mid-thirties.

One way to illustrate this phenomenon is to compare more or less conventional films made by the same directors and studios on either side of the conversion to sound. Examples that I regularly use are William Wellman's *Wings* (1927), which, its aerial sequences notwithstanding, is a conventionally plotted love story, and Wellman's *Pioneer Builders* (aka, *The Conquerors* [1932]). Whereas the narrative of the former moves fluidly from one classical continuity sequence to the next, despite the frequent intrusion of intertitles, that of the latter grinds to a halt with every exchange of dialogue, interior and exterior, finally making the film painful to watch. It's often possible to find this tension between the dialogue and non-dialogue sequences within the same film—for example, in the Eddie Cantor musical *Whoopee!* (Thorton Freeland, 1930), whose jazzy Busby Berkeley production numbers exist side by side with ponderously staged dialogue scenes. The most illuminating example of this technical schizophrenia, of course, is Hitchcock's *Blackmail* (1929), which was made first as a silent film and then as a sound film and finally cut together with a synchronized music track uniting sequences from both versions. Hitchcock's experiments with camera movement in dialogue sequences here are historically significant, as are his manipulations of the sound track in his next film, *Murder* (1930). Other important transitional films that I frequently show in whole or part include Josef von Sternberg's *Der Blaue Engel* (1930), Rene Clair's *A nous la liberté* (1931), Fritz Lang's *M* (1930), and Lewis Milestone's *The Front Page* (1931), whose overlapping dialogue and moving camera sequences are well worth a classroom discussion.

Major endnotes for Chapter 7 concern the groove-on-film system known as Projectophone or *Madalatone*; the work of Eugene Augustin Lauste, Joseph T. Tykociner, and *P.O. Pedersen/ Valdemar Poulsen*; a comparison of Kinemacolor and Cinerama; early Technicolor cameramen and color consultants; a bibliography of the early sound film scholarship of Barry Salt.

Chapter 8

The Sound Film
and the American Studio System

The coming of sound was attended by a series of mergers and takeovers that by 1935 had concentrated 90 percent of all American production in the hands of eight studios—five vertically integrated majors and three horizontally integrated minors—which also controlled distribution and exhibition through the majors' ownership of 2,600 first-run theaters. These latter represented only 16 percent of the nation's total but generated 75 percent of the revenue. Most people today associate the studio system of the thirties and forties with American filmmaking's Golden Age, and indeed between 1930 and 1945 Hollywood produced more then 7,500 features—a truly stunning, industrial achievement. But it is somewhat sobering to note that throughout the era, only five percent of the majors' total corporate assets went toward production activity and one percent toward distribution, while a whopping 94 percent was consumed by exhibition. As J. Douglas Gomery points out in *The Hollywood Studio System* (New York: St. Martin's Press, 1985), the term "studio" itself is a misnomer for these corporations since the clearest way to characterize them is as, "diversified theater chains, producing features, shorts, cartoons, and newsreels to fill their houses" (p. 8).

Each studio made a distinctive kind of entertainment, depending on such variables as its creative personnel, its management, and its access to finance capital. The largest and wealthiest, Metro-Goldwyn-Mayer (MGM), was also thought to be the most "American" in its high-key lighting style and lavish production designs; while Paramount was identified as the most "European" owing to the high number of Universum Film Aktiengesellschaft-trained directors, designers, and cinematographers it employed. Warner Brothers, newly rich from its successful innovation of sound, retained its cost-consciousness and working-class appeal from the twenties, adopting low-key lighting and fast-paced editing styles to conceal the cheapness of its sets. Fox (20th Century-Fox after 1934) was also noted for its tight budget control, but through 1949, it produced the most films in Technicolor, and the studio became associated in the public mind with attractive visual display and state-of-the-art special effects. These four companies were all about the same size (which was about four times larger than the three minors), while Radio-Keith-Orpheum (RKO) was about 25 percent smaller owing to the circumstances of its creation (hastily assembled in 1929 to market films in the RCA Photophone process) and frequent changes in management. RKO became the producer of a number of innovative features during the studio era, including the popular Astaire-Rogers dance films, *King Kong* (Merian C. Cooper and Ernest B. Schoedsack, 1933), and early work of Orson Welles. Of the minors, Universal and Columbia maintained only production and distribution units, while United Artists functioned exclusively as a distributor.

Below the major and minor studios were about twenty, thinly-capitalized "B" studios which produced hour-long program pictures, or "B-films," for the bottom half of double bills. Whereas the A-film was a studio feature rented to exhibitors for a percentage of the box-office gross, the B-film rented at a modest flat rate, so that its profits were predictable and its costs tightly controlled. The double bill was an important marketing tool for American motion pictures during the Depression and World War II, giving the audience two features, cartoons, and a newsreel for the price of a single admission. (After 1956, the double bill became the province of exploitation producers like American International Pictures [AIP] who would churn out paired B-films for dual promotion and marketing to teenagers—see Chapter 12.) At this point in the course, I usually try to recreate a Depression-style double bill, using a few Andy Panda cartoons (c. 1940), *Made for Each Other* (John Cromwell, 1939), and *Prison Train* (Gordon Wiles, 1938); even though *Made for Each Other* was produced independently by Selznick International, it has all the characteristics of a classical, studio feature.

After the structure of the studios themselves, the most important defining feature of the era was the Production Code. The Code's evolution is described in detail on pp. 296-300, and the points I like to emphasize are its relationship to the Payne Fund Studies of 1929–32 (which coincided with the worst excesses of the early sound film) and the authoritative influence of the Catholic Church on the Code's content. The people who wrote the Code and who administered it were all Catholic priests or laymen, and the morality it embodied was quite specifically the one mandated by that religion. The question arises: why should the studio chiefs, who were both immensely powerful and overwhelmingly Jewish, accept this? The answer is complex. For one thing, though the morality imposed by the Code *was* Catholic, there was a national consensus in the wake of Henry James Forman's *Our Movie Made Children* (p. 298) that the regulation of film content was both desirable and necessary. Thus, the moguls found self-censorship more palatable than any other form, and at a time of rampant political anti-Semitism, they were probably happy to accept guidelines proposed by a Christian church. In some ways, too, the Code made for more efficient production by serving as a kind screenwriter's blueprint. In its very specific prescription and proscription of certain behaviors and themes, the Code also furthered the process of gentrification that had begun during the transition to sound. Making films on a yearly schedule according to set formula and type (ten westerns, seven musicals, five gangster films, etc.) could rapidly amortize the cost of sets, costumes, and props—which could be recycled season after season—and even specialized directors and stars. So while the Code inhibited freedom of expression in the American cinema quite severely for at least twenty years, the Code was turned to economic advantage by producers and made an integral part of the studio system. (Some recent books, unmentioned in the text, which are helpful in understanding the dynamics of the studio system are Gene Fernett, *American Film Studios: An Historical Encyclopedia* [Jefferson, N.C.: McFarland & Co, 1988]; Neal Gabler, *An Empire of Their Own: How the Jews Invented Hollywood* [New York: Crown Publishers, 1988]; John Izod, *Hollywood and the Box Office, 1895–1986* [New York: Columbia University Press, 1988]; Tom Stemple, *Framework: A History of Screenwriting in the American Film* [New York: Continuum, 1988]; Thomas Schatz, *The Genius of the System: Hollywood Filmmaking in the Studio Era* [New York: Pantheon Books, 1988]; A. Scott Berg, *Goldwyn: A Biography* [New York: Alfred A. Knopf, 1989]; Leonard J. Leff and Jerold L.

Simmons, *The Dame in the Kimono: Hollywood, Censorship, and the Production Code From the 1920s to the 1960s* [New York: Grove Weidenfeld, 1990]; William MacAdams, *Ben Hecht: The Man Behind the Legend* [New York: Scribner's and Sons, 1990.])

The individual sections on "Major Figures of the Studio Era" (pp. 319–60) are placed in Chapter 8 mainly as a matter of convenience, and can be broken away from it either in whole or in part. Von Sternberg, Howard Hawks, William Wyler, George Cukor, and Frank Capra did so much of their major work during the studio era that it is logically consistent to consider them at this point in the course (and, on a selective basis, I usually do). But John Ford and Alfred Hitchcock produced much of their best work after the Paramount decrees weakened and reconfigured the studio system (1948–52), and it may be useful for some teachers to deal with these directors later, or even in another course. For example, I generally do Hitchcock in conjunction with Chapter 12, referring the students back to the discussions of his work from *Rope* (1948) through *Marnie* (1964), pp. 341–53, having discussed his British Gaumont films (pp. 337–39) as contributions to the early sound era in the unit on Chapter 7.

Major endnotes for Chapter 8 deal with recent theoretical studies of the Hollywood musical; Warner Bros.' supposed social realism; histories of art direction; Fox's experiment with 70mm widescreen cinematography in *The Big Trail* (Walsh, 1930); histories of the B-film; Gaylyn Studlar's work on the "masochistic aesthetic" of von Sternberg; Ford's knowledge of American landscape painting; recent studies of Howard Hawks; the Hitchcock collection in the Margaret Herrick Library; and a bibliography of Hitchcock and voyeurism.

Chapter 9

Europe in the Thirties

The "International Diffusion of Sound" (pp. 361–62) provides a textbook example of the way in which American companies have regularly attempted to dominate the world film industry through patents' control. In this case, their hegemony was successfully challenged by the German cartel Tobis-Klangfilm, with whom they were forced to share the sound film market until World War II. British cinema during this period is important mainly for its rapid decline (pp. 362–63); but Germany experienced a moment of brilliance in the early sound films of Fritz Lang (pp. 364–65). Here, I usually show Lang's *M* (1931), which in addition to its prescient use of sound, suggests some interesting connections between criminality, the police, and the state, in a country that was itself about to become—at least, by postwar definition—a criminal police state. (On Lang's subsequent escape from Berlin to Paris in 1933, see Gosta Werner, "Fritz Lang and Goebbels: Myth and Facts," *Film Quarterly*, 43, 3 [Spring 1990], 24–27; for a fictionalized account, see Howard A. Rodman's novel *Destiny Express* [New York: Atheneum, 1990.) Nazi cinema (pp. 365–67) is worth discussing as a political phenomenon, which serves to underscore the fact that cinema was politicized in nearly every country of the world between the wars. Josef Goebbels' somewhat unique approach was to propagandize selectively through documentaries and a handful of features, but to promote a mainstream cinema of mass entertainment based on Hollywood genres (see, e.g., Eric Rentschler, "The Triumph of the Male Will: *Munchhausen* (1943), *Film Quarterly*, 43, 3 [Spring 1990], 15–23). Such escapist fare would presumably divert public attention from the Nazi's more sinister programs, while the documentary epics of Leni Riefenstahl would focus it on Nazi achievement in the traditional realms of international politics and sports. In this regard, I always show Riefenstahl's *Triumph des Willens* (1935), not only for its cinematic spectacle but for its remarkable portrait of Hitler as a humane leader and judicious statesman. That film form, history, and human stupidity conspired together in 1935 to make this portrait credible offers a chilling insight into the relationship between politics and mass media as it exists even (perhaps, especially) today. (A number of pivotal Nazi features are available on videocassette from International Historic Films, including the anti-Semitic spectacle *Jud Suss* [1940] and the epics *Der Grosse Konig* [1942] and *Kolberg* [1945], all directed by Veit Harlan; the Agfacolor fantasias *Munchausen* [Josef von Baky, 1943] and *Immensee* [Harlan, 1943]; and the hero-worshipping biopics *Bismarck* [Wolfgang Liebeneiner, 1940], *Rembrandt* [Hans Steinhoff, 1942], *Diesel* [1942], and *Paracelsus* [G. W. Pabst, 1943]—see Part IV, below.)

It's worth noting that Goebbels did not fully nationalize the film industry until 1942, by which time the Nazi conquest of Europe had created a huge new market for German films. In Italy (pp. 367–68), Benito Mussolini followed a similar course, manipulating and finally controlling the national film industry without actually nationalizing it, through both L'Unione Cinematografica Educativa (LUCE) and Ente Nazionale Industrie Cinematografiche (ENIC). As in Germany, the result was an escapist cinema (e.g., *"telephono bianco"* films) with a modicum of nationalist propaganda. In the Soviet Union, things were a bit different. First, the earliest Soviet sound systems were technically inferior to their Western counterparts, which meant that sound was slower in coming; second, the transition to sound was made during a time of extreme political reaction, when the doctrine of "socialist realism" (see Chapter 5) was at its height. Stalin's lieutenant Boris Shumiatski ruled supreme over the industry, having replaced the liberal Anatoli Lunacharski, and he rigidly imposed socialist realism on the great montage artists of the twenties, breaking most of them in the process (pp. 368–70). Only Eisenstein (pp. 370–77) refused to yield to pressure, suffering many humiliations but eventually triumphing over Shumiatski in *Alexander Nevski* (1938) and *Ivan the Terrible, Parts I and II* (1945–1946). Even though the latter was banned by Stalin (and not seen in the Soviet Union until 1958), hastening Eisenstein's early death in 1948, he lived to see his genius vindicated by *Nevski* and *Ivan, Part I*. I always show the Battle on the Ice sequence from *Nevski* in class because it pro-

vides such a clear demonstration of Eisenstein's ideas about contrapuntal sound. It's also useful to compare it as a piece of wartime propaganda (although the Nazi-Soviet Nonaggression Pact of 1939 temporarily forestalled Soviet involvement in the war itself) with films like Laurence Olivier's *Henry V* (1944) or Veit Harlan's *Der Grosse Konig* (*The Great King*, 1942), the Nazi-produced tribute to Frederick II's winning the Seven Years' War against overwhelming odds.

In France, the period of avant-garde Impressionism (pp. 377–79) was a very rich one, and it is the subject of a marvelous critical work by Richard Abel, *French Cinema: The First Wave, 1915–1929*, discussed in the endnotes of this manual. The giant of this movement was Abel Gance (pp. 379–83), whose *Napoleon* (1927), as reconstructed by Kevin Brownlow, is one of the cinema's most remarkable epics despite its clear proto-fascist tendencies. The full tryptich reconstruction with a new orchestral score by Carmine Coppola is available on cassette and disc, and though it's a terrible economy to impose on a film of this grandeur, I find that my students can get a pretty clear idea of the film from projected video. Another important figure associated with Impressionism was the Danish director Carl-Theodor Dreyer (pp. 386–88), whose major work during this period was done in France. The definitive critical work on Dreyer is David Bordwell's *The Films of Carl-Theodor Dreyer* (Berkeley: University of California Press, 1981); he is difficult but rewarding to teach undergraduates (*La Passion de Jeanne d'Arc* [1928] is a good place to start), and all of his work is available on both film and tape. René Clair (pp. 388–90) and Jean Vigo (pp. 391–92) both directed avant-garde films during the twenties but did their most influential work in the early sound era, 1929–34. Clair, especially, made important innovations in the use of asynchronous or contrapuntal sound in *Sous les toits de Paris* (1930), *Le Million* (1931), and *A nous la liberté* (1931), while Jean Vigo's *Zéro de conduite* (1933) and *L'Atalante* (1934) laid the foundations for "poetic realism."

The somewhat imprecise term "poetic realism" was coined by the French film historian Georges Sadoul to describe a blend of lyricism and realism that characterized the films of Jacques Feyder, Julien Duvivier, and particularly Marcel Carné and Jacques Prévert during the latter half of thirties (pp. 392–96). Poetic realism was associated politically with the Popular Front movement that united the parties of the left under Leon Blum in May 1936. Though Blum's government lasted only a year, it inspired hope for a new beginning (as well as despair at its collapse in 1937) and was particularly associated with the films of Jean Renoir (pp. 396–406). That many of Renoir's films were politically motivated (*La Vie est à nous* [1936]; *La Marseillaise* [1937]), however, does not detract from their greatness as art, and no one teaching in this era can afford to neglect either *La Grande illusion* (1937) or *La Règle de jeu* (1939). Not only do these films take significant steps toward the creative conquest of sound, but they brilliantly anticipate the deep-focus photography brought to perfection by Orson Welles and Gregg Toland a few years later in *Citizen Kane* (1941). Renoir's use of the depth perspective is so striking in these and other films (e.g., *Toni* [1935]) that I use this section of the text (pp. 399–401) to introduce the fundamental principles of the long take, or sequence shot, in conjunction with deep-focus photography, as well as to provide a thumbnail history of film stocks and lighting technology. This serves to contextualize Renoir's use of deep-focus and off-screen space, as well as to introduce the succeeding chapter on Orson Welles.

Major endnotes for Chapter 9 include a bibliography of scholarship on British cinema during the 1930s; an historical sketch of Fritz Lang's career; a bibliography of works on Nazi cinema; a bibliography and discussion of the Leni Riefenstahl controversy; a bibliography of works on Italian cinema between the wars; notes on Eisenstein's *Que Viva México!* (1929–31), *Bezhin Meadow* (1935), *Alexander Nevski* (1938), *The Great Ferghana Canal*, and *Ivan the Terrible, Parts I and II* (1945–46); a discussion of Richard Abel's *French Cinema: The First Wave, 1915–1929* and some production statistics for the 1920s; notes on Abel Gance's collaborators on *Napoleon* (1927), the several versions of Dreyer's *La Passion de Jeanne d' Arc* (1928), and the film scores of Maurice Jaubert; French industry production statistics from the 1930s; a bibliography on "poetic realism"; and notes on Renoir's politics and aesthetics-of-depth.

Orson Welles and the Modern Sound Film

When I first wrote Chapter 10 in the late 1970s, few knowledgeable people would have disputed the centrality of Orson Welles and *Citizen Kane* (1941) to the history of narrative film. Today, such an argument has become easier to make, but it is still almost impossible to sustain. Thanks largely to the scholarship of Robert Carringer in *The Making of Citizen Kane* (Berkeley: University of California Press, 1985), we now know that the film was the work of many hands at RKO, and that the studio hierarchy, rather than Welles, largely determined their placement. Moreover, we know that many persons directly responsible for the aesthetic texture of *Kane*, such as unit art director Perry Ferguson, did not receive screen credit for their work. Finally, the relationship between Welles and his two key collaborators, Herman Mankiewicz and Gregg Toland, long ambiguous, is now pretty clearly defined and the mutuality of their contributions acknowledged. All of this, however, will trouble only the most extreme and rearguard of auteurists, since it leaves Welles still as the principle author of *Kane* and the film itself as a crucible of film history for reasons having as much to do with the material circumstances of its production as with its themes.

I teach that *Kane* is notable in three distinct categories. First, is the complexity of its narrative—basically a series of overlapping flashbacks connected by dissolves and montage sequences providing a composite picture of the life of a single individual. Second, is the film's use of the deep-focus sequence shot, permitting composition of the image frame in depth. Composition in depth I define as the arrangement of dramatically significant actions and objects on several spatial planes within the frame at once, achieved through manipulating photographic depth of field. Toland achieved extreme depth of field for *Kane* by extending techniques he had used in earlier films like John Ford's *The Long Voyage Home* (1940) and William Wyler's *Wuthering Heights* (1939). These involved the use of Eastman Super XX film stock together with a 24mm wide-angle lens with a radically stopped-down aperture, and high-intensity arc lamps whose lenses were coated with plastic to reduce glare. In *Kane*, Welles and Toland typically used deep-focus effects in combination with stylized camera angles (especially low ones), high-contrast lighting, and moving camera shots. The third category of achievement is *Kane*'s innovative use of sound, a heritage of Welles' broad experience in radio. In the film, Welles uses three basic techniques: the "lightning mix" for time-compression, overlapping dialogue, and directional sound. Bernard Herrmann's brilliant score should be noted here as well. (Herrmann [1911–75] had scored Welles' Mercury Theater radio productions since 1936 and was originally brought to Hollywood to write the music for the *Heart of Darkness*; when this project was abandoned, Welles brought him back for *Kane*, and Herrmann stayed on to become the greatest composer of the studio era, bar none.)

I use a tape demonstration to talk about composition in depth that is quite effective. After briefly describing the *180-degree system* (discussed initially on pp. 65–66) and *continuity editing* (introduced pp. 134–36), I show an excerpt from the golf links scene near the beginning of Howard Hawk's *Bringing Up Baby* (1938). This skillfully edited continuity sequence begins with a master shot establishing the axis of action, followed by a shot-reverse-shot dialogue exchange between Gary Grant and another character standing on the 180-degree line itself. We cut back to the master shot and Grant walks off, frame right, to retrieve a hooked ball, entering the next shot frame left and pointing to someone off-frame right who has apparently taken up his ball. An eyeline match reveals Katharine Hepburn in a medium long shot preparing a stroke. We cut back to Grant moving off-frame laterally from left to right, and then entering Hepburn's shot, frame left. The action continues with the two of them moving through a series of shots from left to right, and Grant occasionally looking off-frame, left, to a shot of the character he has left behind in the master shot. The sequence is paradigmatic in that the 180-degree system works perfectly to maintain consistent screen direction and coherently matching eyelines, yet the narrative space and time it constructs is completely artificial. Next I show the boarding house scene from *Citizen Kane* (as pictured in still 10.5), in which the complicated action of Mrs. Kane signing young Charlie over to Mr. Thatcher's bank is rendered in a single deep-focus sequence shot. The camera begins with a medium full shot of the boy playing with his sled in the snow and pulls slowly back through the window to reveal the interior of the boarding house and three characters inside, finally reaching the "fourth wall" to shoot the principle dialogue exchange (although overlapping dialogue is continuous throughout the shot). The camera then reverses its inward movement to follow Mrs. Kane back to the window for a cut to a reverse angle shot, as she calls Charlie in to pack his things. After this, I ask students to imagine how Hawks and the *Bringing Up Baby* crew might have rendered this same action as a multi-shot continuity sequence. The point is quickly made: we have before us two very different modes of dramatic/cinematic construction which have very different psychological affects. It is the difference between classical Hollywood continuity structure and the sequence shot composed in-depth, of which *Citizen Kane* is inarguably the *locus classicus*, if nothing else.

At this point, I usually outline the film's structure on the board, pointing out how each narrator's version of Kane is colored by a particular bias, even—perhaps, especially, the "News on the March" obituary—and how, in the course of the film, we watch Kane change from someone we like and admire into someone we hate. In a general sense, *Citizen Kane* charts the course of human knowledge from innocence to experience—a journey that the American people, standing on the brink of World War II, were just about to complete. In this regard, *Kane*'s sense of history and of its own precise place in history is acute. It evokes a nation balancing on a fulcrum between the inertia of the Great Depression and the challenge of global leadership, and the death of Charles Foster Kane signals a changing of the guard. Kane—whose world, as the "News on the March" commentator tells us, "is history now"—has represented the imperialist adventurism and hemispheric isolationism of the century's first forty years, and, in his role as media baron, he has manipulated popular opinion and politics to those ends through the mass press. The new world is represented by the thinly disguised Time-Life media empire for whom Rawlston and Thompson work at assembling Kane's obituary—not in the medium of his own ascendency, print, but on celluloid. Theirs is a world of internationalism in politics and motion pictures/broadcasting/photojournalism in communication. The film's grand irony is that the new photographic and electronic media are no more capable of objectively representing reality than the old—an irony compounded by the fact that its own medium is the film *Citizen Kane*. If reality is itself too complex and multiformed for *Kane*'s narrators to capture, either individually or collectively, then media attempts to represent reality are bound to fail. From the open medacity of the Kane press ("Galleons off the Jersey Coast!," "Fraud at Polls!," the trumped-up myth of Susan Alexander Kane's operatic talent) to the mindlessly pugnacious and insensitive quest by Thompson for the meaning of "Rosebud," the essential fraudulence of media representation stands at the core of the film. The "Rosebud" gambit itself, which generates *Kane*'s form, is a cheap trick invented by Rawlston to hype his newsreel, but the fundamental superficiality of *all* media—the idea, in Thompson's terms, that "a word or phrase can sum up a man's life"—is still very much with us in the 1990s, as anyone who reads *People* magazine or watches television newscasts will be aware.

Kane overshadows Welles' other work, but certainly not to the point of exclusion. Had it been released in its 132-minute form, *The Magnificent Ambersons* (1942) would surely have been as great a film, but the surviving 88-minute fragment gives ample proof of the original's epic sweep and majesty. The replacement of Welles by Norman Foster during the shooting of *Journey into Fear* (1942; released 1943) and RKO's unaccountable destruction of the negative for *It's All True* meant that Welles did not complete another film as director until *The Stranger* (1946), a calculated commercial venture closely supervised by producer Sam Spiegel for International Pictures, which Welles nevertheless managed to infuse with a large dose of self-parody. (For a Dossier on *It's All True*, as well as scholarly essays on all aspects of Welles' career and a complete catalogue of his work, see *Persistence of Vision*, No. 7 (1989), a special issue growing out of the Orson Welles Retrospective held at New York University in the Spring of 1988.) *The Lady from Shanghai* (1947) and *Touch of Evil* (1957; restored 1976) are today regarded as paradigmatic *films noirs*, and they nicely book end the histori-

cal contours of that genre. In between came two eccentric but widely acclaimed adaptations from Shakespeare, *Macbeth* (1948; restored 1980) and *Othello* (1952). So did *Mr. Arkadin* (1952), a *Kane*-like identity quest marred by the financial necessity of intermittent and ambulatory production. *The Trial* (1962) and *Chimes at Midnight* (1966) were Welles' last released features and the first over which he had exercised total production control since *Citizen Kane*. The former continues to disappoint critics for not being sufficiently "Kafkaesque," while the latter is "Shakespearean" enough to delight them still (as if Welles hadn't made a career out of turning other people's classics into his own in the first place). *Chimes* is certainly Welles' last major film and the summation of his work in Shakespeare; many hold it to be a masterpiece equal in stature to *Kane*. Beyond that are the several minor works discussed in the endnotes—the 58-minute French telefilm *The Immortal Story* (1969), *F for Fake* (1976; released in France as *Vérités et Mensonges*, 1973), and *Filming Othello* (1978)—the still unfinished *Don Quixote* and the still unreleased *The Other Side of the Wind* (see Audrey Stainton, "Orson Welles' Secret," *Sight and Sound*, 57, 4 [Autumn 1988], 253–60; and Scott Bukatman, "Incompletion, Simulation, and the Refusal of the Real: The Last Films of Orson Welles," *Persistence of Vision*, No. 7 [1989], (83–90).

In assessing the inarguable decline of Welles' later career, it is useful to consider the *totality* of his artistry, as several recent biographers have done (Barbara Leaming, *Orson Welles* [1985]; Charles Higham, *Orson Welles* [1985]; and, best of the lot, Frank Brady, *Citizen Welles* [1989]; see also Bret Wood, *Orson Welles: A Biobibliography* [New York: Greenwood Press, 1990]). Welles was a celebrated theater director from 1931 to 1960 (see Richard France, *The Theatre of Orson Welles* [Lewisburg: Bucknell University Press, 1977]; and Michael Denning, "Towards a People's Theater: The Cultural Politics of the Mercury Theater," *Persistence of Vision*, No. 7, [1989], 24–38), and a prominent theater, film, and television actor from 1931 until his death in 1985 (see, e.g. Robert Sklar, "Welles before *Kane*: The Discourse on a 'Boy Genius,' *Persistence of Vision*, No. 7, 63–72; and Michael Anderegg, "Orson Welles as Performer," *Persistence of Vision*, No. 7, 73–82). His innovations in live broadcasting via "Mercury Theater on the

Air" and its successors are well known, and there is a way in which Welles' latterday incarnations as television storyteller, talk-show guest, and pitchman were logical extensions of his many radio personae. (Our knowledge of Welles' contributions to radio theater has been enhanced through the Voyager Company's 1988 publication of "Theatre of the Imagination: Radio Stories by Orson Welles & The Mercury Theater," six, hour-long cassettes digitally remastered from acetate recordings made at the time of the original broadcasts.) If an artist's early work proceeds his contemporaries by half a century and he lives long enough, then at some point his own life is bound to fall behind it, and that is what happened to Welles. Another director making *The Magnificent Ambersons*, *The Lady from Shanghai*, *Touch of Evil*, and *Chimes at Midnight*, not to mention *Macbeth* and *Othello*, in the same time frame as Welles might have been deemed a remarkable success. But Welles was judged at every turn against the brilliant standard he had set for himself in *Citizen Kane*, a film still universally thought to be among the most influential films ever made. That he understood this and did not become bitter, and he continued to try and make art, successfully or not, quite literally until the night he died should fill us not with regret but with admiration.

Important endnotes for Chapter 10 deal with the controversy over the authorship of the script(s) of *Kane*; Robert Altman's soundtracks and their similarities to Welles'; scholarship on Welles' use of sound; scholarship on the meaning of "Rosebud"; the recent rediscovery of footage from *It's All True* (1942); and Welles' minor and/or unfinished films.

Chapter 11

Wartime and Postwar Cinema: Italy and America, 1940–1951

World War II seems such a distant event to students in the 1990s that I generally remind them of a few of its central facts, especially the material devastation of so much of Western and Eastern Europe at the war's conclusion. Italian neorealism becomes more salient in these circumstances as a truly reconstructive movement in both politics and art. Cinematically, the neorealists were reacting against a national tradition of spectacle (the pre-World War I epic), decadence ("telephono bianco"), and bombast ("calligraphism"). Politically, they were reacting against both Fascism and American economic imperialism (i.e., the Marshall Plan). Their ideological roots were Marxist, and for aesthetic models they naturally looked toward the cinemas of the post-Revolutionary Soviet Union and the Popular Front (i.e., French "poetic realism"). Ironically, however, most had received their training in the state-sponsored film industry created by Mussolini during the thirties, through the establishment of the Centro Sperimentale

della Cinematografia (1935) and the building of the huge Cinecittà studios in Rome (1937); and some neorealists (notably Roberto Rossellini) had actually directed Fascist propaganda films during the war. But the Mussolini regime collapsed in 1943, and Rome was liberated from the occupying Nazis in June 1944, so that the true nature of these filmmakers could finally emerge in *Roma, città aperta* (1954), shot on location by Rossellini and his collaborators in the streets of that city shortly after the Nazi withdrawal.

In fact, the first identifiable neorealist film had appeared two years earlier while Il Duce was still in power. Luchino Visconti's *Ossessione* (1943) was a bleak melodrama shot on location in the countryside around Ferrara, but it was suppressed by the Fascist censors because of its negative portrait of Italian provincial life (pp. 442–43). Thus it fell to *Roma, città aperta* (Roberto Rossellini, 1942) to introduce international audiences to the neorealist hallmarks of documentary texture, postrecorded sound, a mix of professional and nonprofessional actors, improvisation of script, and a focus on the lives of ordinary people caught up in contemporary events (pp. 443–44). *Roma, città aperta*, in fact, became the neorealist paradigm, and Rossellini followed it with *Paisa* (1946) and *Germania, anno zero* (1947) to complete his "war trilogy" (pp. 444–46). Visconti (pp. 448–50) made a second contribution to the movement with *La terra trema* (1948), an epic of Sicilian peasant life which many consider one of the postwar cinema's greatest achievements, while neorealism's third major director emerged in the former matinee idol Vittorio De Sica (pp. 446–48; 452–53). De Sica, working in close collaboration with Cesare Zavattini (pp. 440–43), neorealism's major theorist and spokesperson, produced in *Sciuscià* (1946), *Ladri di biciclette* (1948), and *Umberto D.* (1952) films central to the movement's canon. (Footnotes to pp. 446, 450, and 452–53 extend the discussion of Rossellini and Visconti and De Sica's careers beyond the neorealist era and into the seventies.)

Because its fundamenal subject was the day-to-day reality of a people impoverished and traumatized by war, neorealism as a cohesive national movement did not outlast the rebuilding of Italy's economy by the Marshall Plan, but it was formative of much that came later. As the first postwar cinema to reject Hollywood's narrative conventions and studio production techniques, neorealism had an enormous influence on future European film movements like British "social realism" and the French and Czech New Waves. Furthermore, Third World cinemas that came into being after the war in India, Africa, and Latin America all looked to the example of neorealism at their foundation, just as neorealism itself had forecast, in on-location shooting and postrecorded sound, the mode of production that became the industry standard in the developed world over the next few decades. Finally, the neorealist movement provided the training ground for a number of filmmakers whose work returned the Italian cinema to international prominence in the sixties and seventies, notably Federico Fellini (b. 1920) and Michelangelo Antonioni (b. 1912), and such colleagues as Pier Paolo Pasolini (1922–75), Francesco Rosi (b. 1922), and Lina Wertmüller (b. 1928). Locally, two political factors conspired to defeat neorealism—the Andreotti Law, promulgated in 1949 to protect the Italian industry from foreign (mainly American) domination by establishing import/export quotas, and criticism from the Stalinist Left that neorealism did not sufficiently follow the party line. The Andreotti Law was particularly crippling because it gave the government the power to restrict the export of domestic films that did not present Italy in a "positive" light, as neorealist films hardly ever did and cut the movement off from the foreign markets on which it depended. (It was foreign critical acclaim and foreign earnings that had made neorealism viable in the first place: Italian audiences didn't need to be reminded of the grim circumstances that surrounded them and tended to prefer lighter fare.)

The American section of Chaper 11 breaks almost evenly into wartime and postwar segments. As a prologue to "Hollywood at War" and the Roosevelt administration's direct manipulation of the film industry through the Bureau of Motion Picture Affairs (BMPA), I discuss the industry's (and the country's) prewar isolationism and some of the reasons for it. First among these was the moguls' desire to maintain a stance of neutrality in Nazi-dominated and pro-Nazi markets abroad—which by mid-1940 included Germany, Austria, Czechoslovakia, Poland, Belgium, the Netherlands and France in the former category, and Italy, the Balkans, Spain, Portugal, and Latin America, plus Japan and the countries of its "Greater Southeast Asia Co-Prosperity Sphere" in the latter. Hollywood, in fact, was able to maintain its share in these markets through late 1941, after which its only foreign markets were Switzerland and Sweden through the end of 1945. It's also true that a significant minority of the domestic audience sympathized with fascism and anti-Semitism before 1942, and Hollywood's mainly Jewish studio chiefs wanted to tread lightly around these issues. Beyond these specifics, there was the fiercely isolationist mood of the country in general, and the fact that business relationships existed between U.S. corporations backing the film industry and certain German cartels—RCA/GE had such a relationship with I.E. Siemens, while Allied Chemical (a Rockefeller interest) was aligned with I.G. Farben—all good reasons not to give offense before it was absolutely required.

As President Franklin D. Roosevelt and his advisors saw it, our declaration of war on Japan on December 8, 1941, in the wake of Pearl Harbor, required Hollywood's service—absolutely—and ten days later he created by executive order the Bureau of Motion Picture Affairs (BMPA) within the Office of War Information to mobilize the film industry for the national defense effort (p. 456). Most students today seem surprised that an American president was able to turn Hollywood into an agency of wartime propaganda so quickly and (apparently) effortlessly for nearly four years. In fact, there was no direct coercion, and the studios cooperated voluntarily with the program laid down by the BMPA, which lacked enforcement machinery in any case. But, as the footnote on p. 456 points out, there were more subtle inducements, such as the suspension of the Justice Department's antitrust suit, the Selective Service System's classification of motion pictures as an "essential industry," and Hollywood's new dependence on the domestic market almost exclusively for its profits. (The best account of the frequently uneasy relationship between the studios and the BMPA is contained in Clayton R. Koppes and Gregory D. Black's *Hollywood Goes to War: How Politics, Profits, and Propaganda Shaped World War II Movies* [New York: The Free Press, 1987].)

To illustrate the progression and range of Hollywood's wartime propaganda features, I show excerpts from such lurid (but undeniably effective) anti-Nazi films as *Hitler's Children* (Edward Dymtryk, 1943), which offers up Bonita Granville for an on-screen flogging for refusing to participate in an "Aryan" breeding program (thus violating the Production Code twice in the service of ideology), and such relatively sophisticated combat films as *Destination Tokyo* (Delmer Daves, 1943), with its strident hate-the-godless-Jap rhetoric and its ethnically balanced submarine crew celebrating Thanksgiving amidst exploding depth-charges at the bottom of Tokyo Bay. Out of class, I try to show something upbeat from the "United Nations" (i.e., our allies in arms) category, such as *Casablanca* (Michael Curtiz, 1942) or *Reunion in France* (Jules Dassin, 1942), but I also show the entirely mendacious purge trial sequence from *Mission to Moscow* (Michael Curtiz, 1943) to suggest how some of these films would be perceived as Communist propaganda only a few years later and how, in fact, some of Roosevelt's minions did go farther than necessary

in order to make a point. Not to overlook the non-fiction film, I show an equally extreme entry from Frank Capra's *Why We Fight* series (although it was withdrawn from circulation after only a month's release because the war ended and is generally not listed as part of the canon). Produced over a period of 18 months to prepare both servicemen and civilians for the enormous American casualities (one million, in a best case scenario) projected for a land invasion of the Japanese Island, *Know Your Enemy: Japan* (1945) can only be described as a brilliantly constructed hate film. Assembled mainly from film footage and prewar Japanese feature films, *Know Your Enemy: Japan* is a potent brew of fact and fiction, which uses Eisensteinian montage tactics to overwhelm its audience with fear and loathing for the Japanese. Students find it both fascinating and repellent, which it genuinely is, but it provides an immensely effective lesson in just how desperate those times really were.

Since all of the three major postwar genres manifest in heightened realism, I try to locate some reasons for this in the stylistic influence of wartime documentaries and newsreels (both as such and as integrated into feature films like *Casablanca* [Michael Curtiz, 1942]) and of Italian neorealism, immensely popular in the United States just after the war. Equally important, however, was the economic crisis in the film industry around 1947 which made location shooting cheaper than studio work for the first time since the coming of sound, combined with technological improvements in film stocks and camera equipment that made location shooting more practical. As the cost of set construction and studio overhead rose steadily owing to spiralling postwar inflation, more and more screenplays were tailored for location shooting, which stimulated the rise of "social consciousness" films, semi-documentary melodramas, and *films noir*. At the same time, a new critical scrutiny of American values was in the air, owing in no small part to wartime propaganda's depiction of the society as a perfect democracy, free of racial bigotry, class cleavage, and political corruption—none of which was true. "Social consciousness" films involved a direct (if often too polite) address to these problems, mainly through fictionalized accounts of the effects of racial segregation and restriction. If a film attempted to recreate real cases of racism, anti-Semitism, and racketeering (or espionage or anthing else, for that matter) in actual locations, it was understood to be a semi-documentary melodrama. This form, which we would call "docudrama" today, became closely associated with 20th Century-Fox and producer Louis de Rochemont, creator of *The March of Time* newsreel series, and through such Henry Hathaway-directed films as *The House on 92nd Street* (1945), *13 Rue Madeleine* (1946), and *Call Northside 777* (1948).

Film noir was distinct from "social consciousness" films and semi-documentary films but shared with them the practice of location shooting and an implicitly critical vision of American experience. Discovered by French critics after the war and created largely by German émigré filmmakers who had come to Hollywood to escape Hitler, *film noir* posits a world of moral corruption and betrayal where nothing is what it seems. This instability is rendered visible through a cinematographic style highly reminiscent of German Expressionism and, more recently, *Citizen Kane*—one dependent on wideangle lenses to achieve great depth of field, low-key lighting, night-for-night shooting, and angular, bizarrely distorted compositions within the frame. Most *films noir* were pessimistic crime melodramas with vulnerable but unsympathetic protagonists who are variously entrapped, sold-out, and double-crossed in pursuit of their own lusts and greed. (In the text, I equate *film noir* thematically with pre-martial law Poland's "cinema of moral anxiety" in that it reflects conditions forced upon people living in a mendacious, self-deluding society.) A frequent metaphor in these narratives is the Freudian "return of the repressed"—something welling up from the long-sublimated past to wreck havoc on the present.

It should come as no surprise, then, that *film noir* achieved its paradigmatic formulation at the height of the anti-Communist witch-hunt in Hollywood, when the youthful flirtation of hundreds of writers, actors, and directors with Communism during the Depression was used by the House Un-American Activities Committee (HUAC) to smear them as traitors, and when so many of their former collaborators and friends cheerfully betrayed them for personal gain. According to some historians, the Hollywood blacklist functioned tactically as a form of union-busting, and ideologically as the vengeance of the Right for fourteen years of the New Deal. In human terms, it was a personal tragedy for the 324 film artists who lost their jobs and, in most cases, their careers to the treachery, ignorance, and cupidity of their fellow citizens. But most important for us, the blacklist devastated the American film industry's creative community, as competition was replaced by denunciation, respect by mistrust, and paranoia was rampant everywhere. In this context, the Paramount decrees and the rapid diffusion of television fell like a plague of locusts on the studios, and Hollywood, never far removed from the sewer's brink, fell briefly into it.

Two books that I find especially valuable in teaching American cinema of this period are Dana Polan's *Power & Paranoia: History, Narrative, and the American Cinema, 1940–1950* (New York: Columbia University Press, 1986) and William Manchester's *The Glory and the Dream: A Narrative History of America, 1932–72* (Boston: Little Brown & Co., 1974; 1988). Polan's work is a superb cultural history which challenges many accepted views of the decade and reveals its crucial conflicts submerged in seemingly conventional films, while Manchester's volume is a traditional narrative history, rich in detail and insight, which is particularly illuminating about the psychological shredding of America, 1943–52.

Major endnotes for the Italian section of Chapter 11 concern the Marshall Plan; the involvement of Mussolini's son Vittorio Mussolini in the film industry; "calligraphism;" and the film career of Carlo Lizzani. For the American section major notes deal with the creation of the Office of War Information; the World War II combat film as genre; the impact of the Paramount decrees and their legal status today; a bibliography of scholarly literature on *film noir*; a categorical filmography of *film noir*; a filmography/bibliography of "female gothic" melodramas; a bibliography on Communist activity in Hollywood; Herbert Biberman and *Salt of the Earth* (1954); social and economic reasons for the decline in film attendance in the late forties and fifties; and a bibliography of scholarship on Hollywood's brief attempt to co-opt the television industry.

Chapter 12

Hollywood, 1952–1965

Readers of the First Edition will find this chapter substantially revised. There is significant new material on the conversion to color, stereoscopic 3-D, and all of the widescreen processes, and of course, the eight-page gathering of color stills (which have referents in Chapters 8–18), that occurs between pp. 486–87. Moreover, the section entitled "American Directors in the Early Widescreen Age" (pp. 498–506) contains expanded discussions of Otto Preminger, Elia Kazan, Nicholas Ray, Douglas Sirk, Robert Aldrich, John Huston, Budd Boetticher, Anthony Mann, Samuel Fuller, and others, while the "Comedy" section (pp. 508–11) adds Mel Brooks and Woody Allen. There is much new material on the anticommunist cycle of 1948–55 (pp. 515–17), and the "Science Fiction" section has been expanded in two directions to include both exploitation producers and high-tech, computer-generated special effects.

I spend most of my classroom energies for this unit on the introduction of widescreen, which is poorly understood these days thanks to careless video formatting and multiplex theaters whose screens are too small to contain full widescreen images. Most students have been watching widescreen films on television and video for years without the slightest suspicion that anything is missing (or, in the case of pan-and-scan, added), except for a vague sense of bewilderment regarding squeezed credits. So I spend at least one class period on a tape and lecture presentation that leaves them little doubt about the various widescreen formats and what happens to them on a cathode ray tube. To illustrate the effect of multi-camera/projector widescreen, I show the conclusion of Gance's *Napoléon* (1927), whose Polyvision process was the model for Cinerama. That moment when, as Napoleon addresses his troops on the brink of the Italian campaign, the central Academy frame expands into a three-panel triptych makes the point very nicely that all Cinerama-like processes widen their frame by joining three standard 33mm images side by side, and that the major problem in projection was frame alignment. Next I show an excerpt from *Revenge of the Creature* (Jack Arnold, 1955), the last film released in Natural Vision, to demonstrate that fifties-style 3-D was *not* a widescreen process, as students for some reason nearly always think, but one exploiting the depth-perspective within the Academy frame. (As an experiment with a new optical format, 3-D was, of course, related to widescreen, and 20th Century-Fox muddied the waters in 1954 by advertising CinemaScope as "The Modern Miracle You See Without Glasses.") My tape of *Revenge of the Creature* was encoded in a video 3-D format for broadcast in 1982, and I have several pairs of cardboard polarized glasses which I can distribute if the class is small. Most original Natural Vision films are available only in non-stereo versions today, but even flat excerpts from films like *Charge at Feather River* (Gordon Douglas, 1953) and *Dial M for Murder* (Hitchcock, 1954) can be used to suggest the way in which depth was exploited in the originals.

Anamorphic widescreen, which through its cost-effectiveness and relative simplicity became the vehicle for wholesale industry conversion, is difficult to illustrate on tape, so I use the text (pp. 488–92) to fill in here. This is a good (and, in my presentation, necessary) place to introduce the concept of letter-boxing and its alternatives. It is easy enough for students to see the problem of squeezing films with aspect ratios of 1.85:1 and 2.35:1 onto a screen formatted at 1.33:1 (the Academy frame). But it's another thing for them to appreciate what happens to a widescreen film aesthetically when this occurs. To help, I show examples of several different approaches described in the footnote on p. 490: first, squeezed credits, unsqueezed center-framed film with image loss at both edges of as much as 20 percent (e.g., *White Witch Doctor* [Henry Hathaway, 1953]); second, pan and scan, which induces artificial camera movement and perceptual disorientation (e.g., *The Wild Bunch* [Sam Peckinpah, 1968]); third, frame-cutting, in which opposite sides of the same wide-frame image are cut against each other to produce such lunacies as characters staring each other down without matching eyelines (e.g., *The Roots of Heaven* [John Huston, 1957]; *The Innocents* [Jack Clayton, 1962]; *Kwaidan* [Masaki Kobayashi, 1964]; *In Cold Blood* [Richard Brooks, 1967]; *Little Big Man* [Arthur Penn, 1971]); and fourth, letter-boxing the video frame

to reduce the image size but restore the film's original frame ratio (Akira Kurosawa's *The Hidden Fortress* [1958] available on video in letter-boxed TohoScope, works well here).

To wrap up this discussion of widescreen processes and cover all the bases, I make it clear that Paramount's widescreen alternative Vista-Vision was a nonanamorphic process which, except when roadshown full-frame on horizontal transport projectors, was reduced to a 35mm positive from a 70mm negative and normally shown in the "golden ratio" of 1.85:1. This blowing-down process produced an image of great clarity and resolution which contrasted markedly with the quality of anamorphic prints that, when unsqueezed in projection, were in effect blown up. (Paramount Video's tape of the studio's first VistaVision release *White Christmas* [Michael Curtiz, 1954] actually replicates the original processes' density and saturation, and is worth a look in class if you can find the film.) Wide-film widescreen (pp. 492–94) can be nicely illustrated with a tape of the handsomely letter-boxed "Director's Cut" of David Lean's *Lawrence of Arabia* (1962), which some of the students may actually have seen theatrically in the 1989 roadshow. (Showing a few excerpts from the earlier, non-letter-boxed version of *Lawrence* back to back with their letter-boxed counterparts can hammer home the importance of seeing films in their original ratios.) To conclude the widescreen discussion, I always show something in the European 1.66:1 ratio, usually Antonioni's *L'avventura* (1959) or the recently available (and gorgeous) *Il deserto rosso* (1964).

For the rest of this chapter, students seem to do pretty well on their own, although the large number of titles and dates tends to be anxiety-producing here as elsewhere. In fact, from this point until the end of the course, I tend to emphasize films which exemplify cycles or genres (*My Son John* [Leo McCarey, 1952]; *Kiss Me Deadly* [Robert Aldrich, 1954]; *The Searchers* [John Ford, 1956]), historically significant trends (*Rebel Without a Cause* [Nicholas Ray, 1955] as an avatar of "teenpix"), or the work of certain directors (Hitchcock's *Rear Window* [1956], *Vertigo* [1958], etc.). But there are two points that I like to underscore before leaving this material entirely. One is that the modern science-fiction film, with its dual emphasis on space travel and global catastrophe, was born of World War II: Hitler's V-1 and V-2 rockets implied that our future was in the stars, and the Hiroshima-Nagasaki blasts told us that science and technology were suddenly in a position to determine the destiny of the entire human race. The other is that the 1952 U.S. Supreme Court decision in the *Miracle* case, and its subsequent clarification in lower courts, gave the motion extended First Amendment protection to motion pictures for *the first time* since the 1915 *Mutual v. Ohio* decision (see footnote to p. 81) had specifically excluded them. From a contemporary perspective, it is quite stunning to realize that for their first half century American motion pictures were not regarded as a medium of communication at all and were therefore unprotected by Constitutional guarantees against censorship and prior restraint—a circumstance which goes far toward explaining Hollywood's knee-jerk, self-censorship reflex from the institution of the Hays Office in 1922, through the Production Code Administration of 1934, to the Waldorf Declaration of 1947.

Major endnotes for Chapter 12 deal with color-fading in Eastman-based systems and other preservation issues; a bibliography of scholarship on color technology; a bibliography of scholarship on stereoscopic cinematography; early wide-film systems; a bibliography on stereophonic sound in motion pictures; the work of Arthur Freed; the work of Sergio Leone; the controversy over *My Son John* (Leo McCarey, 1952) and *The Fountainhead* (King Vidor, 1949); the spy film as genre; a bibliography of work on fifties alien-invasion films; a bibliography on the work of George Pal; a bibliography on the horror film and the science-fiction film as genres; a filmography of AIP monster films; a filmography of teenage exploitation films; and traveling matte photography and computer-generated special effects.

The French New Wave and Its Native Context

As a history of French cinema from the Nazi Occupation through the present, with its major focus on the New Wave, Chapter 13 is pretty much self-contained. It's worth noting that the Occupation and postwar era produced many fine films (e.g., Marcel Carne's *Les Enfants du paradis* [1945]; Jean Cocteau's *La Belle et la bête* [1946]; René Clément's *Jeux interdits* [1952]; Jacques Becker's *Casque d'or* [1952]; Henri-Georges Clouzot's *La Salaire de la peur* [1953]—see pp. 538–42), but that they were often excessively literary and heavily scripted. Exceptions occurred in the austere classicism of Robert Bresson (*Le Journal d'un curé de campagne* [1950]; *Un Condamné à mort s'est échappé* [1956]—pp. 542–43), and the absurdist comedy of Jacques Tati (*Les Vacances de M. Hulot* [1953]—pp. 543–44). But the most influential predecessor of the New Wave was the German-born Max Ophüls, whose lushly stylized melodramas *La Ronde* (1950), *Le Plaisir* (1952), *Madame de . . .* (1953) and, above all, *Lola Montès* (1955) are masterworks of *mise-en-scène* (pp. 544–47). Also influential was the postwar documentary movement which provided a training ground for young directors outside the traditional industry system and resulted in such landmark nonfiction films as Georges Rouquier's *Farrebique* [1946], Georges Franju's *Le Sang des bêtes* (1949), and Alain Resnais' *Nuit et brouillard* (1955) (pp. 547–49), as were the examples of independent feature production (pp. 549–50) provided by Jean-Pierre Melville's *Bob le Flambeur* (1955), Agnès Varda's *La Pointe-Courte* (1955), and Roger Vadim's *Et Dieu créa la femme* (1956).

But the main impetus for the New Wave lay in the theoretical writings of Alexandre Astruc and, more prominently, André Bazin (pp. 550–52). Writing in *L'Ecran française* in 1948, Astruc formulated the concept of the *caméra-stylo* ("camera-pen"), in which film is an audiovisual language and the filmmaker a kind of writer in light. Bazin's influential journal *Cahiers du cinéma*, founded in 1951, embraced Astruc's notion and attracted to it a group of young *cinéphiles*—François Truffaut, Jean-Luc Godard, Claude Chabrol, Jacques Rivette, and Eric Rohmer—who first became critics and would soon become the major directors of the *nouvelle vague* (New Wave). Having spent much of their youths immersed in film history as it was projected on the screens of Henri Langlois' amazing Paris archive the Cinémathèque Française, the *Cahiers* group conceived a very large contempt for the mainstream "scenarist tradition," or "tradition of quality" and began a series of attacks on it in the journal's pages. Their position involved two basic premises: first, the superiority of mise-en-scène aesthetics (the long take, composition in depth) to all forms of montage; and second, *la politique des auteurs* ("the policy of authors"), a term coined by Truffaut in 1954 to mean that film should be a medium of personal artistic expression and that the best films are those imprinted with the maker's individual signature (and, ideally, that directors should write their own screenplays and not depend upon literarily oriented "scenarists" at all). Christened "the *auteur* theory" by American critic Andrew Sarris, Truffaut's idea was subjected to various forms of distortion and abuse over the next few decades—both by English-speaking practitioners and by the French themselves—and has today become anathema to academic film scholars of every stripe. *It is crucial to note, however, that the concept of authorship in cinema has never been seriously challenged as a schema for the ordering of historical information*—even by those most hostile to it in theoretical/ideological terms. All of our major reference books in film history are organized by director, producer, or other supervisory personnel; all of our survey histories attribute creative responsibility for films or components of films to individuals, singly or in collaboration; and books on major figures—Dreyer, Hitchcock, Welles, Ford, Rossellini, Yasujiro Ozu, Edwin S. Porter, Griffith, Walter Wanger, to name a few recent subjects—abound, regardless of their approach. Furthermore, the *Cahiers* critics were able to vindicate the *auteur* theory in part, at least, by becoming filmmakers and practicing it.

The first films of the New Wave were 16mm shorts, made between 1956–57, and features appeared from Claude Chabrol (*Le Beau Serge* [1958]; *Les Cousins* [1959], Truffaut (*Les Quatre-cents coups* [1959]), and Jean-Luc Godard (*À bout de souffle* [1959]) soon after (pp. 553–57).

The same year witnessed the emergence of "the Left Bank group" of the New Wave in Alain Resnais' *Hiroshima, mon amour* (1959)—intellectuals like Resnais, Chris Marker, and Agnès Varda, who, while supportive of the *Cahiers* group, drew their inspiration from modernist literature rather than film. Common to the films of both groups, however, was deconstruction of classical Hollywood norms through elliptical editing and location shooting with hand-held 35mm cameras (pp. 557–58). Such methods met the need of New Wave directors to make films quickly and cheaply, and the critical and commercial success of the first New Wave features produced impressive margins of profit. This is important to note, because the New Wave's challenge to the "tradition of quality" within the French industry was economic as well as aesthetic, and for awhile, at least, the films of the movement's three major figures—Truffaut, Godard, and Resnais—made money for their producers hand over fist.

Truffaut (pp. 559–64) was the most commercially successful of all the New Wave directors—so much so, that by the end of his career critics suspected he had begun to make the kind of well-tailored, crowd-pleasing films he had formerly attacked. (See Annette Insdorf, *Francois Truffaut*, [New York: Touchstone/Simon & Schuster, 1978; 1989].) And yet Truffaut's films were *always* works of sense and sensibility, from his "Antoine Doinel" series through *Vivement dimanche* (1983), and, when he died of a brain tumor in 1984 at the age of 52, it was very difficult to argue that he had ever been anything as a director but the passionate cinéphile and charming romantic ironist of his youth. (He was, however, a major innovator of widescreen composition in his first three features—*Les Quatre-cents coups* (1959), *Tirez sur le pianiste* (1960), *Jules et Jim* (1961)—all shot in French versions of CinemaScope, which one wouldn't know today since none are available in their original ratios.) The intellectual/political leader of the New Wave was Jean-Luc Godard (pp. 564–70), whose films of the sixties were so stylistically and ideologically radical as to alienate popular audiences and, after the "events of May" 1968, nearly everyone else. In the seventies Godard abandoned features altogether to make increasingly incomprehensible video essays, returning to commercial features again in the eighties with a kind of cynical, but always interesting, perspective. Of the three major New Wave figures, only Resnais (pp. 570–73) continues to make films according to his original vision, although popular success has eluded him since *Stavisky* in 1975.

Of the less spectacular, but no less sophisticated, original New Wave talents—Chabrol, Louis Malle, Eric Rohmer, Agnès Varda, Jacques Demy, and Jacques Rivette (pp. 575–80)—all are still directing with varying degrees of success. Chabrol, Malle, and Demy have all become mainstream commercial directors, while Rohmer, Varda, and Rivette exist at the margins as cult figures. Indeed, the New Wave is less important today for any of the work of its surviving members (with the possible exception of Resnais) than for the second- and third-generation talents it has nurtured within the French (and Swiss—see Alain Tanner, pp. 581–82) industry—directors like Claude Sautet, Bertrand Tavernier, Maurice Pialat, Bertrand Blier, and Marcel Ophüls (pp. 583–87)—who either trained with or were significantly influenced by New Wave figures. And beyond national boundaries, it is hardly possible to overestimate the influence of the New Wave and its creators in world cinema. In vindicating the concept of personal authorship, they demonstrated that film is an audiovisual language that can be crafted into "novels" and "essays," and by exploding classical Hollywood conventions they added new dimensions to that language which made it capable of expressing a whole new range of internal and external states. In doing so, the *nouvelle vague* helped to revitalize such stylistically moribund cinemas as the British, the American, and the West German, and it created a succession of "second waves" and "third waves" in the already flourishing cinemas of Italy, Poland, Czechoslovakia, Hungary, and Japan. Finally, the movement made France the leading center of modernist and postmodern film and theory, a position it holds to this day.

Major endnotes for Chapter 13 concern a bibliography of criticism on Robert Bresson; a bibliography of the writings of the *Cahiers* critics; French government (CNC) aid for New Wave filmmakers; the work of cinematographers Nestor Almendros and Raoul Coutard; the work of former Godard collaborator Jean-Pierre Gorin; the work of Chantal Akerman and a brief history of Belgian cinema; a note on Swiss French-language filmmakers; an extensive filmography of post-New Wave French filmmakers.

Chapter 14

New Cinemas in Britain and the English-Speaking Commonwealth

The material in this chapter has been detached from the other cinemas of Western Europe (now considered separately in Chapters 13 and 15) because its size has been tripled since the First edition. Furthermore, it now seems culturally correct to consider the cinemas of the major British Commonwealth nations as a unit, since they share a common history and—excepting the province of Quebec in Canada—a common language. The British Commonwealth of Nations began in the first decade of the twentieth century as a series of Imperial Conferences in which representatives of Britain and its self-governing colonies would meet to coordinate foreign policy. During the 1910s and 1920s, as these nations moved toward independence in foreign affairs, Britain declared them all to be equal in rank and united in a free association by their "common allegiance to the Crown"—an association legalized by the Statute of Westminster in 1931. The original Commonwealth was comprised of Australia, Britain, Canada, Ireland, New Zealand,

Newfoundland, and South Africa, but between 1947 and 1980 about 40 more nations joined the association as they became independent of British rule. Today, the Commonwealth functions as a loose confederation of independent states, territories, and dependencies with mutual interests, whose heads of government meet irregularly to coordinate national policies in pursuit of common goals. Membership is voluntary; member nations cover about one-fourth of the earth's land surface and contain about one-fourth of its population.

Although it made an extremely important contribution to documentary form in the work of John Grierson and his followers at the Empire Marketing Board (EMB)/General Post Office (GPO) Film Units, 1933–39, and the Crown Film Unit, 1940–45 (pp. 589–90), British cinema of the postwar era was even more "literary" than in France, relying heavily on the adaptation of classics in the work of such directors as Laurence Olivier (*Henry V* [1944]; *Hamlet* [1948]), David Lean (*Great Expectations* [1946]; *Oliver Twist*

[1948]), and Anthony Asquith (*The Importance of Being Earnest* [1952]). This conservatism was inspired by the cinema's bid to become a part of mainstream British culture, extending even to the work of less conventional directors like Carol Reed (*The Third Man* [1949]) and Michael Powell (*The Red Shoes* [1948]), and was countervailed only by the irreverent comedies of Michael Balcon's Ealing Studios (*The Lavender Hill Mob* [Charles Crichton, 1951]; *The Man in the White Suit* [Alexander Mackendrick, 1951]—pp. 590–91). On the whole, however, postwar British cinema—like the "culture" it aspired to—was elitist and culturally conservative. (See, e.g., Robert Murphy, *Realism and Tinsel: Cinema and Society in Britain 1938–48* [London: Routledge & Kegan Paul, 1989], and Peter Stead, *Film and the Working Class* [London: Routledge & Kegan Paul, 1989].)

As in France, a younger generation of *cinéphiles* led by Lindsay Anderson, Czechoslovakian-born Karel Reisz, and Tony Richardson organized a "Free Cinema" movement in 1954–55, whose stated purpose was to make short, low-budget documentaries about problems of daily life (pp. 592–93). Emerging simultaneously with a larger anti-establishment movement which rejected the traditional British class structure and its elitist values, Free Cinema was grounded in the ideology and practice of Italian neorealism, and it led directly to the "New Cinema" or "social realist" cinema formulated in Reisz' *Saturday Night and Sunday Morning* (1960). Like its successors, this film was shot on location in the industrial Midlands borrowing stylistic devices from the French New Wave, and it had a working-class protagonist and proletarian themes. Other entries were Tony Richardson's *A Taste of Honey* (1961) and *The Loneliness of the Long Distance Runner* (1962), John Schlesinger's *A Kind of Loving* (1962) and *Billy Liar* (1963), Lindsay Anderson's *This Sporting Life* (1963), and Karel Reisz' *Morgan: A Suitable Case for Treatment* (1966). Independently produced on modest budgets, British social realist films (pp. 593–96) attracted large audiences abroad and became the focus of international attention, very much like the New Wave, and for some of the same reasons. Not only were they fresh in both form and content, but they treated the sexual side of human experience more graphically than was then the norm in the United States and other major markets, creating the perception that they offered the best of all possible worlds—serious, stylistically advanced films which were at the same time "sexy."

British New Cinema thus brought prestige and profits to an industry that for much of its life had been culturally hidebound, economically depressed, and dominated to the point near extinction by American distributors (pp. 596–99). The same thing was happening, less surprisingly, in contemporary British literature and theater, and, for the first time ever—thanks to the Beatles, the Kinks, the Who, and the Rolling Stones—popular music. "Swinging" London briefly became the avant-garde pop capital of the Western world, and a major production site for both domestic superhits like Tony Richardson's *Tom Jones* (1963), Schlesinger's *Darling* (1965), and Richard Lester's two Beatles films, *A Hard Day's Night* (1964) and *Help!* (1965), as well as such international coproductions as Roman Polanski's *Repulsion* (1965), Truffaut's *Fahrenheit 451* (1966), Antonioni's *Blow-Up* (1966), and Stanley Kubrick's *2001* (1968) and *A Clockwork Orange* (1971). Like neorealism, then, New Cinema as a social realist movement was destroyed at least in part by its own material success. Yet its achievements inspired a new, more visually oriented generation of British filmmakers—John Boorman, Ken Russell, Nicholas Roeg, and Ridley Scott (pp. 600–3)—who would make their mark in the seventies, even as Britain's national economy began its precipitous decline. By the eighties, many of Britain's most prominent directors had followed a familiar trend and relocated in Hollywood, while domestic industry production reached an all-time low. Bright spots appeared in the work of the Monty Python team (e.g., Monty Python's *Life of Brian* [Terry Jones, 1979]), former Python animator Terry Gilliam (*Brazil* [1985], and narrative avant-gardists Peter Greenaway (*The Draughtsman's Contract* [1982] and Derek Jarman (*Caravaggio* [1986]), as well as in the Goldcrest/Channel 4-funded work of producer David Puttnam (*Chariots of Fire* [Hugh Hudson, 1981]; *My Beautiful Laundrette* [Stephen Frears, 1985])—pp. 603–8. In the present decade, there is clearly enough creative energy for the British cinema to once more overcome its traditionally literary bias and its culturally ingrained technophobia—the only thing to prevent it is capital, which grows scarcer by the month in Thatcherite England and is hardly to be found at all in Scotland, Ireland, and Wales.

While British cinema was entering the doldrums, the English-language film industry began to experience a vigorous and unprecedented challenge from Australia. After nearly two centuries of domination by first British and then American culture, Australia in the 1970s undertook to embrace its own. Early in the decade, the federal government established the Australian Film Development Corporation (after 1975, the Australian Film Commission, or AFC) to stimulate the growth of an indigenous industry, and founded a national film school (the Australian Film and Television School, or AFTS) to populate it with native Australian talent. The financial mechanism for this development was a system of lucrative tax incentives to attract foreign investment capital to the new industry, and between 1970 and 1985 Australia produced nearly 400 films (pp. 608–15). The first began to appear in the early seventies, and within the next few years several talented directors began to receive recognition, including Peter Weir (*Picnic at Hanging Rock* [1975]; *The Last Wave* [1977]), Bruce Beresford (*The Getting of Wisdom* [1977]), Fred Schepsi (*The Chant of Jimmy Blacksmith* [1978]), George Miller (*Mad Max* [1979]), and the first AFTS graduates, Phillip Noyce (*Newsfront* [1978]) and Gillian Armstrong (*My Brilliant Career* [1979]). Many of these directors have subsequently gone to work in other industries, primarily the American, but despite this temporary talent drain and a recent decline in government tax concessions, the Australian cinema remains one of the most influential and creatively vital in the world. New Zealand's industry has successfully modeled itself on the Australian, even though its population of 3.2 million can't support a regular features market and depends primarily on export sales (pp. 615–16).

Canada created the Canadian Film Development Corporation (CFDC), similar to Australia's, in 1967 but by the late seventies had abandoned one of the chief features of the Australian system—the insistence that films made in the country have indigenous casts and crews, regardless of their funding source (pp. 616–19). For much of the time since, Canada has experienced an unprecedented boom in the production of commercial features, most of which lack a specifically Canadian character (p. 620). Indeed, many "Canadian" films are actually shot out of the country with CFDC financing or use Canadian locales to represent other places (Montreal for Paris; any Canadian town or city for its U.S. equivalent), so that by 1982 foreign-dominated film and video distribution companies accounted for 73 percent of Canada's gross film industry revenues. (See R. Bruce Elder, *Image and Identity: Reflections on Canadian Film and Culture* [Waterloo, Ontario: Wilfred Laurier University Press, 1989]; Gerald G. Graham, *Canadian Film Technology, 1896–1986* [Cranbury, N.J.: University of Delaware Press, 1990]; Gerald Pratley, "The Eyes of Canada: The National Film Board at Fifty," *Sight and Sound*, 58, 4 [Autumn 1989]: 229–33; and Kenneth Winikoff, "They Always Get Their Man," *American Film*, 15, 10 [July 1990]: 26–31.) The exception is the French-language cinema of the province of Quebec (pp. 620–21), unique, frequently avant-garde, and fiercely independent (see, e.g., John Harkness, "The Improbable Rise of Denys Arcand," *Sight and Sound*, 58, 4 [Autumn 1989], 234–38).

Major endnotes for Chapter 14 concern the career of Michael Powell with specific regard to *Peeping Tom* (1959); the Losey-Pinter collaboration; thumbnail histories of the cinemas of Ireland, Scotland and Wales; a bibliography of scholarship on the decline of the British film industry in the eighties; and trade information on the industries of Australia and New Zealand.

Chapter 15

European Renaissance: West

It may seem reductive to attribute an entire aesthetic movement to the work of two directors, but in fact Italian film culture in the fifties and sixties was virtually synonymous with Federico Fellini and Michelangelo Antonioni, both of whom had trained as neorealists after the war. Fellini, of course, continues to make films and is still well known today, but Antonioni has been nearly forgotten by the public at large—in part because a cerebral hemorrhage has prevented his working since 1982. In the 1950s, Fellini (pp. 623–26) made an impressive series of films whose form was neorealist but whose content was primarily allegorical—*I vitelloni* (1953); *La strada* (1954); *La notti di Cabiria* (1956)—and then pursued a surrealist course in the sixties with *La dolce vita* (1960), *8 1/2* (1963), *Guilietta degli spiriti* (1965), and *Fellini Satyricon* (1969)—all of which enjoyed great popular success, as much for their perceived "decadence," no doubt, as for their remarkable cinematic style. By the seventies Fellini had acquired the reputation of a flamboyant ironic fantasist which sustained him through such serious and successful films as *Fellini Roma* (1972), *Amarcord* (1974), *Casanova* (1976), *Prova d'orchèstra* (1979), *La città delle donne* (1980), *E la nava va* (1983), and so on.

Compared to Antonioni (pp. 627–30), however, Fellini now seems the lesser figure in several respects. Antonioni's first films were bleak neorealist documentary shorts (e.g., *Netteza urbana* [1948]), but during the fifties he turned increasingly to an examination of the Italian bourgeoisie grounded firmly in *mise-en-scène*—*Cronaca du un amore* (1950); *La signor a senza camelie* (1953); *Le amiche* (1955)—and in the early sixties, he produced a trilogy of middle-class malaise that made him internationally famous. In *L'avventura* (1959), *La notte* (1960), and *L'eclisse* (1962), Antonioni used long-take sequence shots equating film time with real time to create a vision of the numbing emptiness of modern urban life. He went on to use color expressionistically in *Il deserto rosso* (1964) and

Blow-Up (1966) to convey alienation and abstraction from human emotion, and all of his later work in some way concerned the disintegration of personal relationships (*Zabriskie Point* [1969]; *Identificazione di una donna* [1982]) and of identity itself (*The Passenger* [1975]). The films that Antonioni made between 1959 and 1975 were all heavily dependent upon the telephoto and zoom lens, and it is clear today that he was the first major director to use lens technology in a conceptually consistent—and, usually, brilliant way. *Il deserto rosso*, for example, is at one level a film of spatial abstraction achieved through lens optics, while the seven-minute zoom-and-tracking shot that concludes *The Passenger* effaces the identity of its protagonist optically as surely as his own death. Optical tracking, combined with sophisticated montage-style editing, gives the "empty" conclusion of *L'eclisse* and the exploding house sequence in *Zabriskie Point* an impact unlike anything else the cinema has to offer. Because environment was such an important concept for Antonioni, his films can seem dated by their very specific cultural and chronological settings. But they are narratives in a technical sense only, and it is as essays on the surfaces of reality itself that they are best observed.

While Fellini and Antonioni were putting Italy in the vanguard of modernist cinema, the country's second postwar generation of directors emerged. Ermanno Olmi (*Il pòsto* [1961]; *Un certo giorno* [1968]; etc.) continued the neorealist tradition in his tales of ordinary people caught up in systems beyond comprehension or control (p. 631). Pier Paolo Pasolini (pp. 631–32), who had worked as a scriptwriter for Fellini, achieved international reknown for his semi-documentary reconstruction of the life of Christ—*Il vangèlo secondo Matteo* (1964)—and went on to make a series of astounding, sometimes outrageous, films offering Marxist interpretations of history and myth (e.g., *Teorèma* [1968]; *Medea* [1969]; *Salò* [1975]), before his murder in 1975. Bernardo Bertolucci (pp. 633–35) is likewise a Marxist intellectual who attempts to correlate sexuality, ideology, and history in films like *Il conformista* (1970), *Ultimo tango a Parigi* (1972), and *1900* (1976), although this analysis has become increasingly difficult to find in such recent work as *The Last Emperor* (1987). Other important Italian filmmakers (pp. 635–42) include Francesco Rosi (*Salvatore Giuliano* [1962]; *Cronaca di una morte annunciata* [1987], Marco Bellocchio (*I*

pugni in tasca [1965]; *Enrico IV* [1984]), Marco Ferreri (*La grande bouffe* [1973]);' Éttore Scola (*Una giornata speciale* [1977]; *La Nuit de Varennes* [1982]), Paolo and Vittorio Taviani (*Padre, Padrone* [1977]; *La notte di San Lorenzo* [1981]), Lina Wertmüller (*Swept Away* [1974]; *Pasqualino settebellezze* [1976]), and a host of new comedy directors such as Maurizio Nichetti, Nanni Moretti, and Carlo Verdone (pp. 641–42).

I use a videotape presentation to clarify the section on "Contemporary Widescreen Technologies and Styles" (pp. 642–46), which is essentially about the aesthetics of the zoom lens, since this material can be confusing without illustration. Essentially, though, lens optics are quite simple. The wide-angle lens is one of short focal length (as low as 12.5mm) and great depth of field. The telephoto lens reverses this equation, possessing great focal length (as much as 500mm) and little depth of field. The zoom lens is a lens of continuously variable focal length, from extreme wide-angle to extreme telephoto positions (e.g., 25mm–250mm, the standard ratio-zoom-ratio being 1:10). The zoom lens gives cinema the capability of optical tracking (either in depth or, in its telephoto position, laterally), optical hovering (effectively, i.e., moving from close-up, to medium shot, to long shot, without the discontinuity of montage), and cutting on optical movement. The telephoto position can also be used to warp optical space and create expressive abstraction. In my demonstration, I show the betrayal scene from *Bonnie and Clyde* (Arthur Penn, 1967) (15.32) as an example of optical tracking (lateral), and the final confrontation scene from *The Wild Bunch* (Peckinpah, 1969) (15.33) or the opening mess hall sequence from *M*A*S*H* as an example of optical hovering. Since cutting on optical movement is a key feature of the action sequences in *The Wild Bunch* (and nearly every other Peckinpah film), I show part of the concluding massacre as well. Then I show reverse zooms from the winter camp massacre scene of *Little Big Man* ([Penn, 1970] the cavalry approaching from the distance) and *Barry Lyndon* ([Kubrick, 1975] troops marching to slaughter in close military formation) to illustrate the capacity for optical tracking in depth. The reverse track-out, zoom-in from the conclusion of *Alice's Restaurant* (Penn, 1969) makes a nice point about expressive abstraction (the frame seems about to explode from the reverse tension of the camera pulling in one direction and the lens in the other—see also relevant sequences in *Vertigo* (Hitchcock, 1958) and *Adrift* (Ján Kadár, 1971) in this regard), as do telephoto abstractions from *Il deserto rosso* (Antonioni, 1964) and *Shadows of Forgotten Ancestors* (Sergei Parajanov, 1964) (e.g., the 360-degree telephoto track of Ivan and Marichka as they embrace for the first time in the woods). The fact that these brilliant uses of lens optics cluster around the period 1964–75 suggests a period of experiment which preceded the general diffusion of zoom technology, that is now available on the most modestly priced consumer camcorder.

The material on Ingmar Bergman (pp. 647–55) and Luis Buñuel (pp. 655–65) is self-explanatory. It is *auteur* criticism devoted to the life's work of two directors who can hardly be considered anything but *auteurs*, so closely did their own obsessions shape their films. Bergman constructed his exquisite parables of spiritual suffering within the secure (if sometimes stifling) context of a state-supported industry nearly all of his career, while Buñuel spent much of his life turning crassly exploitative projects into subversive, anti-clerical masterpieces under the nose of Roman Catholic censors in Mexico, Spain, and France. This is not to suggest that Bergman and Buñuel somehow lacked a specific material/economic context for their work, any more than

Fellini and Antonioni did at the same time, but rather that in terms of their art—and probably for specific historical reasons—it didn't matter. The situation in the independent distribution and exhibition sectors in the United States for much of the sixties and seventies was such that filmmakers with their status (and this included many French New Wave and British New Cinema figures too) could find audiences and produce a tidy profit for their backers. *Auteurism*, in brief, was for about fifteen years not so theoretical in the American film market, and if for example, you were Roger Corman's New World Pictures distributing Bergman's *Cries and Whispers* (1973) or Fellini's *Amarcord* (1974), it could even make you rich.

But, of course, there was a specific industrial context for the work of both Bergman and Buñuel, and to accommodate this there now exist two long endnotes to Chapter 15 with brief accounts of contemporary cinema in Sweden, Finland, Denmark, Norway, and Iceland, illustrated in the text by the stills on p. 654 (15.50–15.54), and Spanish and Portuguese cinema, illustrated in the text by the stills on p. 660 (15.62–15.66). Other important endnotes for this chapter deal with mainstream Italian directors of the sixties, seventies, and eighties; and with the aesthetics of the zoom lens.

European Renaissance: East

What has been called "the collapse of Communism" and the abrupt end of Soviet hegemony over the countries of Eastern Europe in 1989 have produced profound changes whose effects are yet to be seen. Some of these nations are attempting to adopt a style of Western democratic capitalism for which they have few resources or precedents; others are still experiencing internal struggles for control. Germany has reunited, to the manifest concern of her neighbors, and in the Soviet Union itself, political, economic, and social upheavals have brought several regions dangerously close to civil war. Chapter 16 was revised in galleys to reflect some of these dislocations—the violent overthrow of the Ceaucescu regime in Romania, for example, and the installation of Vaclav Havel as president of Czechoslovakia—but the deep structural changes coming to Eastern Europe will alter its films in ways we can't even guess, so it is better not to try. Since the cinemas and political economies of these nations have been historically interdependent, however, we *can* assume that the alterations will be radical.

It is well known that Lenin said shortly after the Bolshevik Revolution, "The cinema is for us the most important art," and then proceeded to nationalize the Soviet film industry in the service of propaganda and create a state-supported film school (the VGIK). This became the model for the Eastern European countries that fell under Soviet sway after World War II—that is, their cinemas were subsidized (and, in some cases, created) by their newly formed Communist governments, which simultaneously established national film schools to fill them with the creative personnel (pp. 666–67). As in the Soviet Union, in the worst of times, film in Eastern Europe became the medium for party line propaganda; at best, for social and ideological debate. The immediate postwar years were quite repressive, because Party Secretary for Ideological Affairs Andrei Zhdanov demanded strict adherence to the official Soviet style of "socialist realism" (see Chapter 5, pp. 204–16). But Stalin's death in 1953 produced a brief period of liberalization under Nikita Khrushchev, leading to the work of the "Polish School," 1954–63, and laying the foundations for the Czech New Wave, 1962–68, as well as for significant developments in Hungary, Yugoslavia, Bulgaria, and Romania.

Poland had a small film industry before World War II, which went underground with the Polish Army Film Unit during the Nazi occupation and re-emerged as the nationalized Film Polski under the socialist government in 1945. The Łódz Film School (officially, the Leon Schiller State Film School at Łódz) was established under the direction of Jerzy Toeplitz in 1948, and among its first graduates were the three directors who founded the movement known as the Polish School—Jerzy Kawalerowicz (pp. 668–69), Andrzej Munk (pp. 669–70), and Andrzej Wajda (pp. 670–73). The influence of the first two was mainly domestic, but Wajda became an international figure, first with his war trilogy—*A Generation* (1954), *Canal* (1956), and *Ashes and Diamonds* (1958)—and then with a series of films, including *Innocent Sorcerors* (1960), *Everything for Sale* (1969), *Landscape After Battle* (1970), and *Wedding* (1972), among others, that marked him as one of world cinema's leading figures (see Andrzej Wajda, *Double Vision: My Life in Film*, trans. Rose Medina [New York: Henry Holt, 1989]). Meanwhile, a second generation of Polish directors emerged from Łódz whose work was closely identified with the European art film, most prominently Roman Polanski (e.g., *Knife in the Water* [1962] —pp. 673–75) and Jerzy Skolimowski (e.g., *Barrier* [1966]—pp. 675–76), both of whom left Poland in the late sixties for reasons both political and artistic. A third generation, whose work is collectively called the "Third Polish Cinema," stayed on to create the *kino moralnego niepokoju* —"cinema of moral anxiety"—associated with the free labor union movement Solidarity (pp. 679–80). The preeminent figure of this group was Krzysztof Zanussi (pp. 676–77), whose work from *The Structure of Crystal* (1969), through *Camouflage* (1977) and *The Constant Factor* (1980) calmly dissected the mendacity of Polish society, and influenced the films of such newer directors as Krzysztof Kieslowski (*Camera Buff* [1976]), Feliks Falk (*Top Dog* [1978]), and Agnieszka Holland (*Provencial Actors* [1980]). Wajda threw the full weight of his reputation behind the pro-Solidarity movement with *Man of Marble* (1977), *Without Anesthetic* (1978), and *Man of Iron* (1981), and by 1981 the Festival of Polish Films at Gdansk (whose Lenin Shipyard was the birthplace of Solidarity) had be-

come the focus of world attention. The imposition of martial law in December 1981, and the banning of Solidarity and most of the films associated with it, began a period of repression during which Wajda, Zanussi, Holland, and other directors left the country (pp. 681–83). By 1984, however, an uneasy truce was proclaimed between the Polish industry and the Jaruzelski regime, and the Gdansk festival was reopened in August of that year. By the time that a Solidarity-controlled civilian government was installed in August 1989, the Polish cinema had recovered from the crisis of martial law and achieved its pre-1981 level of productivity and internationally acknowledged, creative achievement (pp. 683–84).

Unlike that of Poland, Czechoslovakian film history reached back to the turn of the century and by 1933 the Barrandov studios in Prague had become one of the most sophisticated production facilities in Europe. During the Occupation, the Nazis appropriated it to make German-language films, but Czech cinema was nationalized by the democratic Benes government after the war, and a state film school—the Prague Film Faculty of the Academy of Dramatic Arts (FAMU)—was founded in 1947 (pp. 684–85). When the Benes regime was replaced by a brutal Communist dictatorship in 1948, Czech cinema was turned toward doctrinaire socialist realism which stifled creativity through most of the fifties, except in the brilliant animation work of Jirí Trnka (e.g., *Old Czech Legends* [1953] and Karel Zeman (*The Invention of Destruction* [1958])—see pp. 685–86. Elmar Klos and Ján Kadár's *Three Wishes* (1958) signaled a new concern with contemporary social reality, but it became the subject of a better neo-Stalinist attack at an industry conference in Bánska Bystrica and was banned for the next four years (p. 686). A similar fate loomed for Stephen Uher's stylized allegory *Sunshine in a Net* (1962), but it was vindicated by an official union of critics in Prague and became the first film of the Czech New Wave (p. 687). A deluge of such work followed, most of it formally experimental (the influence of *cinéma vérité* and the French New Wave) and nearly all of it critical in some way of President Antonin Novotny's hardline Communist regime. The major filmmakers associated with this "Czech Film Miracle" (pp. 687–97) were Vera Chytilová (e.g., *Daisies* [1966]), Jaromil Jires (*The Joke* [1968]), Ján Kadár (*The Shop on Main Street* [1965]), Vojtech Jasny (*All My Countrymen*) [1968]), Milos Forman (*Fireman's Ball* [1967]), Jiri Menzel (*Closely Watched*

Trains [1966]), Evald Schorm (*Everyday Courage* [1964]), and Jan Němec (*The Party and the Guests* [1966]). These filmmakers were directly instrumental in creating the context for the "Prague Spring" of 1968—that brief period of democratization extending from Alexander Dubcek's election as Party Secretary in January to the Warsaw Pact invasion of August, when Soviet tanks rolled through the streets of Prague. In the "era of normalization" that followed, the major works of the New Wave were "banned forever" and many directors were forced to relocate abroad. (Forman, for example, moved to the United States, where he became famous as the maker of *One Flew Over the Cuckoo's Nest* [1975], *Ragtime* [1981], and *Amadeus* [1984]; others, like Nemec, were not so lucky and never found work as directors again.) During the seventies and eighties, the Czech government kept a tight rein on the film industry, so that figures like Chytilová, Jireš, and Menzel could hardly ever rise above conventional literary adaptations and genre fare, and the days of Czech domination at international festivals and awards ceremonies receded into the past. In some ways, however, the Czech New Wave was so unique and—like the Irish Literary Renaissance, with which it has been compared—so much a product of its specific socio-political moment that it probably would have ended whether the Soviets had invaded or not. What might have happened then, to both the nation and its films, if Czechoslovakia had gone on to become a democratic state, we may soon have the opportunity to find out.

Like Czechoslovakia, Hungary had a long and distinguished cinematic tradition prior to World War II, which included a brief period of nationalization after Bela Kun's socialist revolution in 1919 and a Hollywood-style studio system during the thirties (pp. 699–700). The film industry was nationalized again by the pro-Nazi Horthy regime during World War II, and the Academy for Dramatic and Cinematographic Art at Budapest was established in 1947 by the postwar republican government. When the Communists gained control the following year, they nationalized the Hungarian cinema yet again in service of socialist realism. When Imre Nagy replaced Mátyás Rákosi as premier after Stalin's death in 1953, Hungary experienced a brief era of liberation which was interrupted by the return of Rákosi in 1955. This led directly to the revolution of October/November 1956 which was brutally crushed by Soviet intervention, crippling Hungary's development for the rest of the decade. Yet János Kádár, a moderate, was installed as the new premier, and he gradually led the country in a realistic course of liberalization and economic growth, culminating in the New Economic Mechanism (NEM) formed in 1968 as a program that successfully integrated socialism and free market practices (pp. 700–1). During the seventies, Hungary became the freest and most economically stable nation of the Warsaw Pact. The film industry, of course, was a prime beneficiary of these changes. As early as 1961, the experimental Béla Balázs Studio began producing the first short works of film school graduates, and soon features appeared from András Kovács (*Difficult People* [1964]; *Cold Days* [1966]) and Miklós Jancsó (*My Way Home* [1964]; *The Round-Up* [1965]) that signaled a major resurgence of Hungarian cinema (pp. 702–3). Over the next decade, Jancsó became internationally famous for such works as *The Red and the White* (1967), *Red Psalm* (1972), *Elektreia* (1974), and *Hungarian Rhapsody* (1979), which are characterized by political symbolism, extremely complicated sequence shots, and striking widescreen composition (pp. 704–7). A younger generation of film school graduates—István Gaál (*The Falcons* [1970]; *Dead Landscape* [1971]); István Szabó (*Father* [1966]); *Budapest Tales* [1976]; *Mephisto* [1981]; Márta Mészáros (*Adoption* [1975]; *Nine Months* [1976]; *Diary for My Children* [1984])—followed Jancsó to distinction in the seventies (pp. 707–12), and, together with such lesser figures as Pál Gábor (*Angi Vera* [1978]), Peter Bacsó (*The Day Before Yesterday* [1982]), Ferenc Kósa (*Snowfall* [1974]), Pál Sándor (*Football in the Good Old Days* [1973]), Judit Elek (*Maybe Tomorrow* [1980]), István Dárday (*Film Novel—Three Sisters* [1979]), and Péter Gothár (*Time Stands Still* [1982]), created what has come to be known the world over as New Hungarian Cinema (pp. 712–24). Hungary's movement toward social democracy since the fall of 1989 can only serve to increase the sophistication of its film industry and enhance its material base.

Yugoslavia's film industry was basically the creation of the postwar government of Marshal Tito, which authorized the construction of the Film City studio complex in Belgrade and the foundation of state film schools (Faculty of Dramatic Arts) at Belgrade and Zagreb in 1950 (pp. 724–25). In the same year, the National

Assembly passed the law on workers' self-management which became the cornerstone of the postwar Yugoslav economy. Tito had broken with Stalin in 1948 and was determined to put his country on a self-financing basis by creating a unique socialist market economy. As reflected in the Basic Law of Film in 1956, this plan replaced state production subsidies with a tax on film admissions and enabled individual production units to raise their own funds by negotiating foreign distribution, leasing, and rental fees (p. 726). The immediate result was a turning away from narrowly focused "national realist" films (patriotic Partisan war epics like Vjekoslav Afríc's *Slavica* [1947]) toward coproductions with West Germany, Italy, and France (p. 727). The next step was a group of domestic films that showed the direct influence of neorealism (Veljko Bulajíc's *Train Without a Schedule* [1959]); France Stiglic's *The Ninth Circle* [1960]) and the rise of the Zagreb Film studio to international prominence through the abstract animation style of Vatroslav Mimica and Montenegrin Dusan Vukotić. In the sixties, with Yugoslav production averaging over thirty features per year, the avant-garde movement called *novi film* ("new film") arose as part of a wider liberalizing trend known as the Second Yugoslav Revolution (pp. 728–29). The major filmmakers associated with *novi film* were Aleksander Petrović (*Three* [1965]; *I Even Met Happy Gypsies* [1967]), Živojin Pavlović (*When I Am Pale and Dead* [1967]), Dušan Makavejev who became an international figure through such avant-garde/surrealist satires as *Man Is Not a Bird* (1965), *The Tragedy of the Switchboard Operator* (1967), and preeminently, *WR—The Mysteries of the Organism* (1971)—pp. 729–32. But *novi film* was repressed as socially negative ("black film") and the film industry was purged in 1971–72, so that Petrović and Makavejev were forced to emigrate and Pavlović was demoted (p. 732). Production declined to less than eighteen features annually for much of the seventies, until the "Prague Group"—Goran Paskaljević, Goran Marković, Lordan Zafranović, Rajko Grlić, and Šrdan Karanović (pp. 732–38)—returned from their studies at FAMU in Prague to reinvigorate Yugoslav cinema, creating a context in which even Petrović, Pavlović, and Makavejev (pp. 737–38) could occasionally work again. Since Tito's death in 1980, Yugoslavia has been a country without consensus as its six nationality groups vied with each other for territorial and political control.

Domestically, however, Yugoslav cinema seems to have become self-sustaining, to the incredibly successful extent of out-selling American films by as much as three-to-one (p. 738)—something that many Western European cinemas would give their eye teeth to achieve.

In Bulgaria there was a small, underdeveloped prewar industry which was nationalized in 1948, two years after the country became a People's Republic, and produced twenty-six features over the next nine years (pp. 738–39). During the next decade, several Bulgarian films won festival awards—notably Rangel Vulchnov's *Sun and Shadows* (1962) and Binka Zheliazkova's *We Were Young* (1961)—but it wasn't until the late sixties that a real cultural thaw took place (pp. 740–41). (Bulgaria's leaders pursued hardline Stalinism much longer than other Eastern bloc countries—as late as 1966, Zheliazkova's absurdist fantasy *The Attached Balloon* was shelved for its sardonic allusions to Stalin and remained unreleased until 1989.) Landmarks of liberalization were Grisha Ostrovski and Todor Stoianov's *Sidetrack* (1967) and Metodi Andonov's *The White Room* (1968), the first Bulgarian films to deal openly with the Stalinist past. Todor Dinov and Hristo Hristov's *Iconostasis* (1969) was Bulgaria's first great national epic and inaugurated a form that would become central to its cinema. In 1971, the film industry was reorganized into three separate production units and the Sofia Film and Television Academy (VITIS) was established in 1973 (pp. 742–43). A bumper crop of award-winning films followed—Metodi Andonov's *The Goat Horn* (1972); Hristo Hristov's *The Last Summer* (1972, 1974); Eduard Zahariev's *Hare Census* (1974), *Villa Zone* (1975), and *Manly Times* (1977); Georgi Djulgerov's *Advantage* (1977); Vulchanov's *The Unknown Soldier's Patent Leather Shoes* (1979); Zheliazkova's *The Swimming Pool* (1977) and *The Big Night Bath* (1980); Liudmil Staikov's *Illusion* (1980)—all of them sharing in some measure a fantastic visual style known as "Bulgarian surrealism" and implicitly critical of their society (pp. 743–47). To celebrate Bulgaria's 1,300th anniversary as a nation (681–1981), the film industry was commissioned to produce four superspectacles commemorating great events from the national past—Zahari Zhandov's *Master of Boiana* (1981), Staikov's *Khan Asparukh* (1981), Georgi Stoianov's three-part *Constantine the Philosopher* (1983), and Borislav Sharaliev's *Boris the First*

(1984)—which together chronicle the history of the Bulgarian people from their first migration from Central Asia, through their adoption of Christianity, to the foundation of the Bulgarian state (pp. 747–49). The execution of such an extraordinary project says volumes about the vitality of the Bulgarian cinema, which in the course of three decades has risen from marginality to a state of sophistication comparable to the cinemas of Czechoslovakia or Hungary (pp. 749–51). Though the Bulgarian Communist Party is still strong, the nation moves today toward a reform government which should benefit the industry both creatively and materially.

Romania's small prewar industry collapsed in 1943, and though an Institute of Theater and Film (IATC) was founded at Bucharest in 1950, the country's postwar economy was so entirely dominated by the Soviets that a truly national cinema could not emerge until the early sixties (p. 751–52). At this time Premier Gheorghe Gheorghiu-Dei broke openly with the Soviets, and the work of the first generation of IATC graduates began to appear in Mircea Drăgan's *Lupeni 29* (1962), Liviu Ciulei's *The Forest of the Hanged* (1965), and Mircea Mureşan's *Blazing Winter* (1965), as well as the animated shorts of Ion Popescu-Gopo. As part of the new "Romanization of Romanian Culture" filmmakers mined the national historical tradition, producing epics like Sergui Nicolaescu's *The Dacians* (1966) and *Michael the Brave* (1971), and even such works of social criticism as Lucian Pintilie's *Reconstruction* (1969). Hopes of liberalization were short-lived, however, because Nicolae Cesausescu had become president in 1965 and had already become extremely repressive by the early seventies (pp. 752–53). Yet, so long as it was apolitical, he showed an inclination to leave the film industry alone, and for this reason, the third generation of postwar Romanian directors—"the Class of the 1970s"—created an art cinema whose social criticism, in general, was deeply submerged (pp. 753–56). Its major figures are Mircea Daneliuc (*Microphone Test* [1980]), Dan Piţa (*The Stone Wedding* [1973]), Mircea Veriou (*Beyond the Bridge* [1977]), and Alexandru Tatos (*Anastasia Passed By/Gently Was Anastasia Passing By* [1980]; *Forest Fruit* [1984]). By the early eighties, Romania was producing an average of thirty films per year (many of them multi-part features for Romanian television), but Cesausescu's plundering of the national economy took its toll as the

decade wore on and production came to a dead stop during the revolutionary year of 1989–90.

The film industries of Turkey (pp. 757–58) and Greece (pp. 758–59) are given brief descriptions in this chapter because both are Balkan nations whose histories and cultures are intertwined with those of Yugoslavia, Bulgaria, and Romania, and because both have recently produced work of signal importance. In Turkey, a movement known as Young Turkish Cinema coalesced around the actor-writer Ylimaz Guney, who began directing his own scripts in the late sixties and produced a body of politically motivated work which kept him in-and-out of jail for most of the seventies. Even in prison, Guney continued to write scripts which were made into films by associates on the outside—most notably *Yol* (Serif Goren, 1983), which shared the Palm d'Or at Cannes with Costa-Gavras' *Missing* (1982). Greece has also produced one figure of international note—Theodore Angelopoulos (*Traveling Players* [1975]; *Alexander the Great* [1980]; *The Beekeeper* [1986])—whose work has inspired a younger generation of directors to produce what is now called New Greek Cinema.

Of all the postwar cinemas of Eastern Europe, the Soviet was most firmly in the grips of Zhdanovian socialist realism since Andrei A. Zhdanov was himself one of Stalin's most trusted lieutenants, until he died in 1948 (probably murdered by Stalin). Production, which had reached a prewar high of 125 films per year, fell to nineteen features in 1946 and five in 1952, because the Central Committee demanded that all films show Stalin personally as the motive force of Soviet history (pp. 759–60). This led to the production of films in a single genre—so-called "artistic documentary," which depicted Stalin (played always by a handsome young actor) forging the Communist Party of the Soviet Union (CPSU) (*The Vow* [Mikhail Chiaureli, 1946]) and conducting the major strategic battles of World War II (*The Fall of Berlin* [Chiaureli, 1949]; *The Battle of Stalingrad* [Vladimir Petrov, 1950])—see pp. 760–61. Three years after his death, these "Stalin-films" were denounced together with the cult of personality they helped to foster by Nikita Khrushchev at the Twentieth Party Congress in 1956, ushering in a thaw in both foreign relations and internal affairs. The effect on the film industry was dramatic, as new work began to appear from recent graduates of the VGIK for the first time since the 1930s and annual output reached 115 features by

1958 (pp. 761–64). Several, such as Mikhail Kalatozov's *The Cranes Are Flying* (1957) and Grigori Chukhrai's *Ballad of a Soldier* (1958) won international awards, but others like Mikhail Romm's *Nine Days in a Year* (1962) and Marlen Khutsiev's *I'm Twenty* (1963) were suppressed as too experimental (both were rereleased in 1987—see p. 776). Khrushchev made several stinging denouncements of liberalism in the arts before his replacement in 1964 by the diumvirate of Leonid Brezhnev and Alexei Kosygin. From 1966, when Brezhnev alone assumed supreme leadership of the Soviet Union, until the Warsaw Pact invasion of Czechoslovakia in 1968, there was a period of uncertainty which produced extraordinary work by Sergei Parajanov, Andrei Tarkovski, and Andrei Mikhalov-Konchalovski, and witnessed the graduation of a whole new generation of directors from the VGIK, both from Russia and from the non-Russian republics (pp. 771–73)—Ukrainia, Georgia, Moldavia, Armenia, Lithuania, Latvia, Estonia, Kirgizia, Uzbekistan, Turkmenistan, and Kazakhstan (see, for example, Forrest S. Ciesol, "Kazakhstan Wave," *Sight and Sound*, 59, 1 [Winter 1989/90], 56–61). By far the most brilliant of the new directors were Parajanov and Tarkovski, both of whom were later persecuted for the unconventionality of their work. Parajanov's greatest film, *Shadows of Forgotten Ancestors* (1964) (available in 16mm from Films Incorporated and videocassette from Connoisseur Video Collection) is the subject of a detailed reading on pp. 765–68 of the text. Tarkovski's work, now widely available in both 16mm and video formats, constitutes a body of work whose seriousness and symbolic resonance had a major impact on world cinema (*Ivan's Childhood* [1962]; *Andrei Rublev* [1966]; *Solaris* [1971; available since 1989, restored and uncut from Kino International]; *A Mirror* [1974]; *Nostalgia* [1983]; *The Sacrifice* [1986]), even though it was frequently tampered with by Soviet censors (pp. 768–70). During the 1970s, the policy of socialist realism (euphemized as "pedagogic realism") was again put into practice, so that only two types of films could safely be made—literary adaptations (Konchalovski's *Uncle Vani* [1972]; Nikita Mikhalkov's *Oblomov* [1980]) and *bytovye*, films of everyday life (Georgi Danelia's *Autumn Marathon* [1979]; Valdmir Menshov's *Moscow Does Not Believe in Tears* [1980])—see pp. 770–71; 773–75. Soviet cinema then experienced a far-reaching liberalization under the regime of Mikhail Gorbachev, elected Party Secretary in 1985, whose policy of *glasnost* ("openness") took control of the industry away from bureaucratic censors and placed it in the hands of the filmmakers themselves (pp. 775–76). That this change was more than cosmetic became clear as formerly suppressed films, such as Elim Klimov's *Agoniia* (1975), were distributed for the first time, together with new films that deal confrontationally with Stalinism (Tengiz Abuladze's *Repentence* [1984]), nuclear war (Konstantin Lopushanski's *Letters from a Dead Man* [1985]), and contemporary social problems (Mikhail Belikov's *How Young We Were Then* [1986]). Today, of course, the future path of the Soviet film industry is no clearer than the future of the Soviet Union itself. But if Gorbachev can continue to hold the nation together, its cinema will surely remain among the most fascinating and vital in the world. (A number of contemporary Soviet films are available on video in the United States from War & Peace Video [Belair, Texas] and the Video Project [Oakland, California]—see Part IV.)

Major endnotes for Chapter 16 deal generally with the Albanian film industry: For Poland—the Warsaw uprising of 1944, other significant members of the Polish School, the history of the Solidarity movement, a filmography of Polish directors who have done significant work in the past two decades; for Czechoslovakia—the "First Wave" of Czech directors during the fifties, the film and theater work of Alfred Radok, the American career of Ivan Passer, the relevance of Kafka and the theater of the absurd of the Czech New Wave, a list of significant Czech films produced during the eighties; for Hungary—a description of the later work of Károly Makk and Zoltán Fábri, a history of Béla Balázs Studio ("BBS Budapest"), Miklós Jancsó's work for Italian television, a filmography of notable Hungarian directors of the seventies and eighties, a bibliography of recent work in English on Hungarian film, for Yugoslavia—an updating of the careers of France Stiglic, Veljko Bulajic, Dušan Vukotić, and Aleksander Petrović, a filmography/bibliography of recent Yugoslavian cinema, for Bulgaria—a filmography of significant work, unmentioned in the text, 1979–88; for Romania—a filmography of members of "The Class of the 1970s" not mentioned in the text; for the Soviet Union—the films of Alexander Dovzhenko's widow, Iulia Solntseva, a bibliography of work in English on Andrei Tarkovski, the origins of the *bytovye*.

Chapter 17

Wind from the East:
Japan, India, and China

Japanese cinema is easier to teach today than formerly thanks to the recent availability of many key films on both 16mm and tape. It is now possible to stock an entire course in the subject through domestic distributors, and even Turner Network Television (TNT) shows Japanese classics as part of its regularly scheduled programming. By contrast, it is much more difficult to locate Indian and Chinese titles, although several distributors for each are noted in Part IV, and such organizations as the Asian Cinema Studies society (through its journal *Asian Cinema*, for example, offer advice on distribution sources. It's also worth noting that thousands of Indian popular films circulate in the West on videocassette through Indian provision stores, and that films from the People's Republic of China, Hong Kong, and Taiwan often appear in 35mm on the festival circuit.

In my own courses, I devote four or five 80-minute class periods to Japan, concentrating mainly on the postwar era. The history that I offer of the silent era is the standard account, focusing on the cultural mediation of *kabuki* and its effect on film form, especially the function of the *benshi* (pp. 778–79). I discuss the restructuring of the industry that followed the Kanto earthquake of 1923 and the subsequent bifurcation of film types into those with pre-Meiji (*jidai-geki*) and post-Meiji (*gendai-geki*) subjects (in practice, most *jidai* films are set during the period of the feudal Tokugawa *shogunate* (1603–1867). This division (pp. 779–80) was made to achieve production economy: period films were henceforth shot in the old capital of Kyoto with its pre-Meiji architecture, while contemporary films were shot in Tokyo, rebuilt and modernized in the aftermath of the quake. (See Scott Nygren, "Reconsidering Modernism: Japanese Film and the Post-Modern Context," *Wide Angle*, 11, 3 [1989], 6–15; and James Petersen, "A War of Utter Rebellion: Kinugasa's *Page of Madness* and the Japanese Avant-Garde of the 1920s," *Cinema Journal*, 29, 1 [Fall 1989], 36–53.) The slowness of the conversion to sound (paralleled in the West only by the Soviet Union) was owed in large measure to the popularity and influence of the *benshi*, but the sound film had become quite popular by 1937, when Japan produced some 400 of them for distribution to its 2,500 theaters (pp. 780–81). Although there was yet no export market for these features, the coming of sound—as in America—facilitated the vertical monopolization of the Japanese industry so that production, distribution, and exhibition were concentrated in the hands of first three, and later five, large corporations. As Japan became increasingly xenophobic and militaristic in the late thirties, its most distinguished directors turned to works of social criticism called "tendency" films (*keiko-eiga*), in response to which the government imposed a strict code of state censorship, retained through the end of World War II, and demanded the production of "national policy films" (*senkyoyo-eiga*)—see pp. 781–83. (See Gregory J. Kasza, *The State and Mass Media in Japan 1918–1945* [Berkeley: University of California Press, 1988]; and D. William Davis, "Back to Japan: Militarism and Monumentalism in Prewar Japanese Cinema," *Wide Angle*, 11, 3 [1989], 16–25.)

Japan's postwar experience was unique among World War II combatants: although more than half of its theaters were destroyed by American bombing, most of its studio facilities remained intact, and films continued to be produced in large numbers during the Allied occupation of 1945–52 (p. 783). Many traditional subjects were proscribed as promoting feudalism by the Allied Command, including all films classified as *jidai-geki*, but it was a film set in the medieval past that brought Japanese cinema to international attention when Akira Kurosawa's *Rashomon* (1950) won the Golden Lion at the 1951 Venice Film Festival. Kurosawa (pp. 784–91) went on to become the most famous Japanese director in the West owing to a series of distinguished *chanbara* (samurai films) which raised the conventions of the form to the state of an art—*Seven Samurai* (1954), *Throne of Blood* (1957), *The Hidden Fortress* (1958), *Yojimbo* (1961), *Sanjiro* (1962), and—near the end of his career—*Kagemusha* (1980) and *Ran* (1985), but he also made masterful crime films, literary adaptations, and films from original material, all of which he scripted himself. (See David Desser, *The Samurai Films of Akira Kurosawa* [Ann Arbor: UMI Research Press, 1983], and "Towards a Structural Analysis

of the Postwar Samurai Film," *Quarterly Review of Film Studies*, 8, 1 [Winter 1983], 25–41; Alain Silver, *The Samurai Film* [Woodstock, N.Y.: The Overlook Press, 1983]; Donald Richie, *The Films of Akira Kurosawa*, Revised Edition [Berkeley: University of California Press, 1984]; Michitaro Tada, "The Destiny of Samurai Films," *East-West Film Journal*, 1, 1 [December 1986], 48–58; Joseph S. Chang, "*Kagemusha* and the *Chushingura* Motif," *East-West Film Journal*, 3, 2 [June 1987], 14–37; Ann Thompson, "Kurosawa's *Ran*: Reception and Interpretation," *East-West Film Journal*, 3, 2 [June 1987], 1–13.) Two older directors, both of whom had begun their careers in the silent era and were more traditionally Japanese in style than Kurosawa, also produced major work during the postwar era. The films of Kenji Mizoguchi (pp. 792–94), whether *jidai-geki* (*Sansho the Bailiff* [1954]; *Crucified Lovers* [1954]) or *gendai-geki* (*Women of the Night* [1948]; *Gion Festival Music* [1953]), his films were frequently critiques of feudalism that focused on the condition of women within the social order. His greatest postwar films—*The Life of Oharu* [1952] and *Ugetsu* [1953]—reveal Mizoguchi as a master of *mise-en-scène*, comparable in many ways to Murnau, Ophüls, and Welles. (See David Bordwell, "Mizoguchi and the Evolution of Film Language," *Cinema and Language*, ed. Stephen Heath [Frederick, Md.: University Publications of America, 1983], 107–17; Keiko McDonald, *Mizoguchi* [Boston: Twayne Publisher, 1984].) Yasujiro Ozu (pp. 794–98) was likewise a supreme stylist, but the majority of his 54 films fall into a single genre—the *shomin-geki*, a variety of *gendai* film treating lower-middle-class family life—and his style was, appropriately, an extremely spare one. Although David Bordwell has corrected the notion that a majority of Ozu's shots are static and assume the eye level of a person seated on a *tatami* mat, it is true that Ozu frequently subordinated camera movement to visual composition and that his camera angle was nearly always low relative to its subject (*Ozu and the Poetics of Cinema* [Princeton: Princeton University Press, 1988], 74–88). Furthermore, Ozu's use of off-screen space and noncentered framing was so consistently brilliant (and, as Bordwell shows, scrupulously deliberate—see *Ozu and the Poetics of Cinema*, pp. 88–102) that it provides an excellent model for the detailed discussion of these concepts offered on pp. 794–98. For classroom demonstration, I use a videotape of the sequence in *Floating Weeds* (1959) from which the 180-degree axial shots in illustration 17.29 derive, often combined with similar—but differently motivated—180-degree cuts from *Vertigo* (1958), *Psycho* (1960), *Shadows of Forgotten Ancestors* (1964). In the screening sessions for this unit, I usually show *Seven Samurai* and *Ugetsu*, both widely available on 16mm and video.

The second postwar generation of Japanese filmmakers was composed mainly of Masaki Kobayashi, Kon Ichikawa, and Kaneto Shindo (pp. 799–801). Kobayashi is best known for his three-part antiwar epic *The Human Condition* (1959–61), set during Japan's brutal occupation of Manchuria, the two graphic *jidai-geki*, *Hara kiri* (1962) and *Rebellion* (1967), and the beautiful ghost film *Kwaidan* (1964). The latter was originally shot in TohoScope but is available today only in a frame-cut version; in this form, it is still gorgeous and strikingly Japanese, but screening it provides an excellent example of how the practice of frame-cutting destroys composition for the widescreen frame. Ichikawa's major works are the pacifist films *The Burmese Harp* (1956) and *Fires on the Plain* (1959), *Conflagration* (1958), *The Key* (1959), and *Tokyo Olympiad* (1965), most of which make bold use of widescreen space, as do his more conventional thrillers (e.g., *Island of Horrors* [1977]) and melodramas (e.g., *An Actor's Revenge* [1963]). Shindo's reputation rests on the poetic semi-documentary *The Island* (1960), the bizarre, folkloristic *Onibaba* (1964), and his prolific work as a scriptwriter. (See Joseph L. Anderson and Donald Richie, *The Japanese Film: Art and Industry*, Expanded Edition [Princeton: Princeton University Press, 1982]; Keiko McDonald, *Cinema East: A Critical Study of Major Japanese Films* [East Brunswick, N.J.: Associated University Presses, 1983]; and Donald Richie, *Japanese Cinema: An Introduction* [Oxford: Oxford University Press, 1990].)

In the sixties and seventies, Japan experienced a New Wave in the work of its third generation of postwar filmmakers on which there is no better source in English than David Desser's *Eros plus Massacre: An Introduction to the Japanese New Wave Cinema* (Bloomington: Indiana University Press, 1988). Some of these directors are important mainly for a single film (Hiroshi Teshigahara—*Woman in the Dunes* [1964]; Susumu Hani—*The Inferno of First Love* [1968]), or work in a single genre, for example, the avant-garde youth film—Yoshishige Yoshida (*Eros*

plus Massacre [1969]; *Martial Law* [1973]; Seijun Suzuki (*Tokyo Drifter* [1963]; *Elegy to Violence* [1966]); the "pink" film—Koji Wakamatsu (*Violated Angels/Violated Women in White* [1967]; *Angelic Orgasm* [1970])—see pp. 801–3. Three New Wave filmmakers, however, have made continuing contributions to Japanese cinema in films of world class. These include Masashiro Shinoda (pp. 802–3)—best known as a supreme stylist in works extending from *Assassination* (1964) and *Double Suicide* (1969) through *Demon Pond* (1979) and *Gonza the Spearman* (1986); and Shohei Imamura (pp. 803–5), whose radical combination of fiction and documentary styles lends anthropological precision to *Pigs and Battleships* (1961), *The Insect Woman* (1964), and *The Pornographer* (1966), and creates the near mythic resonance of *Vengeance Is Mine* (1979), *Eijanaika* (1980), *The Ballad of Narayama* (1983), and *Black Rain* (1989—a restrained account of the atomic bombing of Hiroshima, not to be confused with Ridley Scott's meritricious *policier* of the same title). But the most influential New Wave figure was Nagisa Oshima (pp. 805–6) whose stylistically and politically radical films—*Night and Fog in Japan* (1960), *Death By Hanging* (1968), *The Diary of a Shinjuku Thief* (1968), *Boy* (1969), and *The Man Who Left His Will on Film* (1970); *Empire of the Senses/In the Realm of the Senses*—incarnated his generation's disillusionment with contemporary Japan and the social disintegration wrought by rapid economic expansion. (See Dana Polan, "Politics as Process in Three Films by Nagisa Oshima," *Film Criticism*, 8, 1 [1983], 35–41; Maureen Turim, "Oshima's Cruel Tales of Youth and Politics," *Journal of Film and Video*, 39, 1 [Winter 1987] 42–51; *Wide Angle*, 9, 2 [1987]: Oshima special issue; and Paul Coates, "Repetition and Contradiction in the Films of Oshima," *Quarterly Review of Film and Video*, 11, 4 [1990], 65–71.)

During the 1960s, television plundered the Japanese film audience as it had already done in most countries of the West. Two major studios went bankrupt, and the remaining three turned increasingly to exploitative genre fare—primarily the soft-core "pink" film and violent *yakuza-eiga* but also cheaply made science fiction, cartoons, and "teenpix" (pp. 808–9). A rising post-New Wave generation (pp. 806–8) has achieved some success through independent (i.e., non-studio, non-American-financed) production—e.g., Kohei Oguri's *Muddy River* (1981), Yoshimitsu Morita's *The Family Game* (1983), Mitsuo Yanagimachi's *Fire Festival* (1985), Shinji Somai's *Typhoon Club* (1985), and Juzo Itami's *The Funeral* (1984), *Tampopo* (1986), and *A Taxing Woman* (1987)—but the studios continue to serve up pablum domestically. Although the Japanese industry currently has one of the highest annual production rates in the world, it is well known that serious filmmakers like Kurosawa must seek extra-national funding to realize their projects (p. 810).

The sections of Chapter 17 on India and the three Chinas (the People's Republic of China [PRC], Hong Kong, and Taiwan) are largely self-evident. It is important for students to know that although India is the largest producer of films in the world (averaging 700 per year since 1971), most of these are low-quality "mythologicals" manufactured for consumption by a virtually pre-industrial domestic audience. The small but significant "parallel cinema" inspired by the work of Satyajit Ray is basically a government-subsidized art film movement whose work is intended for export and festival competition. As for PRC, U.S. official recognition in 1972 opened that country up to the West as never before, and with the end of the Cultural Revolution in 1976 there was a steady increase in film production. As Gina Marchetti notes ("Chinese Cinema," *Jump Cut*, No. 34, p. 85), whereas the period between 1949 and the beginning of the Cultural Revolution in 1966 witnessed the development of a uniquely Chinese,

socialist film aesthetic, the "fifth generation" directors (e.g., Chen Kaige, Tian Zhuangzhuang) have produced an artistically provocative cinema clearly influenced by Western modernism, which among other things, makes stunning use of widescreen and Technicolor. The cinemas of Hong Kong and, most recently, Taiwan, have also experienced aesthetic movements of unusual merit, and representative films are not so difficult to locate as titles from PRC, especially since the Tiananmen Square massacre of June 4, 1989.

Major endnotes to Chapter 17 for Japan—deal with the institution of the *benshi*, or "*katsuben*," the later work of Heinosuke Gosho and Mikio Naruse, Japanese film historiography, Yasujiro Ozu scholarship, the Zen aesthetic of discontinuity and early Japanese film projection, *bunraku* puppet theater, David Desser's study *Eros plus Massacre* (1988), the *ni-ni-roku* coup d'etat attempt, and post-New Wave comic directors; for India—Indian film audiences, the Indian films of James Ivory and Ismail Merchant, the International Film Festival held at Delhi, James Lester Peries and the Sri Lankan film industry, and the Pakistani film industry; for the Chinas—the Mongolian film industry, a bibliography of work in English on PRC cinema, a bibliography of work in English on Hong Kong and Taiwanese cinema; other cinemas of the Pacific rim—Thailand, Vietnam, Indonesia, Malaysia, North and South Korea, and the Philippines.

Chapter 18

The Seventies and the Eighties: Colonies of the Mind and Heart

This chapter deals with three phenomena which over the past few decades have significantly affected the course of film history—the emergence of Third World cinema, the renaissance of West German film, and the elephantine conglomeration of the American media industries. Equally important, from our perspective as teachers, has been the rise of academic film studies, especially in the form of feminist and formalist film theory. I hope some day to include a separate chapter on this development in *A History of Narrative Film*, but since it does not affect industrial practice (or, rather, affects it only in very specific ways—as when directors who have attended film school demonstrate an academic influence in their work) I must be satisfied to merely acknowledge it in the Second Edition.

The Third World Cinema section in Chapter 18 is divided into subsections for Latin America (pp. 823–45) and Africa (pp. 845–50), which are further subdivided by country and/or region—all united in having endured long histories of colonial oppression. (Of course, this schema omits the Third World parts of East and Southeast Asia, the Indian subcontinent, and the Middle East, which are either treated in Chapter 17 or in the endnotes to Chapters 17 and 18.) Though modes of production vary according to local political circumstance, most Third World films are made outside the context of established industries and have as their goal the reclamation of an authentic national consciousness from imposed foreign values. Still, in a survey course the sheer diversity of these nations demands either a shotgun approach or focusing on a single, representative example. In the former case, a useful teaching tool for Latin America is Michael Chanan's documentary *New Cinema of Latin America* (1985), available from The Cinema Guild on video with English subtitles and narration. Part I: *Cinema of the Humble* (83 minutes) explores the movement's origins and traces its theoretical/aesthetic positions against the background of U.S. cultural hegemony, focusing on the development of militant cinema in

Cuba and Nicaragua; Part II: *The Long Road* (85 minutes) examines the development of new forms of representation, repression against filmmakers, and the emergence of a new women's cinema. Chanan's film, or excerpts from it, can work nicely with readings from such anthologies as Julian Burton's *Cinema and Social Change in Latin America: Conversations with Filmmakers* (Austin: University of Texas Press, 1986) or the Third World section of *Jump Cut: Hollywood, Politics, and Counter-Cinema*, ed. Peter Steven (New York: Praeger Publishers, 1985). Focusing on the context of a specific Latin American cinema also works well. In the case of Cuba (pp. 840–45), for example, such key films as *For the First Time* (Octavio Cortázar, 1967), *Lucía* (Humberto Solás, 1968), *Memories of Underdevelopment* (Tomás Gutiérrez Alea, 1968), *The First Charge of the Machete* (Manuel Octavio Gómez, 1969), and others are now accessible through such distributors as The Cinema Guild (see Part IV) in both 16mm and video, and excellent cultural studies like Michael Chanan's *The Cuban Image* (London: BFI Publishing, 1985) are available as supplementary texts. As endnotes for this section suggest, the same is true for Mexico (pp. 826–27), Brazil (pp. 828–31), Argentina (pp. 831–34), Chile (pp. 836–38), and parts of Central America (pp. 839–40).

North African (pp. 845–47) and sub-Saharan cinema (pp. 847–50) are more difficult because so much less is available in the West. Nevertheless, there are several recent publications that simplify access, notably Roy Armes' *Third World Film Making and the West* (Berkeley: University of California Press, 1987); Francoise Pfaff's *Twenty-five Black African Filmmakers: A Critical Study with Filmography and Bio-Bibliography* (Westport, Conn.: Greenwood Press, 1988); Nancy Schmidt's *Sub-Saharan African Films and Filmmakers: An Annotated Bibliography* (London: Hans Zell Publishers, 1988); and *Critical Perspectives on Black Independent Cinema*, ed. Mbye B. Cham and Claire Andrade-Watkins (Cambridge, Mass.: MIT Press, 1988). Furthermore, in addition to the various studies of North African and sub-Saharan cinema mentioned in the endnotes, *Variety* publishes a special issue on Egyptian and Maghreb cinema every year and regularly reviews African features appearing at the annual Carthage Film Festival. Finally, the cinemas of several Arabic-speaking Middle Eastern countries are dealt with in the endnotes. (The

omission of Israeli cinema from this volume will be corrected in subsequent editions; in the meantime, there has appeared an excellent study on the subject in Ella Shohat's *Israeli Cinema: East/West and the Politics of Representation* [Austin: University of Texas Press, 1989].)

New German Cinema, like the French New Wave and its reincarnations in many separate film cultures, isn't exactly "new" anymore; and I find it useful at this point in my courses to interrogate the concept of novelty itself as a validation of aesthetic worth. The first "new" movement in the discourse of film history was Italian neorealism, and in an important sense all of the "new" cinema movements thereafter recapitulate that term's most essential meaning—that it was new in the context of a moribund and bankrupt tradition (*telephono bianco*, calligraphism, Fascism), and that it constituted a radical break with what had gone before. Yet neorealism was also conceived as a return to something valued in the prewar years, a rekindling of the spirit of Soviet "expressive realism" and French "poetic realism." This was the case with a vengeance for *Das neue Kino*: the cultural/psychological devastation wrought upon Germany by the rise and fall of the Third Reich seemed irreversible, but there was among the movement's founders a sense of longing for the distinguished cinema of the Weimar past (pp. 850–51). Defeat in World War II and the subsequent partitioning of the country had virtually killed the German film industry, and in 1962 a manifesto produced by twenty-six writers and filmmakers at Oberhausen, West Germany, proclaimed its demise calling for the establishment of a *junger deutscher film* (a "young German cinema") to replace the old one (pp. 851–52). This "Oberhausen manifesto" became the founding document of *Das neue Kino*, which was brought into being materially over the next decade through the establishment of the Kuratorium Junger Deutscher Film (the Young German Film Board, 1965), a Film Subsidies Board (the Filmförderungsanstalt, or FFA, 1967), and the private distribution company, the Filmverlag der Autoren (literally, the "Authors' Film-Publishing Group," 1971), with additional funding from the two West German television networks (pp. 853–54). It was these institutions that financed the first features of the Oberhausen originators (pp. 854–56): Volker Schlöndorff (*Young Törless* [1966]) and Alexander Kluge (*Artists under the Big Top: Disoriented* [1968]), as well as the major work of three younger filmmakers who brought the New German Cinema to international prominence in the seventies—Werner Herzog (*Aguirre, the Wrath of God* [1972], etc.—pp. 861–65), Wim Wenders (*Kings of the Road* [1976], etc. —pp. 865–67), and the astoundingly prolific Rainer Werner Fassbinder (*The Bitter Tears of Petra von Kant* [1972], *Fear Eats the Soul/Ali* [1973], etc.— pp. 857–61). From their obscure beginnings, these directors went on to achieve success in the marketplace and by the eighties were involved in such relatively big-budget projects as *Berlin Alexanderplatz* (Fassbinder, 1980), *Fitzcarraldo* (Herzog, 1982), *Swann in Love* (Schlöndorff, 1984) and *Wings of Desire* (Wenders, 1987)—see pp. 873–74. Most other *neue Kino* directors, including a large number of women (e.g., Margarethe von Trotta [*Rosa Luxemburg*, 1986]—see pp. 856–57), depend mainly on state subsidies or a combination of public and private financing to produce their work. Notable in this category is the mythopoetic Hans Jürgen Syberberg (*Hitler: A Film from Germany* [1977]—pp. 867–68), the French-born Marxist materialist Jean-Marie Straub (*Moses und Aron* [1975]—pp. 870–72), and a score of lesser but important figures whose works fluctuate between contemporary social commentary and the experimental avant-garde (pp. 868–70). A good way to quickly illustrate the stylistic diversity of New German Cinema is to compare excerpts from the work of several directors—the opening sequences, say, of *Kings of the Road*, *Nosferatu* (Herzog, 1979), *The Marriage of Maria Braun* (Fassbinder, 1979), and *Parsifal* (Syberberg, 1982)—all of which are formally unconventional in quite different ways. Such excerpts can also help to explain the relative unpopularity of *Das neue Kino* with domestic audiences, who perceive it as difficult, downbeat and self-consciously arty—all of which, in some sense, it quite deliberately is. (Ironically, the path-breaking work of Konrad Wolf and his protégés in the East German cinema has found audience acceptance in both Germanys, a phenomenon that should become increasingly powerful as the nation reunites. See the GDR endnote for this section of Chapter 18; see also endnotes pertaining to the German-language industries of Switzerland and Austria and the Dutch-language industry of the Netherlands, illustrated by stills 18.53–18.55 on p. 874.)

It was during the 1960s that the American film industry experienced the first wave of mergers that would leave it, by 1990, the most conglomerated in the world (pp. 889–90). In that decade, Universal was acquired by Music Corporation of America (MCA, Inc. [1962]). Paramount by Gulf & Western Industries (1966), United Artists (UA) by Transamerica Corporation (1967), Warner Bros. by Kinney Services (later reincorporated as Warner Communications, Inc., or WCI), and MGM by financier Kirk Kerkorian (1970). By the end of 1970, only Fox, Columbia Pictures Industries, and the family-owned Walt Disney Productions and its wholly-owned distributor Buena Vista remained in veteran industry hands (RKO had been sold to General Tire and Rubber in 1956 and reduced to a broadcast holding company). In the midst of these convulsions, there appeared some of the most exciting films by American directors in a generation, many of them calculated to attract the attention of the nation's youth (pp. 877–87). Whatever their merit as art—and I believe they are considerable—*Bonnie and Clyde* (Arthur Penn, 1967; pp. 877–80), *2001: A Space Odyssey* (Stanley Kubrick, 1968; pp. 880–82), and *The Wild Bunch* (Sam Peckinpah, 1969; pp. 882–84) all borrowed heavily from the stylistic arsenal of the New Wave and other sophisticated sources (Kubrick from Antonioni, e.g., and Peckinpah from Kurosawa) in ways that appealed to the television-trained audiovisual sensibilities of their young audiences. The success of these films, as well as distinctly lesser ones like *Easy Rider* (Dennis Hopper, 1969), created a short-lived "youth-cult" boom in Hollywood (pp. 885–87) before Paramount struck it rich with *The Godfather* and *The Godfather Part II* (Francis Ford Coppola, 1972; 1974), Universal with *Jaws* (Steven Spielberg, 1975), and Fox with *Star Wars* (George Lucas, 1977), creating a new obsession with mass-appeal blockbusters directed by a film-school-trained *wunderkind* (pp. 887–88; 890–92). Such films, when successful, became mega-hits earning their producers unprecedented fortunes in repeat attendance, sequel rights, and marketing tie-ins. When they flopped, like United Artist's *Heaven's Gate* (Michael Cimino, 1980; pp. 895–96), they could take an entire studio with them. The consequences of this win-all/lose-all mentality produced a second round of mergers starting in 1981, when Transamerica sold United Artists off to Kirk Kerkorian, who combined it with MGM to create MGM/UA Entertainment in 1983. At about the same time, Columbia was acquired by the Coca-Cola Company (1982), Fox was purchased by Denver oil millionaire Marvin Davis (1981) and then sold to Australian media baron Rupert Murdoch (1985), Turner Broadcasting Systems (TBS) bought MGM/UA (1985) to acquire its film library and then resold the company to Kerkorian in the same year. A third and continuing wave of mergers began in 1989, when Warner Communications merged with Time, Inc. to become, as Time Warner, Inc., the world's largest media conglomerate and Gulf + Western spun off its financial services unit to become Paramount Communication, Inc. (PCI), concentrating exclusively on media (pp. 889–90). In 1990, an attempted merger between UA and Australia's Qintex Entertainment failed on a junk bond issue (although it is mistakenly reported as having succeeded in the text), and Sony Corp. of America acquired Columbia from Coca-Cola. Smaller producer/distributors—Orion, the Ladd Company, Tri-Star (merged with Columbia, 1989), Disney's adult market subsidiaries Touchstone and Hollywood Films—exist in close relationship with the majors, but it is the giants who flex the muscle in both the national and international arena.

As the major producer/distributors combined and inflated so too did the mega-hit phenomenon, yielding the "blockbuster summer" of 1989 in which three $40 million (negative cost) productions—Paramount's *Indiana Jones and the Last Crusade* (Steven Spielberg), Columbia's *Ghostbusters II* (Ivan Reitman), and Warner's *Batman* (Tim Burton)—broke all-time box-office records as they were released successively May through June. By the summer of 1990, it was not extraordinary for a mega-hit like Warner's *Gremlins 2: The New Batch* (Joe Dante), Fox's *Die Hard 2* (Renny Harlan), and Tri-Star's (Columbia) *Total Recall* (Paul Verhoven) to court their audiences with negative costs of $50 million, $60 million, and $65 million respectively. New channels of video distribution—cable networks, pay-per-view services, direct broadcast satellites, videocassette and laserdisc rental/sales—insure enormous post-playoff markets for successful blockbusters (pp. 898–99), but it should be clear that only mammoth corporations can afford the initial production investment required for such films. When *The Wall Street Journal* can describe the $32-million-dollar negative cost of Touchstone's *Dick Tracy* (Warren Beatty, 1990) as "relatively low" (*Wall Street Journal*, 7/11/90, p. B1), we are forced to conclude that the American film industry in the 1990s has erected considerable barriers to entry.

It is in this context that the work of Robert Altman in the seventies and early eighties (pp. 892–95) provides a striking example of the kind of films that the industry, and perhaps the culture, will no longer tolerate or afford. Intelligent, stylistically progressive, and individualistic to the point of eccentricity, Altman's best films attempted to treat serious issues in the American social and political experience—often comically or serio-comically—in ways that appealed largely to adults. His work was always handsomely produced in a medium-budget range and featured a remarkably varied and well-directed group of performers. And, while Altman's use of multiple-channel remote sound-recording and zoom lens dynamics often approached the experimental, his films were only rarely inaccessible (*Images* [1972], *Three Women* [1977]), and some were distinctly popular hits (*M*A*S*H* [1970], *McCabe and Mrs. Miller* [1971], *The Long Goodbye* [1973], *Nashville* [1975]). But they were not mega-hits: while *Nashville*, for example, was returning its $1.2 million investment in 1975 seven times, *Jaws* was returning nearly $100 million on an investment of $8 million. In a market turned increasingly toward mass audience exploitation through R-rated "psycho-slashers" (pp. 896–97), PG-13 "teenpix" (pp. 897–98), music-video features (pp. 898–90), and comic book epics (*Superman, Star Wars, Indiana Jones, Batman, Dick Tracy*), a filmmaker like Altman who refused to pander was doomed. Let me make it clear that I carry no particular brief on Robert Altman. I don't like some of his films, and I'd much rather teach Peckinpah or Kubrick (both of whom were compelled to leave the American mainstream, in their separate ways, for the same reasons). But Altman's situation is both representative and symbolic of the American cinema's contemporary malaise. That a filmmaker of his talent and vision no longer even *wants* to work in it, can't be a positive sign for a future that promises both High Definition Television (HDTV) and the wholesale colorization of black-and-white (pp. 902–14) as its norms.

Important endnotes for Chapter 18 include: for Third World Cinema—a bibliography of material on Third World Cinema at large, separate bibliographies of scholarship on Mexican cinema, Brazilian cinema, Argentine cinema, Chilean cinema, Central American cinema, and Cuban cinema, brief accounts of cinema in Lebanon, Syria, Iraq and Iran, and separate bibliographies of scholarship on North African and sub-Saharan cinema; for New German Cinema—an account of the East German film industry (GDR), East and West German attitudes towards the Nazi past; state financing mechanisms for *Das neue Kino*, a filmography/bibliography of posthumous work on Fassbinder, bibliographies of scholarship on Herzog, a filmography of important *neue Kino* figures not mentioned in the text; a bibliography of general works on New German Cinema; an account of the German-language industries of Switzerland and Austria, and the Dutch-language industry of the Netherlands; on the United States—separate bibliographies of work on Kubrick, Peckinpah, and Altman, and a filmography of notable contemporary American directors who are not mentioned in the text.

Part II

Endnotes Keyed to Text

Origins

p. 1 processes involved in the perception of motion: Hugo Munsterberg, *The Photoplay: A Psychological Study* (New York: D. Appleton, 1916), repr. as *The Film: A Psychological Study* (New York: Dover, 1970); R. L. Gregory, *Eye and Brain: The Psychology of Seeing* (New York: McGraw-Hill, 1966; 2nd ed., 1973); Irvin Rock, *An Introduction to Perception* (New York: Macmillan, 1975); Joseph Anderson and Barbara Fisher, "The Myth of Persistence of Vision," *Journal of the University Film Association* 30, 4 (Fall 1978): 3–8; Joseph and Barbara Anderson, "Motion Perception in Motion Pictures," in Teresa de Lauretis and Stephen Heath, eds., *The Cinematic Apparatus* (London: Macmillan, 1981), pp. 76–95; Michael Chanon, *The Dream That Kicks: The Prehistory and Early Years of Cinema in Britain* (London: Routledge & Kegan Paul, 1980), Chapter 4, *passim*; and Susan J. Lederman and Bill Nichols, "Flicker and Motion in Film," in Nichols, *Ideology and the Image* (Bloomington: Indiana University Press, 1981), pp. 293–301.

p. 4 Muybridge . . . refining his process of series photography: Muybridge ultimately became a professor at the University of Pennsylvania, where he undertook motion studies of a wide assortment of men, women, children, and animals. The resulting series photographs—in excess of 100,000—were published by the university in 1887 in an eleven-volume edition that sold for five hundred dollars. This work, *Human and Animal Locomotion*, was republished as a three-volume set by Dover Books in 1979.

p. 6 Dickson . . . the work of Muybridge, Marey, and others: Edison took intellectual credit for his employee Dickson's work after it had proved successful, and for decades Edison allowed himself to be eulogized as the "inventor of the motion pictures." The film historian Gordon Hendricks restored Dickson to his rightful creative place with *The Edison Motion Picture Myth* (Berkeley: University of California Press, 1961), and no one has since doubted Dickson's crucial role in the development of the Kinetograph. For his own account, see W. K. L. Dickson and Antonia Dickson, *History of the Kinetograph, Kinetoscope, and Kinetophonograph* (New York: Albert Bunn, 1895; repr. New York: Arno Press, 1970).

p. 7 Norman C. Raff and Frank R. Gammon: The original marketing syndicate had been formed in June 1892 by Edison's secretary, A. O. Tate, and Thomas Lombard and Erastus Benson, a vice president and concessionaire, respectively, of the Edison-controlled North American Phonograph Company, to exploit the Kinetoscope at the Chicago World's Columbian Exposition; Raff and Gammon were brought in the following year to beef up the syndicate with investment capital. For a more detailed account of these events in the context of Edison's whole career as an inventor and entrepreneur, see Robert Conot, *A Streak of Luck: The Life and Legend of Thomas Alva Edison* (New York: Seaview Books, 1979), pp. 320–33.

p. 10 Le Prince . . . never heard from again: Documents detailing the work of Friese-Greene, Le Prince, and many other pioneering inventors are contained in *The Merritt Crawford Papers*, ed. Eileen Bowser, a five-reel microfilm publication (Frederick, Md.: University Publications of America, 1987). Crawford (1880–1945) was one of the film industry's first historians, and he corresponded regularly with its originating figures.

p. 11 Lumières . . . documentary views: see Alan Williams, "The Lumière Organization and Documentary Realism," in John Fell, ed. *Film before Griffith*, (Berkeley: University of California Press, 1983), pp. 153–61; and Emmanuelle Toulet, *Cinematographe, invention du siecle* (Paris: Decouvertes Gallimard, 1988).

p. 11 editing . . . unthinkable to their makers: About the alleged lack of structure in the Lumière films there is not universal agreement. See, e.g., Marshall Deutelbaum, "Structural Patterning in the Lumière Films, *Wide Angle* 3, 1 (Spring 1979): 28–37, and Dai Vaughan, "Let There Be Lumière," *Sight and Sound* 50, 2 (Spring 1981): 126–27. See also the feature-length compilation film *La Voie Lumière* (*The Lumière Approach*, 1983) prepared under the supervision of Franz Schmitt of the French State Film Archive (Archives du Film, Centre National de la Cinématographie) in Bois d'Arcy.

p. 12 Paul . . . the Theatrograph: See John Barnes, *The Beginnings of the Cinema in England* (London: David and Charles, 1976), and Alan D. Kattell, "The Evolution of Amateur Motion Picture Equipment 1895–1965," *Journal of Film and Video* 38, 3–4 (Summer–Fall 1986): 47–57. See also John Barnes, *The Rise of the Cinema in Great Britain, Volume 2: Jubilee Year 1897*, and *Pioneers of the British Film, Volume 3: 1898: The Rise of Photoplay*.

p. 12 Armat . . . Atlanta, Georgia: See Gene G. Kelkres, "A Forgotten First: The Armat-Jenkins Partnership and the Atlanta Projection," *Quarterly Review of Film Studies* 9, 1 (Winter 1984): 45–58.

p. 14 Méliès . . . illusionist possibilities: See Charles Musser, "The Eden Musée in 1898: The Exhibitor as Creator, "*Film and History* (December 1981): 73–83 ff. For a detailed account of the reciprocal relationship between professional magic shows and primitive cinema, see Erik Barnouw, *The Magician and the Cinema* (New York: Oxford University Press, 1981). See also Katherine Singer Kovács, "Georges Méliès and the *Feérie*, "*Cinema Journal* 16, 1 (Fall 1976): 1–13; and Lucy Fischer, "The Lady Vanishes: Women, Magic, and the Movies," *Film Quarterly* 33, 1 (Fall 1979), repr. in Fell, *Film before Griffith*, pp. 339–54.

p. 17 scenes are arranged . . . as follows: adapted from the *Star Film Catalogue* (Paris, 1903).

p. 21 Georges Sadoul, Kenneth Macgowan, and Barry Salt: Georges Sadoul, *Histoire du cinéma mondial* (Paris, 1949): Kenneth Macgowan, *Behind the Screen* (New York: Delacorte Press, 1965); and Barry Salt, *Film Style and Technology: History and Analysis* (London: Starword, 1983).

p. 21 the low survival rate of the era's films: In 1978 the International Federation of Film Archives (FIAF, Brussels), at its annual conference at Brighton, made the first complete survey of surviving prints from a single period. It was concluded that some 1,500 films made between 1900 and 1906 have been preserved and that at least three times that number have been lost, a survival ratio of one to four.

On the other hand, a marvelous example of what can be gleaned from the surviving one-fourth was provided by the American Federation of the Arts' 1987 exhibition *Before Hollywood: Turn-of-the-Century Film from American Archives*. Curated by Jay Leyda and Charles Musser, this exhibition offered six programs representing the gamut of early cinema genre—actualities, comedies (including trick films, animation, and chases), drama, and socially oriented melodramas—from a broad range of production companies, and it was the most extensive ever devoted to the first two decades of American film, 1895–1915. The exhibition catalogue, *Before Hollywood: Turn-of-the-Century American Film* (New York: Hudson Hills Press, 1987), not only contains writings and primary source documents supplied by Leyda and Musser but additional essays by John L. Fell, Stephen Gong, Neil Harris, Richard Koszarski, Jay Leyda, Judith Mayne, Brooks McNamara, Russell Merritt, Charles Musser, and Alan Trachtenberg, and is a considerable scholarly resource in itself. Other useful material on the subject of early film representation is contained in John L. Fell, "Motive, Mischief and Melodrama: The State of Film Narrative in 1907," *Film Quarterly* 33, 3 (Spring 1980): 30–37, repr. in Fell, *Film before Griffith*, pp. 272–83; Barry Salt, "The Early Development of Film Form," Fell, *Film before Griffith*, pp. 284–98; Paul Kerr, "Re-Inventing the Cinema," *Screen* 21, 4 (Winter 1980): 80–84, and two essays in *Screen* 23, 2 (July–August 1982), Ben Brewster, "A Scene at the 'Movies' " (4–15), and Nöel Burch, "Narrative/Diegesis—Thresholds, Limit" (16–33), prepared in conjunction with the Society for Education in Film and Television (SEFT) conferences "Inventing the Cinema, 1895–1911," (South West Arts, December 1980) and "Putting Narrative in Place: the Cinema 1906–1916" (East Midlands Arts, December 1982). See also Jan-Christopher Horak, "The Magic Lanterne Moves: Early Cinema Reappraised," *Film Reader 6: Investigations in Film History and Technology* (1985): 93–101; Jean-Pierre Geuens, "Morning Light: A Study of the Visual Signifiers between 1895 and 1915," *The Spectator* 7, 1 (Fall 1986), 7–9; and Tom Gunning, "Le style non-continu du cinema des premiers temps (1900–1906)," *Les cahiers de la cinemathéque* no. 29 (Winter 1979): 24–34, and "An Unseen Energy Swallows Space: The Space in Early Film and Its Relation to American Avant-Garde," in Fell, *Film before Griffith* pp. 355–66, and "The Cinema of Attraction: Early Film, Its Spectator and the Avant-Garde," *Wide Angle* 8, 3 & 4 (Autumn–Winter 1986): 63–77.

See also *Motion Picture Catalogues by American Producers and Distributor's, 1894–1908*, ed. Thomas A. Edison Papers, a 35 mm microfilm publication (six reels) with printed guide (Frederick, Md.: University Publications of America, 1987).

p. 21 *Life of an American Fireman* . . . released in January 1903: Barry Salt claims that Porter's *Life of an American Fireman* (1903) is an imitation of Williamson's *Fire!* (1901) and that *The Great Train Robbery* was based on the Mottershaw's *Daring Daylight Burglary* (Sheffield Photo Company, 1903). But as Charles Musser points out in his painstakingly researched "The Early Cinema of Edwin Porter" *Cinema Journal* 19, 1 [Fall 1979]: 1–38), " . . . Porter's borrowings tended towards the pro-filmic elements of set construction and gesture (which were themselves highly conventionalized and obviously did not originate with Williamson) rather than specifically cinematic strategies of decaupage" (p. 28). See Barry Salt, "Film Form, 1900–1906," *Sight and Sound* 47, 3 (Summer 1978): 148–53; two articles by Martin Sopocy, "A Narrated Cinema: The Pioneer Story Films of James A Williamson, *Cinema Journal* 28, 1 (Fall 1978), 1–20, and "French and British Influences on Porter's *American Fireman*," *Film History* 1, 2 (1987): 137–48; also, Allan T. Sutherland, "The Yorkshire Pioneers," in Fell, *Film before Griffith*, pp. 92–98.

p. 24 parallel editing . . . newspaper comic strips: For discussions of precedents for parallel editing, see Nicholas A. Vardac, *Stage to Screen* (Cambridge: Harvard University Press, 1949); Alan J. Spiegel, *Fiction and the Camera Eye* (Charlottesville: University of Virginia Press, 1976); John L. Fell, *Film and the Narrative Tradition* (Norman: University of Oklahoma Press, 1975); Burns Hollyman, "Alexander Black's Picture Plays: 1893–1894," *Cinema Journal* 16, 2 (Spring 1977): 26–33; William C. Darrah, *The World of Stereographs* (Gettysburg, Pa.: W. C. Darrah, 1977); Pierre Couperie et al., *A History of the Comic Strip*, trans. Eileen B. Henessy (New York: Crown, 1968); Winsor McCay, *Little Nemo* (New York: Nostalgia Press, 1972); and Francis Lacassin "The Comic Strip and Film Language" (translated with "Supplementary Notes" by David Kunzle), *Film Quarterly* 26, 1 (Fall 1972): 11–23. For an argument placing all of these phenomena of serial presentation and projection, as well as cinema proper, within a larger context of screen history, see Charles Musser, "Toward a History of Screen Practice," *Quarterly Review of Film Studies* 9, 1 (Winter 1984): 60–69. See also André Gaudreault, "Temporality and Narrativity in Early Cinema, 1895–1908," in Fell, *Film before Griffith*, pp. 311–29; and Stephen Bottomore, "Shots in the Dark: The Real Origins of Film Editing," *Sight and Sound* 57, 3 (Summer 1988): 200–204.

p. 24 completely autonomous actions: For more on the controversy, see Roman Gubern, "David Wark Griffith et l'articulation cinématographique," and Barthélemy Amengual, "*The Life of an American Fireman* et la naissance du montage," *Cahiers de la Cinématheque*, 17 (Christmas 1975): and Charles Musser, "The Early Cinema of Edwin Porter," and André Gaudreault, "Detours in Film Narrative: The Development of Cutting," *Cinema Journal* 19, 1 (Fall 1979). For an engaging ideological approach both to Porter's films and to the historiography of the primitive period, see Nöel Burch, "Porter, or Ambivalence," *Screen* 19, 4 (Winter 1978–79), 91–105. (A third print of the film, which seems to support the authenticity of the Copyright Version, was found in 1978 but hadn't been dated at the time of publication.)

p. 25 the violence of armed crime: Macgowan, *Behind the Screen*, p. 114.

p. 27 Edison Catalogue: *Edison Catalogue* (New York, 1904); quoted in Lewis Jacobs, *The Rise of the American Film*, rev. ed. (New York: Teachers College Press 1948), p. 46.

p. 30 leasing a complete film service . . . to the vaudeville houses: For more on the relationship between film and vaudeville in the "novelty period" and beyond, see Robert C. Allen, "Contra the Chaser Theory," *Wide Angle* 3, 1 (1979), repr. in Fell, *Film before Griffith*, pp. 105–15; Jean Thomas Allen, "Copyright and Early Theater, Vaudeville, and Film Competi-

tion," *Journal of the University Film Association* 29, 3 (Summer 1977), repr. in Fell, *Film before Griffith*, pp. 176–85; Charles Musser, "Another Look at the Chaser Theory," *Studies in Visual Communication* 10, 4 (Fall 1984): 24–44; Robert C. Allen, "Looking at 'Another Look at the Chaser Theory'," *SVC* 10, 4: 44–50; and Charles Musser, "Musser's Reply to Allen," *SVC* 10, 4: 51–52.

p. 30 narration, music, and **sound effects**: Musser, "Nickelodeon," p. 4.

p. 31 producers . . . could not meet demand: Robert C. Allen, *Vaudeville and Film, 1895–1915: A Study in Media Interaction* (Ph.D. diss. University of Iowa, 1977; repr. New York: Arno Press, 1980), p. 43. Allen's information is based on figures provided by George Kleine, which were inflated less by an increase in domestic production than by a sudden influx of new foreign films in March 1907. According to Charles Musser, American production itself increased very little in the period in question. (Musser to author, April 14, 1988.)

p. 31 new economies of production, distribution, and exhibition: For more on the nickelodeon boom and the various controversies surrounding it, see Russell Merritt, "Nickelodeon Theaters: Building an Audience for the Movies, *Wide Angle* 1, 1 (1979): 4–9, repr. in Tino Balio, ed., *The American Film Industry*, rev. ed. (Madison: The University of Wisconsin Press, 1985); Garth S. Jowett, "The First Motion Picture Audiences," *Journal of Popular Film* 3, 1 (Winter 1974), repr. in Fell, *Film before Griffith*, pp. 196–206; Robert C. Allen, "Motion Picture Exhibition in Manhattan, 1906–1912: Beyond the Nickelodeon," *Cinema Journal* 18, no. 2 (Spring 1979): 2–15, and repr. in Gorham Kindem, ed., *The American Movie Industry: The Business of Motion Pictures* (Carbondale: Southern Illinois University Press), pp. 12–24, and repr. in Fell, *Film before Griffith*, pp. 162–75; Charlotte Herzog, "The Movie Palace and the Theatrical Source of its Architectural Style," *Cinema Journal* 20, 1 (Spring 1981): 15–37, and "The Archaeology of Cinema Architecture: The Origins of the Movie Theater," *Quarterly Review of Film Studies* 9, 1 (Winter 1984): 11– 32; Jon Gartenberg, "Vitagraph before Griffith: Forging Ahead in the Nickelodeon Era," *Studies in Visual Communication* 10, 4 (Fall 1984): 7–23; Charles Musser, "The Nickelodeon Era Begins: Establishing the Framework for Hollywood's Mode of Representation," *Archaeology of the Cinema* 8: 4–11; and Q. David Bowers *Nickelodeon Theaters and Their Music* (Vestal, N.Y.: The Vestal Press, Ltd., 1986).

Both in the scholarly articles cited here about and in the superb documentary *Before the Nickelodeon: The Early Cinema of Edwin S. Porter*. (A Film for Thought Production, 1982), written and directed by Musser, which traces Porter's career from his days as a projectionist at the Eden Musée through the termination of his Edison contract in 1909, providing in the process a casebook on the evolution of the overlapping continuity and the problems of spatial, temporal, and narrative relationships it attempted to solve. See also John Fell, "Before the Nickelodeon," *Film Quarterly* 36, 4 (Summer 1983): 21–25, and Robert Pearson, "The Filmmaker as a Scholar and Entertainer: An Interview with Charles Musser," *Cineaste* 13, 3 (1984): 22–24.

International Expansion, 1907–1918

pp. 33–34 Jacobs . . . movie-making as a shabby occupation: Lewis Jacobs, *The Rise of the American Film* (New York: Teachers College Press, 1948), pp. 58–59.

p. 34 technical competence . . . marginally adequate: For the several minor exceptions to this statement, see Lewis Jacobs' chapter on the "First School of Directors: Specialization of Crafts," in *The Rise of the American Film*, 2nd ed., pp. 120–35.

p. 36 *Republic* . . . the state's right of censorship: See Nancy J. Rosenbloom, "Between Reform and Regulation: The Struggle Over Film Censorship in Progressive America, 1909–22," *Film History* 1, 4 (1987): 307–25.

p. 36 MPPC . . . Arthur Knight: Arthur Knight, *The Liveliest Art* (New York: New American Library, 1957), p. 30.

p. 40 new theaters . . . the major Hollywood studios in the 1920s: For a thoroughgoing account of the demographics of "dream palace" proliferation in the twenties, see Douglas Gomery, "The Picture Palace: Economic Sense or Nonsense?" *Quarterly Review of Film Studies* 3, 1 (Winter 1978): 23–36, "The Movies Become Big Business: Public Theaters and the Chain-Store Strategy," *Cinema Journal* 28, 2 (Spring 1979), repr. in Kindem, *American Movie Industry*, pp. 104–16, and "U.S. Film Exhibition: The Formation of a Big Business," in Balio, *American Film Industry*, pp. 218–28. On surviving dream palace structures, see David Naylor, *Great American Movie Theaters: A National Trust Guide* (Washington, DC: The Preservation Press, 1987).

p. 42 mass migration . . . between 1907 and 1913: For a fascinating account of the early motion-picture industry in the East, see Paul C. Spehr, *The Movies Begin: Making Movies in New Jersey, 1887–1920* (Newark: Newark Museum, 1977). See also Rita Ecke Altomara, *Hollywood on the Palisades. A Filmography of Silent Features Made in Fort Lee, New Jersey, 1903–1927* (New York: Garland Publishing, 1983).

p. 44 Wilson administration in 1912: The government brief in this case, *United States of America v. Motion Picture Patents Company and Others* (1914), has been published as a special issue of *Film History* 1, 3 (1987).

p. 45 Paramount . . . theaters across the nation: Jacobs, p. 93.

p. 48 *The Film: A Psychological Study* [1916]: Vachel Lindsay, *The Art of the Moving Picture* (New York: Macmillan 1915; repr. New York: Liveright, 1970); and Hugo Münsterberg, *The Film: A Psychological Study* (New York: D. Appleton, 1916; repr. New York: Dover Books, 1970).

p. 48 United States . . . nearly all of them: Jacobs, p. 249.

p. 48 undisputed economic . . . leadership: For a full-blown analysis of Hollywood's hegemonic conquest of the international motion-picture market, see Kristen Thompson, *Exporting Entertainment: America in the World Film Market, 1907–1934* (London: BFI Publishing, 1985).

p. 49 Georges Sadoul . . . Charles Pathé: Georges Sadoul, *The French Film* (London: Falcon Press, 1953), p. 7.

p. 50 Mack Sennett . . . Keystone Kops: For more on the work of Zecca, Linder, and the stage comedians André Deed (1884–1938) and Rigadin (Charles Petit-Demange [1872–1933]) at Pathé, as well as that of Jean Durand, Roméo Bosett, Calino (Clément Migé), Onésime (Ernest Bourbon), and "Les Pouics" at Gaumont, see David Robinson, "Rise and Fall of the Clowns: The Golden Age of French Comedy, 1907–14," *Sight and Sound* 56, 3 (Summer 1987): 198–203. See also "1895–1910: Les Pionniers du Cinéma Française," *L'avant scène cinéma* 3, no. 334 (November 1984).

p. 51 Alice Guy: Most sources list Guy's birthdate as 1873, but her daughter Simone Blaché insists on the later date. See Anthony Slide, *Early Women Directors* (New York: Da Capo, 1984) and *The Memoirs of Alice Guy Blaché*, translated by Roberta and Simone Blaché, ed. Anthony Slide (Metuchen, N.J.: Scarecrow Press, 1986).

p. 52 David Robinson . . . Feuillade: David Robinson, *The History of World Cinema* (New York: Stein & Day, 1973), pp. 79–80.

p. 53 Émile Cohl . . . the father of modern animation: Cohl may have been preceded in this by the Spaniard Segundo de Chomón, who supposedly discovered the principle of stop-motion animation while shooting some title cards for Ferdinand Zecca at Pathé in 1902. Between that year and 1908, when he left to work as a cinematographer for Italia Film in Turin, Chomón may have collaborated on drawings. At Italia, Chomón became famous as the cameraman for Giovanni Pastrone's *Cabiria* (1914, q.v.). See Donald Crafton, *Before Mickey: The Animated Film, 1898–1928* (Cambridge, Mass.: MIT Press, 1982), pp. 23–25, *passim*, and Émile Cohl, *Caricature, and Film* (Princeton: Princeton University Press, 1990). Even earlier, the Englishman Arthur Melbourne-Cooper seems to have animated matchsticks in *Matches Appeal* (1899), a propaganda effort for the Boer War, and later to have animated objects in *The Enchanted Toymaker* (1904) and several subsequent films. Also, Edwin Porter had used animated titles in a series of films made in 1905 (e.g., *How Jones Lost His Roll, The Whole Damm Family and the Damm Dog*).

p. 54 Kenneth Macgowan . . . Film d'Art: Kenneth Macgowan, *Behind the Screen: The History and Techniques of the Motion Picture* (New York: Dell, 1965), p. 108.

p. 55 David Robinson . . . historical costume films: Robinson, p. 52.

p. 58 1909–11 . . . flood of historical films: These were also the years of the first great flowering of Italian film comedy in the work of Italia's "Cretinetti" (André Deed, lured away from Pathé), Ambrosia's "Robinet" (Marcel Fabre), the Cines Company's "Tontolini"/"Polidor" (both Fernando Guillaume) and "Kri Kri" (Raymond Fran), and many others. See David Robinson, "The Italian Comedy," *Sight and Sound* 55, 2 (Spring 1986): 105–12.

p. 59 cast of one thousand extras: Vernon Jarratt, *The Italian Cinema* (London: Falcon Press, 1951), p. 16.

p. 59 *Cabiria* . . . Vernon Jarratt: Jarratt, p. 18.

D. W. Griffith and the Consummation of Narrative Form

p. 63 *Rescued from an Eagle's Nest*: Griffith had played bit parts in several other films before *Rescued*—see Eileen Bowser, "Griffith's Film Career before *The Adventures of Dollie*," *Quarterly Review of Film Studies* 6, 1 (Winter 1981): 1–9; Russell Merritt, "Rescued from a Perilous Nest: D. W. Griffith's Escape from Theatre into Film," *Cinema Journal* 21, 1 (Fall 1981): 2–30; and Richard Schickel, *D. W. Griffith: An American Life* (New York: Simon & Schuster, 1984). Schickel suggests that Griffith was cast in *Rescued* not by Porter but by his consultant and "secondary director" J. Searle Dawley (p. 92).

p. 63 K. M. C. D. Syndicate: See Paul C. Spehr, "Filmmaking at the American Mutoscope and Biograph Company 1900–1906," *The Quarterly Journal of the Library of Congress* 37, 3–4 (Summer–Fall 1980): 413–21.

p. 64 450 one- and two-reelers: The vast majority are one-reelers, and remarkably, all but eight of Griffith's Biograph films are known to have survived. Like the Edison Company, Biograph regularly deposited paper print rolls with the U.S. Copyright Office, which contained a transfer of every frame from the original 35mm films (the prevailing copyright laws covered photographs but not yet motion pictures). Today, the Paper Print Collection at the Library of Congress has restored these rolls and transferred them back on to film stock (16mm and, increasingly, 35mm), and it represents one of the most comprehensive resources for the study of the transition from the primitive to the classical cinema anywhere in the world. In 1975, MoMA held a retrospective screening of nearly one hundred Griffith Biograph Films to commemorate the centennial of his birth. In 1985, a catalogue of all of Griffith's Biograph films as a director and supervising producer was compiled by Cooper C. Graham, Steven Higgins, Elaine Mancini, and João Luiz Viera, titled *D. W. Griffith and Biograph Company* (Metuchen, N.J.: Scarecrow Press, 1985).

p. 65 Kristin Thompson: Kristin Thompson, with David Bordwell and Janet Staiger, *The Classical Hollywood Cinema: Film Style and Mode of Production to 1960* (New York: Columbia University Press, 1985), pp. 157–58.

p. 65 Barry Salt: See Barry Salt, *Film Style and Technology: History and Analysis* (London: Starwood, 1983). For more on the 180-degree system, see Chapter 16, "Yasujiro Ozu and the Use of Off-Screen Space." See also Bordwell et al., *The Classical Hollywood Cinema*; Fell, *Film before Griffith*; Annette Kuhn, "The History of Narrative Codes," in Pam Cook, ed., *The Cinema Book* (London, British Film Institute, 1985); Robert B. Ray, "Classic Hollywood's Formal and Thematic Paradigms," in *A Certain Tendency of the Hollywood Cinema, 1930–1980* (Princeton: Princeton University Press, 1985); and David Bordwell and Kristin Thompson, *Film Art: An Introduction*, 2nd ed. (New York: Knopf, 1986).

p. 66 *The Greaser's Gauntlet*: See Thomas R. Gunning, "D. W. Griffith and the *Narrator-System*: Narrative Structure and

Industry Organization in Biograph Films, 1908–1909 (diss. New York University, 1986), pp. 132–45 and 171–84. Gunning, "Weaving a Narrative: Style and Economic Background in Griffith's Biograph Films," *Quarterly Review of Film Studies* 6, 1 (Winter 1981): 11–12, and Joyce E. Jesionowski, *Thinking in Pictures: Dramatic Structure in D. W. Griffith's Biograph Films* (Berkeley: University of California Press, 1987).

p. 66 *A Corner in Wheat*: The shot from *A Corner in Wheat* referred to is a *tableau vivant*. See Eileen Bowser, "The Reconstitution of *A Corner in Wheat*," *Cinema Journal* 15, 2 (Spring 1976): 42–55, and "Addendum to the Reconstitution of *A Corner in Wheat*," *Cinema Journal* 19, 1 (Fall 1979): 101–2. On the social content of this and other Griffith Biograph films, see Kay Sloan, *The Loud Silents: Origins of the Social Problem Film* (Urbana: University of Illinois Press, 1988).

p. 67 close-up . . . fill the frame: For an informative article on the historical evolution of the close-up, see Andrew Sarris, "About Faces," *American Film* 4, 8 (June 1979): 54–61.

p. 67 Linda Arvidson Griffith: Linda Arvidson Griffith, *When the Movies Were Young* (New York: E. P. Dutton, 1925, p. 66; repr. New York: Dover Books, 1969).

p. 68 Lewis Jacobs: Lewis Jacobs, *The Rise of the American Film* (New York: Teachers College Press, 1948), p. 103.

p. 68 intercutting . . . prior to 1909: *A History of Films* (New York, 1979). Fell notes that intercutting was practiced in Vitagraph's 1906 short *The Hundred-to-One Chance*, where the filmmakers cut back and forth several times between a racing car and events taking place at its destination (p. 38). Barry Salt ("*Der Arzt des Schlosses*," *Sight and Sound* 54, 4 [Autumn 1985]: 284–85) notes intercutting in Pathé's *Le Cheval emballé* (*The Runaway Horse*, 1907) and *Der Arzt des Schlosses* (*The Physician of the Castle*, 1908). See also Rich Altman, "*The Lonely Villa* and Griffith's Paradigmatic Style," *Quarterly Review of Film Studies* 6, 2 (Spring 1981): 123–34.

p. 68 Arthur Knight . . . psychological tension in the audience: Arthur Knight, *The Liveliest Art* (New York: New American Library, 1957), p. 32.

p. 71 narrative panning shots: See Jon Gartenberg, "Camera Movement in Edison and Biograph Films 1900–1906," *Cinema Journal* 19, 2 (Spring 1980): 1–16.

p. 74 *The Massacre*: Jacobs, p. 114.

p. 76 Jacobs . . . *Judith of Bethulia*: Jacobs, p. 116.

p. 78 Thomas E. Dixon, Jr.: See *Southern Horizons: The Autobiography of Thomas Dixon* (Alexandria, Va.: IWV Publishing, 1984).

p. 79 Lillian Gish: Lillian Gish quoted in "The Making of *The Birth of a Nation*," in *Focus on "The Birth of a Nation*," ed. Fred Silva (Englewood Cliffs, N.J.: Prentice-Hall, 1971), p. 47.

p. 80 *The Birth of a Nation* . . . forty-eight million dollars: See for example, Janet Wasko, "D. W. Griffith and the Banks," *Journal of the University Film Association* 30, 1 (Winter 1978): 15–20, and *Movies and Money: Financing the American Film Industry* (Norwood, N.J.: Ablex, 1982), ch. 2, pp. 33–45.

p. 80 excised material has never been recovered: Some of the excised material exists on the original nitrate stock at the

Library of Congress as individual frames from each shot filed for copyright purposes, but no original print of *The Birth of a Nation* is known to have survived. In 1979, Research Publications, Inc. (Woodbridge, Conn.), published a microfiche version of the film assembled by John Cuniberti from a 1921 release print (from which 16mm tinted versions derive today) and a slightly longer version preserved by MoMA, together with material from censorship and licensing boards and from Griffith's own papers. Cuniberti's reconstruction contains 1,610 scenes (1,377 shots, plus 233 titles)—only 31 scenes short of the original 1,641 submitted for copyright—and is accompanied by a computerized shot analysis indicating the original tints for each scene and the original musical cues.

In 1984, University Publications of America (Frederick, Md.) published on microfilm the *D. W. Griffith Papers 1897–1954*, containing over 50,000 pages of documentation on Griffith's life and work. This invaluable scholarly resource includes screenplays, dialogue, synopses, and cast and shot lists for filmed and proposed motion pictures, as well as scripts written by Griffith and others; financial reports, copyright registrations, bills, lab reports, leasing agreements, capital stock reports, and income tax returns; documentation of the formation of United Artists, including correspondence among the four principals, bylaws, contracts, and minutes of meetings of the board of directors; payroll records, production costs, and box-office statements for many of Griffith's films; clippings from newspapers across the country on all Griffith's films beginning with *The Birth of a Nation*; from a number of Griffith's contemporaries, a series of transcripts of oral history interviews and long letters describing Griffith's personality and his creative techniques. Billy Bitzer's handwritten memoirs of his partnership with Griffith; detailed legal files on such matters as contracts with actors and actresses, Griffith's role in the Triangle Company (with Mack Sennett and Thomas Ince). Griffith's production agreements with Adolph Zukor (for Paramount) and with Famous Players-Lasky, and his involvement in the fight against censorship of films; as well as voluminous correspondence with many of the leading figures in the film industry during Griffith's career: Douglas Fairbanks, Mary Pickford, Lillian and Dorothy Gish, Mack Sennett, Charlie Chaplin, William Randolph Hearst, Adolph Zukor, and hundreds of other personal and business acquaintances. Obviously, these papers are an essential source of primary material not merely on the work of Griffith but on the formative years of the motion-picture industry at large.

p. 80 Oswald Garrison Villard: Oswald Garrison Villard quoted in Peter Noble, "The Negro in *The Birth of a Nation*," in Silva, ed., *Focus on "The Birth of a Nation*," p. 131.

p. 80 race riot . . . modern Ku Klux Klan: One immediate response to *The Birth of a Nation* within the black community was an attempt to create an indigenous Afro-American cinema, which ultimately resulted in Selig Polyscope's swindle-ridden, fragmentary epic of black history, *The Birth of a Race* (1918). A complete six-reel nitrate print of this rare all-black film was discovered near Canyon, Texas, in 1980 by representatives of the American Film Institute and is currently available to scholars in the AFI Collection at the Library of Congress. See Thomas Cripps, *Slow Fade to Black: The Negro in American Film, 1900–1942* (New York: Oxford University Press, 1977), pp. 70–75. In another black counteroffensive, a brief epilogue, filmed on the campus of the Hampton Institute (since July 1984, Hampton University),

Hampton, Virginia, apparently by professional photographers on the Hampton staff, was in some cities added to *The Birth of a Nation* itself. This "Hampton Epilogue" stressed the advancement of the Negro race since Reconstruction and its contributions to American social and industrial progress. Griffith permitted the addition to silence protest against his film, but its mitigating effect was negligible. See Nickie Fleener, "Answering Film with Film: The Hampton Epilogue, a Positive Alternative to the Negative Black Stereotypes Presented in *The Birth of a Nation*," *The Journal of Popular Film and Television* 7, 4 (Summer 1980): 400–25.

pp. 80–81 Wilson . . . specious ends: For more on the public reaction to *The Birth of a Nation* and on its historical context, see Daniel J. Leab, "*The Birth of a Nation* as a Public Event," and A. Marshall Deutelbaum, "Reassessing *The Birth of a Nation*," in "*The Birth of a Nation*" and 1915 (Society for Cinema Studies, 1976), pp. 4–14.

p. 81 Griffith's . . . regional conditioning: Robert Henderson, *D. W. Griffith: His Life and Work* (New York: Oxford University Press, 1972), p. 151.

p. 84 MoMA: Theodore Huff, *A Short Analysis of D. W. Griffith's "The Birth of a Nation"* (New York: Museum of Modern Art Film Library, 1961). Copyright © 1961. Excerpted by permission.

p. 89 Woodrow Wilson: Woodrow Wilson, *A History of the American People*, 5 vols. (New York, 1902), vol. 5, pp. 58–59.

p. 89 Bruce F. Kawin: The issue of the relationship between film and mental process was raised as early as 1916 in a footnote to Hugo Münsterberg's *The Photoplay: A Psychological Study* (reprinted as *The Film: A Psychological Study* [New York: Dover Books, 1970]). Like Kawin, Münsterberg concluded that motion pictures obey "the laws of the mind," where a variety of spatial and temporal relationships can exist simultaneously, "rather than those of the outer world."

pp. 90–91 tributaries flowing . . . Vachel Lindsay: Vachel Lindsay, *The Art of the Moving Picture* (New York Macmillan, 1915; repr. New York: Liveright, 1970), p. 41.

p. 91 breathlessly moving camera . . . Vachel Lindsay: Lindsay, p. 49.

p. 92 glowing portrait of the Ku Klux Klan: See Maxim Simcovitch, "The Impact of Griffith's *Birth of a Nation* on the Modern Ku Klux Klan," *Journal of Popular Film* 1, 1 (Winter 1972): 45–54.

p. 93 Harry M. Geduld: Harry M. Geduld, ed., *Focus on D. W. Griffith* (Englewood Cliffs, N.J.: Prentice-Hall, 1971), p. 8.

p. 94 Woodrow Wilson: Woodrow Wilson quoted in Everett Carter, "Cultural History Written with Lightning: The Significance of *The Birth of a Nation*," in Silva, ed., *Focus on "The Birth of a Nation*," p. 133.

p. 95 3.26: illustration of Babylonian set of *Intolerance*: For a marvelous interpretation of this image in relation to the film's thematic structure, see Russell Merritt, "On First Looking into Griffith's Babylon: A Reading of a Publicity Still," *Wide Angle* 1, 2 (Spring 1979): 12–21.

p. 97 contemporary interviewer: Griffith re *Intolerance*, see Geduld, p. 47.

p. 98 Iris Barry . . . *Intolerance*: Iris Barry, *D. W. Griffith: American Film Master* (New York: MoMA, 1940), p. 25.

p. 99 pompous titles . . . Iris Barry: Barry, p. 24.

p. 99 Jay Leyda . . . Griffith's death: Jay Leyda quoted in Geduld, p. 165.

p. 99 John Dorr: John Dorr, "The Griffith Tradition," *Film Comment* 10, 2 (March–April 1974): 54.

p. 101 Griffith's rejoinder . . . pacifist statement: On the influence of the progressive movement and World War I on the film's reception, see William M. Drew, *D. W. Griffith's "Intolerance": Its Genesis and Its Vision* (Jefferson, N.C.: McFarland & Co,, 1968), chapters 5 and 6, and Miriam Hansen and Martin Christadler, "David Wark Griffith's *Intolerance* (1916): Zum Verhältnis von Film und Geschichte in der Progressive Era," *Amerikastudien/American Studies* 21, 1 (1976): 7–37. See also Miriam Hansen, "Rätsel der Mütterlichkeit: Studie zum Wiegenmotiv in D. W. Griffith's *Intolerance*," trans. Nele Löw-Beer, *Frauen und Film* 41 (December 1986): 32–48; "Universal Language and Democratic Culture: Myths of Origin in Early American Cinema," *Myth and Enlightenment in American Literature: In Honor of Hans-Joachim Lang*, Erlanger Forschungen, series A, vol. 38 (Erlanger, W. Germany: University of Erlangen-Nürnberg, 1985), 321–51; "The Hieroglyph and the Whore: Rescue Fantasies in D. W. Griffith's *Intolerance*," *South Atlantic Quarterly* (Fall 1988), forthcoming; *Babel and Babylon: Spectatorship in American Silent Cinema* (Cambridge; Harvard University Press 1988); and "Griffith's Real *Intolerance*," *Film Comment* 25, 5 (September–October 1989): 28–29. See also Jean E. Tucker, "Voices from the Silents," *The Quarterly Journal of the Library of Congress* 37, 3–4 (Summer–Fall 1980): 387–412 for an oral history of the production of the film; and Nell Irvin Painter, *Standing at Armageddon: The United States 1877–1919* (New York: Norton, 1987), for a history of the entire progressive era.

p. 102 *Broken Blossoms* . . . hopelessly old-fashioned: See Dudley Andrew, "*Broken Blossoms*: The Art and the Eros of a Perverse Text," *Quarterly Review of Film Studies* 6, 1 (Winter 1981): 81–90.

p. 102 *Hearts of the World* . . . enormously popular: On the troubled production and marketing of *Hearts of the World* (through a shameless anti-German publicity campaign that Griffith deliberately used to smear censors who had opposed *The Birth of a Nation*), see Russell Merritt, "D. W. Griffith Directs the Great War: The Making of *Hearts of the World*," *Quarterly Review of Film Studies* 6, 1 (Winter 1981): 45–65. See also Nicholas Reeves, *Official British Propaganda During the First World War* (London: Croom Helm, 1986), chap. 3: "Film Production."

p. 103 Robert Henderson . . . Griffith imprimatur: Henderson p. 209

p. 103 Lillian Gish . . . no retakes: Lillian Gish quoted in Georges Sadoul, *Dictionary of Films*, trans. and ed. Peter Morris (Berkeley: University of California Press, 1972), p. 43.

p. 105 ice flow montage . . . *Mother*: On the shooting of this scene, see Arthur Lennig, "The Birth of *Way Down East*," *Quarterly Review of Film Studies* 6, 1 (Winter 1981): 105–16.

p. 108 *The Struggle* . . . better film than *Abraham Lincoln*: see Edward Wagenknecht and Anthony Slide, *The Films of D. W. Griffith* (New York: Crown Publishers, 1976).

p. 109 human history . . . Good and Evil: Sergei Eisenstein, *The Film Form*, trans. and ed. Jay Leyda (New York, Meridian Books, 1949), pp. 233, 235.

German Cinema of the Weimar Period, 1919–1929

p. 111 Siegfried Kracauer . . . *Der Student von Prag*: Siegfried Kracauer, *From Caligari to Hitler: A Psychological History of the German Film* (Princeton, N.J.: Princeton University Press, 1947), p. 31.

p. 114 minor exceptions . . . Alf Sjoberg: See Forsyth Hardy, *Scandinavian Film* (London: Falcon Press, 1952); Ebbe Neergaard, *The Story of Danish Film*, trans. Elsa Gress (Copenhagen: Danish Institute, 1962); Ron Mottram, *The Danish Cinema Before Dreyer* (Metuchen, N.J.: Scarecrow Press, 1988); Bengt Idestam-Almquist, *Victor Sjöström* (Paris, 1965); Hans Pensel, *Seastrom and Stiller in Hollywood* (New York: Vantage Press, 1969); Peter Cowie, *Sweden, Screen Series*, 2 vols., Rev. ed. (Cranberry, N.J.: A. S. Barnes, 1969); Aleksander Kwiaikowski, *Swedish Film Classics: A Pictorial Survey of 25 Films from 1913 to 1957* (New York, 1983); John Fullerton, "AB Svenska Biografteatem: Aspects of Production," in Bruce A. Austin, ed., *Current Research in Film: Audiences, Economics, and Law*, vol. 1 (Norwood, N.J., 1985); and Graham Petrie, *Hollywood Destinies: European Directors in America, 1922–1931* (London, 1985).

p. 115 As Kracauer points out: Kracauer, pp. 38–39.

p. 115 Expressionism . . . prominent in the arts: See *Passion and Rebellion: the Expressionist Heritage*, ed. Stephen Eric Bronner and Douglas Kellner (New York: Universe Books, 1983). See also Eberhard Roters et al., *Berlin 1910–1933*, trans. Marguerite Mounier (New York: Rizzoli, 1982).

p. 116 Lewis Jacobs . . . Lubitsch: Lewis Jacobs, *The Rise of the American Film* (New York: Teachers College Press, 1948), p. 303.

p. 116 Kracauer . . . variables: Kracauer, p. 49.

p. 119 exemplar of the German Expressionist cinema: See Barry Salt, *Film Style and Technology* (London: Starword, 1983), pp. 157–59; see also Frank Tomasulo, "*Cabinet of Dr. Caligari*: History/Psychoanalysis/Cinema," *On Film* 11 (Summer 1983): pp. 2–7; Michael Budd, "Retrospective Narration in Film: Rereading 'The Cabinet of Dr. Caligari'," *Film Criticism* 4 (Fall 1979): 35–43; "'The Cabinet of Dr. Caligari': Conditions of Reception," *Cine-Tracts* 3 (Winter 1981): 41–49; and "The National Board of Review and the Early Art Cinema in New York: 'The Cabinet of Dr. Caligari' as Affirmative Culture," *Cinema Journal* 26, 1 (Fall 1986): 3–18.

p. 119 *The Haunted Screen*: Lotte H. Eisner, *The Haunted Screen: German Expressionism and the Influence of Max Reinhardt*, trans. Richard Greaves (Berkeley: University of California Press, 1969).

p. 120 Lewis Jacobs . . . *Caligari*: Jacobs, p. 303.

p. 120 Arthur Knight . . . UFA: Arthur Knight, *The Liveliest Art: A Panoramic History of the Movies* (New York: New American Library, 1957), p. 58.

p. 121 Paul Rotha . . . German studies: Paul Rotha, *The Film Till Now* (London, 1930), p. 255.

p. 122 Cultural pessimism . . . *The Decline of the West*: Kracauer, p. 88.

p. 124 *Nosferatu* . . . a classic of the genre: See Alain Silver and James Ursini, *The Vampire Film* (New York: A. S. Barnes, 1975); Barry Pattison, *The Seal of Dracula* (New York: Bonanza Books, 1975); David Pirie, *The Vampire Cinema* (London: Tantivy Press, 1977); Gregory A. Waller, *The Living and the Undead: From Stoker's Dracula to Romero's Dawn of the Dead* (Urbana, Ill.: University of Illinois Press, 1986); and Judith Mayne, "Dracula in the Twilight: Murnau's *Nosferatu* (1922) in *German Film and Literature*, ed. Eric Rentschler (New York: Methuen, 1986), pp. 25–39.

p. 126 Béla Balázs . . . *Nosferatu*: Béla Balázs, *The Visible Man, or Film Culture* (Halle, Germany, 1924); quoted in Kracauer, p. 78

p. 127 that the camera be put into . . . continuous motion: In *Film Style and Technology* (London: Starword, 1983), Barry Salt ascribes the new wave of camera mobility to Lupu Pick's 1923 *Sylvester* (also known as *New Year's Eve*), which he says contained many tracking shots through a set showing city streets (these executed by cameraman Guido Seeber, according to Kracauer, on "a tripod moving on rails" [*From Caligari to Hitler*, p. 105]). Initially, *Sylvester* was conceived as the second film in a Mayer-Pick *Kammerspielfilme* trilogy, beginning with *Scherben* (*Shattered*, 1921) and concluding with *Der letzte Mann*. Pick was replaced by Murnau as the result of a quarrel with Mayer, and it was *his* film that led to a widespread renewal of interest in the possibilities of the moving camera for the first time since Griffith. (It should be noted, however, that a few tracking shots occur in the 1923 films of the French avant-garde—Abel Gance's *Au secours!*, e.g., Jean Epstein's *L'Auberge rouge*, and Louis Delluc's *L'Inondation*; and Bruce Kawin has pointed out to me a 360-degree pan halfway through Gance's *La Roue* [1922].) For an ambitious, thoroughly researched history of camera movement "executed with the action related to it for dramatic purposes," see Lutz Bacher, *The Mobile Mise-en-Scène* (New York: Arno Press, 1978).

p. 129 possibilities inherent in the subjective camera: For the most thorough treatments of subjectivity and self-conscious narration available in English, and their relationship to narrative point of view, see Bruce F. Kawin, *Mindscreen: Bergman, Godard, and the First-Person Film* (Princeton: Princeton University Press, 1978), and Edward Branigan, *Point of View in the Cinema: A Theory of Narration and Subjectivity in Classical Film* (New York and Berlin: Mouton, 1984). See also Bruce F. Kawin, "An Outline of Film Voices," *Film Quarterly* 38, 2 (Winter 1984–85): 38–46; and Maureen Turim, *Flashbacks in Film: Memory and History* (New York: Routledge, 1989).

p. 130 Murnau's biographer: Lotte H. Eisner, *Murnau* (Berkeley: University of California Press, 1973), p. 167.

p. 130 Lewis Jacobs . . . *Variety*: Jacobs, p. 307.

p. 132 migration . . . was random and temporary: Other German and Central European film artists who ultimately emigrated to Hollywood, most of them to escape Hitler, were the directors Fritz Lang, Max Ophüls, Detlef Sierck (who would become Douglas Sirk, master of that quintessential fifties genre, the widescreen melodrama, and a formative influence upon the work of Rainer Werner Fassbinder, a leading figure in the New German Cinema of the seventies; see Chapter 17), Kurt and Robert Siodmak, William Dieterle, Billy Wilder, Edgar G. Ulmer, Fred Zinnemann, Max Reinhardt, Otto Preminger, Reinhold Schünzel, William Thiele, Ernö Metzner, Hermann Kosterlitz (Henry Koster), Gustav Machaty, Stephan Székely, Joe May, Richard Oswald, Henrik Galeen, Kurt (Curtis) Bernhardt, Hans (John) Brahm, Paul Czinner, Charles Vidor, and André De Toth, and the cinematographers Eugen Schüfftan and Rudolph Maté. Other important *émigrés* are as follows. Actors and actresses: Albert Basserman, Elizabeth Bergner, Helmut Dantine, Marlene Dietrich, Peter van Eyck, Hugo Haas, Paul Henreid, Oscar Homolka, Hedwig Kiesler (Hedy Lamarr), Fritz Kortner, Franz (Francis) Lederer, Peter Lorre, Paul Lukas, Luise Rainer, Sigfried Rumann, S. Z. Sakall, Joseph Schildkraut, and Walter Slezak. Writers: Bertolt Brecht, Lion Feuchtwanger, Bruno Frank, Georg Fröschel, Heinz Herald, Hans (John) Kafka, Fritz (Frederic) Kohner, Emil Ludwig, Alfred Neumann, Wolfgang Reinhardt, Walter Reisch, and Franz Schulz (Francis Spencer). Composers: Paul Dessau, Hanns Eisler, Bronislau Kaper, Erich W. Korngold, Miklós Rózsa, Hans Salter, Max Steiner, Franz Wachsmann (Waxman), and Kurt Weill. There were many, many others less prominent. All told, Hollywood managed to absorb more talent from the German cinema than was left to the Nazis when they took over the industry in 1933, and, for a while, Los Angeles became known as "the new Weimar." See the Exhibition Catalogue *German Film Directors in Hollywood: Film Emigration from Germany and Austria*, ed. Ernst Schürmann (San Francisco: The Goethe Institutes of North America, 1978). Anthony Heilbut, *Exiled in Paradise: German Refugee Artists and Intellectuals in America from the 1930s to the Present* (New York: Viking, 1983), John Russell Taylor, *Strangers in Paradise: The Hollywood Émigrés, 1933–1950* (New York: Holt, Rinehart, and Winston, 1983), and *The Muses Flee Hitler: Cultural Transfer and Adaptation, 1930–1945*, ed. Jarrell C. Jackman and Carla M. Borden (Washington: Smithsonian Institution Press, 1983).

p. 132 Murnau's work declined: See, for example, Murnau's *Our Daily Bread* (completed 1928, re-edited and released by Fox as the part-talkie *City Girl* [1930]). But see also Graham Petrie's reassessment of Murnau's and Lubitsch's American careers in *Hollywood Destinies: European Directors in America, 1922–1931* (London, Methuen, 1985), pp. 26–102. (In the recut version, the film's first five reels were left nearly intact and the second five reshot with sound by a studio technician and compressed to two; in 1983, the complete ten-reel silent version was rediscovered in the vaults at Fox and has since been preserved, revealing a constrained and compromised but still vital Murnau.)

p. 135 motivated point-of-view: For a rigorous taxonomy of the point-of-view shot, see Ch. 5 of Edward Branigan's *Point of View in the Cinema* (New York: Mouton, 1984). See also Kawin's *Mindscreen*; *Film Reader 4*, ed. Blaine Allan et al. (Evanston, Ill., 1979), pp. 105–236; George M. Wilson's *Narration in Light: Studies in Cinematic Point of View* (Baltimore: Johns Hopkins, 1986); *Wide Angle* 8, 3–4 (Fall 1986); *Narrative/Non-narrative*, ed. Edward Branigan, "Point of View in the Fiction Film," 4–52; and, especially, David Bordwell's *Narration in the Fiction Film* (Madison, Wis.: University of Wisconsin, 1985).

Soviet Silent Cinema
and the Theory of Montage, 1917–1931

p. 141 seven hundred domestic features: See Vance Kepley, Jr., and Betty Kepley, "Foreign Films on Soviet Screens, 1922–1931," *Quarterly Review of Film Studies* 4, 4 (Fall 1979); 429–42, and V. Kepley, Jr., "The Origins of Soviet Cinema: A Study of Industry Development," *Quarterly Review of Film Studies* 10, 1 (Winter 1985): 22–38. See also Richard Taylor, "A 'Cinema for the Millions': Soviet Socialist Realism and the Problem of Film Comedy," *Journal of Contemporary History* 18 (1983): 439–61; and V. Kepley, Jr., "Building a National Cinema: Soviet Film Education, 1918–1934," *Wide Angle* 9, 3 (Summer 1987): 4–20.

p. 142 radical manifestoes: Vertov's manifestoes are collected in *Kino-Eye: The Writings of Dziga Vertov*, trans. Kevin O'Brien and ed. Annette Michelson (Berkeley: University of California Press, 1984). See also Vlada Petríc, "Dziga Vertov as Theorist," *Cinema Journal* 18, 1 (Fall 1978): 29–44, and "The Difficult Years of Dziga Vertov: Excerpts from His Diaries," *Quarterly Review of Film Studies* 7, 1 (Winter 1982): 7–21; Seth Feldman, " 'Cinema Weekly' and 'Cinema Truth': Dziga Vertov and the Leninist Film Proportion," in *"Show Us Life": Toward a History and Aesthetics of the Committed Documentary*, ed. Thomas Waugh (Metuchen, N.J.: Scarecrow Press, 1984), pp. 3–20; and Sergei Drobashenko, "Soviet Documentary Film, 1917–40," in *Propaganda, Politics, and Film, 1918–45*, ed. Nicholas Pronay and D. W. Spring (London: Macmillan, 1982), pp. 249–69.

p. 143 *Kino-glaz* . . . one critic: Sadoul, *Dictionary of Films*, trans. and ed. Peter Morris (Berkeley: University of California Press, 1972), p. 178.

p. 143 *The Man with a Movie Camera*: For a definitive reading of *The Man with a Movie Camera* in its technical, formal, and cultural contexts, see Vlada Petríc, *Constructivism in Film: The Man with the Movie Camera: A Cinematic Analysis* (Cambridge, Eng.: Cambridge University Press, 1987). See also Judith Mayne, *Kino and the Woman Question: Feminism and Soviet Silent Film* (Columbus: Ohio State University Press, 1989), Chapter 6, pp. 154–82.

p. 143 David Bordwell: David Bordwell, "Dziga Vertov," *Film Comment* 8, 1 (Spring 1972): 41.

p. 143 *Enthusiasm*: See Lucy Fischer, "Enthusiasm: From Kino-Eye to Radio-Eye," *Film Quarterly* 31, 2 (Winter 1977–78): 25–35; in *Film Sound: Theory and Practice*, ed. Elisabeth Weis and John Belton (New York: Columbia University Press, 1985), pp. 247–64.

p. 145 Iris Barry . . . ten years: Iris Barry, *D. W. Griffith: American Film Master* (New York: MoMA, 1940), p. 26.

p. 145 Jay Leyda . . . *Intolerance*: Jay Leyda, *Kino* (London: George Allen & Unwir, 1960), p. 143.

p. 146 Pudovkin: V. I. Pudovkin, *Film Technique and Film Acting* (London: 1929), p. 168.

p. 147 Ron Levaco . . . *perception*: Ron Levaco, "Kuleshov," *Sight and Sound* 40, 2 (Spring 1971): 88.

p. 147 Sergei Eisenstein: Sergei Eisenstein, *The Film Form*, trans. and ed. Jay Leyda (New York: Meridian Books, 1949), p. 240.

p. 149 *Art of Cinema*: V. I. Pudovkin, "Foreword" to *The Art of Cinema*; reprinted in *Kuleshov on Film*, ed. Ronald Levaco (Berkeley: University of California Press, 1947), p. 41.

p. 149 half of the major Soviet directors since 1920: Levaco, "Kuleshov," p. 86.

p. 149 obtains differing results: Pudovkin, *Film Technique and Film Acting*, pp. 166–67.

p. 149 Futurist and Formalist experimentation: Bordwell, "Dziga Vertov: An Introduction," *Film Comment* (Spring 1972): 38. See also *The Film Factory: Russian and Soviet Cinema in Documents, 1896–1939*, ed. and trans. Richard Taylor (London: Routledge & Kegan Paul, 1988).

p. 151 Meyerhold . . . claimed: "Chaplin and Chaplinism," in *Meyerhold on the Theater*, ed. Edward Braun (London, 1969), pp. 311–12.

p. 151 Oriental theater: Peter Wollen, *Signs and Meaning in the Cinema*, 2nd ed. (Bloomington, Ind., 1972), pp. 46–55.

p. 152 certain emotional shocks: Reprinted in Sergei Eisenstein, *The Film Sense*, trans. and ed. Jay Leyda (New York: Harcourt Brace Jovanovich, 1942), pp. 166–67.

p. 153 agitational aspects of his work: Eisenstein, *The Film Sense*, p. 39.

p. 153 Yon Barna: Yon Barna, *Eisenstein* (Bloomington, Ind., 1973), p. 70.

p. 154 *Strike* . . . according to Eisenstein: quoted in Barna, p. 78.

p. 154 Kuleshov Workshop . . . VGIK: Whether or not Eisenstein was officially enrolled at the VGIK when he studied with Kuleshov is unclear. Kuleshov told Eisenstein's biographer Yon Barna that Eisenstein had been a student in the workshop in 1923 "at the beginning of his film career" (*Eisenstein*, p. 71). In a "bio-interview" with Steven P. Hill, Kuleshov elaborated: "Eisenstein got his first lessons in film direction from me. True, he didn't study with me very long—about three months—but Eisenstein himself said that any man can be a director, only one needs to study three years and another three hundred years. . . . Together with Alexandrov, he attended our workshop in the evening (in the attic of Meyerhold's Theater), and together we did some work on developing shooting scripts mostly for crowd scenes. . . . We studied together how to work out editing scenes on paper, when there wasn't any film. That was before his début—that is, before *Strike*." *Film Culture* 44 (1967): 1–41.

p. 155 Eisenstein . . . "kino-fist": quoted in Barna, p. 88.

p. 157 mutiny . . . bloody aftermath: For a full historical account of the mutiny, see Richard Hough, *The Potemkin Mutiny* (Englewood Cliffs, N.J.: Prentice-Hall, 1960); on the making of the film *Potemkin*, see a recent "revisionist" commentary by Steven Hill in *Film Culture* 44 (1977): 1–41, which corrects some widely quoted mistaken accounts of the film's production.

p. 159 *Potemkin* . . . plate . . . montages: for an extended semiotic analysis of this important sequence, see Daniel L. Selden, "Vision and Violence: The Rhetoric of *Potemkin*," *Quarterly Review of Film Studies* 7, 4 (Fall 1982): 308–29.

p. 175–76 *Potemkin*'s . . . stone lion: For alternate interpretations of this stone lion montage sequence, see Herbert Marshall, "The Puzzle of the Three Stone Lions" (*The Battleship Potemkin: The Greatest Film Ever Made* [New York, 1978], pp. 264–75.

p. 176 Arthur Knight: Arthur Knight, *The Liveliest Art* (New York: New American Library, 1957), p. 80.

p. 179 Meisel . . . Eisenstein: quoted in Barna, p. 109.

p. 179 Max Reinhardt . . . *Potemkin*: quoted in Marie Seton, *Sergei M. Eisenstein* (London, 1952), p. 86.

p. 179 popular . . . Eisenstein: quoted in Barna, p. 104.

p. 180 Eisenstein defined montage . . . industrial metaphor: Sergei Eisenstein, "The Cinematographic Principle and the Ideogram" (excerpted from *The Film Form*); reprinted as "Collision of Ideas" in *Film: A Montage of Theories*, ed. Richard Dyer MacCann (New York: E. P. Dutton, 1966), p. 36.

p. 181 Eisenstein . . . theoretical essays: *The Film Form*, pp. 45–63, 150–78.

p. 182 brotherly feeling—in both moments: *The Film Form*, pp. 164–65.

p. 183 general *tone* of the piece: *The Film Form*, p. 75.

p. 184 Eisenstein . . . overtone: *The Film Form*, p. 69.

p. 184 Eisenstein . . . God: *The Film Form*, p. 82.

p. 185 Bazin . . . analytical fragmentation: André Bazin, "The Evolution of the Language of the Cinema," in *What Is Cinema?*, trans. Hugh Grey, 2 vols. (Berkeley: University of California Press, 1967; 1971), vol. 1, pp. 35–36.

p. 186 Paul Seydor . . . critical of Eisenstein: Paul Seydor, "Eisenstein's Aesthetic: A Dissenting View," *Sight and Sound* 43, 1 (Winter 1973–74): 38–43.

p. 186 Eisenstein . . . *The Film Sense*: Eisenstein, *The Film Sense*, p. 32.

p. 186 a measure of its limitations: For a detailed analysis of Eisenstein's theoretical formulations (many of them still unavailable in English) as they relate systematically to his work, see Jacques Aumont, *Montage Eisenstein*, trans. Lee Hildreth, Constance Penley, and Andrew Ross (Bloomington: Indiana University Press, 1987).

p. 187 Yon Barna . . . October: Barna, p. 125.

p. 187 Eisenstein . . . *Film Form*: Eisenstein, *Film Form* and *The Film Sense*, ed. and trans. Jay Leyda (New York: Meridian Books, 1967), p. 58.

p. 189 Russian peasant village . . . collective farm: On the historical context of collectivization as a key to understanding the ideological content of several Soviet films (1928–31), see Paul E. Burns, "Cultural Revolution, Collectivization, and Soviet Cinema: Eisenstein's *Old and New* and Dovzhenko's *Earth*," *Film & History* 11, 4 (December 1981): 84–105. On the murderous process itself, see Robert Conquest, *The Harvest of Sorrow: Soviet Collectivization and the Terror Famine* (New York: Oxford, 1986) and the PBS documentary by the same title (October 1986).

p. 190 Eisenstein . . . *Old and New*: *The Film Form*, p. 69.

p. 190 neorealist successors, Eisenstein wrote . . . *The Film Form*, p. 66.

p. 191 outer limits of the legitimate stage: quoted in Barna, p. 70.

p. 194 Léon Moussinac: quoted in Barna, p. 115.

p. 194 Pudovkin . . . *Potemkin*: Pudovkin, *Film Technique and Film Acting*, p. 95.

p. 196 *Film Technique and Film Acting*: Pudovkin, *Film Technique and Film Acting*, p. 24.

p. 198 Dovzhenko . . . Odessa: quoted in Georges Sadoul, *Dictionary of Film Makers*, trans. and ed. Peter Morris (Berkeley: University of California Press, 1972), p. 68.

p. 198 reminiscent of . . . Gogol: quoted in *Alexander Dovzhenko: The Poet as Filmmaker*, trans. and ed. Marco Carynnyk (Cambridge, Mass: MIT Press, 1973), p. xv.

p. 198 Dovzhenko . . . *Zvenigora*: quoted in *Alexander Dovzhenko*, p. 14.

p. 199 Eisenstein . . . *Arsenal*: quoted in Leyda, *Kino*, p. 252.

p. 199 Jay Leyda . . . *Arsenal*: Leyda, quoted in *Alexander Dovzhenko*, p. xvii.

p. 200 Lewis Jacobs . . . *Earth*: Lewis Jacobs, *The Rise of the American Film* (New York: Teachers College Press, 1948), p. 560.

p. 201 Ivor Montagu: Ivor Montagu, "Dovzhenko: Poet of Eternal Life," *Sight and Sound* 26, 3 (Summer 1957): 47. Quoted in *Alexander Dovzhenko*, p. xxi.

p. 202 Dovzhenko: The definitive account of Dovzhenko's life and work (in English) is contained in Vance Kepley, Jr.'s, *In the Service of the State: The Cinema of Alexander Dovzhen-ko* (Madison: The University of Wisconsin Press, 1986).

p. 203 Esther Shub: See Vlada Petric, "Esther Shub: Cinema Is My Life" and "Esther Shub's Unrealized Project," *Quarterly Review of Film Studies* 3, 4 (Fall 1978): 429–56; "Esther Shub: Film as Historical Discourse," in *"Show Us Life": Toward a History and Aesthetics of the Committed Documentary*, pp. 21–46; and Sergei Drobashenko, "Soviet Documentary Film, 1917–40," in *Propaganda, Politics, and Film 1918–45*, pp. 258–69.

p. 205 Stalin . . . blunt: quoted in Richard Taylor, *The Politics of the Soviet Cinema, 1917–1929* (London: Cambridge University Press, 1979), p. 64.

p. 206 Socialist realism: *Marxism, Communism, and Western Society*, ed. C. D. Kernig, 8 vols. (New York, 1973), vol. 8, p. 1.

p. 206 Soviet Union . . . creative sterility: For a detailed scholarly account of how the Soviet cinema was turned from a revolutionary agitational movement into "a mouthpiece for Stalinist orthodoxy," see Richard Taylor, *The Politics of the Soviet Cinema, 1917–1929* (London: Cambridge University Press, 1979). For a revisionist perspective, which argues that socialist realism did not merely reflect "Stalin's primitive personal tastes" but was part of a worldwide 1930s trend toward "cinema realism," see Denise J. Youngblood, *Soviet Cinema in the Silent Era, 1918–1935* (Ann Arbor: University of Michigan, 1985).

Hollywood in the Twenties

p. 209 all trained at Inceville: Borzage, King, Ingraham, and Hillyer directed Westerns for the American Film Company's "Flying A" and "Mustang" brands in Santa Barbara before coming to work for Ince. See Timothy J. Lyons, *The Silent Partner: The History of the American Film Manufacturing Company, 1910–1921* (New York: Arno Press, 1974).

p. 209 Ince . . . contributed to the cinema: A retrospective of Ince's work as an actor, director, and producer in forty films, from the Biograph short *His New Lid* (Frank Powell, 1910) through *Anna Christie* (John Griffith Wray, 1923), was held by the Museum of Modern Art in October 1986. See Tom Gunning, "Thomas H. Ince, American Filmmaker," *Domitor Bulletin* 1, 2 (December 1986): 6, and Jean Mitry, "Thomas H. Ince: His Esthetic, His Films, His Legacy," trans. Martin Sopocy with Paul Attallah, *Cinema Journal* 22, 2 (Winter 1983): 2–25.

p. 210 John Ford: Quoted in David Robinson, *Hollywood in the Twenties* (New York: Paperback Library, 1970), p. 91.

p. 210 madcap improvisation: An archive of synopses, continuities, and postproduction materials for some sixty Sennett films is now on file in the Sennett Collection at the Margaret Herrick Library of the Academy of Motion Picture Arts and Sciences. See Tom Stemple, "The Sennett Screenplays," *Sight and Sound* 55, 1 (Winter 1985–86): 58–60.

p. 213 Chaplin's . . . sound films: For more on Chaplin's sound films, see "Chaplin and Sound," *Journal of the University Film Association* 31, 1 (Winter 1979 [special issue]); Julian Smith, *Chaplin*, Chapter 4, "The Transition to Sound," and Chapter 5, "The Doomed Tyrant" (Boston: Twayne, 1984); and David Robinson, *Chaplin: The Mirror of Opinion* (Bloomington: Indiana University Press, 1984) and *Chaplin: His Life and Art* (New York: McGraw-Hill, 1985).

p. 216 Chaplin the filmmaker: See Gavin Millar, "The Unknown Chaplin," *Sight and Sound* 52, 2 (Spring 1983): 98–99; Charles Silver, "*Chaplin Redux*" 9, 10 (September 1984); and Leonard Maltin, "Silent Film Buffs Stalk and Find a Missing Tramp," *Smithsonian* 18, 4 (July 1986): 46–58. Another aid to studying Chaplin will be *Chapliniana* (Bloomington: Indiana University Press, 1987–89), Harry M. Geduld's three-volume commentary on Chaplin's eighty-one films prepared to commemorate the centenary of his birth. The first volume deals with his thirty-five Keystone comedies made in 1914; the second with his twenty-seven Essanay and Mutual films, 1915–16; and the third with his nineteen First National and feature films made between 1918 and 1967.

p. 221 Walter Kerr . . . *The General*: Walter Kerr, *The Silent Clowns* (New York: Knopf, 1975), p. 246.

p. 222 Keaton . . . miracles: Rudi Blesh, *Keaton* (New York: Macmillan, 1966), p. 12.

p. 222 Keaton . . . one-take scene: David Robinson, *Buster

Keaton (Bloomington, Ind.: Indiana University Press, 1969), p. 165.

p. 222 Keaton . . . newsreel: P. Demun, quoted in Sadoul, *Dictionary of Films*, trans. and ed. Peter Morris (Berkeley: University of California Press, 1972), p. 51.

p. 223 Keaton was the superior director: Working in a constellation identical to that which created *The Unknown Chaplin*, Kevin Brownlow and David Gill are producing a Thames Television documentary on Keaton in collaboration with his widow, Eleanor, and archivist distributor Raymond Rohauer, who controls the rights to most of Keaton's films. Among other items, the program will contain footage from the lost short *Hard Luck* (1921) and the recently rediscovered French feature *Le Roi des Champs Elysees* (Max Nosseck, 1934).

p. 225 Lloyd . . . Walter Kerr: Kerr, pp. 190–92.

p. 225 Hardy . . . native of Georgia: Hardy, known as Babe to his friends, had appeared as a "fat boy" in numerous Patents Company releases before joining the Vim Comedy Company in Jacksonville, Florida, where between 1915 and 1917 he became something of a star. See Richard Alan Nelson, "Before Laurel: Oliver Hardy and the Vim Comedy Company, a Studio Biography," *Current Research in Film*, vol. 2, ed. Bruce A. Austin (Norwood, N.J.: Ablex, 1986), pp. 136–55.

p. 226 decidedly minor by comparison: For a closely reasoned alternative view of Harry Langdon, see Joyce Rheuban, *Harry Langdon: The Comedian as Metteur-en-Scène* (Rutherford, N.J.: Associated University Presses, 1983), especially Chapter 8, "Langdon, Lloyd, Keaton, and Chaplin," pp. 189–204.

p. 228 implicated both women in the murder: In *A Cast of Killers* (New York: Dutton, 1986), Sidney D. Kirkpatrick claims that director King Vidor solved the mystery forty-five years later in the course of doing research for a screenplay, proving in late 1966 that Taylor was killed by Minter's wealthy and domineering mother Charlotte Shelby in a fit of sexual jealousy. He further claims that Shelby arranged to conceal her guilt through multiple payoffs to investigators for the Los Angeles Police Department.

p. 229 to paraphrase Arthur Knight: Arthur Knight, *The Liveliest Art* (New York: New American Library, 1957, revised edition, New York: Mentor Books, 1978).

p. 230 Antitrust litigation: See J. Douglas Gomery, "Hollywood, the National Recovery Administration, and the Question of Monopoly Power," *Journal of the University Film Association* 31, 2 (Spring 1979): 47–52.

p. 232 Paul Fejos: For more on Fejos, Christensen, Sjöström, and the European directors working in Hollywood during this period, see Graham Petrie, "Paul Fejos in America," *Film Quarterly* 32, 2 (Winter 1978–79): 28–37; "Fejos," *Sight and Sound* 47, 3 (Summer 1978): 175–77, and most prominently, *Hollywood Destinies: European Directors in America, 1922–1931* (London, 1985).

p. 234 David Robinson . . . lost frontier: David Robinson, *Hollywood in the Twenties* (New York: Paperback Library, 1970), pp. 38–39.

p. 235 *The Thief of Bagdad*: Restored to its original 140-minute form in a newly hand-tinted and toned print with a new orchestral score by Carl Davis based on themes from Rimsky-Korsakov, the reconstructed *The Thief of Bagdad* was premiered in a video version produced by Thames Television in association with Raymond Rohauer on PBS's *Great Performances* series in January 1987.

p. 235 *Nanook of the North*: In 1947, a reedited version of *Nanook* was released by United Artists with narration and a musical score; prints of this version have subsequently found their way into many university film collections. But in 1976, David Shepard reconstructed the film using Flaherty's original intertitles and a newly commissioned score; this version, distributed by the Museum of Modern Art, is now considered to be authoritative. (See Steve Dobi, "Restoring *Nanook of the North*," *Film Librarian's Quarterly* 10 [1984]: pp. 16–18.)

p. 235 Flaherty . . . tilts and pans: Flaherty filmed *Nanook* with two Ackeley cameras, which had been invented by the naturalist Carl E. Ackeley in 1917 to photograph wild animals in their habitats. The Ackeley had a gyroscopic tripod head that permitted panning and tilting simultaneously; on the Bell & Howell 2709 and other standard professional cameras of the day, the two movements could be performed only by cranking two separate geared handles. The Ackeley also had extremely long lenses that could be sighted through while shooting, and it became standard for newsreel photography until the coming of sound. In the late twenties and early thirties, Ackeleys became widely used at the major studios for aerial scenes (e.g., in Paramount's *Wings* [William Wellman, 1927]), fights, chases, and races (e.g., in MGM's *Ben Hur* [Fred Niblo, 1926]). The Ackeley's only drawback was its 200-foot film magazine, half the size of the Bell & Howell or the Mitchell magazine.

p. 237 Benjamin Hampton . . . 1,500 per cent: *A History of the American Film Industry* (New York: Covicin, 1931, pp. 205–07, repr. New York: Dover, 1931), p. 684.

p. 246 *The Merry Widow* . . . made a fortune for MGM: MGM's books showed a profit of 1,271,054 dollars, but von Stroheim's lawyers, author Samuel Marx (*Mayer and Thalberg* [New York: Random House, 1975]), and others have claimed that the figure was close to 4.5 million dollars. Whatever the case, the 25 percent share promised to von Stroheim by his *Merry Widow* contract disappeared when MGM charged off "losses" from *Greed* against it (apparently, the latter film was deliberately underdistributed in Europe to produce these). In 1933, when MGM was planning a remake of *The Merry Widow* under the direction of Ernst Lubitsch, Thalberg offered von Stroheim 5,000 dollars for his interest in it, which the director accepted out of sheer financial necessity.

p. 250 André Bazin . . . von Stroheim: André Bazin "The Evolution of the Language of the Cinema," in *What Is Cinema?* trans. Hugh Grey, 2 vols. (Berkeley: University of California Press, 1967; 1971), vol. 1, p. 27.

p. 251 eccentric talent . . . von Stroheim: For example, in 1927 the powerful Wall Street brokerage firm of Hayden, Stone and Company, bankers to Associated First National and other studios, published an influential report sharply critical of the high cost of feature films and advising the industry in future to keep all budgets under 150,000 dollars and to abandon independent production as the costliest form of filmmaking. See Janet Wasko, *Movies and Money: Financing the American Film Industry* (Norwood, N.J.: Ablex, 1982), and Halsey, Stuart & Company, "The Motion Picture Industry as a Basis for Bond Financing," *The American Film Industry*, rev. ed., ed. Tino Balio (Madison: University of Wisconsin Press, 1985), pp. 195–217.

The Coming of Sound, 1926–1932

p. 254 Harry M. Geduld . . . musical accompaniment: Harry M. Geduld, *The Birth of the Talkies* (Bloomington: Indiana University Press, 1975), p. 36.

p. 255 to sound-on-film systems: Around 1916 there was a brief flurry of interest in a groove-on-film system known alternatively as Projectophone or Madalatone, after its inventors, Katherina and Ferdinand von Madaler. This was a variation of the sound-on-disk systems, in which a single continuous groove impressed directly onto the film strip served the same function as the concentric grooves of a disk recording, so that a stylus and sound box on the projector could convert fluctuations in the groove into sound waves for amplification. Madalatone was marketed on the Continent from 1927 to 1928 but was too imprecise to compete with the optical sound-on-film systems.

p. 255 Eugene Augustin Lauste: A native of France, Lauste (1856–1935) also worked with Major Woodville Latham on the development of the wide-gauge "Eidoloscope" projector, c. 1895, and he was the director of American Mutoscope and Biograph's Paris laboratory for several years around the turn of the century. He developed "Photocinematophone" at a studio in Brixton, London, with the initial backing of some British exhibitors.

p. 255 Joseph T. Tykociner: More than twenty years later, in 1922, Tykociner (1877–1969) gave a public demonstration of a program of sound-on-film clips at the University of Illinois that he had produced by modulating high-frequency currents through a photoelectric cell. He tried briefly and unsuccessfully to interest the film industry in the process, which went unnamed and unexploited, although when he died, the *New York Times* described him as the "inventor of the first talking motion picture process." See John R. Lewis, "J. T. Tykociner: A Forgotten Figure in the Development of Sound," *Journal of the University Film Association* 33, 3 (Summer 1981): 33–40.

p. 256 Tobis-Klangfilm: On the corporate history of Tobis-Klangfilm, see Douglas Gomery, "Tri-Ergon, Tobis-Klangfilm, and the Coming of Sound," *Cinema Journal* 16, 1 (Fall 1976): 51–61, and "Economic Struggle and Hollywood Imperialism: Europe Converts to Sound, *Yale French Studies* 60 (1980): 80–93. A rival optical process developed by the Danish engineers P. O. Pederson and Valdemar Poulsen in 1923 used an oscillograph to modulate light in recording and a selenium cell in reproduction, apparently to obviate the Tri-Ergon patents. This process was marketed as Tonfilm in Germany and was licensed by Gaumont in France and British Acoustic, Ltd., in England.

p. 258 Refrigerated* Warner Theater: On air-conditioned movie theaters, see Douglas Gomery, "The Growth of Movie Monopolies: The Case of Balaban & Katz," *Wide Angle* 3, 1 (Spring 1979): 54–62.

p. 258 Michael Pupin: Pupin quoted in Geduld, p. 142.

p. 258 Harry M. Geduld: Geduld, p. 142.

p. 260 to adopt a uniform sound system: See Douglas Gomery, "The Warner-Vitaphone Peril: The American Film Industry Reacts to the Innovation of Sound," *Journal of the University Film Association* 28, 1 (Winter 1976): 11–19; repr. in Gorham Kindem, ed., *The American Movie Industry: The Business of Motion Pictures* (Carbondale: Southern Illinois University Press, 1982), pp. 119–35.

p. 262 Richard Griffith: Richard Griffith, *The Movies* (New York: Simon and Schuster, 1957; revised edition, 1970), p. 341.

p. 263 prepared itself for the conversion to sound: See Douglas Gomery, "The Coming of Sound: Technological Change in the American Film Industry," *Film Sound: Theory and Practice*, Elisabeth Weis and John Belton (New York: Columbia University Press, 1985), pp. 5–24.

p. 264 Alexander Walker: Alexander Walker, *The Shattered Silents: How the Talkies Came to Stay* (London: Elm Tree Books, 1978), p. vii.

p. 264 market valuation . . . for fiscal year 1928: See also Douglas Gomery, "Hollywood Converts to Sound: Chaos or Order?", in *Sound and the Cinema:. The Coming of Sound to American Film*, ed. Evan W. Cameron (Pleasantville, N.Y.: Redgrave, 1980), pp. 24–37.

p. 264 Arthur Knight: sound engineers: Arthur Knight, *The Liveliest Art* (New York: New American Library, 1957, rev. ed., New York: Mentor Books, 1978), p. 150.

p. 265 7.10: A Critique of Klingender and Legg's analysis is contained in Janet Wasko, *Movies and Money* (Norwood, N.J.: Ablex, 1982), Chapter 3, "The Introduction of Sound and Financial Control (1927–1939)," pp. 47–102.

p. 266 Kenneth Macgowan . . . receiverships: Macgowan, *Behind the Screen: The History and Techniques of the Motion Picture* (New York: Dell, 1985), p. 287.

p. 267 process was used . . . well into the thirties: See the feature-length compilation film *Aux Sources des Colours, de son et de l'animation* (*The Beginnings of Color, Sound and Animation*) prepared under the supervision of Franz Schmitt in 1983 at the French State Film Archive in Bois d'Arcy.

p. 269 Kinemacolor films . . . shown regularly in thirteen countries: As Steve Neale points out in *Cinema and Technology: Image, Sound, Colour* (Bloomington: Indiana University Press, 1985), the success of Kinemacolor was analogous to the later success of Cinerama: ". . . it involved long runs of a limited number of films and programmes at a limited and particular number of cinemas . . . [which was] emphasized all the more by the types of film made in Kinemacolor and by the types of film that proved especially popular: news, actuality, and nonfiction in general at a time when fiction (dramas and comedies) tended overwhelmingly to dominate mainstream production" (p. 127).

p. 269 Gorham Kindem . . . Kinemacolor: Gorham Kindem, "The Demise of Kinemacolor," in *The American Movie Industry*, ed. Gorham Kindem, p. 144.

p. 273 work closely with the Technicolor cameraman: Among the early Technicolor cameramen who achieved distinction were Ray Rennahan (*La Cucaracha*, 1933, *Becky Sharp*, 1935; Academy Awards for *Gone with the Wind*, 1939, *Blood and Sand*, 1941); W. Howard Greene (*The Garden of Allah*, 1936, *A Star Is Born*, 1937, *The Private Lives of Elizabeth and Essex*, 1939, *Blossoms in the Dust*, 1941; Academy

Award for *Phantom of the Opera*, 1943); Allen Davey (*Cover Girl*, 1944, *Life with Father*, 1947); William V. Skall (*Northwest Passage*, 1940, *Reap the Wild Wind*, 1942, *Quo Vadis*, 1951; Academy Award, with Winton Hoch, for *Joan of Arc*, 1948; Winton Hoch Academy Awards for *She Wore a Yellow Ribbon*, 1949, *The Quiet Man*, 1952, with Archies Stout); and Arthur Arling *The Captain from Castille*, 1948; Academy Award for *The Yearling*, 1946, with Charles Rosher and Leonard Smith).

As for the "color consultant," from 1936 through 1948 this was the legendary Nathalie Kalmus (b. 1892), a former art student and wife of Herbert Kalmus (they had been secretly divorced in 1921 but continued to work and live together). As head of Technicolor's Color Advisory Service, Ms. Kalmus and her associates, Henri Jaffe and William Fritzsche, prepared a color chart for every scene, sequence, set, and character in a Technicolor script on the basis of its dominant mood. She exercised what many filmmakers felt to be an inordinate degree of control over lighting, costuming, makeup, and set design in actual production, for which she received screen credit as "Color Consultant." Ms. Kalmus's theories on the "language of color" were notoriously dogmatic, and she became a force to be reckoned with in the industry during the period of Technicolor's ascendance.

p. 281 Arthur Knight . . . dictatorial rule: Knight, p. 148.

p. 281 Paul Rotha . . . natural instincts: Paul Rotha, *The Film Till Now* (New York: Funk and Wagnalls, 1950), p. 405.

p. 281 "Sound and Image" manifesto: Eisenstein, Pudovkin, and Alexandrov quoted in Léon Moussinac, *Sergei Eisenstein*, trans. D. S. Petry (New York: Crown Publishers, 1970), pp. 154–55.

p. 282 Eisenstein . . . titles: For an engaging essay on the structural function of intertitles in silent films, see William F. Van Wert, "Intertitles," *Sight and Sound* 49, 2 (Spring 1980): 98–105.

p. 282 René Clair . . . sound film: René Clair, "The Art of Sound" (excerpted from his *Reflections on the Cinema*); reprinted in Richard Dyer McCann, ed., *Film: A Montage of Theories* (New York: Dutton, 1966) pp. 38–40.

p. 283 Pudovkin . . . human speech: V. I. Pudovkin, *Film Technique and Film Acting* (London, 1929; repr. New York: Grove Press, 1970), p. 184.

p. 283 the future of the sound film: For more on the theoretical and practical aspects of the debate about synchronous sound, see Lucy Fischer, "René Clair, *Le Million*, and the Coming of Sound," *Cinema Journal* 16, 2 (Spring 1977): 34–50, and "*Applause*: The Visual and Acoustic Landscapes," in *Sound and the Cinema*, ed. Cameron, pp. 182–210.

p. 284 Lewis Jacobs . . . detachment of sound: Lewis Jacobs, *The Movies as Medium* (New York: Farrar, Straus, & Giroux, 1970), p. 245.

p. 287 Arthur Knight . . . Post-Synchronization: Knight, p. 153.

p. 288 variable density and variable area: See Barry Salt, "Film Style and Technology in the Thirties," *Film Quarterly* 30, 1 (Fall 1976): 19–32; repr. in part as "Film Style and Technology in the Thirties: Sound," *Theory and Practice of Film Sound*, eds. Weis and Belton, pp. 37–43. See also Salt's *Film Style and Technology: History and Analysis* (London: Starwood, 1983).

The Sound Film
and the American Studio System

p. 290 new genres . . . musical film: In his excellent, comprehensive structural study, *The American Film Musical* (Bloomington: Indiana University Press, 1987), Rich Altman concludes that the genre was most prominent and culturally influential during the short period between the coming of sound to film and the coming of hi-fi, stereo, and television to the American home, making it "the last bridge, the last holdout in the passage from live to mechanical and electronic reproduction" (p. 356). See also Jane Feuer, *The Hollywood Musical* (Bloomington: Indiana University Press, 1982), for a similarly thought-provoking cultural analysis.

p. 293 the gangster as social victim: Robert Warshow, "The Gangster as Tragic Hero," in *The Immediate Experience* (New York: Doubleday, 1962), pp. 127–34.

p. 295 writer-director Preston Sturges: See James Curtis, *Between Flops: A Biography of Preston Sturges* (New York: Harcourt, Brace, 1982); Elliot Rubenstein, "The Home Fires: Aspects of Sturges's Wartime Comedy," *Quarterly Review of Film Studies* 7, 2 (Spring 1982): 131–41; Ray Cywinski, *Preston Sturges: A Guide to References and Resources* (Boston: G. K. Hall, 1984): Andrew Dickos, *Intrepid Laughter: Preston Sturges and the Movies* (Metuchen, N.J.: Scarecrow Press, 1985); *Five Screenplays by Preston Sturges*, ed. Brian Henderson (Berkeley: University of California Press, 1985); Brian Henderson, "Sturges at Work," *Film Quarterly* 39, 2 (Winter 1985–86), 16–28; Geoff Brown, "Preston Sturges, Inventor,"

Sight and Sound 55, 4 (Autumn 1986): 272–77. On the screwball form itself, see Stanley Cavell, *Pursuits of Happiness: The Hollywood Comedy of Remarriage* (Cambridge: Harvard University Press, 1981); William Paul, *Ernst Lubitsch's American Comedy* (New York: Columbia University Press, 1983), pp. 114–55; Wes D. Gehring, *Screwball Comedy: A Genre of Madcap Romance* (Westport, Conn.: Greenwood Press, 1986); James Harvey, *Romantic Comedy in Hollywood, from Lubitsch to Sturges* (New York: Knopf, 1987); and Duane Byrge and Robert Milton Miller, *A Critical Study of the Screwball Comedy Film* (Ann Arbor: UMI Research Press, 1989).

p. 297 Lewis Jacobs . . . new managerial figures: Lewis Jacobs, *The Rise of the American Film* (New York: Harcourt, Brace, 1939; repr. New York: Teachers College Press, 1968), p. 228.

p. 297 David Robinson . . . bureaucrats and accountants: David Robinson, *Hollywood in the Twenties* (Cranbury, N.J.: A. S. Barnes, 1968), p. 33.

p. 297 producer's role as supervisor: See Janet Staiger, "The Producer-Unit System," Bordwell, Thompson, and Staiger, *The Classical Hollywood Cinema* (New York: Columbia University Press, 1985), ch. 2.

p. 300 Raymond Moley . . . Production Code: Raymond Moley, *The Hays Office* (Indianapolis: Bobbs-Merrill, 1945), p. 132.

p. 301 exhibition sector . . . Douglas Gomery: Douglas Gomery, *The Hollywood Studio System* (New York: St. Martin's Press, 1986), p. 8.

pp. 301–02 David Robinson . . . the nature of art: David Robinson, *The History of World Cinema* (New York: Stein & Day, 1973) p. 178.

p. 302 Charles Higham . . . conformed to studio style: Charles Higham, *Warner Brothers* (New York: Scribner's, 1975), p. 108.

p. 302 John Baxter . . . largest output: John Baxter, *Hollywood in the Thirties* (London: A. S. Barnes & Company, 1968), p. 16.

p. 305 John Baxter . . . Paramount: Baxter, *Hollywood in the Thirties*, p. 34.

p. 307–08 Warner's . . . social realism: For an ideological reading of Warners' Depression-era films within the context of the studio system, see Nick Roddick, *A New Deal in Entertainment: Warner Brothers in the 1930's* (London: BFI Publishing, 1983). See also Thomas Schatz, " ' A Triumph of Bitchery': Warner Bros., Bette Davis and *Jezebel*," *Wide Angle* 10, 1 (Winter 1988): 16–29.

p. 308 Warners . . . art directors: For a brilliant, authoritative history of the work of art directors, see Léon Barsacq, *Caligari's Cabinet and Other Grand Illusions: A History of Film Design*, rev. and ed. Elliott Stein (New York: New American Library 1978). See also Eugene Lourie, *My Work in Films* (New York: Harcourt, Brace, 1985), the detailed memoirs of a world-renowned art director who worked at various points in his career for studios in Paris, London, Madrid, Rome, Hollywood, and Tokyo. See also John Hambley and Patrick Downing, "Fifty Years of Art Direction," in *The Art of Hollywood*, a Thames Television program guide (London: Victoria and Albert Museum, 1979); Howard Mandelbaum and Eric Myers, *Screen Deco: A Celebration of High Style in Hollywood* (New York: St. Martin's, 1985); and Donald Albrecht, *Designing Dreams: Modern Architecture in the Movies* (New York: Harper & Row/MoMA, 1988).

p. 310 Fox . . . special effects department: William Fox seems to have been personally fascinated by film technology, and the studio's reputation as an innovator in the field, of course, began with his promotion of Movie-Grandeur, which was used to shoot the epic Western *The Big Trail* (Raoul Walsh, 1930) and sparked a brief widescreen revolution among the majors. Shot almost entirely on location in the Grand Tetons at the cost of 2 million dollars, *The Big Trail* was billed as the "picture of the century," and its popularity forced the debuts of Natural Vision (65mm—RKO), Magnafilm (56mm—Paramount), Realife (70mm—MGM), and Vitascope (65mm—Warners) before the effects of the Wall Street crash curtailed such extravagance later in the year. (*The Big Trail* was recently restored to its widescreen format from the original 70mm negative by MoMA—see Ronald Hauer, "Trail Blazing," *American Film* 11, 7 (May 1986): 17–19.) Twenty-three years later, Fox would catalyze the industry's permanent conversion to widescreen with the introduction of CinemaScope, an anamorphic process.

p. 314 fn. *The Adventures of Sherlock Holmes*: See Robert W. Pohle and Douglas C. Hart, *Sherlock Holmes on the Screen* (London: A. S. Barnes, 1977); Chris Steinbrunner and Norman Michaels, *The Films of Sherlock Holmes* (Secaucus, N.J.: Citadel, 1978); and Ron Haydock *Deerstalker! Holmes*

and Watson on the Screen (Metuchen, N.J.: Scarecrow Press, 1978).

p. 315 New Deal optimism . . . one critic: Jeffrey Richards, *Visions of Yesterday* (London: Routledge, 1973), p. 254.

p. 318 B-features . . . bottom half of double bills: For a detailed history of the American B-film from 1933 to 1945, see Don Miller, *"B" Movies* (New York: Curtis Books, 1973); also, *Kings of the Bs: Working Within the Hollywood System*, ed. Todd McCarthy and Charles Flynn (New York: Dutton, 1975) provides an excellent anthology of history and criticism, as does Wheeler W. Dixon's *The "B" Directors: A Biographical Directory* (Metuchen, N.J.: Scarecrow Press, 1985). See also Gene Fernett, *Poverty Row* (Satellite Beach, Fla.: Coral Reef Publications, 1973); Robin Cross, *B Movies* (New York: St. Martin's Press, 1981); Richard Maurice Hurst, *Republic Studios: Between Poverty Row and the Majors* (Metuchen, N.J.: Scarecrow Press, 1979); Jon Tuska, *The Vanishing Legion: A History of Mascot Pictures, 1927–1935* (Jefferson, N.C.: McFarland, 1982); and *Producers Releasing Corporation: A Comprehensive Filmography and History*, ed. Wheeler Dixon (Jefferson, N.C.: McFarland, 1986).

p. 322 Sergei Eisenstein . . . *Morocco*: Eisenstein telegram quoted in Josef von Sternberg, *Fun in a Chinese Laundry* (London: Secker and Warburg, 1965), p. 45.

p. 322 *Shanghai Express* . . . Herman G. Weinberg: Herman G. Weinberg, *Josef von Sternberg* (New York: E. P. Dutton, 1967), p. 60.

p. 323 *The Devil Is a Woman* . . . humiliated by a temptress: For a feminist-psychoanalytic reading of the relationship of the theme of sexual domination in the von Sternberg/Dietrich films to their visual style and narrative structure, see Gaylyn Studlar's *In the Realm of Pleasure: von Sternberg, Dietrich, and the Masochistic Aesthetic* (Champaign: University of Illinois Press, 1988). See also Studlar, "Masochism and the Perverse Pleasures of the Cinema," *Quarterly Review of Film Studies* 9, 4 (Fall 1984) in *Movies and Methods*, vol. 2, ed. Bill Nichols (Berkeley: University of California Press, 1985), pp. 602–21; Studlar, "Visual Pleasure and the Masochistic Aesthetic," *Journal of Film and Video* 37, 2 (Spring 1985): 5–26; and Lèa Jacobs and Richard de Cordova, "Spectacle and Narrative Theory" (on *The Scarlet Empress*), *Quarterly Review of Film Studies* 7, 4 (Fall 1982): 293–307. See also Peter Baxter, "The Birth of *Venus*," *Wide Angle* 10, 1 (Winter 1988): 4–15.

p. 324 John Grierson . . . visually extravagant: quoted in John Baxter, *The Cinema of Josef von Sternberg* (New York: A. S. Barnes, 1971) p. 15.

p. 325 *The Black Watch* . . . one critic: Tag Gallagher, *John Ford: The Man and His Films* (Berkeley: University of California Press, 1986), p. 61.

p. 327 Monument Valley . . . symbolic landscape: There is a story that when John Ford was a boy in Portland, Maine, his older brother would earn pocket money in the summer by ferrying picnickers back and forth to a small coastal island in a rowboat. One summer, the brother fell ill, and the ferry business devolved upon John at a very young age. Among his clients for that summer was an elderly artist who would stay on the island all day long painting landscapes. According to the story, Ford was so fascinated by the painter that he spent the entire summer watching him work. The artist was the great American landscape painter Winslow Homer (1838–1910).

(Told to the author by Murray Golden, Hollywood, May 1979.) On artists of the American West, specifically, and the ideology of the Western, see Edward Buscombe, "Painting the Legend: Frederic Remington and the Western," *Cinema Journal* 23, 4 (Summer 1984): 12–27.

p. 328 *The Long Voyage Home*: See Matthew Bernstein, "Hollywood's 'Arty Cinema': John Ford's *The Long Voyage Home*" *Wide Angle* 10, 1 (Winter 1988): 30–45.

p. 333 *Scarface . . .* cause célèbre: For an excellent analysis of Hawk's major films within the narrative tradition, see Gerald Mast, *Howard Hawks: Storyteller* (New York: Oxford, 1982). For more on Hawks's actual working methods, see Bruce Kawin's Introduction to *To Have and Have Not* (1980), Lawrence Howard Suid's Introduction to *Air Force* (1983), and Gerald Mast's Introduction to *Bringing Up Baby* (1988), all from the Wisconsin/Warner Bros. screenplay series (Madison: University of Wisconsin Press).

p. 335 Henry Langlois . . . Hawks: Henry Langlois quoted in Georges Sadoul, *Dictionary of Film Makers*, trans. and ed. Peter Morris (Berkeley: University of California Press, 1972), p. 112.

p. 336 Sarris . . . Hitchcock: Andrew Sarris, *The American Cinema* (New York: E. P. Dutton, 1968), p. 57.

p. 337 *Blackmail . . .* dubbed as sound film: The original silent version of *Blackmail* is preserved in the archives of the British Film Institute. See Charles Barr, "Blackmail: Silent and Sound," *Sight and Sound* 52, 2 (Spring 1983): pp. 122–26.

p. 337 fn. only child, Patricia: Hitchcock's daughter, now named Patricia O'Connell, donated her father's entire collection of scripts, papers, notes, photographs, and memorabilia to the Margaret Herrick Library of the Academy of Motion Picture Arts and Sciences in 1984; they include extensive documentation of his early British career. See also, Tom Ryall, *Alfred Hitchcock and the British Cinema* (Urbana: University of Illinois Press, 1986).

p. 340n Hitchcock . . . Selznick International: For an exhaustively researched, if controversial, account of this relationship, see Leonard J. Leff, *Hitchcock and Selznick: The Rich and Strange Collaboration of Alfred Hitchcock and David O. Selznick in Hollywood* (New York: Weidenfeld & Nicholson, 1987).

p. 345 *Rear Window . . .* moral complicity of the voyeur: There is an enormous volume of literature on the theme of voyeurism in Hitchcock, much of it highly theoretical and psychoanalytic in focus. Some good starting places are Robin Wood, *Hitchcock's Films* (London: Tantivy, 1965); David Thomson, *Movie Man* (New York: Stein & Day, 1967); Raymond Durgnat, *The Strange Case of Alfred Hitchcock* (Cambridge, Mass.: MIT Press, 1974); Donald Spoto, *The Art of Alfred Hitchcock* (New York: Hopkinson and Blake, 1976); David Thomson, "The Big Hitch," *Film Comment* 15, 2 (March–April 1979): 26–29; and Dave Kehr, "Hitch's Riddle," *Film Comment* 20, 3 (May–June 1984): 9–18. Beyond these, see Laura Mulvey, "Visual Pleasure and Narrative Cinema," *Screen* 16, 3 (1975): 6–18; the essays contained in the Hitchcock/Bellour special issue of *Camera Obscura* no. 3–4 (1979); William Rothman, *Hitchcock—The Murderous Gaze* (Cambridge, Mass.: Harvard University Press, 1982); the essays contained in *A Hitchcock Reader*, ed. Marshall Deutlebaum and Leland Pogue (Ames: Iowa State University Press, 1986); and Tania Modleski, *The Woman Who Knew Too Much* (New York: Methuen, 1987).

p. 348 Robin Wood . . . *Vertigo*: Robin Wood, "Fear of Spying," *American Film* 9, 2 (November 1983): 35.

p. 349 Samuel Taylor: Samuel Taylor quoted in Donald Spoto, *The Dark Side of Genius* (Boston: Little, Brown, 1983), p. 402.

p. 349 Hitchcock . . . Lehman: Hitchcock quoted in Spoto, *Dark Side*, p. 440.

pp. 352–53 Robert Boyle . . . Munch's *The Scream*: Robert Boyle quoted in Spoto, *Dark Side*, p. 455.

pp. 353–54 Yet the tendency . . . both a formalist and moralist: For a persuasively argued opposing viewpoint, see David Thomson, "The Big Hitch," *Film Comment* 15, 2 (March–April 1979): 26–29. Here, Hitchcock is neither "moral scientist nor teacher" but "a torturer," a position nicely countervailed by Leslie Brill's *The Hitchcock Romance: Love and Irony in Hitchcock's Films* (Princeton: Princeton University Press, 1988).

p. 354 Hannah Arendt: Hannah Arendt, *Eichmann in Jerusalem* (New York: Meridian, 1963).

Europe in the Thirties

p. 362 Tobis-Klangfilm . . . decline in Hollywood's influence: For more on these corporate maneuvers, see Douglas Gomery, "Economic Struggle and Hollywood Imperialism: Europe Converts to Sound," *Yale French Studies: Cinema/ Sound* no. 60 (1980): 80–93, repr. in *Film Sound: Theory and Practice*, ed. Elizabeth Weis and John Belton (New York: Columbia University Press, 1985), pp. 25–43.

p. 363 British films . . . international scale: For a fascinating social analysis of British films of this period, see the "Cinema of Empire" section in Jeffrey Richards, *Visions of Yesterday* (London, 1973). See also, Elizabeth Sussex, *The Rise and Fall of the British Documentary* (Berkeley: University of California Press, 1975); Rachael Low, *Documentary and Educational Films of the 1930's* (The History of British Film, vol. 5 [London: Allen & Unwin, 1979]); Don MacPherson, ed., *Traditions of Independence: British Cinema in the Thirties* (London; BFI, 1980); Jack C. Ellis, "Changing of the Guard: From the Grierson Documentary to Free Cinema," *ORFS* 7, 1 (Winter 1982): 23–35, and "The Final Years of British Documentary as the Grierson Movement," *JFV* 34 (Fall 1984): 41–48; *British Cinema History*, ed. James Curran and Vincent Porter (Totowa, N.J.: Barnes and Noble, 1983); Jeffrey Richards, *The Age of the Dream Palace: Cinema and Society in Britain, 1930–1939* (London: Routledge & Kegan Paul, 1984); and Rachael Low, *Film Making in 1930s Britain* (The History of British Film, vol. 6 [London: Allen & Unwin,

1985]); *Cinema, Literature and Society: Elite and Mass Culture in Interwar Britain* (London: Croom Helm, 1987); Bert Hogem Kaup, *Deadly Parallels: Film and the Left in Britain, 1929–39* (London: Lawrence and Wishart, 1987; and Ian Aitken, *Film and Reform: John Grierson and the Documentary Film Movement* (London: Routledge, 1990).

p. 364 Goebbel's offer . . . UFA: Lang: " . . . [Goebbels] told me that, many years before, he and the Führer had seen my picture *Metropolis* in a small town, and Hitler had said at the time that he wanted me to make the Nazi pictures" (*New York World Telegram*, June 11, 1941, "Fritz Lang"; quoted in Siegfried Kracauer, *From Caligari to Hitler* [Princeton, N.J.: Princeton University Press, 1947], p. 164). But see Lucy Fischer, "Dr. Mabuse and Mr. Lang," *Wide Angle* 3, 3 (Fall 1979): 18–26.

p. 365 Lang . . . United States: Lang's American films include social melodramas (*You and Me*, 1938; *Clash by Night*, 1952; *Human Desire*, 1954), Westerns (*The Return of Frank James*, 1940; *Western Union*, 1941; *Rancho Notorious*, 1952); espionage thrillers (*Manhunt*, 1941; *The Ministry of Fear*, 1945; *Cloak and Dagger*, 1946); anti-Nazi films (*Hangmen Also Die*, 1943); war films (*An American Guerrilla in the Philippines*, 1950): period films (*Moonfleet*, 1955—his first film in CinemaScope); and, above all, a wide range of *films noir* (*The Woman in the Window*, 1944; *Scarlet Street*, 1945; *The Secret Beyond the Door*, 1948; House by the River, 1950;

The Blue Gardenia, 1953; *While the City Sleeps*, 1956; *Beyond a Reasonable Doubt*, 1956). Of these, *Manhunt, The Woman in the Window*, and *Rancho Notorious* are considered his best. In 1958, Lang returned to Germany to make an exotic two-part costume epic based on a 1920 screenplay by Theo van Harbou, *Der Tiger von Eschnapur* (*The Tiger of Eshnapur*) and *Das indische Grabual* (*The Indian Tomb*), both released in 1959. These were poorly received, as was his last effort, *Die Tausend Augen des Dr. Mabuse* (*The Thousand Eyes of Dr. Mabuse*, 1961), and updated pastiche of his Mabuse films. Subsequently, Lang retired, much honored around the world until his death in 1976. See Lotte Eisner, *Fritz Lang* (London: Secker and Warburg, 1976); Frederick W. Ott, *The Films of Fritz Lang* (Secaucus, N.J.: Citadel Press, 1979); *Fritz Lang: The Image and the Look*, ed. Stephen Jenkins (London: BFI, 1981); Matthew Bernstein, "Fritz Lang, Incorporated," *The Velvet Light Trap*, no. 22 (1986): 33–52; and Reynold Humphries, *Fritz Lang: Genre and Representation in His American Films* (Baltimore: The Johns Hopkins University Press, 1989).

p. 365–66 *anti-Semitic . . . Nazi Party:* The most widely read work on Nazi film in English is David Stewart Hull's *Film in the Third Reich* (Berkeley: University of California Press, 1969), which is nicely supplemented by the German documentarist (*Mein Kampf*, 1959) and journalist Erwin Leiser's *Nazi Cinema* (London: Macmillan, 1974). More recent works include Richard Traubner, "The Sound and the Führer," *Film Comment* 14, 4 (July–August 1978): 17–23; and "Berlin II. The Retrospective," *American Film* 4, 7 (May 1979): 67–69—both on the German escapist cinema, 1933–45; Julian Petley, *Capital and Culture: German Cinema 1933–45* (London, 1979), where it is argued (against the conventional wisdom) that the reorganization of the German film industry during the Third Reich was not an act of "subversion" but a collective undertaking "by the government and the most powerful sectors of the industry . . . working in closest cooperation and very much to the latter's advantage" (p. 1), and David Welch, *Propaganda and the German Cinema, 1933–1945* (Oxford: Oxford University Press, 1983), a comprehensive analysis of Goebbels' propaganda films as reflections of National Socialist ideology. See also Ward Rutherford, *Hitler's Propaganda Machine* (London: Bison Books, 1978); Thomas G. Plummer et al, eds., *Film and Politics in the Weimar Republic* (New York: Holmes & Meier, 1982); and David Welch, ed., *Nazi Propaganda* (London: Croom Helm, 1983).

p. 366 *Triumph des Willens:* See *"Triumph of the Will": A Documentary History*, ed. David Culbert, a 35mm microfilm publication (one reel) of selected period documents, with printed guide (Frederick, Md.: University Publications of America, 1987).

p. 366 *Hitler's architect Albert Speer:* Leni Riefenstahl quoted in Georges Sadoul, *Dictionary of Films*, trans. and ed. Peter Morris (Berkeley: University of California Press, 1972), p. 383.

p. 366 *1936 Berlin Olympics:* Riefenstahl has always maintained that *Olympiad* was financed by her own production company, Olympic Film Company, and commissioned by the International Committee for the Olympic Games, over Goebbels' protests. But official documents recently brought to light reveal that the Olympic Film Company was a front for the Nazi government and that the film was made with the full approval of Goebbels. The same documents show that the

government made a handsome profit by distributing *Olympiad* internationally through Tobis-Klangfilm. See Hans Barkhausen, "Footnote to the History of Riefenstahl's *Olympia*," *Film Quarterly* 1 (Fall 1974): 8–12; Glenn B. Infield, *Leni Riefenstahl: The Fallen Film Goddess* (New York: Crowell, 1976); Susan Sontag, "Fascinating Fascism," in *Women and the Cinema*, ed. Karyn Kay and Gerald Peary (New York: E. P. Dutton, 1977), pp. 35–76; David B. Hinton, *The Films of Leni Riefenstahl* (Metuchen, N.J.: Scarecrow, 1978) and Cooper C. Graham, *Leni Riefenstahl and Olympia* (Metuchen, N.J.: Scarecrow, 1986).

Riefenstahl made two other notable films in her controversial career, in both of which she played leading roles. (She also appeared anonymously in the nude dancing sequence of the Prologue to *Olympia*.) *Das blaue Licht* (*The Blue Light*, reissued in 1952 as *Die Hexe von Santa Maria*, with a new soundtrack and score) is a semimystical "mountain film" shot on location in Spain with a script by the Hungarian film theorist Béla Balázs, *Tiefland* (1954) is a version of Eugen D'Albert's opera, also set in Spain, adapted by Riefenstahl with a score by Herbert Wind. Production of the latter began in Spain in 1940 and was moved at various points during the war to studios in Bavaria and finally Prague, where shooting was completed in late 1944. Occupying French forces seized the film in Berlin, where, according to Riefenstahl, significant portions were lost. When it was finally returned to her in 1953, she edited what remained. She released *Tiefland* to considerable critical acclaim the following year but subsequently withdrew it on the grounds that it was a mutilated work. In 1983, however, a West German television documentary charged that Riefenstahl purposely destroyed the missing portions of the film herself, to avoid revealing that she used, as extras, a large number of Gypsy slave laborers bound for the gas chambers at Auschwitz.

p. 368 *LUCE:* LUCE was the state "educational" film service established by Mussolini in 1924. See Elaine Mancini, *Struggles of the Italian Film Industry during Fascism, 1930–1935* (Ann Arbor, Mich.: UMI Research Press), pp. 121–60; Peter Bondanella, *Italian Cinema: From Neorealism to the Present* (New York: Ungar, 1983), pp. 1–14; Sam Rohdie, "Capitalism and Realism in the Italian Cinema: An Examination of Film in the Fascist Period," *Screen* 24, 4–5 (July–October 1983): 37–46; and James Hay, *Popular Film Culture in Fascist Italy: The Passing of the Rex* (Bloomington: Indiana University Press, 1987), pp. 201–32.

p. 370 *Eisenstein . . . Que viva México!:* Eisenstein quoted in Sadoul, *Dictionary of Films*, p. 302.

p. 370 *MoMA . . . Que viva México!:* See Ivor Montagu, *With Eisenstein in Hollywood* (New York: International Publishers, 1969), Harry M. Geduld and Ronald Gottesman, *The Making and Unmaking of "Que Viva México!"* (Bloomington, Ind.: Indiana University Press, 1971); Greg Mitchell, "The Greatest Movie Never Made," *American Film* 8, 4 (January–February, 1983) 53–85; and Inga Karetnikova, "Eisenstein's Mexican Drawings: Communicators of Cinematic Ideas," *LAMP* (1985): pp. 5–11.

p. 372 *Pravda . . . ideological errors:* About 60 percent of *Bezhin Meadow* had been shot when the project was canceled. The official Soviet position is that this footage was stored in a Mosfilm vault that was destroyed by German bombardment in 1942. In all likelihood it was destroyed by Shumiatski in 1937. Whatever happened to the original, Elfir Tobak, the film's editor, preserved a number of frames which were assembled into a montage of stills by Eisenstein's friends Sergei Iutkevich and Naum Kleiman in 1956. Released as *Bezhin Meadow*, this film was provided with a score from the symphonies of Prokofiev and had a running time of 25 minutes. Its continuity was based on the original script. See Sergei Eisenstein, *Nonindifferent Nature*, trans. Herbert Marshall (Cambridge: Cambridge University Press, 1987), and *S. M. Eisenstein: Selected Works, Vol. 1: Writings 1922–34*, a new English-language edition, ed. and trans. Richard Taylor (London: Bloomington, 1988). See also *Eisenstein at Ninety*, eds. Ian Christie and David Elliot, a catalogue to accompany the exhibition "Eisenstein: His Life and Work," Museum of Modern Art, Oxford, England, 17 July–28 August, 1988.

p. 372 Georges Sadoul . . . visual rhythms: Sadoul, *Dictionary of Films*, p. 6.

p. 372 *Alexander Nevski*: On the techniques of psychological manipulation in the film, see Leon Balter, M.D., "*Alexander Nevski*," *Film Culture* 70–71 (1983): 43–87.

p. 373 *The Great Ferghana Canal* . . . cancelled: See Eisenstein, *Immoral Memories: An Autobiography*, trans. Herbert Marshall (Boston: Houghton Mifflin, 1983), pp. 249–60. Test shots for the film were later edited into a short documentary on the construction of the canal.

p. 374 Goebbels . . . Russian culture: Quoted in Jay Leyda and Zina Voynow, *Eisenstein at Work* (New York: Pantheon Books/MoMA, 1982), p. 111.

pp. 474–75 Eisenstein . . . lighting: Eisenstein quoted in Peter Wollen, *Signs and Meaning in the Cinema*, 2nd ed. (Bloomington, Ind.: Indiana University Press, 1972), p. 60.

p. 375 *Ivan the Terrible*: The stylized use of color in *Part II* seems to have originated in the extensive planning Eisenstein had done in 1940 for a film on the life of the great Russian writer Alexander Pushkin (1799–1837) to be entitled *The Love of a Poet*. His sketches and notes for the project propose a unique "psychological" approach to color; they also suggest the influence of Pushkin's political tragedy *Boris Godunov* (1825, published 1830) and the Mussorgski opera adapted from it (1870). On *Ivan*'s style in general, see Leyda and Voynow, *Eisenstein at Work*, pp. 116–22.

p. 375 incomparable formal beauty . . . design: Eisenstein quoted in Sadoul, *Dictionary of Films*, p. 162.

p. 375 *Parts I* and *II*: For an impressive and exhaustive structural reading of the two *Ivans*, see Kristin Thompson's *Eisenstein's Ivan the Terrible: A Neoformalist Analysis* (Princeton, N.J.: Princeton University Press, 1981).

p. 378 Abel Gance . . . making feature films: The definitive study of "impressionist" period in French film history is Richard Abel's *French Cinema: The First Wave, 1915–1929* (Princeton: Princeton University Press, 1984), which, among other splendid resources, contains detailed textual analysis of every film mentioned in this section of the text. It's worth noting here that, despite the intellectual prominence of French cinema during this era, by 1917 half of the films shown in Paris were American; by 1918 French productions made up only 20 percent of Paris' cinema programs; and until the coming of sound, French films held a minority position in their own domestic market. As Alexander Sesonske has put it, "While the number of movie theaters in France doubled between 1919 and 1922 and exhibitors grew prosperous showing American films, the normal state of the French cinema

industry became one of crisis" ("A la Recherche du Temps Perdu," *Quarterly Review of Film Studies* 10, 3 [Summer 1985]: 261–65. See also Richard Abel, *French Film Theory and Criticism: A History/Anthology, 1907–1939*, 2 vols. (Princeton: Princeton University Press, 1988; and Sandy Flitterman-Lewis, *To Desire Differently: Feminism and the French Cinema* (Urbana: University of Illinois Press, 1990).

p. 378 *populisme* . . . Lumiereé shorts: Georges Sadoul, *The French Film* (London: Falcon Press, 1953), pp. 28–29.

p. 379 Langlois . . . Debussy: Henri Langlois quoted in Sadoul, *Dictionary of Films*, p. 63.

p. 380 *La Roue* . . . avant-garde filmmakers: *La Roue* is currently under reconstruction by Marie Epstein (Jean Epstein's sister) at the Cinémathèque Française. For a detailed study of this work, see Richard Abel, "Abel Gance's Other Neglected Masterwork: *La Roue* (1922–23)," *Cinema Journal* 22, 3 (Winter 1983): 26–41.

p. 382 *Napoléon* . . . tricolor: Gance and his cinematographer Burel apparently shot test reels of the concluding triptychs of *Napoléon* in a "natural" color process and 3-D. See Kevin Brownlow, *Napoléon: Abel Gance's Classic Film* (New York: Knopf, 1983), pp. 134–35. It's worth noting here that both men worked on *Napoléon* with an unusually talented team of assistants—Gance: the directors Alexandre Volkoff, Victor Tourjansky, Henry Krauss, Henri Andréani, Maurius Nalpas, and Anatole Litvak; Burel: the cameramen Juls Kruger, J. P. Mundviller, Bourgassov, Lucas, Roger Hubert, and Emile Pierre. Art direction was by the Russian-born architect Schildknecht; Ivan Lochakoff; and Diaghilev's chief set designer, Alexandre Benoit; technical direction by Simon Feldman.

p. 383 Brownlow . . . hands of a genius: Kevin Brownlow, *The Parade's Gone By* (New York: Knopf, 1968), p. 547

p. 383–84 Georges Sadoul has written: Sadoul, *The French Film*, pp. 33–34.

p. 387 Danish director . . . *La Passion de Jeanne d'Arc*: *La Passion de Jeanne d'Arc* exists today in several versions, owing to a stormy postproduction history during which it was cut by S.G.F. to accommodate French censors (notably, the Archbishop of Paris, who objected to its theology) and because the negative was accidentally destroyed in a laboratory fire. A negative discovered by the French film historian LoDuca in 1951 became the basis for a sonorized print distributed the following year, with selections from Albioni, Vivaldi, Scarlatti, and Bach, but Dreyer rejected this version as destroying the rhythms of his montage. In 1983, the Danish Film Museum unveiled a newly reconstructed and subtitled print using footage from foreign archives, to be accompanied by an original score by Ole Schmidt. but this version was about seven hundred feet shorter than that deposited in the Cinémathèque Française and distributed in the United States by MoMA. Finally, a nitrate print of the 1928 original was discovered in a psychiatric hospital near Oslo in 1985, which essentially validates the reconstruction but contains more idiosyncratic camera angles and montage. In 1987 a version of this print was scored with traditional and electronic music by Arnaud Petit at Ircam, the Paris-based center for musical-acoustical research directed by Pierre Boulez, for theatrical distribution in France in 1988.

p. 387 Jean Cocteau . . . *La Passion de Jeanne d'Arc*: Jean Cocteau quoted in Sadoul, *Dictionary of Films*, p. 276.

p. 387 David Bordwell: David Bordwell, *The Films of Carl-Theodor Dreyer* (Berkeley: University of California Press, 1981), p. 66.

p. 390 Clair . . . returned to France: see León Barsacq, *Caligari's Cabinet and Other Grand Illusions: A History of Film Design* (New York: New American Library, 1976), pp. 74–90.

p. 391 Jaubert . . . eerie and playful: Maurice Jaubert employed imaginative scoring and recording techniques for some of the era's most important films in addition to *Zéro de conduite*. These included Clair's *Quatorze juillet* and *Le Dernier milliardiare*, Vigo's *L'Atalante*, Ophüls' *Mayerling*, Duvivier's *Un Carnet de bal*, and Carné's *Drôle de drame*, *Quai des brumes*, *Hôtel du Nord*, and *Le Jour se lève*—all discussed in the text. Between 1929 and 1939, he wrote thirty-eight film scores. Jaubert was killed in combat in June 1940, the day before Marshal Pétain signed the armistice with Hitler; but his legacy survives in the work of François Truffaut, who used Jaubert's music in four of his later films—*L'Histoire d'Adèle H* (1975), *L'Argent de poche* (1976), *L'Homme qui aimait les femmes* (1977), and *La Chambre verte* (1978).

See Annette Insdorf, "Maurice Jaubert and François Truffaut: Musical Continuities from *L'Atalante* to *L'Histoire d'Adèle H*," *Yale French Studies: Cinema/Sound* (1980): 204–18: Catherine A. Surow, "Maurice Jaubert: Poet of Music," in *Rediscovering French Film*, ed. Mary Lea Bandy (New York: MoMA, 1983), pp. 87–88: and Maurice Jaubert, "Music in the Film," *Rediscovering French Film*, pp. 89–90.

p. 392 Georges Sadoul . . . *L'Atalante*: Sadoul, *The French Film*, p. 63.

p. 392 French production . . . single films: Examining the credits for 1,305 French features made between 1929 and 1939, the film historian Raymond Borde finds that 285 French companies produced a single film apiece, 76 produced 2, 32 produced 3, 17 produced 4, and 16 produced 5, for a total of 681 movies; another 29 companies produced from 6 to 14 features each during the same period, a total of 255; while only 6—the largest being Pathé-Natan (64) and Gaumont (21)—produced more than 15 apiece, for a total of 166. See Borde, "'The Golden Age': French Cinema of the '30s," in *Rediscovering French Film*, ed. Bandy, pp. 67–81.

p. 393 a blend of lyricism and realism: For more on poetic realism as an aesthetic and cultural phenomenon, see Dudley Andrew, "Sound in France: The Origins of a Native School," *Yale French Studies: Cinema/Sound* no. 60 (1980): 94–114, repr. in *Rediscovering French Film*, ed. Bandy, pp. 57–65; and "Poetic Realism" in *Rediscovering French Film*, pp. 115–19. See also, the feature-length documentary *Carné: l'Homme à la Camera* (*Carné: The Man Behind the Camera*, 1985), directed by Christian Jacque; and the critical biography by Edward Baron Turk, *Child of Paradise: Marcel Carné and the Golden Age of French Cinema* (Cambridge: Harvard University Press, 1989).

p. 393 Georges Sadoul . . . René Clair and Jean Vigo: Sadoul, *Histoire du cinéma mondial*, p. 274 (my translation).

p. 395 Carné . . . blamed for the storm: Carné quoted in Sadoul, *Dictionary of Films*, p. 299.

p. 395 *Les Enfants du paradis* . . . classic of the French cinema: In 1979, the French Academy of Cinema Arts and Techniques voted *Les Enfants du paradis* the best French film since the coming of sound. Second was Jean Renoir's *La Grande illusion* (1937), followed by Jacques Becker's *Casque d'or* (1952), Renoir's *La Regle du jeu* (1939), Jacques Feyder's *La Kermesse heroique* (1935), Jean-Luc Godard's *Pierrot le fou* (1965), Alain Resnais' *Hiroshima, mon amour* (1959), René Clement's *Jeux interdits* (1952), Marcel Carné's *Quai des brumes* (1938), and Henri-Georges Clouzot's *Le Salaire de la peur* (1953). (All are discussed in either Chapter 9 or Chapter 13.) For more on *Les Enfants du paradis*, see Edward Baron Turk, "The Birth of *Children of Paradise*," *American Film* 4, 9 (July–August): 42–49; Marc Mancini, "Prévert: Poetry in Motion Pictures," *Film Comment* 17, 6 (November–December 1981): 24–37; and Claire Blakeway, *Jacques Prévert: Popular French Theater and Cinema* (Rutherford, N.J.: Associated University Presses, 1990).

p. 397 in Renoir's words: Jean Renoir quoted in Sadoul, *History of Films*, p. 380.

p. 397–98 *La Vie est à nous* . . . rebellion of the late sixties: On Renoir's political sympathies, see Elizabeth Grottle Strebel, "Renoir and the Popular Front," *Sight and Sound* 49, 1 (Winter 1979–80): 36–41; Jonathan Buchsbaum, "Vote for the Front Populaire! Vote Communiste! *La Vie est à nous*," *Quarterly Review of Film Studies* 10, 3 (Summer 1985): 184–212, and "Toward Victory: Left Film in France, 1930-35," *Cinema Journal* 25, 3 (Spring 1986): 25–52; and Christopher Faulkner, *The Social Cinema of Jean Renoir* (Princeton: Princeton University Press, 1986); and Stephen Tifft, "Theater in the Round: The Politics of Space in the Films of Jean Renoir," *Theater Journal* 39, 3 (October 1987): 328–46. See also Jonathan Buchabaum, *Cinema Engagé: Film in the Popular Front* (Urbana: University of Illinois Press, 1988).

p. 401 Renoir . . . compose his shots in depth: For a carefully researched study of the use of depth of field before Renoir (and for an argument that this use was *not* limited by existing technology), see Charles H. Harpole, *Gradients of Depth in the Cinema Image* (New York: Arno Press, 1978). See also Harpole's article, "Ideological and Technological Determinism in Deep-Space Cinema Images," *Film Quarterly* 33, 3 (Spring 1980): 11–21.

p. 402 *La Régle du jeu*: *La Régle du jeu* is so prominent within the Renoir canon that a special issue of *Quarterly Review of Film Studies* 7, 3, ed. Nick Browne, was devoted to it entirely in Summer 1982. The definitive study of Renoir's work to this point is Alexander Sesouske, *Jean Renoir: The French Films, 1924–1939* (Cambridge, Mass.: Harvard University Press, 1980). Beyond that, see Pierre Leprohon, *Jean Renoir*, trans. Brigid Elson (New York: Crown, 1971): André Bazin, *Jean Renoir* (New York: Simon & Schuster, 1973); Christopher Faulkner, *Jean Renoir: A Guide to References and Resources* (Boston: G. K. Hall, 1979), and selected scholarly journals.

p. 406 André Bazin . . . new aesthetic: Bazin, p. 38.

p. 406 Renoir . . . story-teller: quoted in Roy Armes, *French Cinema Since 1946*, 2 vols. (London: A. S. Barnes & Company, 1970), vol. 1, p. 46.

Orson Welles and the Modern Sound Film

p. 407 unprecedented six-film contract: According to Frank Brady in *Citizen Welles: A Biograph of Orson Welles* (New York: Scribner's, 1989), the original RKO contract, signed on July 22, 1939, was actually a two-film contract, which gave Welles a remarkable degree of control over production on the set but also gave the studio the right of pre-production story refusal and post-production "consultation" on the release print (pp. 199–200). The exaggeration of the contract's terms was probably the work of RKO's publicity department.

p. 407 Welles . . . Herman J. Mankiewicz: Since the publication of Pauline Kael's essay "Raising Kane" in *The New Yorker* (February 20 and 27, 1971) and its subsequent appearance as the introduction to *The Citizen Kane Book* (Boston: Little, Brown, 1971), there has been much controversy over the authorship of the script of *Citizen Kane*. On the basis of what later proved to be largely unconfirmed evidence, Kael maintained that Welles did not write a single line of the script and that he consciously contrived to steal the credit from Mankiewicz after the fact. In response, a substantial body of convincing evidence to the contrary was mounted by such critics as Peter Bogdanovich ("The Kane Mutiny," *Esquire*, October 1972), Andrew Sarris ("The Great Kane Controversy," *World*, January 16, 1973), and Joseph McBride (*Orson Welles* [New York: Viking, 1972]).

In 1978 the film scholar Robert Carringer examined a complete set of script records in the archives of RKO Pictures in Hollywood and reached the conclusion that the principal author was Welles: "In the eight weeks between the time [Mankiewicz's original script] passed into Welles' hands and the final draft was completed, the *Citizen Kane* script was transformed, principally by him, from a solid basis for a story into an authentic plan for a masterpiece." (Robert Carringer, "The Scripts of *Citizen Kane*," *Critical Inquiry* 5, 2 (Winter 1978): 400. Subsequent research in the previously inaccessible Welles collection at RKO, however, led Carringer to conclude that the script of *Kane* was the result of a genuine collaboration in which both men were fundamentally important:

> [Mankiewicz's] principal contributions were the story frame, a cast of characters, various individual scenes, and a good share of the dialogue. . . . Welles added the narrative brilliance—the visual and verbal wit, the stylistic fluidity, and such stunningly original strokes as the newspaper montages and the breakfast table sequence. He also transformed Kane from a cardboard fictionalization of Hearst into a figure of mystery and epic magnificence" (*The Making of Citizen Kane* [Berkeley: University of California Press, 1985], p. 35).

p. 412 Robert Altman . . . soundtracks: Robert Altman's method of recording overlapping sound differs markedly from Welles in *Kane*. Altman usually has his actors arranged in large, spread-out groupings. Initially he recorded his sound "wild" on location—i.e., separately from the film strip, or magnetic tape. Since *California Split* (1974), however, he has used a wireless eight-track recording system in which each performer is equipped with a small microphone that broadcasts sound to a receiving unit. Each actor has one channel whose sound can be individually controlled while shooting, and all the actors can speak at once without grouping around a centrally located microphone. On the soundtrack, the effect is frequently an indistinct blur or hum which Altman uses deliberately to characterize an environment rather than to evoke individual personalities (see *M*A*S*H* [1970]; *Nashville* [1975]; *Three Women* [1977]).

Welles, on the other hand, produced his carefully modulated soundtrack for *Kane* in 1940 using the full resources of a sophisticated studio recording system, complete with its own orchestra. Furthermore, because Welles is primarily concerned with individual character, one never loses the individual identity of speaker and voice in his overlapping dialogue sequences, as one does in some of Altman's films (see Chapter 18).

p. 412 Welles' subtle refinement of sound: For more on Welles' use of sound in *Kane* and other films, see Phyllis Goldfarb, "Orson Welles's Use of Sound," in *Focus on Orson Welles*, ed. Ronald Gottesman (Englewood Cliffs, N.J.: Prentice-Hall, 1976), pp. 85–94; Evan William Cameron, "*Citizen Kane*: The Influence of Radio Drama on Cinematic Design," in *Sound and Cinema: The Coming of Sound to American Film*, ed. Evan William Cameron (Pleasantville, N.Y.: Redgrave, 1980), pp. 202–16; Dudley Andrew, "Echoes of Art: The Distant Sounds of Orson Welles," in *Film in the Aura of Art* (Princeton: Princeton University Press, 1984), pp. 152–71; Penny Mintz, "Orson Welles's Use of Sound," in *Film Sound: Theory and Practice*, ed. Elisabeth Weis and John Belton (New York: Columbia University Press, 1985), pp. 289–97; and Kathryn Kalinak, "The Text of Music: A Study of the Magnificent Ambersons," *Cinema Journal* 27, 4 (Summer 1988): 45–63.

p. 425 symbol of Kane's inability . . . to love: On the continuing controversy over the significance of "Rosebud," see Leonard J. Leff, "Reading *Kane*," *Film Quarterly* 39, 1 (Fall 1985): 10–21; Robin Bates with Scott Bates, "Fiery Speech in a World of Shadows: Rosebud's Impact on Early Audiences," *Cinema Journal* 26, 2 (Winter 1987): 3–26; "Dialogue: Jonathan Rosenbaum, Leonard Leff, and Robin Bates on Viewer Response to *Citizen Kane*," *Cinema Journal* 26, 4 (Summer 1987): 60–66; Bert Cardullo, "The Real Fascination of *Citizen Kane*," *Indelible Images: New Perspectives on Classic Films* (Lanhar, Md.: University Press of America, 1987), pp. 179–99; Ian Jarvie, "*Citizen Kane* and the Essence of a Person," *Philosophy of the Film: Epistemology, Ontology, Aesthetics* (New York: Routledge & Kegan Paul, 1987), pp. 267–94.

p. 426 *Kane*'s 1946 Paris premiere: François Truffaut, "Foreword" to André Bazin, *Orson Welles: A Critical View*, trans. Jonathan Rosenbaum (New York: Harper & Row, 1972), p. 1.

p. 428 *It's All True* . . . Santa Monica Bay: In 1986, 18 to 20 hours of Welles' Brazilian footage was found in the Paramount stock-shot vault (Paramount having bought Desilu Studios, which had earlier acquired RKO's production facili-

ties), and the AFI produced a 22-minute documentary on the film, entitled *It's All True: Four Men on a Raft*, in preparation for a full-length version. (In the same year, a Brazilian docudrama, *Nem tudo e verdade* [*Not Everything Is True*, Rogério Sganzerla], recounted the film's troubled production history from a Latino perspective.)

p. 430 *The Stranger* (1946) for RKO: RKO was the distributor. Technically, *The Stranger* was produced by Sam Spiegel for International Pictures, which merged with Universal to form Universal-International later that year.

p. 431 *Macbeth* . . . restored to its original form: The restored *Macbeth* is now available on cassette by Republic Home Video.

p. 432 *Othello* . . . Grand Prix at Cannes: *Othello* shared the Palm d'Or in 1952 with the Renato Castellani comedy *Due soldi di speranza* (*Two Pennyworth of Hope*).

p. 436 *The Other Side of the Wind* . . . finished: Welles quoted in "Journals: Todd McCarthy, from L.A.," *Film Comment* 15, 2 (March–April 1979): 6.

p. 436 *King Lear* . . . remained unfinished: Welles made several important films of less-than-feature length that are not mentioned in the text. *The Immortal Story* (*Histoire immortelle*, 1968), based on a novella by Isak Dinesen, was written and directed by Welles for France's nationalized television company, ORTF. Running 58 minutes, it was Welles' first film in color and starred Welles, Jeanne Moreau, and Fernando Rey. *The Deep* (also called *Dead Calm* or *Dead Reckoning*), was written and directed by Welles, and was shot by Gary Graver off the Dalmatian coast of Yugoslavia between 1967 and 1969. Based on the novel *Dead Calm* by Charles Williams, the film starred Welles, Jeanne Moreau, Laurence Harvey, Oja Kodar, and Michael Bryant. There is a useful plot summary of *The Deep*, based on an early version of the script, in James Naremore's *The Magic World of Orson Welles* (New York: Oxford University Press, 1978); *The Deep* was completed but remains unreleased because of continuity gaps resulting from the death of Harvey in 1973 and the undubbed part of Moreau. In 1969 Welles shot an abridged color version of *The Merchant of Venice* in Trogir, Yugoslavia, and Asolo, Italy, which was completed, edited, scored, and mixed, but remains unreleased due to the theft of two of its reels; Kodar is currently at work on a reconstruction. Finally—and most significantly—Welles wrote and co-directed with the French documentarist François Reichenbach *F for Fake* (1976; released in France as *Vérités et mensonges*, 1973), a hybrid documentary about the dynamic of fakery. It focuses on the famous art forger Elmyr de Hory; his biographer (and the fraudulent pseudo-biographer of Howard Hughes), Clifford Irving; and Welles himself, who as director of the film, is the chief illusionist among them. According to William Johnson in his *Film Quarterly* review of *F for Fake* (Summer 1976), the film provides a "commentary on the ontology of the film medium" and that medium's "specious realism." In 1978 the documentary *Filming Othello* (also known as *The Making of Othello*) was produced for West German television by Klaus and Jeurgen Hellweg; it featured interviews with the cast and crew of the 1952 Mercury Films Production and narrated footage of the original films—all of it directed by Welles.

Wartime and Postwar Cinema:
Italy and America, 1940–1951

p. 438 Marshall Plan . . . prewar levels of production: Regarding the Marshall Plan, it should be noted that its beneficence is not universally acknowledged—see, e.g., Charles L. Mee, Jr., *The Marshall Plan: The Launching of the Pax Americana* (New York: Simon and Schuster, 1985), and Tyler Cowen, "The Great Twentieth Century Foreign-Aid Hoax," *Reason* 17, 11 (April 1986): 37–41.

p. 439 *Cinema* . . . Vittorio Mussolini: Vittorio Mussolini, a professional aviator, was a film enthusiast who worked in the industry as both a producer and screenwriter under the pseudonym Tito Silvio Mursino. As *Cinema* editor, he became a friend of Rossellini and other future neorealists, and was sympathetic to their agitation for a "new realism." Ultimately, however, the unflattering portrait of rural Italy in Visconti's *Ossessione* (see pp. 442–43) turned him against it.

p. 439 Ted Perry: Ted Perry, "The Road to Neo-Realism," *Film Comment* 14, 6 (November–December 1978): 13.

p. 440 Calligraphism . . . decorative formalism: De Santis used the term calligraphism contemptuously to attack *bello scrivere* (beautiful writing) in cinema, but in fact it was the calligraphers' lack of social engagement rather than their mannered style that made them distasteful to the neorealists. See Roy Armes, *Patterns of Realism: A Study of Italian Neo-Realist Cinema* (London: Tantivy Press, 1971), 35–40; Peter Bondanella, *Italian Cinema: From Neo-Realism to the Present* (New York; Ungar, 1983), pp. 19–25; and Mira Liehm,

Passion and Defiance: Italian Film from 1942 to the Present (Berkeley: University of California Press, 1984), pp. 30–40.

p. 440 Rossellini . . . Fascist trilogy: See Gianni Rondolino, "Italian Propaganda Films: 1940–1943," in *Film and Radio Propaganda in World War II*, ed. K. R. M. Short (Knoxville: The University of Tennessee Press, 1983), pp. 230–44.

p. 441 Zavattini . . . write later: See Zavattini's autobiography, *Sequences from a Cinematic Life*, trans. William Weaver (Englewood Cliffs, N.J.: Prentice-Hall, 1970).

p. 441 revolutionary agitation for a popular . . . cinema: The excitement of the moment may be glimpsed in *Springtime in Italy: A Reader in Neo-Realism*, ed. and trans. David Overbey (Hamden, Conn.: Archon Books, 1979), an anthology of essays, diatribes, and manifestoes from the pages of *Bianco e nero, Cinema, Revista del cinema italiano, Cinema nuovo*, and other contemporary journals.

p. 441 Italian neorealism . . . Soviet expressive realism: Roy Armes, p. 49.

p. 442 *Ossessione*, Angelo Pietrangeli: Angelo Pietrangeli quoted in Georges Sadoul, *Dictionary of Films*, trans. and ed. Peter Morris (Berkeley: University of California Press, 1972), p. 264.

p. 444 Penelope Houston . . . national reputation: Penelope Houston, *The Contemporary Cinema* (Baltimore: Penguin Books, 1963), p. 23.

p. 444 Paisà . . . predecessor: For a critique of commonly received notions of realism in both *Roma, città aperta* and *Paisà*, see Peter Brunette, "Rossellini and Cinematic Realism," *Cinema Journal* 25, 1 (Fall 1985): 34–49.

p. 450 fn. Marxist intellectual . . . Lizzani: Lizzani functioned in the same capacity for many other neorealist films, including De Santis' *Riso amaro* (1948) and *Non c'e pace tra gli ulivi* (1949), and Rossellini's *Germania, anno zero* (1947). Since 1951 (*Achtung banditi!*), he has been writer-director for his own films, most recently *Fontamara* (1980), *La casa del tappetto giallo* (*The House of the Yellow Carpet*, 1983), *Nucleo zero*, (*Nucleus Zero*, 1984), *La sonata a Kreutzer* (*The Kreutzer Sonata*, 1985—from the Tolstoi novella), and *Caro Gorbaciov* (*Dear Gorbachev*, 1988). Today, with thirty features to his credit, Lizzani is a ranking figure within the Italian film industry. He is also the author of the first major history of Italian postwar cinema, *Il cinema Italiano* (1953), which is, to date, unavailable in the United States.

p. 452 Roy Armes . . . Chaplinesque: Armes, pp. 60–61,

p. 453 Penelope Houston . . . affluence of the fifties: Houston, p. 29.

p. 453 George Huaco . . . 71 percent were American: George Huaco, *The Sociology of Film Art* (New York: Basic Books, 1965), p. 185.

p. 454 Raymond Durgnat . . . melodramatists: Quoted in Andrew Sarris, *The American Cinema* (New York: E. P. Dutton, 1968), p. 110.

p. 454 André Bazin . . . neorealism: André Bazin, "An Aesthetic of Reality," in *What is Cinema?*, vol. 2 (Berkeley: University of California Press), pp. 18–19.

p. 454–55 Penelope Houston . . . neorealist heritage: Houston, p. 33.

p. 456 Office of War Information . . . national defense effort: The classical account of the creation and operation of the Office of War Information is contained in Richard Dyer MacCann's *The People's Films: A Political History of U.S. Government Motion Pictures* (New York: Hastings House, 1973), pp. 118–72. See also David Culbert, ed., *Information Control and Propaganda: Records at the Office of War Information* (Frederick, Md.: University Publications of America, 1988); and John Morton Bloom, *V Was for Victory* (New York: Harcourt, Brace, 1976).

p. 456 Lewis Jacobs . . . our associates: Lewis Jacobs, "World War II and the American Film," *Cinema Journal* 7, 2 (Winter 1967–68); reprinted in *The Movies: An American Idiom*, ed. Arthur F. McClure (Rutherford, N.J.: Fairleigh Dickinson University Press, 1971), p. 164.

p. 458 Fascism . . . actual power of the enemy: For a full account of how the image of the Nazis has evolved historically in American films since the war, see John Mariani, "Let's Not Be Beastly to the Nazis," *Film Comment* 15, 1 (January–February 1979): 49–53.

p. 458–59 Lewis Jacobs . . . personal kind of cinema: Jacobs quotation in McClure, *The Movies*, p. 173. On combat films, see Colin Shindler, *Hollywood Goes to War: Films and American Society, 1939–52* (London: Routledge & Kegan Paul, 1979; Kathryn Kane, *Visions of War: Hollywood Combat Films of World War II* (Ann Arbor, Mich.: UMI Research Press, 1982); Bernard F. Dick, *The Star-Spangled Screen: The American World War II Film* (Lexington: The University Press of Kentucky, 1985); Jeanine Basinger, *The World War II Combat Film: Anatomy of a Genre* (New York: Columbia University Press, 1986); and Clayton R. Kopper and Gregary D. Black, *Hollywood Goes to War* (New York: The Free Press, 1987).

p. 459 democratic ideals . . . serious question: See John Costello, *Virtue Under Fire: How World War II Changed Our Social and Sexual Attitudes* (Boston: Little, Brown, 1986), and Allen L. Woll, *The Hollywood Musical Goes to War* (Chicago: Nelson-Hall, 1983).

p. 460 Lewis Jacobs . . . concerned with Fascism and war: Jacobs, in McClure, *The Movies*, p. 176.

p. 460 The American military establishment: For an excellent historical account of the U.S. military's influence on the production of American war films, see Lawrence H. Suid, *Guts and Glory: Great American War Movies* (Reading, Mass.: Addison-Wesley, 1978).

p. 462 efficiency . . . order of the day: Charles Higham and Joel Greenberg, *Hollywood in the Forties* (Cranberry, N.J.: A. S. Barnes, 1968), pp. 15–16.

p. 462 fn. Supreme Court . . . at the exhibitor's expense: See Michael Conant, *Antitrust in the Motion Picture Industry* (Berkeley and Los Angeles: University of California Press, 1960); and Lea Jacobs, "The Paramount Case and the Role of the Distributor," *Journal of the University Film and Video Association* 35, 1 (Winter 1983): 44–49. The ultimate effect of the consent decrees was to promote both independent production and exhibition, but scholars such as James Monaco and Jay E. Korinek believe that if the studios had analyzed their situation more carefully (e.g., with regard to selling films to television, which they refused to do for nearly a decade), the antitrust decision would have had only a minor impact. In the short term, this is probably true, But in fact the Paramount decrees catalyzed and hastened a major structural change in the industry that shifting demographics and the new technology of television would have eventually caused anyway.

The decrees are still in effect today but are often considered economically irrelevant. They prohibit the majors' divested theater chains from engaging in the production or distribution of films without special permission from the district court, and in March 1980, Loew's Inc., was granted such a permit (although the company was still barred from distributing its own products to its own theaters). The decision was rendered by Judge Edmund L. Palmieri in recognition of the fact that in the present film-industry economy (one in which as few as twenty films can account for 85 percent of the rentals in any given year), "Loew's entry into production and distribution will represent the entry of a new competitor and a probable increase in the supply of successful feature films" (Palmieri, as quoted in *Variety*, March 5, 1980). At the other end of the business, the eighties witnessed the aggressive movement of distributors back into exhibition, including the successful petitioning of the courts in 1986 and 1987 by the parents of two majors—Gulf & Western (Paramount) and Warner Communications (Warner Bros.)—to begin the acquisition of theater chains once more (see Thomas Guback, "The Evolution of the Motion Picture Theater Business in the 1980s," *Journal of Communications* 37, 2 [Spring 1987]: 60–77; and Richard Trainor, "Major Powers," *Sight and Sound* 57, 1 [Winter 1987/78]: 27–30. As in the case of so many other corporate mergers during the Reagan era, the antitrust division of the Justice Department simply looked away.

pp. 463–64 postwar disillusionment . . . Depression: Paul Schrader, "Notes on *Film Noir*," *Film Comment* 8, 1 (Spring 1972): 9–10.

p. 466 Louis de Rochemont . . . *The March of Time*: On de Rochemont and *The March of Time* series, see Raymond Fielding, *The March of Time, 1935–1951* (New York: Oxford University Press, 1978), and Max Hastings, "Time Marches On!" *Sight and Sound* 54, 4 (Autumn 1985): 274–77.

p. 467 James Agee . . . actual places: James Agee, *Agee on Film*, Vol. 1: *Reviews and Comments* (Boston: Beacon Press, 1958), p. 376.

p. 467 *film noir* . . . French critics in 1946: The scholarly literature on *film noir* has become rich and quite extensive. Some excellent starting points are Alan Silver and Elizabeth Ward, *Film Noir* (London: Secker & Warburg, 1979); *Women in Film Noir*, ed. E. Ann Kaplan (London: BFI, 1980); Robert Ottoson, *A Reference Guide to Film Noir* (Metuchen, N.J.: Scarecrow Press, 1981); Foster Hirsch, *Film Noir: The Dark Side of the Screen* (San Diego: A. S. Barnes, 1981); Paul Kerr, "My Name Is Joseph H. Lewis," *Screen* 24, 4–5 (July–October 1983): 48–66; Spencer Selby, *Dark City: The Film Noir* (Jefferson, N.C.: McFarland, 1984); Jon Tuska, *Dark Cinema: American Film Noir in Cultural Perspective* (Westport, Conn.: Greenwood Press, 1984); J. P. Telotte, "*Film Noir* and the Dangers of Discourse," *Quarterly Review of Film Studies* 9, 2 (Spring 1984): 102–12, "*Film Noir* and the Double Indemnity of Discourse," *Genre* 18, 1 (Spring): 57–73, and "Siodmak's Phantom Women and *Noir* Narrative," *Film Criticism* 11, 3 (Spring 1987): 1–10; Dana Polan, "College Course File: *Film Noir*," *Journal of Film and Video* 37 (Spring 1985): 75–26, and *Power and Paranoia: History, Narrative, and the American Cinema, 1940–1950* (New York: Columbia University Press, 1986); Paul Kerr, "Out of What Past? Notes on the B *Film Noir*," *The Hollywood Film Industry*, ed. Paul Kerr (London: BFI, 1986), pp. 220–44; and Tom Conley, "Stages of *Film Noir*," *Theater Journal* 39, 3 (October 1987): 347–63. On modes of voice-over narration so common in *film noir* and other postwar genres, see Sarah Kozloff, *Invisible Storytellers: Voice-Over Narration in American Fiction Film* (Berkeley: University of California Press, 1988).

p. 467 *Double Indemnity* . . . "pity or love": Higham and Greenberg, p. 28.

p. 467 fn. horrors of war . . . hypocrisies of postwar American society: See James Damico, "*Film Noir*: A Modest Proposal," and Raymond Borde and Etienne Chaumeton, "The Sources of *Film Noir*," trans. Bill Horrigan, both in *Film Reader* 3, ed. Bruce Jenkins et al. (Evanston, Ill.: Northwestern University Press, 1978), pp. 48–57, 58–66 for alternative points of view.

pp. 468–69 fn. murderous *femmes fatales*: Many other notable *films noir* accommodate the antiheroic schema of *femmes fatales*, including Robert Siodmak's *Phantom Lady* (1944) and *The File on Thelma Jordan* (1950); Fritz Lang's twin tributes to Renoir's *La Chienne*: *The Woman in the Window* and *Scarlet Street* (both 1945); Michael Curtiz's *Mildred Pierce* (1945); Lewis Milestone's *The Strange Love of Martha Ivers* (1946); Jack Berhard's *Decoy* (1946); Andre De Toth's *The Pitfall* (1948); Byron Haskin's *Too Late for Tears* (1949); Max Ophüls' *The Reckless Moment* (1949); and John Far-

row's *Where Danger Lives* (1950). *Films noir* about disturbed private eyes include Howard Hawks' *The Big Sleep* (1946); Henry Hathaway's *The Dark Corner* (1946); John Brahm's *The Brasher Doubloon* (1947); Robert Florey's *The Crooked Way* (1949). About fugitive criminals there were Edward Dmytryk's *Cornered* (1945); Harold Clurman's *Deadline at Dawn* (1946); Irving Pichel's *They Won't Believe Me* (1947); Vincent Sherman's *Norma Prentiss* (1947); Anatole Litvak's *The Long Night* (1947; a remake of Carné's *Le jour se lève*); Steve Sekeley's *Hollow Triumph* (1948); Fred Zinnemann's *Act of Violence* (1949); Richard Fleischer's *Armored Car Robbery* (1950); Maxwell Shanes' *City Across the River* (1949); Gordon Douglas' *Kiss Tomorrow Goodbye* (1950); Cy Endfield's *Try and Get Me* also known as *The Sonth of Fury* (1950); Richard Quine's *Pushover* and *Drive a Crooked Mile* (both 1954). Films on con-men and racketeers include Joseph L. Mankiewicz's *Somewhere in the Night* (1946); Irving Reis' *Crack-Up* (1946); Charles Vidor's *Gilda* (1946); Arthur Ripley's *The Chase* (1946); Robert Montgomery's *Ride a Pink Horse* (1947); Edmund Goulding's *Nightmare Alley* (1947); John Farrow's *The Night Has a Thousand Eyes* (1948); Abraham Polonsky's *Force of Evil* (1948); Otto Preminger's *Whirlpool* (1949); William Dieterle's *Dark City* (1950). Some films featuring psychopaths were Robert Siodmak's *Christmas Holiday* (1944), *The Spiral Staircase* (1946), and *The Dark Mirror* (1946); Curtis Bernhardt's *Conflict* (1945) and *The High Wall* (1947); Roy William Neill's *Black Angel* (1946); Michael Curtiz's *The Unsuspected* (1947); Robert Wise's *Born to Kill* (1947); Edward J. Montagne's *The Tattooed Stranger* (1950); Gerald Mayer's *Dial 1119* (1950); Joseph Losey's American remake of Fritz Lang's *M* (1951); Harry Horner's *Beware, My Lovely* (1952); Edward Dmyktryk's *The Sniper* (1952); Arnold Laven's *Without Warning* (1952); Roy Rowland's *Witness to Murder* (1954). About corrupt cops there were Otto Preminger's *Fallen Angel* (1946); Vincent Sherman's *Nocturne* (1946); Roy Rowland's *Scene of the Crime* (1949); and *Rogue Cop* (1954); William Wyler's *Detective Story* (1951); John Cromwell's *The Racket* (1952); Don Siegel's *Private Hell 36* (1954); Edmund O'Brien and Howard W. Koch's *Shield for Murder* (1954). Assorted fifties degenerates appear in Billy Wilder's *Sunset Boulevard* (1950) and *Ace in the Hole* (1951); Mark Robson's *Edge of Doom* (1950); George Sherman's *The Sleeping City* (1950); Hugo Fregonese's *One Way Street* (1950); John Farrow's *His Kind of Woman* (1951); Harold Daniels' *Roadblock* (1951); Joseph Losey's *The Big Night* and *The Prowler* (both 1951); David Miller's *Sudden Fear* (1952); Phil Karlson's *Scandal Sheet* (1952); Fritz Lang's *Clash by Night* (1952), *The Blue Gardenia* (1953), and *Human Desire* (1954; a remake of Renoir's *La bête humaine*); Otto Preminger's *Angel Face* (1952) and *The Thirteenth Letter* (1951; a remake of Clouzot's *Le corbeau*); John H. Auer's *The City That Never Sleeps* (1953); Ida Lupino's *The Hitchhiker* (1953); Harry Essex's *I, the Jury* (1953); Hugo Haas' *The Other Woman* (1954); Richard Quine's *Pushover* (1954); Stuart Heisler's *I Died a Thousand Times* (1955; a remake of Walsh's *High Sierra*); Edgar G. Ulmer's *Murder Is My Beat* (1955); Robert Aldrich's *The Big Knife* (1955); and Joseph H. Lewis' *The Big Combo* (1955). This list is by no means inclusive. Hitchcock, for example, is omitted as *sui generis*, even though *Suspicion* (1941), *Shadow of a Doubt* (1943), *Notorious* (1946), *The Paradine Case* (1948), *Strangers on a Train* (1951), and *The Wrong Man* (1957) are clearly part of the cycle—for (much, much) more, see Alain Silver and Elizabeth Ward, eds., *Film Noir: An Encyclopedic Reference Guide to the American Style, 1940–1958* (Woodstock, N.Y.: Overlook Press, 1979; rev. ed., 1989); Robert Ottoson, *A Reference Guide to the American Film Noir, 1940–1958* (Metuchen, N.J.: Scarecrow Press, 1981); Spencer Selby, *Dark City: The Film Noir* (Jefferson City, N.C.: McFarland, 1984), which among them refer to some 500 films.

p. 469 antitraditional cinematography: J. A. Place and L. S. Peterson, "Some Visual Motifs of *Film Noir*," *Film Comment* 10, 1 (January–February 1974): 30–31.

p. 470 fn. gothic romances . . . *My Cousin Rachael*: Other important female gothic titles are *All This and Heaven Too* (Anatole Litvak, 1940), *The Lodger* (John Brahm, 1944), *Dark Waters* (André Toth, 1944), *Jane Eyre* (Robert Stevenson, 1944), *The Unseen* (Lewis Allen, 1945), *The Suspect* (Robert Siodmak, 1945), *Temptation* (Irving Pichel, 1946), *Ivy* (Sam Wood, 1947), *The Lost Moment* (Martin Gable, 1947), *The Woman in White* (Peter Godfrey, 1949), *The Black Book* (Anthony Mann, 1949), *Under Capricorn* (Hitchcock, 1949), and *House by the River* (Fritz Lang, 1950). Other representative "women's films" are *Intemezzo* (Gregory Ratoff, 1939), *When Tomorrow Comes* (John M. Stahl, 1939), *Waterloo Bridge* (Mervyn LeRoy, 1940), *Kitty Foyle* (Sam Wood, 1940), *Lydia* (Jacques Duvivier, 1941; a remake of his *Un carnet du bal*), *The Great Lie* (Edmund Goulding, 1941), *Guest in the House* (John Brahm, 1944), *Lady in the Dark* (Mitchell Leisen, 1944), *The Enchanted Cottage* (John Cromwell, 1945), *Love Letters* (William Dieterle, 1945), *To Each His Own* (Leisen, 1946), *A Stolen Life* (Curtis Bernhardt, 1946), *My Reputation* (Bernhardt, 1946), *Possessed* (Bernhardt, 1946), *The Two Mrs. Carrolls* (Peter Godfrey, 1947), *Humoresque* (Jean Negulesco, 1947), *Daisy Kenyon* (Otto Preminger, 1947), *The Unfaithful* (Vincent Sherman, 1947; a remake of *The Letter*); *The Secret Beyond the Door* (Fritz Lang, 1948), *A Woman's Vengeance* (Zoltán Korda, 1948), *A Letter to Three Wives* (Joseph L. Mankiewicz, 1948), *My Foolish Heart* (Mark Robson, 1949), *Beyond the Forest* (King Vidor, 1949), and *A Life of Her Own* (George Cukor, 1950). On both film types, see Tania Modleski, *Loving with a Vengeance: Mass-Produced Fantasies for Women* (Hamden, Conn.: Archon, 1982), and "Never To Be Thirty-Six Years Old: *Rebecca* as Female Oedipal Drama," *Wide Angle* 5, 1 (1982): 34–41; Lucy Fischer, "Two-Faced Women: The 'Double' in Women's Melodrama of the 1940's," *Cinema Journal* 23, 1 (Fall 1983): 24–43; Diane Waldman, "'At Last I Can Tell It to Someone!' Feminine Point of View and Subjectivity in the Gothic Romance Film of the 1940's," *Cinema Journal* 23, 2 (Winter 1983): 29–40; Tania Modleski, "Time and Desire in the Woman's Film," *Cinema Journal* 23, 3 (Spring 1984): 19–30; Andrea S. Walsh, *The Women's Film and Female Experience, 1940–1950* (New York: Praeger, 1984); Mary Anne Doane, "The 'Woman's Film': Possession and Address," in *Re-vision: Essays in Feminist Film Criticism*, eds. Mary Anne Doane, Patricia Mellencamp, and Linda Williams (Frederick, Md.: University Publications of America and the AFI, 1984), and *The Desire to Desire: The Woman's Film of the 1940s* (Bloomington: Indiana University Press, 1987); and Jeffrey Sconce, "Narrative Authority and Social Narrativity: The Cinema's Reconstitution of Bronte's *Jane Eyre*," *Wide Angle* 10, 1 (Winter 1988): 46–61; Murray Smith, "*Film Noir*, the Female Gothic, and 'Deception,' " *Wide Angle* 10, 1 (Winter 1988): 62–75. See also M. Joyce Baker, *Images of Women in Film: The War Years, 1941–1945* (Ann Arbor, Mich.: UMI Research Press, 1980), and Michael Renov, *Hollywood's Wartime Women: A Cultural Perspective* (Ann Arbor, Mich.: UMI Research Press, 1987). See also Barbara Demming, *Running Away from Myself: A Dream Portrait of America Drawn from the Films of the Forties* (N.Y.: Grossman Publishers, 1969), and Carol Traynor Williams, *The Dream Beside Me: The Movies and the Children of the Forties* (Rutherford, N.J.: Fairleigh Dickinson University Press, 1980).

p. 470 Raymond Durgnat . . . low-budget horror cycle . . . Val Lewton: See Raymond Durgnat, "Paint It Black: The Family Tree of *Film Noir*," *Cinema* (August 1976): 49–56; also, Joel E. Siegel, *Val Lewton: The Reality of Terror* (New York: Viking, 1973); and J. P. Telotte, *Dreams of Darkness: Fantasy and the Films of Val Lewton* (Urbana: University of Illinois Press, 1985).

p. 472 David Caute . . . atomic espionage: David Caute, *The Great Fear: The Anti-Communist Purge Under Truman and Eisenhower* (New York: Simon and Schuster, 1978), pp. 64–69.

p. 472 John Howard Lawson . . . wholly laughable: John Howard Lawson, *Film: The Creative Process* (New York: Hill & Wang, 1967), p. 156.

p. 472 apolitical *films noir*: See Philip Kemp, "From the Nightmare Factory: HUAC and the Politics of *Noir*," *Sight and Sound* 55, 4 (Autumn 1986): 266–71.

p. 472 HUAC subcommittee report: Quoted in Caute, p. 491.

p. 472 Communist Party affiliation: On the true nature of Communist activity and influence within the American film industry see David Caute, *The Great Fear: The Anti-Communist Purge Under Truman and Eisenhower* (New York: Simon and Schuster, 1978); Larry Ceplair and Steven Englund, *The Inquisition in Hollywood: Politics in the Film Community, 1930–1960* (Garden City, N.Y.: Doubleday, 1980; repr. Berkeley: University of California Press, 1983); Victor Navasky, *Naming Names* (New York: Simon and Schuster, 1980); Nancy Lynn Schwartz, *The Hollywood Writer's War* (New York: Knopf, 1982). See also John Cogley, *Report on Blacklisting*, 2 vols. (New York: Fund for the Republic, 1956); Otto Friedrich, *City of Nets: A Portrait of Hollywood in the 1940s* (New York: Harper and Row, 1986); Pat McGilligan, "Tender Comrades," *Film Comment* 23, 6 (November–December 1987): 38–48; and the film *Legacy of the Hollywood Blacklist* (Judy Chaikin, 1988), available from Direct Cinema Limited (P.O. Box 69799, Los Angeles, CA 90069).

p. 476 Herbert Biberman: In 1954, however, Herbert Biberman (1900–71), in complete defiance of the blacklist and the tenor of the times, directed *Salt of the Earth*, one of the great social documents of the era. Loosely based on the bitter 1951–52 strike by Mexican-American miners against Empire Zinc of Silver City, New Mexico, this film was shot on location with a largely nonprofessional cast drawn from the members of Local 890 of the International Union of Mine, Mill, and Smelter Workers, and their families. But at the level of production it was a showcase for blacklisted talent—independently produced by Paul Jarrico (with miners union funds), written by Michael Wilson, directed by Biberman, scored by Sol Kaplan and featuring Will Geer as the Anglo sheriff. Plagued by boycotts, vigilante raids, and the deportation as an "illegal alien" during production of its female

Mexican lead, Rosaura Revueltus, *Salt of the Earth* was widely attacked as "communist propaganda" and received only limited North American distribution because union projectionists (members of the racket-infested I.A.T.S.E.) refused to screen it. It was a great success in Europe, however, winning major awards in France and Czechoslovakia, and was given a general American rerelease in 1965, by which time audiences wondered what all the shouting had been about. Biberman directed only one other film before his death, *Slaves* (1969), a sort of revisionist *Uncle Tom's Cabin* notable mainly for featuring his blacklisted wife Gail Sondergaard in her first role in twenty years. See Herbert Biberman, *Salt of the Earth: The Story of a Film* (Boston: Beacon Press, 1965): Deborah Silverton Rosenfelt, *Salt of the Earth* (New York, 1978), and "Ideology and Structure in *Salt of the Earth*," *Jump Cut* 30 (December 1979); and Tom Miller, "*Salt of the Earth* Revisited," *Cineaste* 13, 3 (1984): 30–36. See also the 1984 documentary on the making of the film, *A Crime to Fit the Punishment*, narrated by Lee Grant, and the following related publications: William Alexander, *Film on the Left: American Documentary Film from 1931 to 1942* (Princeton: Princeton University Press, 1981), and Russell Campbell, *Cinema Strikes Back: Radical Filmmaking in the United States, 1930–1942* (Ann Arbor, Mich.: UMI Research Press, 1982).

p. 476 Lester Cole . . . outside salesmen: See Dalton Trumbo, *The Time of the Toad: A Study of Inquisition in America and Two Related Pamphlets* (New York: Perennial Library, 1972), Lester Cole, *Hollywood Red: The Autobiography of Lester Cole* (Palo Alto, Cal.: Ramparts Press, 1981), Elia Kazan; *A Life* (New York: Knopf, 1988), and Terence Butler, "Polonsky and Kazan: HUAC and the Violation of Personality," *Sight and Sound* 57, 4 (Autumn 1988): 262–67.

p. 478 alternate sources of audiovisual entertainment: For a challenging counterargument, see Michael Pye and Lynda Myles, *The Movie Brats: How the Film Generation Took Over Hollywood* (New York: Holt, Rinehart, and Winston, 1979).

The authors maintain that it was neither the rapid growth of television nor the divestiture orders of 1948 which caused the steady decline in film attendance and the crumbling of the studio system throughout the late forties and fifties, but rather a basic change in the organization of American society in the years following World War II. As Americans turned from the business of war to a preoccupation with home and *suburban* family life, they argue, the solitary and *urban*-centered experience of attending theatrical motion pictures gave way to forms of entertainment—such as spectator sports, recreational travel, and, of course, watching television—more symbolic of community and family. In "The Coming of Television and the 'Lost' Motion Picture Audience," Douglas Gomery offers an economic demand analysis of the same circumstance, pointing out, among other phenomena, that wages and salaries doubled during World War II while consumption was necessarily deterred until the war had ended, and that 80 percent of the total population growth of the United States from 1945 to 1960 took place in the suburbs (*Journal of Film and Video* 37, 3 [Summer 1985]: 5–11). Whatever the case, it is clear that in 1946, 20 percent of every dollar spent on recreation in the United States went for motion-picture entertainment; by 1950, the figure had dropped to 12 percent; in 1974, it accounted for less than 4 percent.

p. 478 fn. Paramount . . . Dumont network: See Eric Smoodin, "Motion Pictures and Television, 1930–1945: A Pre-History of the Relations Between the Two Media," *Journal of the University Film and Video Association* 34, 3 (Summer 1982): 3–8; and Douglas Gomery, "Failed Opportunities: The Integration of the U.S. Motion Picture and Television Industries," *Quarterly Review of Film Studies* 9, 3 (Summer 1984): 219–28, and "Theater Television: The Missing Link of Technological Change in the U.S. Motion Picture Industry," *The Velvet Light Trap*, no. 21 (Summer 1985): 54–61.

Hollywood, 1952–1965

p. 480 fn. Color production declined . . . total by 1970: See Gorham A. Kindem, "Hollywood's Conversion to Color: The Technological, Economic, and Aesthetic Factors," *Journal of the University Film Association* 31, 2 (Spring 1979): 29–36; repr. in Gorham Kindem, ed., *The American Movie Industry: The Business of Motion Picture* (Carbondale, Ill.: Southern Illinois University Press, 1982), pp. 146–58. See also Ed Buscombe, "Sound and Color," *Jump Cut* (April 1978): 25 ff; Edward Branigan, "Color and Cinema: Problems in the Writing of History," *Film Reader 4*, ed. Blaine Allan et al. (Evanston, Ill.: Northwestern University Press, 1979), pp. 16–33; Dudley Andrew, "The Postwar Struggle for Color, *Cinema Journal* 18, 2 (Spring 1979): 41–52; repr. in *The Cinematic Apparatus*, ed. Teresa de Lauretis and Stephen Heath (New York: St. Martin's Press, 1980), pp. 61–75; Brian Winston, "A Whole Technology of Dyeing," *Daedalus* (Fall 1985): 105–23; and Steve Neale, *Cinema and Technology: Image, Sound, and Colour* (Bloomington: Indiana University Press, 1985).

p. 482 fn. problem with Eastman-based systems . . . archivists today: Depending on how it is processed, a color print may have a lifetime as short as five years (dye-coupling, at its worst) or as long as forty (imbibition). Preservation is possible through black-and white separations but was, until recently, prohibitively expensive (25,000 to 35,000 dollars per feature); cold storage is effective but impractical.

Nevertheless, a new technique invented by Dr. Charles S. Ih at the University of Delaware in 1977 promises nearly perfect preservation through holography, or lensless photography. Using laser beams at three different wavelengths, the process superimposes the red, green, and blue color elements on a single black-and-white film strip. Since the ratio between the three different wavelengths is established when the hologram is made, the original color can always be duplicated from the black-and-white print. For long-term preservation, the hologram could even be imprinted on metal. (See Dr. Charles S. Ih, "Holographic Process for Color Motion Picture Preservation," *Society of Motion Picture and Television Engineers Journal* 87, 2 [December 1978].) Other hopeful developments spring from the Ciba-Geigy Company and from Eastman Kodak itself, both of which are experimenting with new color stocks whose dye is many times more stable than that of Technicolor imbibition prints. (See Bill O'Connell, "Fade Out," *Film Comment* 15, 5 [September–October 1979]: 11–18; and Paul C. Spehr, "Fading, Fading, Faded: The Color Film Crisis," *American Film* [November 1979]: 56–61.)

At least as distressing to preservationists as color fading is the problem of transferring cellulose nitrate prints to acetate–based safety stock. Virtually all films made before 1951 were printed on celluloid, a highly unstable substance that can ignite at temperatures as low as 106 degrees, burns twenty times faster than wood, and is subject under the best conditions to steady chemical disintegration. Of the estimated 21,000 films produced in the United States before the postwar conversion to acetate, over half have been lost to willful destruction or deterioration. Early producers regularly burned their prints after exhibition, often melting them down for their silver content. Although after World War I most major studios adopted the practice of retaining a single master negative per film, as late as 1947 Universal Pictures destroyed its entire library of silent films in a huge bonfire, figuring that there was no market left for them. Under the cost-conscious regime of Harry Cohn, Columbia wore out many of its master negatives in the process of striking prints, with the result that such classics as *It Happened One Night* (Capra, 1934), *The Awful Truth* (Leo McCarey, 1937), and *Mr. Smith Goes to Washington* (Capra, 1939) no longer exist in negative form. At United Artists the original negative of John Ford's *Stagecoach* (1939) was cut to pieces to make previews of coming attractions. Today Columbia, Fox, Walt Disney, and MGM Entertainment (currently owed by TBS) are all active in the preservation of their own libraries. Four institutional archives supported in part by public funds and loosely coordinated by the AFI's National Center of Film and Video Preservation exist—the Library of Congress, the UCLA Film and Television Archive, the International Museum of Photography at George Eastman House in Rochester, N.Y., and MoMA. Much of what has survived on nitrate in these archives is in imminent danger of decay, with the costs of transfer to acetate ranging from 10,000 dollars for a black-and-white feature to 40,000 dollars for color. At these prices, it is a safe bet that much of America's pre-1951 film heritage will not survive into the next century.

p. 485 fn. stereoscopy . . . both are flat: See Brian Coe, *The History of Movie Photography* (Westfield, N.J.: Eastview Editions, 1981), pp. 156–61; Hall Morgan and Dan Symmes, *Amazing 3-D* (Boston: Little, Brown, 1982); Lenny Lipton, *Foundations of the Stereoscopic Cinema: A Study in Depth* (New York: Van Nostrand Reinhold, 1982); and *American Cinematographer* 64, 7 (July 1983), special 3-D issue.

p. 486 addition of a twin-lens Natural Vision camera: Arthur Knight, *The Liveliest Art* (New York: New American Library, 1957), p. 289.

p. 492 in 1955 a 70mm wide-film process: The negative of a Todd-AO film was 65mm; the positive was 70mm, with 65mm used for the image and 5mm for the magnetic stereophonic soundtrack. Like stereoscopy, wide format films appeared a few years after cinema's invention, with Dickson's Biograph, for example, using 68mm film as a matter of course and the Lumières creating a 70mm film for the Paris Exposition of 1900. After the 35mm format was standardized by Edison, little happened until the late twenties (an exception was Panoramico Alberini, a 70mm process devised by the Italian producer Filoteo Alberini and used for a sequence in Enrico Guazzoni's *Il Sacco di Roma* [*The Sack of Rome*, 1923]). The coming of sound sparked a renewal of interest in wide-film systems, and every major studio in Hollywood rushed to acquire one. In 1930, RKO produced several features in the Spoor-Berggren 63.5mm "Natural Vision" process (not to be confused with Arch Oboler's identically named 3-D process of 1952–54, *Dixiana* (Luther Reed, 1930), and *Danger Lights* (George B. Sertz, 1930) among them. This system employed an optical soundtrack running on a separate

film strip, and was plagued by problems of synchronization. Fox's Grandeur, on the other hand, was a 70mm system with an integral soundtrack which produced high-quality images and sound. It was used in such critically acclaimed big-budget features as *Fox Movietone Follies of 1929* (David Butler, 1929) and Raoul Walsh's *The Big Trail* (1930; nationally released in 35mm but restored to its original 70mm format in 1985 by MoMA under a grant from the AFI-NEA Preservation program). Paramount used a 56mm system called Magna Film (*You're in the Army Now*, 1929). Warner Bros. (*Kismet*, John Francis Dillon, 1931) and United Artists (*The Bat Whispers*, Roland West, 1930) both used a 65mm system called Vitascope (the same name as Edison's Armat-designed projector, patented in 1896). And MGM used a 65mm system called Realife (King Vidor's *Billy the Kid*, 1930; *The Great Meadow*, Charles Brabin, 1931). All of these systems failed commercially, if not technically, due to public apathy and exhibitor resistance to installing new equipment on the heels of the costly conversion to sound. See Michael Z. Wysotsky, *Wide-Screen Cinema and Stereophonic Sound*, trans. A. E. C. York, ed. Raymond Spotiswoode (New York: Hastings House, 1971); Robert E. Carr and R. M. Hayes, *Wide Screen Movies: A History and Filmography of Wide Gauge Filmmaking* (Jefferson, N. C.: McFarland, 1988); and John Belton, "The Shape of Money," *Sight and Sound* 57, 1 (Winter 1987/88): 44–47, "The Age of Cinerama: A New Era in the Cinema," *The Perfect Vision* 1, 4 (Spring/Summer 1988): 78–90, and "CinemaScope and Historical Methodology," *Cinema Journal* 28, 1 (Fall 1988): 22–44. See also *The Velvet Light Trap*, no. 21 (Summer 1985), "American Widescreen" special issue, and *American Cinematographer* 71, 3 (March 1990), "Wide Screen Formats: Their Future" special issue.

p. 494 Dolby . . . increasingly common: See Philip Beck, "Technology as Commodity and Representation: Cinema Stereo in the Fifties," *Wide Angle* 7, 3 (Summer 1986): 62–73; and Ron Haver, "The Saga of Stereo in the Movies," *The Perfect Vision* 1, 1 (Winter 1986/87): 64–73, and "The Saga of Stereo in the Movies: Part II," *The Perfect Vision* 1, 3 (Indiana, Summer 1987): 51–71; and Michael Arick, "In Stereo: The Sound of Money!" *Sight and Sound* 57, 1 (Winter 1987/88): 35–42.

p. 495 Henry King said: Henry King, quoted in David Robinson, *The History of World Cinema* (New York: Stein & Day, 1973), p. 281.

p. 495 André Bazin: André Bazin, *What Is Cinema?*, vols. 1 and 2 (Berkeley: University of California Press, 1967; 1971).

p. 495 Charles Barr: Charles Barr, "Cinemascope: Before and After," *Film Quarterly* 16, 4 (1963): 4–24.

p. 506 *The Pirate* . . . *Gigi*: Also worthy of note among Freed's musicals are *Girl Crazy* (Norman Taurog, 1943), *Cabin in the Sky* (Minnelli, 1943, *Ziegfield Follies* (Minnelli, 1946), *Take Me Out to the Ball Game* (Busby Berkeley, 1949), *The Barkleys of Broadway* (Walters, 1949), *Annie Get Your Gun* (George Sidney, 1950), *Royal Wedding* (Walters, 1949), *Show Boat* (Sidney, 1951), and *Bells Are Ringing* (Minnelli, 1960). Of his nonmusicals, three—*The Clock* (Minnelli, 1945), *Crisis* (Richard Brooks, 1950), and *Light in the Piazza* (Guy Green, 1962)—retain considerable interest. See Gerald Mast, *Can't Help Singin': The American Musical* *on Stage and Screen* (Woodstock, N.Y.: Overlook Press, 1987), Chapter 14 (" 'And Best of All, He's American': Arthur Freed and MGM").

p. 512 Andrew Sarris . . . Michelangelo Antonioni: Andrew Sarris, *The American Cinema: Directors and Directions, 1929–1968* (New York: E. P. Dutton, 1968), p. 98.

p. 512 *Leone . . . Once Upon a Time in the West:* Leone's other work includes the Westerns *Duck, You Sucker* (also known as *A Fistful of Dynamite*, 1971), *My Name Is Nobody* (1973), and the epic gangster film *Once Upon a Time in America* (1984), which was subject to not only multiple cuts but a radical restructuring of its narrative by its American producer (The Ladd Company). It was finally released in three separate versions running 250, 226, and 144 minutes. For more on Leone and other key figures of the spaghetti Western, see Christopher Frayling, *Spaghetti Westerns: Cowboys and Europeans from Karl May to Sergio Leone* (London: Routledge & Kegan Paul, 1981); Ignacio Ramonet, "Italian Westerns as Political Parables," *Cineaste* 15, 1 (1986): 30–35; and Robert C. Cumbow, *Once Upon a Time: The Films of Sergio Leone* (Metuchen, N.J.: The Scarecrow Press, 1987).

p. 517 controversial since the day of its release: Otis L. Guerney, Jr., wrote of *My Son John* in the *New York Herald-Tribune*, April 10, 1952: "In effect, McCarey's picture of how America should be is so frightening, so speciously argued, so full of warnings against intelligent solution of the problem, that it boomerangs upon its own cause and becomes, by mistake, a most vivid demonstration that two wrongs don't make a right." *Variety* on the same date faulted the film's "snide attitude toward intellectuals, its obvious pitch for religious conformity, and its eventual wholehearted endorsement of its Legionnaire's [John's father] stubborn bigotry." The only other American film of the era that can touch *My Son John* in these terms is King Vidor's ambitious adaptation of Ayn Rand's best-selling "objectivist" novel *The Fountainhead* (1949). This philosophically pretentious film, which Peter Biskind has correctly labeled "a Wagnerian soap opera for the radical right" (*Seeing Is Believing* [New York: Pantheon, 1983], p. 316), concerns the rise of an unconventional architectural genius named Howard Roark and, in its contempt for the common man, virtually equates democracy with communism. But whereas *The Fountainhead* is finally laughable, if visually impressive, *My Son John* is downright scary because the viewer is forced to confront a strain of native American fascism that we all know exists. See, in addition to the Biskind work cited above, Andrew Dowdy, *The Films of the Fifties: The American State of Mind* (New York: Morrow, 1975); Nora Sayre, *Running Time: Films of the Cold War* (New York: The Dial Press, 1982); Michael Rogin, *Ronald Reagan, the Movie and Other Episodes in Political Demonology*, Chapter VIII, "Kiss Me Deadly: Communism, Motherhood, and Cold War Movies" (Berkeley: University of California Press, 1987); and Thomas Doherty, "Hollywood Agit-Prop: The Anti-Communist Cycle, 1948–1954," *Journal of Film and Video* 40, 4 (Fall 1988): 15–27.

p. 517 State of moral confusion . . . never emerged: It is possible, of course, to see the anti-Red and James Bond-type films as part of a larger category of spy films. In the sound era, this category would include films as diverse as *Dishonored* (Josef von Sternberg, 1931), *Mata Hari* (George Fitzmaurice, 1932), *The Man Who Knew Too Much* (Alfred Hitchcock, 1934; remade 1956), *The Scarlet Pimpernel* (Harold Young, 1935), *The Thirty-Nine Steps* (Hitchcock, 1935), *The Lady Vanishes* (Hitchcock, 1938), *Confessions of a Nazi Spy* (Anatole Litvak, 1939), *Across the Pacific* (John Huston, 1942), the Sherlock Holmes and Charlie Chan espionage cycles (1940–45), *Ministry of Fear* (Fritz Lang, 1945), *The House on 92nd Street* (Henry Hathaway, 1945), *13 Rue Madeleine* (Hathaway, 1946), *Notorious* (Hitchcock, 1946), *Five Fingers* (Joseph L. Mankiewicz, 1952), *The Man Between* (Carol Reed, 1953), North by Northwest (Hitchcock, 1959), *The Manchurian Candidate* (John Frankenheimer, 1962), *The Ipcress File* (Sidney J. Furie, 1965), *The Spy Who Came in from the Cold* (Martin Ritt, 1965), *The Quiller Memorandum* (Michael Anderson, 1966), *Funeral in Berlin* (Guy Hamilton, 1966), *Torn Curtain* (Hitchcock, 1966), *Billion Dollar Brain* (Ken Russell, 1967), *The Deadly Affair* (Sidney Lumet, 1967), *Topaz* (Hitchcock, 1969), *The Tamerind Seed* (Blake Edwards, 1974), *The Odessa File* (Ronald Neame, 1974), *Three Days of the Condor* (Sydney Pollack, 1975), *Telefon* (Don Siegel, 1977), *Hopscotch* (Neame, 1980), *The Eye of the Needle* (Richard Marquand, 1981), *The Osterman Weekend* (Sam Peckinpah, 1983), *The Jigsaw Man* (Terence Young, 1984), *Target* (Arthur Penn, 1985), *Edge of Darkness* (Martin Campbell, 1985; BBC), and *Yuri Nosenko, KGB* (Mick Jackson, 1986; HBO). See James Robert Parish and Michael R. Pitts, *The Great Spy Pictures* (Metuchen, N.J.: Scarecrow, 1974) and *The Great Spy Pictures II* (Metuchen, N.J.: Scarecrow, 1986).

p. 519 paranoid politics . . . science fiction boom: See Bill Warren, *Keep Watching the Skies: American Science Fiction Movies of the Fifties, vol. 1 1950–1957* and *vol. 2 1958–1962* (Jefferson, N.C.: McFarland, 1982; 1986); Peter Biskind, *Seeing Is Believing*, Part II: "Us and Them" and Patrick Lucanio, *Them or Us: Archetypal Interpretations of Fifties Alien Invasion Films* (Bloomington: Indiana University Press, 1988).

p. 520 *The Seven Faces of Dr. Lao:* See Gail Morgan Hickman, *The Films of George Pal* (New York: A. S. Barnes, 1977); the feature-length documentary *The Fantasy World of George Pal* (Arnold Leibovit, 1986); Ray Harryhausen, *Film Fantasy Scrapbook*, 2nd ed., rev: (New York: A. S. Barnes, 1974); Roy Fry and Pamela Fourzon, *The Saga of Special Effects* (Englewood Cliffs, N.J.: Prentice-Hall, 1977); and Roy Kinnard, *Beasts and Behemoths: Prehistoric Creatures in the Movies* (Metuchen, N.J.: Scarecrow, 1988).

p. 520 Hammer films . . . the generic fence between science fiction and horror: On the Hammer phenomenon, see Raymond Durgnat, *A Mirror for England: British Movies from Austerity to Affluence* (New York: Praeger, 1971), Chapter 6; David Pirie, *A Heritage of Horror: The English Gothic Cinema, 1946–1972* (London: Gordon Fraser, 1973); Allen Eyles et al., eds., *The House of Horror: The Complete Story of Hammer Films* (New York: Lorrimer 1973; 1984); John Brosnan, *The Horror People* (New York: St. Martin's, 1976), Chapter 6; and Leslie Halliwell, *The Dead That Walk* (London: Grafton, 1986). Good introductions to the horror genre are Carlos Clarens, *An Illustrated History of the Horror Film* (New York: Capricorn, 1968); Ivan Butler, *Horror in the Cinema* (New York: A. S. Barnes, 1970); Roy Huss and T. J. Ross, eds., *Focus on the Horror Film* (Englewood Cliffs, N.J.: Prentice-Hall, 1972); William K. Everson, *Classics of the Horror Film* (Secaucus, N.J.: Citadel, 1974); *Living in Fear: A History of Horror in the Mass Media* (New York: Scribner's

1975); Charles Derry, *Dark Dreams: A Psychological History of the Modern Horror Film* (New York: A. S. Barnes, 1977); S. S. Prawer, *Caligari's Children: The Film as a Tale of Terror* (New York: Oxford, 1980); Barry Keith Grant, ed., *Planks of Reason: Essays on the Horror Film* (Metuchen, N.J.: Scarecrow, 1984); and James B. Twitchell, *Dreadful Pleasures: An Anatomy of Modern Horror* (New York: Oxford, 1985); Gregory A. Waller, ed., *American Horrors: Essays on the Modern American Horror Film* (Champaign: University of Illinois Press, 1988); Tom Weaver, *Interviews with B Science Fiction and Horror Movie Makers* (Jefferson, N.C.: McFarland, 1988); Andrew Tudor, *Monsters and Mad Scientists: A Cultural History of the Horror Movie* (London: Basil Blackwell, 1989); and Noel Carroll, *The Philosophy of Horror: Paradoxes of the Heart* (New York: Routledge, 1990).

The bibliography on science fiction films is enormous. Good beginnings are John Baxter, *Science Fiction in the Cinema* (New York: A. S. Barnes, 1970); William Johnson, ed., *Focus on the Science Fiction Film* (Englewood Cliffs, N.J.: Prentice-Hall, 1972); Edward Edelson, *Visions of Tomorrow: Great Science Fiction from the Movies* (New York: Doubleday, 1975); Jeff Roven, *A Pictorial History of Science Fiction Films* (Secaucus, N.J.: Citadel, 1975) and *S-F 2: A Pictorial History of Science Fiction Films from "Rollerball" to "Return of the Jedi"* (Secaucus, N.J.: Citadel, 1984); Douglas Menville, *A Historical and Critical Survey of the Science Fiction Film* (New York: Arno Press, 1975); Douglas Menville and R. Reginald, *Things to Come: An Illustrated History of the Science Fiction Film* (New York: Times Books, 1977) and *Future Visions: The New Golden Age of the Science Fiction Film* (North Hollywood, Ca.: Newcastle, 1985); John Brosnan, *Future Tense: The Cinema of Science Fiction* (New York: St. Martin's, 1978); Danny Peary, ed., *Omni's Screen Flights/Screen Fantasies: The Future According to Science Fiction* (New York: Doubleday, 1984); Phil Hardy, ed., *Science Fiction* (New York: Morrow, 1984); George Slusser and Eric C. Rabkin, eds., *Shadows of the Magic Lamp: Fantasy and Science Fiction in Film* (Carbondale and Edwardsville: Southern Illinois University Press, 1985); Vivian Sobchak, *Screening Space: The American Science Fiction Film*, 2nd ed. (New York: Ungar, 1987); and *Camera Obscura/15: Science Fiction and Sexual Difference* (Los Angeles: Camera Obscura, 1988). Important reference works are Donald Willis, *Horror and Science Fiction Films: A Checklist and Horror and Science Fiction Films II* (Metuchen, N.J.: Scarecrow, 1972; 1982); Walt Lee, ed., *Reference Guide to Fantastic Films: Science Fiction, Fantasy and Horror*, 3 vols. (Los Angeles: Chelsea-Lee Books, 1972; 1973; 1974); James Robert Parish and Michael R. Pitts, *The Great Science Fiction Pictures* (Metuchen, N.J.: Scarecrow, 1977); A. W. Strickland and Forest J. Ackerman, *A Reference Guide to American Science Fiction Films* (Bloomington, Ind.: T.I.S. Publications, 1981); Alan Frank, *The Science Fiction and Fantasy Film Handbook* (Totowa, N.J.: Barnes & Noble, 1983); and Donald Willis, ed., *Variety's Complete Science Fiction Reviews* (New York and London: Garland, 1985); and James Robert Parish and Michael R. Pitts, *The Great Science Fiction Pictures II* (Metuchen, N.J.: Scarecrow, 1990).

p. 522 *Rodan . . . Destroy All Monsters*: Other Honda-Tsuburaya collaborations were *Half-Human* (also known as *The Monster Snowman*, 1955), *The H-Man* (1958),

Matanga—Fungus of Terror (1963), *Dogora—The Space Monster* (1964), and *Latitude Zero* (1969). So successful was the work of this team both at home and abroad that it was widely imitated in other Japanese films—e.g., *Gigantis, the Fire Monster* (Motoyoshi Odo, 1955; 1959), *Ultraman* (Hajime/Tsuburaya, 1967), Noriaki Yuasa's "Gamera" series (*Destroy All Planets* [also known as *Gamera vs. Viras*, 1968], *Gamera vs. Monster X*, 1970, *Gamera vs. Zigra*, 1971), Jun Fukuda's *Godzilla vs. the Sea Monster* (1966; 1969), *Son of Godzilla* (1968), *Godzilla vs. Gigan* (1971), *Godzilla vs. the Smog Monster* (1972), *Godzilla vs. Megalon* (1973), and *Godzilla vs. Mechagodzilla* (1974). Furthermore, after Tsuburaya's death in 1970, Honda continued to make monster films (*kaiju-eiga*) on his own (e.g., *Yog—Monster from Space*, 1971). On *Godzilla*'s nuclear origins and iconography, see Chon Noriega, "Godzilla and the Japanese Nightmare: When *Them!* Is Us," *Cinema Journal* 27, 1 (Fall 1987): 47–62.

p. 524–25 *Monster from the Ocean Floor . . . The Wasp Woman*: Other representative AIP monster/horror titles include *The Beast with 1,000,000 Eyes* (David Kramarsky, 1955), *The Phantom from 10,000 Leagues* (Dan Milner, 1955), *The She Creature* (Edward L. Cahn, 1956), *Invasion of the Saucer Men* (also known as *The Hell Creatures*, Cahn, 1957), *The Astounding She-Monster* (Ronnie Ashcroft, 1958), *The Brain Eaters* (Bruno Ve Sota, 1958), *Night of the Blood Beast* (Bernard Kowalski, 1958), *Terror from the Year 5,000* (Robert J. Gurney, 1958), *Attack of the Giant Leeches* (Kowalski, 1959), *The Amazing Transparent Man* (Edgar G. Ulmer, 1960), *The Angry Red Planet* (Ib Melchior, 1960), *Beyond the Time Barrier* (Ulmer, 1960), *Journey to the Seventh Planet* (Sidney Pink, 1961), *The Phantom Planet* (William Marshall, 1961), *The Brain That Wouldn't Die* (Joseph Green, 1962), *Invasion of the Star Creatures* (Ve Sota, 1962), *Panic in the Year Zero* (Ray Milland, 1962), and *The Crawling Hand* (Herbert L. Strock, 1963).

p. 525 fn. Teenage exploitation films . . . *Don't Knock the Rock*: Simultaneously Elvis Presley vehicles were launched by Fox with *Love Me Tender* (Robert D. Webb, 1956), *Loving You* (Hal Kanter, 1957), and *Jailhouse Rock* (Richard Thorpe, 1957); its more "wholesome" Pat Boone films (*Bernadine* [Henry Levin, 1957]; *April Love* [Henry Levin, 1957]) also targeted the teenage market.

Other teenage films were Fox's *The Girl Can't Help It* (Frank Tashlin, 1956), Universal-International's exploitative exposé series (*High School Confidential!* [Jack Arnold, 1958]; *College Confidential!* [Albert Zugsmith]), and AIP's own "hotrod" cycle (*Dragstrip Girl* [Edward L. Cahn, 1957]; *Motorcycle Gang* [Cahn, 1957]; *Dragstrip Riot* [David Bradley, 1958]; *The Cool and the Crazy* [William Witney, 1958]; *High School Hellcats* [Edward Bernds, 1958]; *Hot Rod Gang* [Lew Landers, 1958]; *Daddy-O* [Lew Place, 1959]).

But the *Beach Party* movies—recently parodied in *Surf II* (Randall Badat, 1984) and *Back to the Beach* (Lyndall Hobbs, 1987)—reflected a shift in teenage styles from the East Coast to the West and a cleaning up of teens' public image as forecast by Columbia's *Gidget* (Paul Wendkos, 1959) and its sequels (*Gidget Goes Hawaiian* [Wendkos, 1961], *Gidget Goes to Rome* [Wendkos, 1963], etc.), starring Sandra Dee as a sort of pubescent Doris Day. These films mixed teenaged performers (usually some combination of Annette Funicello, Frankie Avalon, Dwayne Hickman, and

Harvey Lembeck) with veteran talent (e.g., Robert Cummings, Dorothy Malone, Keenan Wynn, Don Rickles, Paul Lynde, Vincent Price, and, somewhat sadly, Buster Keaton) in comic plots involving teenage surfside romance adult cupidity, and of course, songs sung by Avalon and Funicello, California-style.

AIP then produced a cycle of "protest" films triggered by the popularity of Corman's *The Wild Angels* in 1966. These included *Riot on Sunset Strip* (Arthur Dreifuss, 1987), *Psych-Out* (Richard Rush, 1968), *Born Wild* (Muary Dexter, 1968), *Wild in the Streets* (Barry Shear, 1968), *Three in the Attic* (Richard Wilson, 1968), *Up in the Cellar* (Theodore J. Flicker, 1970), and *Gas-s-s-s* (Robert Corman, 1970). The studio also continued to mine the stylish horror vein of the Poe films with *The Conqueror Worm* (Michael Reeves, 1968), *The Oblong Box* (Gordon Hessler, 1969), and the continental Poe anthology *Spirits of the Dead* (Roger Vadim, Louis Malle, Federico Fellini, 1969).

p. 527 In 1970, Corman left AIP: In the early seventies, AIP continued its line of medium-budget horror films with *Count Yorga, Vampire* (Robert Kelljan, 1970) and *The Return of Count Yorga* (Kelljan, 1971), *The Dunwich Horror* (Daniel Haller, 1970), *Murders in the Rue Morgue* (Gordon Hessler, 1971), and *The Abominable Dr. Phibes* (Robert Fuest, 1971) and *Phibes Rises Again* (Fuest, 1971). It also ventured several interesting, if controversial, animated features (*Heavy Traffic* [Ralph Bakshi, 1973]; *The Nine Lives of Fritz the Cat* [Robert Taylor, 1974]), and even a handful of intelligent literary adaptations (*Wuthering Heights* [Robert Fuest, 1970]; *The Wild Party* [James Ivory, 1975]; *Crime and Passion* [Ivan Passer, 1976]). However, AIP continued to subsist mainly on exploitation genres, especially "blaxploitation" (films made by whites mainly for urban black audiences—see Chapter 17) such as *Blacula* (William Crain, 1972), *Slaughter* (Jack Starrett, 1972), *Black Caesar* (Larry Cohen, 1973), *Black Mama, White Mama* (Eddie Romero, 1973), *Coffy* (Jack Hill), *Scream Blacula, Scream* (Bob Kelljan, 1973), *Slaughter's Big Rip-Off* (Gordon Douglas, 1973), *Abby* (William Girdler, 1974), *Foxy Brown* (Jack Hill, 1974), *Hell Up in Harlem* (Larry Cohen), and *Cooley High* (Michael Schultz, 1975). In 1975, Arkoff announced that AIP would thenceforth produce mainstream films in the 3-to 4-million-dollar range, a plan that resulted in a number of remarkably dull but well-produced films (*The Island of Dr. Moreau* [Don Taylor, 1977]; *Force Ten from Navarone* [Guy Hamilton, 1978]; *The Amityville Horror* [Stuart Rosenberg, 1979]; *Meteor* [Ronald Neame, 1979]; *Love at First Bite* [Stan Dragoti, 1979]. In July 1979 the company was merged with Filmways, which three years later became Orion Pictures. See Mark Thomas McGee, *Fast and Furious: The Story of American International Pictures* (Jefferson, N.C.: McFarland, 1984) and Robert L. Ottoson, *American International Pictures: A Filmography* (New York: Garland, 1985). See also Paul Willeman, et al., *Roger Corman: The Millennic Vision* (Edinburgh, Scotland: Edinburgh Film Festival, 1970; J. Phillip De Franco, ed., *The Movie World of Roger Corman* (New York: Chelsea House, 1979); the documentary feature *Roger Corman, Hollywood's Wild Angel* (Christian Blackwood, 1979), Ed Naha, *The Films of Roger Corman: Brilliance on A Budget* (New York: Arco Press, 1982); David Chute, "The New World of Roger Corman," *Film Comment* 18, 2 (March–April, 1982); 27–32; and Gary Morris, *Roger Corman* (New York: Twayne, 1985).

p. 529 *The Last Starfighter* . . . generated entirely by the computer: The space travel sequences in *Star Wars*, like those in *2001*, were made through a process known as traveling matte photography in which models of space ships and other miniatures are manipulated for the camera in front of a blue screen that leaves the background of the shot unexposed. The background is then superimposed—or "matted in"—in the printing process via double exposure. Any number of images can be layered in this way on the same piece of film, but the matching of them must be absolutely precise. Traveling matte shots were torturously difficult and time-consuming before the intervention of computers. The process was so expensive, in fact, that the use of even twenty or thirty traveling mattes, even in a spectacular production like *2001*, was considered extreme. The innovation wrought by *Star Wars*, which used 365 traveling matte special effects, was a computerized motion-control system designed by effects director John Dykstra and patented as "Dykstraflex." The heart of the system is a motorized camera mount, governed by multitrack magnetic tape, which permits the camera to pan, tilt, roll, and perform 8 feet of vertical and 42 feet of horizontal tracking movement. Operators can "program" their cameras through complicated plotted motions one frame at a time, and the whole sequence can be repeated precisely by numeric control, making traveling matte work cost-effective for the first time. Since the development of Dykstraflex, numerous refinements in motion-control systems have taken place (e.g., Walt Disney Productions' automated camera effects system, or ACES, which used computer automation to control the movement of both camera *and* model, and the same studio's Matte-Scan, first used in the abysmal *The Black Hole* [Gary Nelson, 1979], which permits the integration of matte paintings with live scenes in which the camera is moving). But the most remarkable interaction between electronics and special effects in recent years has been the advent of computer-generated imagery, or CGI, in which scenes are digitalized and printed directly onto the film stock without the intervention of photography. The first film to employ CGI at any length was Disney's *Tron* (Steven Lisberger, 1982), for which Digital Production, Inc., created approximately five minutes of completely digitalized high-resolution imagery with a 6.5-million dollar Ramtek Cray-1 computer. For *The Last Starfighter*, Digital Productions leased Ramtek's 10.5-billion-dollar supercomputer, the Cray X-MP, to generate 230 scenes or about twenty-seven of its one hundred minutes, making it the first feature film in history to simulate *all* of its special effects. Although the simulation cost 4.9 million dollars of *Starfighter*'s 14-million-dollar budget, the film's producers (Lorimar) figured that it had been completed in one third the time and half the expense of traditional effects.

p. 531 United Artists . . . by 1956: See Tino Balio, "When Is an Independent Producer Independent? The Case of United Artists After 1948," *The Velvet Light Trap* 22 (1986): 55–64; and *United Artists: The Company that Changed the Film Industry* (Madison: University of Wisconsin Press, 1987).

p. 534 Alexander Walker . . . transitional period: Alexander Walker, *Stardom* (New York: Stein & Day, 1970), p. 332.

p. 536–37 Cultural taboo . . . violence: Regarding extant film taboos, see Amos Vogel, *Film as a Subversive Art* (New York: Random House, 1974).

The French New Wave
and Its Native Context

p. 543 Bresson . . . those of sound: On Bresson, see Michel Ciment, "The Poetry of Precision," *American Film* 9, 1 (October 1983): 70–73; Mirella Jona Affron, "Bresson and Pascal: Rhetorical Affinities," *Quarterly Review of Film Studies* 10, 2 (Spring 1985): 118–34; Tom Milne, "Angels and Ministers," *Sight and Sound* 56, 4 (Autumn 1987); and Linda Hanlon, *Fragments: Bresson's Film Style* (Rutherford, N.J.: Fairleigh Dickinson University Press, 1986). For Bresson's own views, see his *Notes on the Cinematographer*, trans. Jonathan Griffen (London: Quartet Books, 1986). See also the Dutch feature-length documentary *De Weg Naar Bresson* (*The Way to Bresson*, 1984), directed by Jurrien Rood and Leo de Boer.

p. 545 Ophüls . . . remarking of Lola: Ophüls is quoted in Roy Armes, *French Cinema Since 1946*, vol. 2, *The Great Tradition* (Cranberry, N.J.: A. S. Barnes, 1970), p. 62.

p. 546 Andrew Sarris . . . movement itself: "Max Ophüls: An Introduction by Andrew Sarris," *Film Comment* 7, 2 (Summer 1971): 57.

p. 550 *The Wild Palms*: See Bruce Kawin, *Faulkner and Film* (New York: Ungar, 1977), pp. 146–49. According to Kawin, Varda, Resnais, and Chris Marker—all friends—were part of "the Left Bank group" of the New Wave, as distinct from "the *Cahiers* group." The former drew much of their inspiration from modernist literature, whereas the latter were more exclusively devoted to film as film.

p. 551 Astruc . . . long take: Astruc's article was reprinted in *The New Wave*, ed. Peter Graham (Garden City, N.Y.: Doubleday, 1968), p. 20.

p. 551 *Cahiers du cinéma* . . . New Wave: Classical *Cahiers* criticism is collected in *Cahiers du Cinéma: The 1950s: Neo-Realism, Hollywood, New Wave* (Cambridge: Harvard University Press, 1985) and *Cahiers du Cinéma: The 1960's: New Wave, New Cinema, Reevaluating Hollywood* (Cambridge: Harvard University Press, 1986), both edited by Jim Hillier. (A third volume, *Cahiers du Cinema, 1969–72: The Politics of Representation*, edited by Nick Brown [Harvard, 1990], offers an interesting perspective on the New Wave era but contains no writing by the original *Cahiers* group.) Individual critics are collected in François Truffaut, *The Films in My Life*, trans. Leonard Mayhew (New York: Simon and Schuster, 1975; 1985); Jean-Luc Godard, *Godard on Godard*, ed. Jean Narboni and Tom Milne (New York: Viking, 1972) and Eric Rohmer, *Le Goût de la beauté* (Paris: Editions de l'Etoile, 1985). On Bazin and his contemporary impact on French film practice, see Dudley Andrew, *André Bazin* (New York: Oxford University Press, 1978); "Bazin Before *Cahiers*," *Cineaste* 12, 1 (1962): 11–15; and *Wide Angle* 9, 4, André Bazin Special Issue, ed. Dudley Andrew (includes Andrew's "Preface": 4–6; Philip Rosen, "History of Image, Image of History: Subject and Ontology in Bazin": 7–35; Pamela Falkenberg, " 'The Text! The Text!': André

Bazin's Mummy Complex, Psychoanalysis and the Cinema":
35–55; Jean Narboni, "André Bazin's Style": 56–60; Jean-Charles Tacchella, "André Bazin from 1945 to 1950: The Time of Struggles and Consecration": 61–73; and John Belton, "Bazin Is Dead! Long Live Bazin!": 75–81).

p. 552 François Truffaut . . . 1954 essay: Truffaut's essay is reprinted in *Movies and Methods*, ed. Bill Nichols (Berkeley: University of California Press, 1976), pp. 224–37.

p. 552 Andrew Sarris . . . personal artistic expression: Andrew Sarris, "Notes on the *Auteur* Theory in 1962," in *Film Theory and Criticism*, 2nd ed., ed. Gerald Mast and Marshall Cohen (New York: Oxford University Press, 1979), pp. 650–65.

p. 552 French writer-directors . . . studio system: The New Wave's challenge to the "tradition of quality" was economic as well as aesthetic. Under the system that prevailed from 1953 to 1959, government aid was awarded to productions by the Centre National de la Cinématographie (CNC, founded 1946) on the basis of reputation, so potential directors needed an established record of success, and very few new people could hope to enter the industry. (Short films, called "films of art and essay," of which over three hundred were funded from 1950 to 1960, were virtually the only mode of entry for apprentice directors. The French distribution system demanded such short films because double features had been prohibited since before the war.) But in 1959, the laws relating to aid for film productions were changed to allow first films to be funded by the state on the basis of a submitted script alone, enabling hundreds of new filmmakers to become their own producers and creating the economic context for the New Wave. Moreover, the international commercial success of films like *Les Quatre-cents coups*, which was produced for 75 thousand dollars and brought 500 thousand dollars for its American distribution rights alone, dramatically increased the number of private producers willing to finance new work. Thus, for a while at least, until the failures mounted, Truffaut's concept of *un cinéma d'auteurs* was realized in France by placing the control of the conception of a film in the same hands that controlled the actual production. As Steve Lipkin has remarked: "The New Wave was . . . not only a new style of making films, it was also . . . a way of producing a 'personally' created work—in direct opposition to the more formulaic establishment output of the preceding years." ("The New Wave and the Post-War Film Economy," *Current Research in Film: Audiences, Economies, and Law*, vol. 2. ed. Bruce A. Austin [Norwood, N.J.: Ablex, 1986], pp. 156–85, p. 183.)

p. 561 Franscope . . . CinemaScope: For a convincing argument that in his first three features Truffaut became a major innovator of widescreen composition, see Richard T. Jameson's moving eulogy, "Wild Child, Movie Master," *Film Comment* 21,1 (January–February 1985): 34–41. At present 16mm prints of these films are generally unavailable in their original anamorphic formats.

p. 561 Truffaut . . . book-length interview with Alfred Hitchcock: Truffaut's book was updated and revised as *Hitchcock*, by François Truffaut with the collaboration of Helen G. Scott (New York: Simon and Schuster, 1983).

p. 562 fn. Almendros . . . Schroeder: Almendros has also worked with Maurice Pialat, Jean Eustache, Roberto Rossellini, Jack Nicholson, Robert Benton, and Alan Pakula.

In 1984 Almendros wrote and directed with Orlando Jiminez-Leal *Improper Conduct*, a documentary about the suppression of civil rights—specifically those of homosexuals—in Castro's Cuba. See his autobiography, *A Man with a Camera*, trans. Rachel Phillips Belash, with a preface by Truffaut (New York: Farrar, Straus, Giroux, 1984).

p. 564 Coutard . . . director of photography: Coutard (b. 1924) would later try his hand at direction in the polemical documentaries *Hoa Binh* (1970), shot in Vietnam, and *Le Legion saute sur Kolwezi* (English title: *Operation Leopard*, 1980), shot in Zaire. *S.A.S. à San Salvador* (*S.A.S.—Terminate with Extreme Prejudice*, 1982) was his first narrative feature.

p. 567 Godard . . . capitalism in its purest form: Godard is quoted in Georges Sadoul, *Dictionary of Film Makers* (Berkeley: University of California Press, 1972), p. 101.

p. 568 fn. Brecht's . . . theories of theater: See Hans-Bernhard Moeller, "Brecht and 'Epic' Film Medium: The Cinéaste Playwright/Film Theoretician and His Influence," *Wide Angle* 3, 4 (Winter 1980); and George Lellis, *Bertolt Brecht, Cahier du Cinema, and Contemporary Film Theory* (Ann Arbor, Mich.: UMI Research Press, 1982).

p. 568 fn. political crisis in May 1968: See Sylvia Harvey, *May '68 and Film Culture* (London: British Film Institute, 1978). And, for a personal summary of leftist politics during the sixties by an intensely committed filmmaker who participated in them, see Chris Marker's *Le Fond de l'aire est rouge* (Paris, 1979).

p. 569 Roy Armes puts it: Roy Armes, *French Film* (New York: E. P. Dutton, 1970), p. 140.

p. 569 Gorin in 1973: Gorin, who frequently co-directed with Godard between 1968 and 1973, has since become a filmmaker in his own right with the American-West German feature *Poto and Cabengo* (1979), a fascinating documentary about the effects of language on children, and the French-British coproduction *Routine Pleasures* (1986), which intercuts a study of model-railroad enthusiasts with paintings by American film critic Manny Farber.

p. 569 Godard . . . contradictory perspectives: Godard's most easily discernible influence in the seventies was upon the materialist cinema of Jean-Marie Straub and Danièle Huillet, his wife (discussed in Chapter 18); upon the omnibus film essays of Hans-Jürgen Syberberg; and upon the extraordinary work of Belgian filmmaker Chantal Akerman (b. 1950), creator of *Jeanne Dielman, 23 quai de Commerce, 1080 Bruxelles* (1977); *News from Home* (1977); *Les Rendez-vous d'Anna* (*The Meetings of Anna*, 1978), which won the Best Director Prize at the 1978 Paris Film Festival; *Toute une nuit* (1982); *Les Années 80* (1983); *L'Homme a la valise* (1984); and *Golden Eighties* (1986).

Before Akerman, the best-known name in Belgian cinema was that of Henri Storck (b. 1907), a former assistant to Jean Vigo who established an international reputation with the socially committed documentaries *L'Histoire du soldat inconnu* (*The Story of the Unknown Soldier*, 1932), *Borinage* (*Misery in the Borinage*, codirected with Joris Ivens, 1932), and *Les Maisons de la misere* (*Houses of Misery*, 1937), but who also became a leading figure in the feature film *Le Banquet des fraudeurs* (*The Smuggler's Banquet*, 1951) and the experimental avant-garde *La Fenetre ouverte* (*The Open Window*, 1952). Storck helped to found both Belgium's Royal

Film Archive in 1938 and its film school at the Institut des Arts de Diffusion (IAD) in Brussels in 1962. Long dominated by the French and American industries, Belgian production came into its own in the seventies and the eighties in the work of such film school graduates as Harry Kummel (*Malpertius* [*Daughters of Darkness*, 1972]); André Delvaux (*Belle*, 1973; *Benvenuta*, 1983; *Babel Opera*, 1985; *L 'Oeuvre au noir* [*The Abyss*, 1988]); Thierry Michel (*Hiver 60*, 1983); Patrick Le Bon (*Zaman*, 1983); Marion Hansel (*Le Lit* [*The Bed*, 1983]; *Dust*, 1985; *Les Noces barbares* [*The Barbarous Wedding*, 1987]); and Peruvian-born Mary Jimenez (*Du Verbe aimer* [*The Word Love*, 1985]; *La Moitie de l' amour* [*Half of Love*, 1985]). During the eighties, a Flemish-language cinema emerged in the work of Hugo Claus (*Vrijdag* [*Friday*, 1980]); Jan Gruyaert (*De Vlaschaard* [*The Flax Field*, 1983]); and Marc Didden (*Brussels by Night*, 1983). Claus' one-million-dollar *De Leeuw van Vlaanderen* (*The Lion of Flanders*, 1984), an epic account of the Flemings' revolt against France and their victory at the Battle of the Golden Spurs in 1302, culminated Flemish cinema. At this writing, however, French and American films still account for 80 to 90 percent of box office receipts in Belgium.

p. 571 Resnais remarked, *Marienbad*: Resnais is quoted in Armes, *French Cinema Since 1946*, vol. 2, p. 123.

p. 573 Resnais . . . Eisenstein: Resnais is quoted in Peter Harcourt, "Alain Resnais," *Film Comment* 9, 6 (November–December 1973): 47.

p. 573 *The Technique of Film Editing*: Karel Reisz, *The Technique of Film Editing* (London: Focal Press; 1953).

p. 573 Chabrol . . . book on Hitchcock: Chabrol's book, written in collaboration with his *Cahiers* associate Eric Rohmer, was published in Paris in 1957. It is now available in English as *Hitchcock: The First Forty-four Years*, trans. Stanley Hochman (New York: 1979).

p. 576 Pauline Kael . . . major figure long ago: Pauline Kael, *Deeper into Movies* (Boston: Little, Brown, 1973), p. 307.

p. 578 Rivette's film, they wrote: Quotation about Rivette's film appears in Georges Sadoul, *Dictionary of Films*, trans. and ed. Peter Morris (Berkeley: University of California Press, 1972), p. 274.

p. 582 Tanner . . . Swiss television: Lesser but still important Swiss French-language filmmakers are Clarisse Gabus (*Melancholy Baby*, 1979); Maya Simon (*Polenta*, 1980); Jean-Francois Amiguet (*Alexandre*, 1983); Pierce Maillard (*Campo Europa*, 1984); Francis Reusser (*Derborence*, 1985); Richard Dembo (*La Diagonale du fou* [*Dangerous Moves*, 1986]); Jean-Pierre Menoud (*Jour et nuit* [*Day and Night*, 1986]); and Denis Berry (Last Song, 1986).

p. 585 post–New Wave directors . . . Kurys: French directors of note who have been less involved with the New Wave are: Jacques Deray (b. 1929): *Borsalino* (1974); *Un Papillon sur l'épaule* (*A Butterfly on the Shoulder*, 1978); *Un Printemps en hiver* (*A Springtime in Winter*, 1980; *Le Marginal* (*The Outsider*, 1983); *On ne meurts que deux fois* (*You Only Die Twice*, 1986); Yves Boisset (b. 1939): *L'Attentat* (*The Outrage/The French Conspiracy*, 1972); *Un Taxi mauve* (*A Mauve Taxi*, 1977; shot in Ireland); *La Clé sur la porte* (*The Key in the Door*, 1978); *La Femme flic* (*The Female Cop*, 1979); *Allons Z'enfants* (*The Boy Soldier*, 1981); *Le Prix du danger* (*The Prize of Peril*, 1983); *Canicule* (*Dog Day*, 1984);

Bleu comme l'enfer (*Blue Like Hell*, 1986); André Téchiné (b. 1943): *Souvenirs d'en France* (English title: *French Provincial*, 1975); *Barocco* (1977); *Les Soeurs Brontë* (*The Brontë Sisters*, 1978); *Hotel des Ameriques* (*Hotel of the Americas*, 1982); *Rendezvous* (1985); *Le Lieu de crime* (*The Scene of the Crime*, 1986); *Les Innocents* (*The Innocents*, 1988); Jean-Charles Tacchella (b. 1926): *Cousin, cousine* (1976); *Le pays bleu* (*Blue Country*, 1977); *Il y a longtemps que je t'aime* (*It's a Long Time I've Loved You*, 1979); *Soupçon* (1980); *Croque la vie* (*A Bite of Life*, 1982); *Escalier C* (*Staircase C*, 1985); *Travelling avant* (*Dolly In*, 1987—a feature about postwar cinephilia); Jean-Jacques Annaud: *La Victoire en chantant* (English title: *Black and White in Color*, 1976); *Coup de tête* (English title: *Hothead*, 1979); *Quest for Fire* (U.S., 1980) *The Name of the Rose* (W. German-Italian-French, 1986); Marguerite Duras (b. 1914): *India Song* (1975); *Des journées entières dans les arbres* (*Days in the Trees*, 1976); *Le Camion* (*The Truck*, 1977); *Le Navire night* (1980); *Aurelia Steiner* (1979); *Agatha et les lectures illimites* (1981); *L'Homme Atlantique* (1981); *Les Enfants* (*The Children*, 1985); Michel Deville (b. 1931): *Le Mouton enragé* (English titles: *Love at the Top/The French Way*, 1974); *L'Apprenti salaud* (*The Apprentice Bastard*, 1977); *Le Dossier 51* (1978—a film about surveillance shot entirely with a subjective camera); *Le Voyage en douce* (English title: *Sentimental Journey*, 1979); *Eaux profondes* (*Deep Water*, 1981); *Le Petite bande* (*The Little Bunch*, 1983); *Peril en la deneuve* (*Danger in the House*, 1985); *Le Paltoquet* (*The Nonentity*, 1986); Gérard Blain (b. 1930): *Les Amis* (*The Friends*, 1971); *Le Pelican* (*The Pelican*, 1973); *Un Enfant dans le foule* (*A Child in the Crowd*, 1976); *Utopia* (1978); *Le Rebelle* (*The Rebel*, 1980); *Pierre et Djemila* (1986); Pierre Kast (b. 1920): *Le Soleil en face* (*Face to the Sun*, 1980); Jacques Doillon: *La Femme qui pleure* (*The Crying Woman*, 1979); *La Drôlesse* (*The Hussy*, 1980); *La Fille prodigne* (*The Prodigal Daughter*, 1981); *La Pirate* (1984); *La Vie de famille* (*Family Life*, 1985); *La Tentation d'Isabelle* (*The Temptation of Isabelle*, 1985); *Comedie!* (1987); Coline Serreau: *Pourquoi pas!* (*Why Not!*, 1979); *Mais qu'est-ce qu'elles veulent?* (*But What Do These Women Want?*, 1979); *Qu'est-ce qu'on attend pour etre heureux!* (*What're We Waiting For to Be Happy!*, 1982); *Trois hommes et un coffin* (*Three Men and a Basket*, 1985); Christine de Chalonge (b. 1937): *L'Argent des autres* (*Other People's Money*, 1987); *Malevil* (1981); Pierre Schoendoerffer (b. 1928): *The Anderson Platoon* (U.S., 1967); *Le Crabe tambour* (*The Crab Drum*, 1977); *L'Honneur d'un capitaine* (*A Captain's Honor*, 1982); René Allio (b. 1924): *La Vieille dame indigne* (*The Shameless Old Lady*, 1964); *L'Une et l'autre* (1967); *Rude journee pour la reine* (1973); *Moi, Pierre Rivère, ayant égorgé ma mere, ma soeur, et mon frere* (*I, Pierre Rivère, Have Butchered My Mother, My Sister, and My Brother*, 1978); *Retour a Marseille* (*Return to Marseille*, 1980); *Le Matelot* (*The Seaman*, 1985); Yannick Bellon (b. 1924): *Un Viol d'amour* (*A Rape of Love*, 1977). *L'Amour un* (*Naked Love*, 1981); *La Triche* (*The Cheat*, 1984); René Gainville: *L'Associé* (*The Associate*, 1979); Alain Cavelier (b. 1931): *Ce répondeur ne prend pas de message* (*This Ans-wering Service Takes No Messages*, 1979); *Un Etrange voyage* (English title: *On the Track*, 1981); *Therese* (1986); Jean-Louis Comolli: *La Cecilia* (1978); *L'Ombre rouge* (*The Red Shadow*, 1981); *Balles perdues* (*Stray Bullets*, 1983); Édouard Molinaro (b.

1928): *L'Homme pressé* (*Man in a Hurry*, 1977); *La Cage aux folles* (English title: *Birds of a Feather*, 1978); *Palace* (1985); *L'Amour en douce* (*Love on the Quiet*, 1985); Paul Vecchiali (b. 1930): *Corps à coeur* (*Body to Heart*, 1979); *C'est la vie!* (*That's Life*, 1980); *En haute des marches* (*At the Top of the Stairs*, 1983); *Rosa-la-Rose, fille publique* (*Rosa-the-Rose, Public Woman*, 1986); Michel Drach (b. 1930): *Les Violons du bal* (*Violins of the Ball*, 1974); *Le Passé simple* (English title: *Replay*, 1977); *Le Pull-over rouge* (*The Red Sweater*, 1979); Christine Pascal: *Félicité* (1979); Nelly Kaplan (b. 1934): *La Fiancée du pirate* (English title: *A Very Curious Girl* (1969); *Néa* (1976); *Le Satellite de Vénus* (*The Satellite of Venus*, 1977); *Au bonheur des dames* (*To the Good Luck of Ladies*, 1979); Luc Béaud: *La Tortue sur le dos* (*Turtle on Its Back*, 1979); *Plein sud* (*Heading South*, 1981); Jean-François Stevénin: *La Passe-Montagne* (*The Mountain Pass*, 1979); *Doubles messieurs*, 1986; Jean-Pierre Denis: *Histoire d'Adrien* (*The Story of Adrien*, 1980); *La Palombiere* (*The Bird Watch*, 1983); *Champ d'honneur* (*Field of Honor*, 1987); Jacques Bral: *Exteriur nuit* (*Exterior Night*, 1980); *Polar*, 1982; the great contemporary stage director Ariane Mnouchkine: *1789*, 1977; the four-hour *Molière* (produced by Claude Lelouch, 1978); Michel Lang (b. 1939): *A nous les petites anglaises* (1975); *L'Hôtel de la plage* (*The Hotel on the Beach*, 1978); *L'Etincelle* (*Tug of Love*, 1984); Jean-Jacques Beineix: *Diva* (1981); *La Lune dans le caniveau* (*The Moon in the Gutter*, 1983); *37.2 Le matin* (English-language title: *Betty Blue*, 1986); Claude Berri: *Un Moment d'engarement* (*One Wild Moment*, 1977); *Je vous aime* (*I Love You*, 1981); *Le Maître d'école* (*The Schoolmaster*, 1981); *Tchao Pantin* (*So Long, Sucker*, 1983); *Jean de Florette* (1986) and *Manon des sources* (*Manon of the Springs*, 1986), a magnificent two-film adaptation of a two-volume novel by Marcel Pagnol; Daniel Vigne: *Le Retour of Martin Guerre* (*The Return of Martin Guerre*, 1982); *Une Femme ou deux* (*One Woman or Two*, 1985); the American Bob Swaim: *La Nuit de Saint-Germain-des-Prés* (1977); *La Balance* (*The Nark*, 1983); *Masquerade* (U.S., 1988); Jean-Louis Bertuccelli: *Ramparts of Clay* (French-Tunisian, 1971); *Lucie sur Seine/Interdit aux moins de 13 ans* (1982); *Stress* (1984); Gerard Oury: *L'As des as* (1982); *Le Vengeance du serpent à plumes* (*The Vengeance of the Winged Serpent*, 1984); Claude Zidi: *Les Ripoux* (English-language title: *My New Partner*, 1984); *Les Rois du Gag* (*The Gag King*, 1985); Catherine Binet: *Les jeux de la comtesse Dolingen de Gratz* (*The Games of the Countess Dolingen of Gratz*, 1981); Alexandre Arcady: *Le Coup de Sirocco* (1979); *Le Grand Carnival* (*The Big Carnival*, 1983); Luc Besson: *Le Dernièr combat* (*The Final Battle*, 1982); *Subway* (1985); Claude

Feraldo (b. 1936): *Deus lions au soleil* (*Two Lions in the Sun*, 1980); Christopher Frank: *Femmes de personne* (*Nobody's Women*, 1984); *Spirale* (1987); Laurent Heyne-mann: *Il Faut tuer Birgitt Haas* (*Kill Birgitt Haas*, 1981); *Stella* (1983); *Les Mois d'avril sont meurtriers* (*April Is a Deadly Month*, 1987); Benoit Jacquot (b. 1947): *Les Enfants de placard* (1977); *Les Ailes de la colombe* (*The Wings of the Dove*, 1981; adapted from Henry James); *Corps et biens* (*With All Hands*, 1986); Laurent Perrin: *Passage sécret* (*Secret Passage*, 1985); *Buisson ardent* (*Burning Bush*, 1987). Also worth noting is the work of two militantly independent French avant-garde filmmakers—Marcel Hanoun (*L'Authentique procés de Carl Emmanuel Jung* [1966]; *L'Été* [1968]; *L'Hiver* [1969]; *Le Printemps* [1970]; *L'Automne* [1972]; *La Verité sur imaginaire passion d'un inconnu* [1974]; *Le Régard* [1976]; *La Nuit claire* [1978]) and Philippe Garrel (*Marie pour memoire* [1967]; *La Concentration* [1968]; *Le Révelateur* [1969]; *La Cicatrice interieure* [1972]; *L'Enfant sécret* [codirected with Anne Wiazemsky, 1983]; *Liberté, la nuit* [1984])—both of whom have a hard-core following of critics. Newcomers to the commercial field include: Bertrand Van Effenterre: *Le Batârd* (*The Bastard*, 1983); Patrick Chaput: *La Bête noir* (1983); the Algerian-born gypsy Tony Gatlif: *Les Princes* (*The Princes*, 1983); *Rue du départ* (*Street of Departures*, 1986); Francis Girod: *Le Bon plasir* (1984); *Descente aux enfers* (*Descent into Hell*, 1986); Leos Carax: *Boy Meets Girl* (1984); *Mauvais sang* (*Bad Blood*, 1986); Jean-Loup Hubert: *La Smala* (*The Tribe*, 1984); Virginie Thevenet: *La Nuit porte jarretelles* (*The Night Wears Suspenders*, 1985); Jean-Pierre Limosin: *Gardien de la nuit* (*Night Guardian*, 1986); Juliet Berto: *Le Havre* (1986); Marie-Claude Treilhou: *Il était une fois la télé* (*Once Upon a Time There Was Television*, 1986); Thomas Gilou: *Black Mic-Mac* (*Black Hanky-Panky*, 1986); Monique Dartonne and Michel Kaptur: *High Speed* (1986); Regis Wargnier: *La Femme de ma vie* (*The Woman of My Life*, 1986); Sebastien Grail: *La Femme sécrete* (*The Secret Wife*, 1986); Claire Devers: *Noir et blanc* (*Black and White*, 1986); Gerard Krawczyk: *Je hais les acteurs* (*I Hate Actors*, 1986); Patrice Chereau: *Hôtel de France* (1987); and Genevieve Lefebvre: *Le Jupon rouge* (*The Red Skirt*, 1987).

p. 586 SLON: The best information in English on this little-known but important group is William F. Van Wert, "Chris Marker: The SLON Films," *Film Quarterly* 32, 3 (Spring 1979): 38–46.

p. 587 *Le Chagrin et la pitié* . . . much attention: See Stanley Hoffmann, "Introduction" to *The Sorrow and the Pity* (New York: Grove Press, 1972).

New Cinemas in Britain
and the English-Speaking Commonwealth

p. 590 Michael Powell . . . Emeric Pressburger: Powell and, to a lesser extent; Pressburger are currently enjoying a revival of critical interest. Among the British cinema's few indisputable *auteurs*, Powell began his career in the early thirties by directing formulaic "quota quickies" for the independent producer Jerome Jackson under the terms of the Cinematograph Film Act (see Chapter 9), but he soon established a critical reputation with such unique films as *The Edge of the World* (1938), a mystical tale of love and death set on the remote Shetland island of Foula, and the fast-paced espionage thriller *The Spy in Black* (1939), his first collaboration with the Hungarian-born scenarist Pressburger and the producer Alexander Korda. Powell then made two semidocumentary war films for the Ministry of Information—*49th Parallel* (1941) and *One of Our Aircraft is Missing* (1942).

Powell and Pressburger formed their own production company, The Archers, in 1942. Although both men shared screen credit for writing, producing, and directing The Archers's films, in fact Pressburger dominated the writing and Powell the directing. Eccentric Archers classics are *The Life and Death of Colonel Blimp* (1943), *A Canterbury Tale* (1944), *I Know Where I'm Going* (1945), *A Matter of Life and Death* (also known as *Stairway to Heaven*, 1946), and the remarkable *Black Narcissus* (1947), a bizarre tale of Anglican nuns becoming unhinged by paganism in a Himalayan

mission which won an Academy Award for Jack Clayton's Technicolor cinematography. Archers also produced the two immensely successful ballet films described in the text. Several productions undertaken for Alexander Korda's London Films—the expressionistic *The Small Back Room* (also known as *Hour of Glory*, 1949), an adaptation of Mary Webb's passionate rural romance, *Gone to Earth* (1950; extensively reshot by Rouben Mamoulian for American release as *The Wild Heart*), and *The Elusive Pimpernel* (1951)—proved to be commercial disasters for The Archers. The company disbanded in 1957 after several more financially unsuccessful productions, including *Oh Rosalinda!!* (1955), an updated version of Strauss's opera *Die Fledermaus*, and the absorbing World War II films *The Battle of the River Platte* (also known as *The Pursuit of the Graf Spee*, 1956) and *Ill Met by Moonlight* (also known as *Night Ambush*, 1957). On his own once more, Powell produced a deeply disturbing masterpiece in *Peeping Tom* (1959), a film so universally reviled on its initial release that it effectively ended the director's British career. In it, Carl Boehm plays Mark, a sexual psychopath who works in a commercial film studio as a focus-puller during the day and murders women at night while simultaneously filming their deaths in tight facial closeup. For this, he uses a 16mm camera rigged with a lethal blade in its tripod and a rear-view mirror that forces his victims to witness and react to their own deaths. This voyeuristic psychosis is shown to have its origins in a horrendous form of child abuse. Mark's psychologist father, played by Powell himself, had used him as a guinea pig for experiments in terror, filming his reactions in the process. In a narrative whose complexity is worthy of Resnais, Powell structures *Peeping Tom* as a series of films within films: those Mark works on at his studio job; those he takes of his victims—both as he sees them in color through his viewfinder at the moment of their deaths and as he later projects them for his pleasure in black and white; those his father has taken of him as a child; and so on. Inevitably, Mark completes the "documentary" begun by his father by committing suicide with his camera while filming it, bringing to full circle this elaborate, brilliant, and profoundly depressing essay on the perverse pleasures of the cinema. *Peeping Tom* is heir to the mantle of *Vertigo* and clear progenitor of *Psycho*, although the mutual influence was denied by both Powell and Hitchcock.

Powell directed several films of modest ambition in Yugoslavia and Australia before ending his career in a reunion with Pressburger in 1972 to produce *The Boy Who Turned Yellow*, a fifty-five–minute fantasy for the Children's Film Foundation. *A Life in the Movies*, the first volume of Powell's autobiography, was published in London by Heinemann in 1986. See also, John Russell Taylor, "Michael Powell: Myths and Supermen," *Sight and Sound* 47, 4 (Autumn 1978): 226–29; David Badder, "Powell and Pressburger: The War Years," *Sight and Sound* 28, 1 (Winter 1978–79): 8–13; Harlan Kennedy and Nigel Andrews, "Peerless Powell," *Film Comment* 15, 3 (May–June 1979): 49–55; Eliott Stein, " 'A Very Tender Film, a Very Nice One': Michael Powell's *Peeping Tom*," *Film Comment* 15, 5 (September–October 1979): 57–59; *Powell, Pressburger, and Others*, ed. Ian Christie (London: British Film Institute 1978); *Arrows of Desire: The Films of Michael Powell and Emeric Pressburger* (London: Waterstone Press, 1985) "Michael Powell (1905–90)," *Film Comment* 26, 3 (May–June 1990): 26–43; and Harlan Kennedy, "A Modest Magician," *American Film* 15, 10 (July 1990): 32–37.

p. 591 *Sequence* . . . assumption of British cinema: Sequence quoted in David Robinson, *The History of World Cinema* (New York: Stein & Day, 1973), p. 292.

p. 598 Losey . . . Harold Pinter: For a detailed account of the Losey-Pinter collaboration, see Beverle Houston and Marsha Kinder, "The Losey-Pinter Collaboration," *Film Quarterly* 32, 1 (Fall 1978): 17–30. See also Christopher C. Hudgins, "Inside Out: Filmic Technique and the Creation of Consciousness in Harold Pinter's *Old Times*," *Genre* 13, 3 (Fall 1980): 355–76. Pinter adapted a number of his own plays to the screen, including *The Caretaker* (American title: *The Guest*; Clive Donner, 1964), *The Birthday Party* (William Friedkin, 1968), *The Homecoming* (Peter Hall, 1973), and *Betrayal* (David Jones, 1983), and he directed an excellent version of Simon Gray's comedy *Butley* (1974) for the American Film Theater.

p. 606 Channel 4 . . . medium-budget features: The cinemas of Ireland, Scotland, and Wales were more or less colonized by English and American films until the eighties, when these countries began efforts to establish film cultures of their own. The Ardmore Studios had been built near Dublin in 1959, and the Irish Film Finance Commission (IFFC) was set up to attract foreign investment. But no specific provisions were made for the production of Irish films or the employment of Irish personnel, so that Ireland largely became a site for international coproductions like David Lean's *Ryan's Daughter* (1971) and John Boorman's *Zardoz* (1973) over the next few decades. In 1980, however, an Irish Film Board (IFB) was set up to help support independent production and its first film, funded in association with Channel Four Television, was Neil Jordan's dark political thriller *Angel* (1982), set in Northern Ireland. Other successful IFB productions have been *The Outcasts* (Robert Wynne-Simmonds, 1983), *Pigs* (Cathal Black, 1984), *The End of the World Man* (Bill Miskelly, 1985), *Eat the Peach* (Peter Ormrod, 1986), *The Fantasist* (Robin Hardy, 1986), and *Reefer and the Model* (Joe Comerford, 1988). (Another film, *Cal* [Pat O'Connor, 1984], was financed by David Puttnam; it was Ireland's official Cannes entry for the year.)

Scotland has been the home of the Edinburgh International Film Festival since 1947, but it, too, had failed to evolve a national film culture until the eighties, when Channel Four began to invest in regional production there. The network's chairman, Scottish-born Neil Isaacs, had been a producer for Scottish Television in the seventies, and at Channel Four he commissioned the production of several notable films utilizing native talent, including *Living Apart Together* (Charles Gormley), *Hero* (Barney Platts-Mill, 1982)—a medieval tale shot entirely in Gaelic—Michael Radford's *Another Time, Another Place* (1983), the documentary *Ill Fares the Land* (Bill Bryden, 1983), and Murray Grigor's radically deconstructive *Scotch Myths—the Movie* (1983). At the same time, the Scottish Film Production Fund was established by the Scottish Film Council, and Scotland received international recognition for the films of Bill Forsyth (b. 1948)—*That Sinking Feeling*, 1979; *Gregory's Girl*, 1981; *Local Hero*, 1982; *Comfort and Joy*, 1984; *Housekeeping*, 1988; and *Breaking In*, 1989—whose work has achieved that rare combination, commercial and critical success.

In Wales, Channel Four has produced both *Giro City* (also known as *Nothing but the Truth*; Karl Francis, 1982) and *Milwr Bychan* (*Boy Soldier*; Karl Francis, 1986). The small native industry has produced a handful of interesting Welsh-language films—*Yr Alcoholig Lion* (*The Happy Alcoholic*; Karl Francis, 1984); *Aderyn Papur* (. . . *And Pigs Might Fly*; Stephen Bayly, 1984), and *Rhosyn a Rhith* (*Coming Up Roses*; Stephen Bayly, 1986). See Kevin Rockett, Luke Gibbons, and John Hill, *Cinema and Ireland* (Syracuse, N.Y.: Syracuse University Press, 1988); Anthony Slide, *The Cinema and Ireland* (Jefferson, N.C.: McFarland & Company, 1988); Brian McIlroy, *World Cinema 4: Ireland* (London: Flicks Books, 1988); *Scotch Reels: Scotland in Cinema and Television*, ed. Colin McArthur (London: BFI, 1982); Steve McIntyre, "New Images of Scotland," *Screen* 25, 1 (January–February 1984): 53–59; John Brown, "A Suitable Job for a Scot," *Sight and Sound* 52, 3 (Summer 1983): 157–63; and "Land Beyond Brigadoon," *Sight and Sound* 53, 1 (Winter 1983/84): 40–46; Scott L. Malcomson, "Modernism Comes to the Cabbage Patch: Bill Forsyth and the 'Scottish Cinema,' *Film Quarterly* 38, 3 (Spring 1985): 16–21; *British Cinema Now*, eds. Martyn Auty and Nick Roddick (London: BFI, 1985); Alastair Michie, "Scotland: Strategies of Centralisation," in *All Our Yesterdays: 90 Years of British Cinema*, ed. Charles Barr (London: BFI, 1986), pp. 252–71.

p. 607 other British filmmakers . . . broad spectrum of styles and themes: See Harlan Kennedy, "The British Are Coming,"

Film Comment 16, 3 (May–June 1980): 57–60; Joseph Coencas, "British Film Renaissance," *Millimeter* 8, 5 (June 1980): 118–23; P. Ruby Rich, "The Very Model of a Modern Minor Industry," *American Film* (May 1983): 47–64; Anne Ross Muir, "The British Film Industry: Dead or Alive?" *Cineaste* 12, 3 (1983): 12–15; Andrew Higson, "Space, Place, Spectacle: Landscape and Townscape in the 'Kitchen Sink' Film," *Screen* 25, 4–5 (July–October 1984): 2–21; James Park, *Learning to Dream: The New British Cinema* (London: Faber and Faber, 1984); John Walker, *The Once and Future Film: British Cinema in the Seventies and Eighties* (London: Methuen, 1985); Vincent Porter, *On Cinema* (London: Pluto Press, 1985); *British Cinema Now*, eds. Martyn Auty and Nick Roddick (London: BFI, 1985); Harlan Kennedy, "The Brits Have Gone Nuts," *Film Comment* 21, 4 (July–August 1985): 51–55; Raymond Durgnat, "The Ploughman's (Just) Desserts," *American Film* (November 1985): 48–54, 80; David Thomson, "Listen to Britain," *Film Comment* 22, 3 (April 1986): 56–63; John Wyver, "The English Channel 4," *American Film* (July/August 1986): 46–49; John Hill, *Sex, Class and Realism: British Cinema 1956–1963* (London: BFI, 1986); *All Our Yesterdays: 90 Years of British Cinema*, ed. Charles Barr (London: BFI, 1986); Paul Swann, *The Hollywood Feature Film in Postwar Britain* (New York: St. Martin's Press, 1987); and Harlan Kennedy, "Whither Britain?" *Film Comment* 12, 1 (February 1987), 50–51.

p. 609 Australia . . . authentic national cinema: For Australian background see Robert Hughes, *The Fatal Shore: The Epic of Australia's Founding* (New York: Knopf, 1987). The Australian film industry's major trade journal is *Cinema Papers*, published bimonthly in Melbourne. There is a major international film festival held each June in Sydney, as well as smaller ones in Melbourne and in Wellington, New Zealand.

p. 614 Paul Cox . . . Australia: See David Stratton, *The Last New Wave: The Australian Film Revival* (Sydney: Angus and Robertson, 1980); Andrew Pike and Ross Cooper, *Australian Film 1900–1977: A Guide to Feature Film Production; The New Australian Cinema*, ed. Scott Murray (Melbourne: Nelson, 1980); Eric Reade, *History and Heartburn: The Saga of Australian Film, 1896–1978* (Rutherford, N.J.: Associated University Presses, 1981); *Australian Motion Picture Yearbook 1983*, ed. Peter Beilby and Ross Lansell (Melbourne: 4 Seasons, 1983); David White, *Australian Movies to the World: The International Success of Australian Films since 1970* (Melbourne: Fontana, 1984); Sue Matthews, *35mm Dreams: Conversations with Five Directors about the Australian Film Revival* (Victoria; Penguin, 1984); Graham Shirley and Brian Adams, *Australian Cinema: The First Eighty Years* (Sydney: Angus and Robertson, 1983; New York: St. Martin's 1985); Dermody Susan and Elizabeth Jacka, *The Screening of Australia: Anatomy of a Film Industry*, vol. 1 (Sydney: Currency Press, 1987), and *The Screening of Australia: Anatomy of a National Cinema*, vol. 2 (Sydney: Currency Press, 1988); Brian McFarlane, *Australian Cinema 1970–1985* (London: Secker and Warburg, 1987); Glen Lewis, *Australian Movies and the American Dream* (New York: Praeger, 1987); Annette Blonski, Barbara Creed, and Freda Freiberg, *Don't Shoot Darling! Women's Independent Filmmaking in Australia* (Richmond, Australia: Greenhouse, 1987); Robert Hughes, *The Fatal Shore: The Epic of Australia's Founding* (New York: Knopf, 1987); *The Imaginary Industry: Australian Film in the Late '80s*, eds. Susan Dermody and Elizabeth Jacka (North Ryde, NSW: Australian Film, Television, and Radio School Publications, 1988); and Harlan Kennedy, "The New Wizards of Oz," *Film Comment* 25, 5 (September–October, 1989): 73–77.

European Renaissance: West

p. 626 Foster Hirsch has put it: Foster Hirsch's Review of Amarcord, *Film Quarterly* 1, 29 (Fall 1975): 50.

p. 628 trilogy . . . modern world: Some critics see it as a tetralogy, extending through *Il deserto rosso*. See, for example, Seymour Chatman, *Antonioni, or, the Surface of the World* (Berkeley: University of California Press, 1985), and Sam Rhodie, *Antonioni* (London: BFI, 1990).

p. 630 *L'avventura* . . . Cannes premiere: Michelangelo Antonioni, *L'avventura* (New York: Grove Press, 1969), pp. 214–15.

p. 641 *Swept Away* . . . Sardinian isle: Other mainstream Italian directors who have done major work during the sixties, seventies, and eighties are Mario Monicelli (b. 1915—*Il bell Antonio*, 1960; *I compagni* (English title: *The Organizer*, 1963); *Un borghese piccolo piccolo* (*A Very Petty Bourgeois*, 1977); *Travels with Anita*, 1979; *Il Marchese del Grillo* (*The Marquis of Grillo*, 1982); *Bertoldo, Bertoldino, e Cacasenno*, 1984; *Le due vite di Mattia Pascal* (*The Two Lives of Mattia Pascal*, 1985, adapted from Pirandello, produced for RAI presentation); *Speriamo che sia femmina* (*Let's Hope It's a Girl*, 1986); *I Picari* (*The Picaros*, 1987); Dino Risi (b. 1916)—*Il sorpasso* (*The Easy Life*, 1962); *I mostri* (*The Monsters*, 1963); *Sesso matto* (*How Funny Can Sex Be?*, 1973); *I nuovi mostri* (*The New Monsters/Viva Italia*, 1977, codirected with Monicelli and Scola); *Caro papa* (*Dear Dad*, 1979); *Fantasma d'amore* (*Ghost of Love*, 1981); *Le bon roi Dagobert* (*Good King Dagobert*; 1984); *Un ragazzo e una ragazza* (*A Boy and a Girl*, 1984); *Scemo di guerra* (*Madmen at War*, 1985); Mauro Bolognini (b. 1923)—*La grand bourgeoisie/Fatti di gente perbene* (English title: *The Drama of the Rich*, 1974); *Dove vai in vacanze?* (*Where Are You Going on Holiday?*, 1978); *La vera storia della Signora delle Camelie* (*The True Story of Camille*, 1981); *La Veneziana* (*The Venetian Woman*, 1986); *Moscow addio* (*Moscow Farewell*, 1988); Mario Vicario—*La mogliamente* (*Wife-Mistress*, 1978); *Il cappotto di asktrakan* (*The Persian Lamb Coat*, 1980); Valerio Zurlini (1926–82)—*La prima notti di quiete* (*The First Night of Quiet*, 1972); *Il deserto dei tartari/Le Desert des tartares* (*The Desert of the Tartars*, 1976); Franco Zeffirelli (b. 1923)—*The Taming of the Shrew*, 1967; *Romeo and Juliet*, 1968; *Fratello sole, sorella luna* (*Brother Sun, Sister Moon*, 1973); *Gesu di Nazareth* (*Jesus of Nazareth*, 1977, produced for RAI presentation); *The Champ*, 1978; *Endless Love*, 1981; *La Traviata*, 1983; *Othello*, 1986; Dario Argento (b. 1943)—*L'ucello dalle piumi di cristallo* (*The Bird with the Crystal Plumage*, 1970); *Il gatto a nove coda* (*The Cat-o'Nine-Tails*, 1971); *Quattro mosche de velluto grigio* (*Four Flies on Black Velvet*, 1971); *Profondo rosso* (*Deep Red*, 1976); *Suspiria*, 1978; *Inferno*, 1979; *Tenebrae*, 1982; *Phenomena*, 1985; *Opera*, 1987; Franco Brusati (b. 1923)—*Pane e cioccolata* (*Bread and Chocolate*, 1974, released 1978); *Dimenticare Venezia* (*To Forget Venice*, 1980); *Il buon soldato* (*The Good Soldier*, 1982).

p. 642 *Julia e Julia* . . . 35mm distribution: Other Italian directors who have produced notable films in the eighties are Fabio Carpi—*Il quartetto basileus* (*The Basel Quartet*, 1982); Giuliana Berlinguer—*Il disertore* (*The Deserter*, 1983); Florian Furtwangler—*Tommaso Blu*, 1986; Caludio Sestieri—*Dolce assenza* (*Sweet Absence*); Francesco Maselli—*Storia d'amore* (*Love Story*, 1986); Giuseppe Ferrara—*Il caso Moro* (*The Moro Affair*, 1986); and Francesco Calogero—*La gentilezza del tocco* (*The Gentle Touch*, 1988).

p. 645 Paul Joannides has written: Paul Joannides, "The Aesthetics of the Zoom Lens," *Sight and Sound* 40, 1 (Winter 1970–71): 41.

p. 646 Future cinema . . . Joannides noted: Joannides, p. 41.

p. 646 Composing for the lens rather than for the frame: See John Belton and Lyle Tector, "The Bionic Eye: The Aesthetics of the Zoom," *Film Comment* 16, 5 (September–October 1980): 11–17: "Symptomatic of the evolution of film language since the New Wave, spatially distorting and inherently self-conscious, the zoom reflects the disintegration of cinematic codes developed before the Second World War." Without Belton's permission, this article was edited and rewritten by *Film Comment*'s editorial staff and was bylined collectively by the name "Lyle Tector"—a conflation of the two Gorch brothers' first names in Sam Peckinpah's *The Wild Bunch* (1969), one of the greatest films ever made with the zoom. The original, which is more scholarly and specific theoretically, appears as "The Bionic Eye: Zoom Esthetics" in *Cineaste* 10, 1 (Winter 1980–81): 20–27. See also Mark Schubin, "Lenses: The Depth of the Field," *Videography* (February 1986): 39–44.

p. 653 fn. other Swedish directors . . . native land: Arne Sucksdorf (b. 1917)—*My Home Is Copacabana* (*Mitt hem är Copacabana*, 1966), Bo Widerberg (b. 1930)—*Raven's End* (*Kvarteret korpen*, 1963); *Elvira Madigan*, 1967; *Adalen 31*, 1969; *The Ballad of Joe Jill* (Joe Hill, 1970); *Fimpen* (*Stubby*, 1974); *The Man on the Roof* (*Mannen på taket*, 1976); *Victoria*, 1979; the former actress Mai Zetterling (b. 1925)—*Loving Couples* (*Alskande par*, 1966); *Night Games* (*Nattlek*, 1967); *Dr. Glas* (*Doktor Glas*, 1968); *The Girls* (*Flickorna*, 1968); Vilgot Sjöman (b. 1924)—*My Sister, My Love* (*Syskonbädd*, 1966); *I Am Curious—Yellow* (*Jag är nyfiken—gul*, 1967); *I Am Curious—Blue* (*Jag är nyfiken—blå*, 1968); *Linus*, 1979; Jan Troell (b. 1931)—*Here Is Your Life* (*Här har du ditt liv*, 1966); *The Emigrants* (*Utvandrarna*, 1972); *The New Land* (*Nybyggarna*, 1973); *Zandy's Bride*, 1974; *The Hurricane*, 1979; the former Bergman actress Gunnel Lindblom (b. 1931)—*Paradise Place*, 1977; Christer Dahl—*The Score* (*Lyftet*, 1978); Kjell Grede (b. 1936)—*Harry Munter*, 1970; and Stefan Karl (b. 1941)—*A Respectable Life* (*Ett anständigt liv*, 1970). During the 1980s, film attendance declined sharply in Sweden due to the country's wholesale embrace of VCR technology, and the Swedish Film Institute became increasingly active in funding production by government mandate in 1982. Important films that have appeared from Sweden in this context are Kay Pollak's *Children's Island* (*Barnens o*, 1980) and *Love Me!* (*Älska mej!*, 1984); Gunnel Lindblom's *Sally and Freedom* (1981) and *Summer Nights on the Planet Earth* (*Sommar-*

kväller på jorden, 1987); Lárus Oskársson's *The Second Dance* (*Andra dansen*, 1982); Jan Troell's *The Flight of the Eagle* (*Ingenjor andrées luftfard*, 1982) and *Fairyland* (1987); Hans Alfredson's *The Simple-Minded Professor* (*Den enfaldige mördaren*, 1982), winner of the Silver Bear in Berlin, and *False as Water* (*Falsk som vatten*, 1985); Stefan Jarl's *Nature's Revenge* (*Naturens hämnd*, 1984) and *The Threat* (*Uhkkadus*, 1985); Agneta Elers-Jarleman's *Beyond Sorrow, Beyond Pain* (*Smärtgränsen*, 1983); Jon Lindström's *The Last Summer* (Den sista leken, 1984); Allan Edwall's *Åke and His World* (*Åke och has varld*, 1985); Christer Dahl's *At Last!* (*Antligen!*, 1985); Lasse Hallström's *My Life as a Dog* (*Mit liv som hund*, 1985), winner of the 1987 American Academy Award for Best Foreign Film; Mai Zetterling's *Amorosa* (1986); Bo Widerberg's *The Man from Majorca* (*Mannen fran Mallorca*, 1985) and *The Serpent's Way* (*Ormens väg på hälleberget*, 1987); Susan Osten's *The Mozart Brothers* (*Bröderna Mozart*, 1986); and Kjell Brede's *Hip, Hip Hurrah!* (1987). The Finnish writer/director Jöm Donner (b. 1933) played an important role in Swedish cinema during the sixties: as film critic for the Stockholm paper *Dagen nyheter* he ran a series of scathing attacks on Bergman; then he married one of Bergman's talented actresses, Harriet Andersson, and cast her in four features that he directed for Svensk Filmindustri—*A Sunday in September* (*Ensondag i september*, 1963); *To Love* (*Att älska*, 1964); *Adventure Starts Here* (*Här börjar äventyret*, 1965); and *Roof-Tree* (*Tvarbalk*, 1967). In 1967, Donner returned to Finland, where he directed several striking features—*Black on White* (*Mustaa valkoisella*, 1967); *69*, 1969. *Fuck Off! Images from Finland* (*Perkele! Kuvia suomesta*, 1971)—in the manner of Godard. He inspired a brief New Wave in the state-subsidized Finnish cinema, exemplified in the work of such young filmmaker as Risto Jarva (1934–77)—*Worker's Diary* (*Työmiehen päiväkirja*, 1967); *Rally* (*Bensaa suonissa*, 1970); *The Year of the Hare* (*Jäniksen vuosi*, 1977); Rauni Mollberg (b. 1929)—*Earth Is a Sinful Song* (*Maa on syntinen laulu*, 1973); *Pretty Good for a Human Being* (*Aika hyvä ihmiseksi*, 1977); *Milka*, 1980; and *The Unknown Soldier* (*Tuntematon sotilas*, 1985), a remake of Finland's most famous postwar film (the original was directed by Edvin Laine in 1955); Erkko Kivikoski (b. 1936)—*Gunshot in the Factory* (*Laukaus tehtaala*, 1973); Jaakko Pakkasvirta (b. 1934)—*Home for Christmas* (*Jouluksi kotiin*, 1975); *The Elegance of Life* (*Elämän koreus*, 1979); *Poet and Muse* (*Runoilija ja muusa*, 1979); *Sign of the Beast* (*Pedon Merkii*, 1981); Eija-Elina Bergholm—*Poor Maria* (*Marja pieni!*, 1972); Pirjo Honkasalo and Pekka Lehto—*Flame Top* (*Tulipaa*, 1980); Tapio Suominen—*Right On, Man!* (*Taalta tullaan, elama*, 1980); Marrku Lahmuskallio (b. 1938)—*The Raven's Dance* (*Korpinpolska*, 1980); *Skierri—Land of the Dwarf-Birch* (*Skierri—vaivaiskoivujen maa*, 1982); *Blue Mammy*, 1985; *Inusuk*, 1987; Anssi Mänttäri (b. 1941)—*The Holy Family*, 1976; *Toto*, 1982; *Regina and the Men*, 1983; *April Is the Cruelest Month*, 1983; *The Clock* (*Kello*, 1984); *Nothing But Love* (*Rakkauselokuva*, 1984); *Morena*, 1986; *The King Goes Forth to France*, 1986; *Goodbye, Farewell*, 1986; Mika (b. 1955) and Aki Kaurismäki (b. 1957)—*The Worthless* (*Arvottomat*, 1982; Mika); *Crime and Punishment* (*Rikos ja rangaistus*, 1983. Aki); *The Clan* (*Klanni*, 1984; Mika); *Calamari Union* (1985; Aki); *Rosso* (1985; Mika); *Shadows in Paradise* (*Varjoja paratiisissa*, 1986. Aki); *Helsinki-Napoli—All Night Long* (1987; Mika); *Hamlet* (1987; Aki);

and Lauri Törhönen (b. 1947)—*Burning Angel (Palava enkeli*, 1984); *The Undressing (Riisuminen*, 1986); *Tropic of Ice*, 1987. During the eighties, most Finnish production was subsidized by the state-owned Finish Film Foundation, a necessity for a nation of less than five million inhabitants which makes an average of twenty features annually. The Finns have recently experimented with coproduction (e.g., with the United States in *Born American*, Renny Harlin, 1985). Donner returned to Stockholm in 1972 and served as director of the Archive at the Swedish Film Institute until 1975. He has since completed a feature-length documentary on Bergman (*The Bergman File*, 1976), and has become a producer for several Young Swedish and Finnish filmmakers. In 1978 Donner was named president of the Swedish Film Institute; his most recent film as a director is the satiric Swedish-Finnish coproduction *Men Can't Be Raped (Män kan inte våldtas/Meistä ei voi raiskata*, 1979).

Of the other Scandinavian countries, Denmark, Norway, and Iceland all have small film industries. Denmark with its population of 5,200,000 produces 10–15 features annually; since 1981 its film industry has had the financial support of the Danish Film Institute, a department of the Ministry of Cultural Affairs. Major Danish directors of the past decade have been Erik Clausen (b. 1942)—*The Casablanca Circus (Cirkus Casablanca*, 1982); *Felix*, 1983; *Rocking Silver*, 1984; *The Man in the Moon (Manden i Manen*, 1986); *Rami and Julie*, 1987; Bille August (b. 1948)—*In My Life*, 1976; *Zappa*, 1983; *Twist and Shout*, 1984; *Pelle the Conqueror*, 1987; Soren Kragh-Jacobsen (b. 1947)—*Wanna See My Beautiful Navel?* 1978; *Rubber Tarzan*, 1981; *Icebirds (Isfugle*, 1983); *Emma*, 1987; Jon Bang Carlsen (b. 1940)—*A Fisherman in Hastholm*, 1977; *Nest Stop Paradise*, 1980; *Phoenix Bird (Flugl fonix*, 1985); *Ophelia Comes to Town (Ofelia kommer til byen*, 1985); *The Voyage to America*, 1988; and Lars von Trier (b. 1956)— *Element of Crime (Forbrydelsens element*, 1984); *Epidemic*, 1987. Denmark has also been the site of several recent coproductions (e.g., the Danish-French *The Wolf at the Door*, Henning Carlsen, 1986; *Babette's Feast*, Gabriel Axel, 1987, winner of the 1987 American Academy Award for Best Foreign Film, and *Pelle the Conqueror*, Bille August, winner of the 1988 Golden Palm at Cannes. Norway (population 4,150,000) gained international recognition in 1986 when director Oddver Einerson (b. 1949) won the Silver Lion at Venice for his first feature, *X* (1986); Vibeke Lokkeberg's *Skin (Hud)* was officially selected for Cannes' "Un Certain Regard"; and Ola Solum's (b. 1943) *Orion's Belt (Orions belte)* became the nation's first worldwide release. Norway's leading directors are Lasse Glomm (b. 1944)—*Black Crows (Savarte fugler*, 1984); *Northern Lights (Havlandet*, 1985); *Sweetwater*, 1987; Anja Breien (b. 1940)—*Wives (Hustruer*, 1975); *Witch Hunt (Forgoegelslen*, 1981); *Paper Bird (Papirfuglen*, 1984); *Wives—Ten Years After (Hustruer ti ar etter*, 1985); and Vibeke Lokkeberg (b. 1945)—*The Revelation (Alpenbaringen*, 1978); *The Betrayal/The Story of Kamilla (Loperjenten*, 1981); *Skin/The Wild One*, 1986. Notable recent coproductions are the Swedish-Soviet-Norwegian *Mio in the Land Far Away* (1987) and the Norwegian-Lapp epic, *Pathfinder (Ofelas*, Nils Gaup, 1987), the first Lapp-language feature and the second Norwegian-backed film to receive international distribution. Icelandic cinema remains a cottage industry, yet that a country of only 240,000 inhabitants

supports a film industry at all is nothing short of astounding. Iceland did not begin postwar production until 1977, but its breakthrough came in 1980 when a film by Agust Gudmundsson (b. 1947)— *Land and Sons (Land og synir)*—and one by Hrafn Gunnlaugsson's (b. 1948)—*Ancestral Estate (Odal fedranna)*—both concerned with the tensions between rural and urban society, were noted at several international festivals. Similar attention was accorded Gudmundsson's rock musical *On Top (Men allt a hre inu*, 1982) and Gunnlaugsson's saga-inspired Viking epic *When the Raven Flies (Hrafninn flygus*, 1984), both of which also became domestic smash hits. Other Icelandic directors are Thrainn Bertelsson (b. 1944)—*Pastoral Life*, 1984—and Thorsteinn Johnsson (b. 1946)—*The Atomic Station (Atomstodin*, 1984). Iceland now produces an average of four features per year, all receiving some support from the government-sponsored Icelandic Film Fund. See Stig Björkman, *Film in Sweden: The New Directors* (London: Tantivy Press, 1976); Brian McIlroy, *World Cinema 2: Sweden* (London: Flicks Books, 1986); Ingmar Bergman, *The Magic Lantern: An Autobiography* (London: Hamish Hamilton, 1988); Jim Hillier, *Cinema in Finland: An Introduction* (London: BFI, 1975); Peter Cowie, *Finnish Cinema* (London: Tantivy Press, 1976); and William Fisher, "Aki Kaurismäki Goes Business," *Sight and Sound* 58, 4 (Autumn 1989): 252–55.

p. 653 Bergman . . . has declared many times: Ingmar Bergman, "Self-Analysis of a Film-Maker," *Films and Filming* (September 24, 1956), p. 19.

p. 655 glory of God . . . he has written: Ingmar Bergman. "Introduction: Bergman Discusses his Film-Making," is *Four Screenplays*, trans. Lars Malstrom and David Kushner (New York: Simon and Schuster, 1960), p. xxii.

p. 659 fn. Palme d'Or . . . Marshall Plan: Both Bardem and Berlanga during the Franco era made interesting satirical films *Muerte de un ciclista (Death of a Cyclist*, Bardem 1955), winner of the International Critics Award at Cannes; and *El Verdugo (The Executioner*, Berlanga, 1963), but neither could effect the rejuvenation of Spanish national cinema for which they had hoped. Later, Berlanga returned from self-imposed exile in France to direct *La escopeta nacional (The National Shotgun*, 1977), a satire on the final years of the Franco dictatorship, and several popular sequels, while Bardem made such post-Franco political thrillers as *Siete dias de enero (Seven Days in January*, 1978) without much success. During the sixties, Carlos Saura (b. 1932) established himself as Spain's leading resident director with a series of black comedies clearly influenced by Buñuel: *La caza (The Hunt*, 1963); *Peppermint Frappé*, 1967; *El jardín de las delicias (The Garden of Delights*, 1970). During the crucial decade of the seventies—which witnessed the death of Franco in 1975, the first free elections in over forty years and the abolition of censorship in 1977, and the approval of a democratic constitution in 1978—Saura directed *Ana y los lobos (Ana and the Wolves*, 1972), *La prima Angélica (Cousin Angelica*, 1973), *Cría cuervos (Raise Ravens*, 1975), *Elisa, vida mia (Elise, My Life*, 1977), *Los ojos vendados (Blindfolded Eyes/Blindfolded*, 1978), and *Mama cumple 100 años (Mama Turns 100*, 1979). Today Saura is clearly a major international figure with such recent award-winning films to his credit as *Deprisa, Deprisa (Hurry, Hurry*, 1980), the Antonio Gades dance trilogy *Boldas de sangre (Blood*

Wedding, 1981, adapted from Lorca's verse tragedy), *Carmen* (1983, adapted from Bizet's opera), and *El amor brujo* (*A Love Bewitched*, 1986, adapted from Manuel de Falla's ballet), and *El Dorado* (1988), an historical epic of the conquistador Lope de Aguirre's ill-fated expedition up the Amazon in 1560 (also the subject of Werner Herzog's *Aguirre, the Wrath of God*, 1972). Saura was, with Jose Luis Borau (b. 1929) who directed *Furtivos* (*Poachers*, 1975), *La Sabina*, 1979, *Rio abajo* (*On the Line*, 1984, USA), *Tata Mia* (*My Nanny*, 1986)—the founder of the new Spanish cinema, a phenomenon forecast in Victor Erice's *El spiritu de la colmena* (*The Spirit of the Beehive*, 1973), a densely symbolic account of life on the loser's side of post–Civil War Spain. The second generation of directors involved in this now immensely rich movement includes Pilar Miro (b. 1940), whose *El crimen de Cuenca* (*The Cuenca Crime*, 1979) became a *cause célèbre* of critics of limitations on freedom of expression in Spain. (It had been briefly suppressed by the military to still discussion of the brutal torture of two innocent peasants accused of murder by the Civil Guard, but released in 1981.) *El crimen de Cuenca* quickly established itself as the highest-grossing film in Spanish film history, and Miro was appointed General Director of Cinematography by the newly elected socialist prime minister Felipe Gonzalez in December 1982. Others in the second generation are: Jaime Chavarri (b. 1943)—*El descencanto* (*The Disenchantment*, 1976); *A un dios descon-ocido* (*To an Unknown God*, 1977); *Dedicatoria* (*Dedication*, 1980); *Bearn* (*La sala de las muneras*, 1983); *Las bicicletas son para el vernano* (*Bicycles Are for Summer*, 1984); *El rio de oro* (*Golden River*, 1986); Jaime Camino (b. 1936)—*La vieja memoria* (*The Old Memory*, 1977); *La campanada*, 1980; *El balcon abierto* (*The Open Balcony*, 1984); *Luces y Sombras* (*Light and Shadows*, 1988); Victor Erice (b. 1940)—*El sur* (*The South*, 1983); Ricardo Franco (b. 1949)—*Pascual Duarte*, 1975; *Los restos del naufragio* (*The Remains of the Shipwreck*, 1978); *San Judas de la frontera* (1984; Mexico); Jose Luis Garci (b. 1944)—*Solos en la madrugada* (*Alone in the Early Hours*, 1978); *Las verdes graderas* (*Green Pastures*, 1979); *El crack* (*The Crack*, 1980); *Volver a empezar* (*To Begin Again*, 1982, winner of the American Academy Award for Best Foreign Film); *El crack II*, 1983; *Sesion continua* (*Double Feature*, 198:); Antonio Drove (b. 1942)—*La verdad sobre el caso Savolta* (*The Truth in the Savolta Case*, 1978); Manuel Gutierrez Aragon (b. 1942)—*Camada negra* (*Black Brood*, 1977, winner of the Directors Prize, Berlin 1979): *Sonambulos* (*Sleepwalkers*, 1977); *El corazon del bosque* (*The Heart of the Forest*, 1978); *Maravillas* (*Marvels*, 1980); *Demonios en el jardin* (*Demons in the Garden*, 1982); *Feros* (*Wild*, 1984); *La noche mas hermosa* (*The Most Beautiful Night*, 1984); *La mitad del cielo* (*Half of Heaven*, 1986); *Malaventura* (*Misadventure*, 1988); Jose Juan Bigas Luna (b. 1946)—*Bilbao, una historia de amor* (*Bilbao, a Love Story*, 1978); *Caniche* (*Poodle*, 1979); Renacer (*Reborn*, 1981, U.S.A.); *Lola*, 1985; *Angustia* (*Anguish*, 1987); Eloy de la Iglesia (b. 1944)—*Los placeres ocultos* (*Hidden Pleasures*, 1977); *El diputado* (*The Deputy*, 1978); *Navajeros* (*Knife Fighters*, 1980); *Colegas* (*Pals*, 1982); *El pico* (*The Shoot*, 1983); *El pico II*, 1984; *Otra vuelta de tuerca* (*The Turn of the Screw*, 1985), Pedro Almodovar (b. 1949)—*Labertinto de pasiones* (*Labyrinth of Passions*, 1982); *Entre tinieblas* (*In the Dark*, 1983); *Que he hecho yo para merecer esta?* (*What Have I Done to Deserve This?*, 1984); *Matador*, 1986; *La ley del deseo* (*The Law of Desire*, 1987); *Mujeres al borde de un ataque de nervios* (*Women on the Verge of a Nervous Breakdown*, 1988); and Augusti Villaronga—*Tras el cristal* (*In a Glass Cage*, 1986). As Marsha Kinder has pointed out in several contexts, the new Spanish cinema is a phenomenon worthy of intense and detailed critical scrutiny, as demonstrated in such recent books as Peter Besas, *Behind the Spanish Lens: Spanish Cinema Under Fascism and Democracy* (Denver: Arden Press, 1985); Ronald Schwartz, *Spanish Film Directors (1950–1985): 21 Profiles* (Metuchen, N.J.: Scarecrow, 1986); John Hopewell, *Out of the Past: Spanish Cinema After Franco* (London: BFI, 1986); J. M. Caparrós-Lera and Rafael de Espana, *The Spanish Cinema: An Historical Approach* (Spain: Film-Historia Publishers, 1987); and Virginia Higginbottom, *Spanish Film Under Franco* (Austin: University of Texas Press, 1988). See also Vicente Molina-Foix, *New Cinema in Spain* (London: BFI, 1978); Marsha Kinder, "Carlos Saura: The Political Development of Individual Consciousness," *Film Quarterly* 32, 3 (Spring 1979): 14–25; by the same author, "Jose Luis Borau *On the Line* of the National/International Interface in the Post-Franco Cinema," *Film Quarterly* 60, 2 (Winter 1986–87): 35–48, and "Pleasure and the New Spanish Cinema: A Conversation with Pedro Almodovar," *Film Quarterly* 41, 1 (Fall 1987): 33–44; Annette Insdorf, "Spain Also Rises," *Film Comment* 16, 4 (July–August 1980): 13–17; special issue on "New Spanish Cinema," ed. Katherine S. Kovacs, *Quarterly Review of Film Studies* 8, 2 (Spring 1983); special issue on "New Spanish and Portuguese Cinema," ed. Richard Pena, *Journal of the University Film and Video Association* 35, 2 (Summer 1983); George De Stefano, "Post–Franco Frankness," *Film Comment* (June 1986): 58–60; Emilio C. Garcia Fernandez, *Historia Illustrada del Cine Espanol* (Madrid: Planeta, 1985); and Katherine S. Kovacs, "Demarginalizing Spanish Film," *Quarterly Review of Film and Video* 11, 4 (1990): 73–82.

Portugal (population 10 million, as compared with Spain's 41 million) has a small film industry that since the overthrow of the Salazarist dictatorship in 1974 has produced about seven films a year. Its major directors are Alberto Seixas Santos—*Brandos costumes* (*Gentle Customs*, 1977); *Gestos & Fragmentos* (*Gestures and Fragments*, 1982); Margarida Cordeiro and Antonio Reis—*Tras-os-Montes*, 1977; *Ana*, 1983; Antonio-Pedro Vasconcelo—*Oxala*, 1980; *O lugar do morto* (*Place of the Dead*, 1985), documentarist Rui Simoe—*Good Portuguese People* (*Bom povo portugues*, 1980); Joao Cesar Monteiro—*Silvestre*, 1981; Paulo Rocha—*A Ilha dos amores* (*The Island of Love*, 1982); and Portugal's single world-class director, Manoel de Oliveira (b. 1908)—*Passado e o presente* (*Past and Present*, 1971); *Benilde, ou a virgem mae* (*Benilde: Virgin and Mother*, 1975); *Amor de perdicao* (*Doomed Love*, 1978); *Francisca*, 1981; *Le Soulier de satin* (*The Satin Slipper*, 1985, coproduced with France); *O meu caso* (*My Case*, 1986, coproduced with France); *Os Canibais* (*The Cannibals*, 1988). Like many of his colleagues within the Portuguese industry, Olivira manifests a taste for a highly literary and theatrical style. (See, however, Alan Stanbrook, "Hard Times for Portuguese Cinema," *Sight and Sound* 58, 2 [Spring 1989]: 118–21.)

p. 660 Raymond Durgnat . . . social roles: Raymond Durgnat, *Luis Buñuel* (Berkeley: University of California Press, 1970), p. 128.

p. 664 Marsha Kinder . . . narrative: Marsha Kinder, "The Tyranny of Convention in *The Phantom of Liberty*," *Film Quarterly* 28, 4 (Summer 1975): 20.

p. 665 John Russell Taylor has written: John Russell Taylor, *Cinema Eye, Cinema Ear* (London: Methuen, 1964), p. 113.

European Renaissance: East

p. 666 fn. Albania . . . closed to the West: Albanian filmmakers are apparently self-taught. At the Giffoni Valle Piana (Italy) International Festival for Children and Youth, held from July 27 to August 5, 1985, in the wake of the death of Enver Hoxha (1908–85), Albania's Communist leader since 1944, the world got its first major opportunity to see Albanian cinema. There it was learned that Albania produces an average of fourteen features, forty documentaries, and twenty animated films a year at its Kinostudio Shaiperia e re (New Albanian Film Studio, established 1953) under the auspices of the Albanian State Film Enterprise in Tiranë. These films are intended entirely for domestic consumption in three hundred theaters nationwide, where the goal is to show films to as large a segment of the population as possible; the price of admission is the equivalent of two cups of coffee in the city and is free in rural areas and to students and youth everywhere. All Albanian films are played on state-run television after several months of theatrical exhibition. Two feature genres were evident—World War II Partisan films and historical dramas about the Albanian revolution against the Turks in 1912. All the country's films were heavily laden with old-style Zhdanovian social realism and ponderously made by Western standards. Domestic product accounts for 80 percent of the box office, with Turkish, Greek, Egyptian, and a few Italian and French films making up the rest. Although it imports National Geographic specials and some Disney cartoons, Albania has been completely isolated from American features since World War II.

p. 670 Warsaw uprising of 1944: When Poland was invaded and occupied by the Nazis in September 1939, the Polish cabinet fled to Paris and set up a government-in-exile. (After the Nazi invasion of France in 1940, the Poles moved to London.) They left behind them in Warsaw a large but ill-equipped resistance force dubbed the Home Army, which was charged with effecting an uprising against the Nazis when the time came. The moment arrived in July 1944, when the Red Army approached Warsaw from the east across the Vistula River and liberation seemed imminent. But the Soviet troops were as hostile to the Poles as were the occupying Nazis, so in late July the Home Army rose up, unaided, against both. It was a hopeless if heroic struggle against superior manpower, airpower, and weaponry. The Poles had only enough ammunition, food, and other supplies for five days, but they stretched these out until the inevitable surrender on October 4, 1944. At the end of the battle, many resistance fighters died while attempting to escape the Nazis through the Warsaw sewer system. After the surrender, Hitler ordered that the city be razed, so that virtually nothing of old Warsaw survives today. Over 200,000 Poles, most of them noncombatants, lost their lives in the uprising; German and Soviet losses were insignificant.

p. 673 Polish School . . . negative view of everyday Polish life: Other significant members of the Polish School had been Kazimierz Kutz (b. 1929)—*Cross of Valor (Krzy walecznych,* 1959); *Nobody Is Calling (Nikt nie wola,* 1960); *People on a Train (Ludzie z pociagu,* 1961); *Salt of the Black Earth (Sól ziemi czarnej,* 1970); *Pearl in the Crown (Perla w koronie,* 1971); *The Beads of One Rosary (Paciorki jednego rozanca,* 1980); *I Shall Always Stand Guard (Na strazy swej stac bede,* 1984)—and Wojciech Jerzy Has (b. 1925)—*The Noose (Petla,* 1957); *Farewells (Poegnania,* 1958); *How to Be Loved (Jak by kochana,* 1963); *The Saragossa Manuscript (Rekopis znaleziony w Saragossie,* 1964); *Ciphers (Szyfry,* 1966); *The Doll (Lalka,* 1968); *The Sandglass (Sanatorium "Pod Klepsydra,"* 1973); *Write and Fight (Pismak,* 1985); *The Memoirs of a Sinner (Osobisty pamietnik grzesznika przez niego samego spisany,* 1986).

p. 679 Solidarity . . . Lech Wałęsa: Intimidated by the massive strikes of August and suffering from internal disorganization, the Central Committee of the Polish Communist Party—the Polish United Workers' Party (*Polska Zjednoczona Partia Robotnicza,* or PZPR)—forced the resignation of Edward Gierek as first secretary and elected Stanislaw Kania in his place. The PZPR officially recognized Solidarity in November 1980, hoping that the "free" union movement (that is, free of the party) would remain confined to the Baltic ports. But Solidarity grew with astounding speed, claiming 10 million members by the end of the year and gaining the support of the vast majority of the Polish people. In May 1981, the government was forced to recognize Rural Solidarity as an independent farmers' union, and the authority of the Kania regime began to crumble amid spreading food shortages and other economic dislocations. In October 1981, the Central Committee forced Kania's resignation and replaced him with General Wojciech Jaruzelski, who was also premier and minister of defense. Early in the morning of Sunday, December 13, 1981, Jaruzelski staged a military coup, imposing martial law and suspending the activities of Solidarity indefinitely. The union was officially declared illegal in October 1982, but it continued to exist underground, emerging triumphantly in the summer of 1989 to form a coalition government with Jaruzelski's Communists.

p. 684 Kiéslowski . . . completed in 1989: Among the most promising Polish directors of the last two decades are Janusz Majewski (b. 1931)—*The Sub-Tenant (Sublokator,* 1967); *The Bear (Lokis,* 1970); *Epitaph for Barbara Radziwill* (1983); *Day Dream* (video, 1985); Witold Leszczyński (b. 1933)—*The Life of Matthew (Zywot Mateusza,* 1967); *Konopielka* (1982); Marek Piwowski (b. 1935)—*Cruise (Rejs,* 1970); *Hair* (1973); *Foul Play (Przepraszam, czy tu bija,* 1977); Andrzej Żulawski (b. 1940)—*Third Part of a Night (Trzecia cześć nocy,* 1971); *Devil (Diabel,* 1971, banned); *Possession* (1981); *La Femme publique (The Public Woman,* 1984); *Mad Love (L'Amour braque,* 1985); *The Silver Globe [Na srebruym globie;* begun 1977, completed for the KADR Unit of Film Polski, 1988]; Antoni Krauze (b. 1940)—*God's Finger (Palec Boży,* 1973); *The Weather Forecast (Prognoza Pogody,* 1981; 1985); Stanislaw Różewicz (b. 1924)—*Passion (Pasja,* 1978); *Lynx (Rys,* 1981); *Mrs. Latter's Pension (Pensja Pani Latter,* 1984); *Woman in a Hat (Robieta w Kopeluszy,* 1985); Grzegorz Królikiewicz (b. 1939)—*Through and Through (Na wylot,* 1973); *Endless Complaints (Wieczne pretensje,* 1974); *The Dancing Hawk (Tánczacy*

jastrzab, 1977); *Killing Auntie (Zabicie Ciotki,* 1985); Krzysztof Kieślowski (b. 1941)—*Staff (Personel,* 1976); *The Scar (Blizna,* 1976); *Amateur/Camera Buff (Amator,* 1976); *The Chance (Przypadek,* 1981); *Calm (Spokoj,* 1976; 1981); *A Short Day's Work (Krótki dzieu pracy,* 1982); *Without End (Bez konca,* 1985]); Edward Żebrowski (b. 1935)—*Salvation (Ocalenie,* 1972); *Hospital of Transfiguration (Szpital przemienienia,* 1979); *In Broad Daylight (W biaty dzien,* 1981); Andrzej Trzos-Rastawiecki (b. 1933)—*Leprosy (Trad,* 1971); *The Record of a Crime (Zapis zbrodni,* 1974); *Condemned (Skazany,* 1976); *Wherever You Are, Mr. President (Gdziekolwiek jesteś, panie prezydencie,* 1979); *Objection* (1985); Agnieszka Holland (coscenarist of Wajda's *Without Anesthesia* (1978)—*Sunday Children* (1978); *Test Shot/Film Test (Zdjecia próbne,* 1978); *Provincial Actors (Aktorzy prowincjonalni,* 1980); *Fever (Goraczka,* 1981); *The Lonely Woman (Kobieta samotna i chromy,* 1981); *Angry Harvest* (1984); Krzysztof Wojciechowski—*Antique* (1977); *A Family* (1978); Feliks Falk—*Top Dog (Wodzirej,* 1978); *Chance (Szansa,* 1980); *There Was Jazz (Byl Jazz,* 1981); *The Idol (Idol,* 1985); *Hero of the Year (Bohater roky,* 1987, a sequel to *Top Dog);* Marek Piestrak—*Test Pilot Pirx (Test Pilota Pirxa,* 1979); *The She-Wolf (Wilczyca,* 1983); Janusz Kidawa—*The Sinful Life of Franciszek Bula (Grzeszny zywot Franciszka Buly,* 1980); Piotr Szulkin—*Golem* (1979); *The War of the Worlds—Next Century (Wojna światownastepne stulecie,* 1981); *O-Bi, O-Ba—The End of Civilization (Ó-Bi, O-Ba—Koniec Cywilizacji,* 1985); Filip Bajon (b. 1947)—*Aria for an Athlete (Aria dia Atlty,* 1979); *Inspection of the Scene of a Crime, 1901 (Wizia lokalna 1901,* 1980); *Limousine/The Consul (Daimler-Benz Limuzyna,* 1982); *Employment* (1985); Janusz Kijowski (b. 1948)—*Index (Indeks,* 1977); *Kung-Fu* (1979); *Voices (Glosy,* 1980); *Before the Battle (Avant la bataille,* 1983); Piotr Andrejew (b. 1947)—*Clinch (Klinch,* 1979); Thomasz Zygadlo—*The Moth (Cḿa,* 1980); Barbara Sass—*Without Love (Bez milósci,* 1980); *The Outsider* (1982); *The Scream (Krzyk,* 1983); Janusz Zaorski (b. 1947)—*Mother of Kings (Matka Królow,* 1982); *The Baritone (Baryton,* 1985); Zbigniew Rybczynski—*Tango* (1983, an animated feature, winner of Poland's first Oscar); Andrzej Kondratiuk—*The Four Seasons (Cztery pory roku,* 1985); Radoslaw Piwowatski—*Yesterday* (1985); Juliusz Machulski—*Va Banque/Go for Broke (Vabank,* 1981); *Sex Mission (Seksmisja,* 1984); *Va Banque II* (1985); and Andrzej Barański (b. 1941)—*The Woman from the Provinces (Kobieta z prowincji,* 1985); Krzysztof Wojciechowski—*Charge (Szarza,* 1981); *The Fetish (Fetysz,* 1984); Stanislaw Bareja—*Teddy Bear (Mis,* 1981); Jerzy Domaradzki—*The Tailor's Planet (Planeta Krawiec,* 1983); Wieslaw Saniewski—*Probation (Nadzór,* 1983); Henryk Jacek Schoen—*The Whirlpool (Wir,* 1984). See Frank Bren, *World Cinema 1: Poland* (London: Flicke Books, 1986); Oskar Sobanski, *Polish Feature Films: A Reference Guide, 1945–1985* (West Cornwall, Conn.: Locust Hill Press, 1987); Boleslaw Michalek and Frank Turaj, *The Modern Cinema of Poland* (Bloomington: Indiana University Press, 1988); Frank Turaj, "Poland: The Cinema of Moral Concern," in Daniel J. Goulding, ed., *Post New Wave Cinema in the Soviet Union and Eastern Europe* (Bloomington: Indiana University Press, 1989), pp. 143–71.

p. 686 Vojtěch Jasny . . . alive: Jasny was the leader of what Peter Hames in *The Czechoslovak New Wave* calls the First

Wave—"that group of directors which prepared the way for the developments of the 1960s through thematic and formal breaks with the conventions of Socialist Realism" (p. 35). With the exception of Kadár, all made their first features in the late fifties following Khrushchev's de-Stalinization speech of 1956. Many—like Jasný, Stefan Uher (see text), and Karel Kachyňa (b. 1924; *That Christmas* [*Tenkrát o vánocích*, 1958]; *Coach to Vienna* [*Kočár do Vidne*, 1966]; *Night of the Bride* [*Noc nevěsty*, 1967])—were FAMU graduates. Others were not, such as Kadár, František Vláčil (see text), Zbyněk Brynych (*A Local Romance* [*Žižkovská romance*, 1958]; *Skid* [*Smyk*, 1960]; *The Fifth Horseman Is Fear* [. . . *a pátý jezdec je strach*, 1964]), and Ladislav Helge (*School for Fathers* [*Skolo otců*, 1957]; *The Great Seclusion* [*Velka samota*, 1959]).

p. 691 fn. Radok . . . socialist realism: Radok's only other films as a director were *The Magic Hat* (*Divotvorny klobouk*, 1952), the first Czech musical, and *Old-Man Motorcar* (*Dědeček automobil*, 1956), a playfully experimental history of the automobile. Radok continued to experiment with film form in *Laterna Magika* (*Magic Lantern*), a mixed-media show that he developed for the Brussels Exposition of 1958 with the assistance of Miloš Forman, Ivan Passer, Jaroslav Papoušek, and other young filmmakers who later created the New Wave. *Laterna Magika* combined multiple cinemascope film and slide projections, stereophonic music, and live action to create a new kind of theater—in Forman's words, "a kind of cybernetic machine one had to keep one's eye on all the time." But its programs were too controversial for the Czech authorities, and Radok and his collaborators were forced to withdraw from the project. Radok returned to stage directing, and emigrated to Sweden in 1968. But he left a lasting legacy to Czech cinema in his formal experimentation and in his mentorship of younger artists.

p. 693 Ivan Passer: After the Soviet-led invasion, Passer left Czechoslovakia permanently to work in the United States, where he has made five films, including the comedy-dramas *Born to Win* (1971) and *Law and Disorder* (1976) and the chillingly effective film noir *Cutter and Bone* (released, recut, as *Cutter's Way*, 1981). Papoušek stayed in Czechoslovakia, and since the New Wave, he has made three popular social comedies focusing on the petit bourgeois Homolka family—*Ecce Homo Homolka* (1969), *Big Shot Homolka* (*Hogo fogo Homolka*, 1979), and *Homolka and the Purse* (*Homolka a tobolka*, 1971).

p. 694 fn. *Josef Kilián* . . . May 1963: Peter Hames wrote of this event that "coming to terms with Kafka was not solely an attempt to catch up with Western intellectuals but an important national experience linked to both cultural and political events" (*The Czechoslovak New Wave*, p. 159). In fact, the relevance of Kafka's work to the everyday realities of life in an authoritarian state extends to all of the countries of Eastern Europe. As the Polish critic Roman Karst said in 1975: "Kafka has an absolutely explosive effect for anyone who lives in a world that is founded on untruth and lack of freedom." Appropriately, the years 1963–65 also witnessed Czech stage productions of the absurdist dramatists Eugène Ionesco, Samuel Beckett, and Edward Albee. See Antonín J. Liehm, "Franz Kafka in Eastern Europe," *Telos* 23 (Summer 1975): 72–86; and Marketa Goetz Stankiewicz, "The Theater of the Absurd in Czechoslovakia," *Survey* 21 (Winter–Spring 1975): 85–100.

p. 695 Škvorecký . . . New Wave directors: Škvorecký's account of these years is contained in his autobiographical history of the Czech New Wave, *All the Bright Young Men and Women* (Toronto: Peter Martin Associates, 1973). He now lives and works in the United States and Canada.

p. 699 simultaneously changed the shape of international cinema: With production at the Barrandov and Koliba Bratislava studios now averaging fifty features per year, several new talents have emerged, including Martin Holly (*Death Made to Order* [*Smrt sita na mieru*, 1979], *Signum Laudis* [1980], *Salt Is Worth More Than Gold* [*Sol nad zlato*, 1982]; Vladimír Kavčiak (*Karla's Marriage* [*Karline manzelstva*, 1980]); Karel Smyczek (*Goslings* [*Housata*, 1979], *Just a Little Whistle* [*Jen si tak trochu písknout*, 1980], *Why?* [*Proc?*, 1987]); Zoro Záhon (*The Assistant* [*Pomocnik*, 1982]); and Jaroslav Soukup (*The Wind in My Pocket* [*Vítr v kapse*, 1983]). In addition, new films by veteran directors have appeared recently: Juraj Herz has directed *I Was Caught in the Night* (*Zastihla me noc*, 1986); Dušan Hanák, *Silent Joy* (*Ticha radost*, 1986, winner of the grand prize at the San Remo Film Festival); Karel Kachyňa, *Death of a Beautiful Woman* (*Smrt krásnych srnců*, 1987); Jaromil Jireš, *The Lion with the White Mane* (*Lev & bilou, hrivou*, 1987); Stefan Uher, *The Sixth Sentence* (*Siesta veta*, 1986); Jiří Menzel, *My Sweet Little Village* (*Vesnicko ma strediskova*, 1986, winner of the Special Jury Award at Venice); Juraj Jakubisko, *I'm Sitting on a Branch and Feeling Fine* (*Sedim na Konari a je mi dobre*, 1989), and *The End of the Good Old Days* (*Konec Starych casu*, 1989); and Věra Chytilová, *Wolf's Lair* (*Vici bouda*, 1986) and *The Jester and the Queen* (*Sasek a kralovna*, 1988). See Peter Hames, "Czechoslovakia: After the Spring," in *Post New Wave Cinema in the Soviet Union and Eastern Europe*, ed. Daniel J. Goulding, pp. 102–42.

p. 701 Béla Balázs Studio . . . make their first films: Because the Academy overproduces filmmakers and because industry feature output is relatively low (fifteen to twenty per year through 1980), competition for feature funding in Hungary has always been extremely keen. At the Béla Balázs Studio (known to its staff as "BBS Budapest"), young filmmakers not yet able to command feature-length resources are given a chance to start their careers and gain practical experience directing shorts. Each year, the Studio receives a production budget from the state, and production policy is set by elected leaders in consultation with the membership. Between 1963 and 1965, the Studio attempted several features, but the policy of shorts prevailed and has contributed materially to the growth of Hungarian cinema at home and its reputation abroad. Among the founders of the Béla Balázs Studio are Judit Elek, István Gaál, Pál Gábor, and István Szabó. Among its award-winning shorts are Sándor Sára's *Gypsies* (*Ciganyok*, 1962), Szabó's *You* (*Te*, 1963), Ference Kardos' *On Top of the World* (*Miénk a világ*, 1963), Zoltán Huszárik's *Elegy* (*Elégia*, 1965), Elek's *How Long Does a Man Matter?* (*Meddig él az ember?* 1967), and Ferenc Kosa's *Suicide* (*Ongyilkosság*, 1967). In 1985, the American Federation of the Arts mounted an impressive exhibition of eighteen Béla Balázs shorts entitled "BBS Budapest: Twenty Years of Hungarian Experimental Film," a program still available as of this writing.

p. 701-2 Fábri . . . and Makk: Makk's films tend to focus on individuals in crisis, and he is best known for *Love* (*Szerelem*, 1971), winner of the Jury Prize at Cannes, *Catsplay*

(*Macskajáték*, 1974), and his recent screwball comedy *Lily in Love* (*Játszani Kell*, 1985). Fábri is more closely associated with Hungarian "New Cinema," having made the first film to confront directly the events of 1956 (*Twenty Hours* [*Húsz óra*, 1964]) and the antifascist, anti-Stalinist cycle *The Toth Family* (*Isten hozta, órnagy úr!*, 1969), *One Day More or Less* (*Plusz mínusz egy nap*, 1973), and *141 Minutes from the Unfinished Sentence* (*141 perc a befejezetlen mondatból*, 1974). It testifies to his universal appeal that Fábri's films have twice been nominated for American Academy Awards (*The Boys from Paul Street* [*A Pál utcai fiúk*, 1968] and its sequel, *Bálint Fábián Meets God* [*Fábián Bálint találkozása Instennel*, 1980]) and have twice won prizes at the Moscow International Festival (*141 Minutes* and *The Fifth Seal* (*Az ötödik pecsét*, 1976]). Fábri has also won the Kossuth Prize in his own country three times. His recent films, such as *Requiem* (*Reqiem*, 1981) and *The House-Warming* (*Gyertek el a nevnapomra*, 1984), have concentrated on political themes.

p. 706–7 *L'Aube* . . . made for television: Jancsó also made three features for Italian television during the seventies: *The Pacifist* (*La pacifista*, 1971), about contemporary political terrorism; *Technique and Rite* (*Il technico e il rito*, 1971), a reductive biography of Attila the Hun; and *Rome Needs Another Caesar* (*Roma rivuale cesare*, 1973), set in North Africa immediately following the assassination of Julius Caesar. These films are reportedly much more conventional in form than his Hungarian work.

p. 723 Hungarian cinema . . . in the world today: Other notable Hungarian directors and films include Rezső Szörény—*Reflections* (*Tükörképék*, 1976), *Happy New Year!* (*Búék!* 1979), *Happy Birthday, Marilyn!* (*Boldog születésnapot, Marilyn!* 1981), *Be Tough, Victor!* (*Talpra, Győző!* 1983); János Zsombolyai (b. 1934)—*Don't Lean Out the Window* (*Kihajolni veszélyes*, 1978), *Duty-Free Marriage* (*Vámmentes házasság*, 1981), *Magic-Queen in Hungary* (1987); Sándor Simó—*My Father's Happy Years* (*Apám néhány boldog éve*, 1978), *The Train Killer* (*Viadukt*, 1983), *Farewell to You* (*Isten veletek, Barataim*, 1988); Judit Ember—*Mistletoe* (*Fagyöngyök*, 1979), *The Resolution* (*A határozat*, 1972, released 1983; with Gyula Gazdag); Tamás Rényi (1930–81)—*K.O.* (1977), *Dead or Alive* (*Élve vagy halva*, 1980); Gábor Bódy (1947–85)—*Agitators* (*Agitatorok*, 1969), *American Torso* (*Amerikai anziksz*, 1978), *Narcissus and Psyche* (*Psyché és Narcisz*, 1981), *The Dog's Night Song* (*Kutya éji dala*, 1983 László Ránody (b. 1919)—*No Man's Daughter* (*Aravácska*, 1976), *I Dream About Colors* (*Szinés tintákról álmodom*, 1981); Pál Schiffer—*Gyuri* (*Cséplö Gyuri*, 1978), *On Parole* (*Á párfogolt*, 1982), *Cowboys* (*Cowboys*, 1986), *Magyar Stories* (1988); Gyula Gazdag (b. 1947)—*Whistling Cobblestone* (*A sipóló macskakó*, 1971, first distributed abroad, 1985), *The Resolution* (*A hatarosat*, 1972, released 1983; with Judit Ember), *Lost Illusions* (*Elveszett illúziok*, 1983), *The Package Tour* (*Társasutázas*, 1985), *A Hungarian Fairy Tale* (*Hol vot, hol nem volt*, 1987); György Révész (b. 1927)—*Land of Angels* (*Angyalok földje*, 1962), *Helter Skelter* (*Hanyatt-homlok*, 1984), *Miklós Akli* (*Akli Miklós*, 1987); Gyula Máar (b. 1934)—*At the End of the Road* (*Vegül*, 1973), *Mrs. Déry, Where Are You?* (*Déryné, hol van?*, 1975), *Flare and Flicker* (*Teketória*, 1977), *Passing Fancy* (*Felhójáték*, 1984), *My First 200 Years* (*Első kétszaz evem*, 1986), *Mills of Hell* (*Malom a pokolban*, 1987); Ferenc András—*It's Rain and Shine Together* (*Veri as ördög fele-*

ségét, 1977), *The Vulture* (*Dögkeselyü*, 1983), *The Great Generation* (*A nagy generacio*, 1986); *Time* (*Ido van*, 1985), *Just Like America* (1985); Péter Szász—*On the Sideline* (*Szépek és bolondok*, 1977), *How to Forget the Greatest Love of One's Live?* (*Hogyan felejtsük el életünk legnagyobb szerelmét?*, 1982); László Lugossy (b. 1939)—*We're Getting Along* (*Köszönöm, Megvagyunk*, 1981), *Petals*, György Dobray—*The Victim* (*Az ázaldozat*, 1980), *Blood Brothers* (*Vérszerzödes*, 1983), *Love Till First Blood* (*Szerelem elso verig*, 1986); Péter Gothar (b. 1945)—*A Priceless Day* (*Ajándék ez a nap*, 1980), *Time Stands Still* (*Megáll az ido*, 1982), *Flowers, Wreaths* (*Szirmok, virágok, koszorúk*, 1985, Special Jury Prize, Berlin); Béla Tarr—*A Piece of Ground* (*Földfolt*, 1981), *Prefab People* (*Panelkapcsolat*, 1982), *Autumn Almanac* (*Oszi almanach*, 1984), *Damnation* (*Karhozat*, 1988); Gábor Koltai—*The Concert* (*A koncert*, 1982), *Stephen, the King* (*István, a király*, 1984), *Mercenaries* (Idegenlegiosok, 1987); Miklós Szurdi—*Midnight Rehearsal* (*Határvadászok*, 1983); Janos Xantus—*Eskimo Woman Feels Cold* (*Eszkimó asszony fazík*, 1984), *Idiots May Apply* (*Hulgeség nem akadly*, 1986); György Szomjas—*Light Physical Injuries* (*Kőnnyú testi sértés*, 1984), *Falfuro* (*The Wall Drillers*, 1986); Péter Gardos—*The Philadelphia Attraction/My God* (*Uramisten*, 1985), *Whooping Cough* (*Szamarkohoges*, 1987; Just for Kicks [*a Hecc*, 1989]); Ferenc Grunwalszky—*Requiem for a Revolutionary* (*Vörös rekviem*, 1975), *To See the Light* (*Eszmélés*, 1985); and Pál Erdöss—*Countdown* (*Szaszamlalas*, 1986), *Tolerance* (*Gondoviseles*, 1987).

p. 724 Hungarian film . . . coproduction with the West: See Karen Jaehne, "István Szabó: Dreams of Memories," *Film Quarterly* 32, 1 (Fall 1978), 30–41; Daniel Bickley, "Socialism and Humanism: The Contemporary Hungarian Cinema," *Cineaste* 9, 2 (Winter 1978–79), 30–35; and Graham Petrie, *History Must Answer to Man: The Contemporary Hungarian Cinema* (London: Tantivy Press, 1979); J. Hoberman, "Budapest's Business," *Film Comment* 22, 3 (May–June 1986): 68–71; and David Paul, "The Esthetics of Courage: The Political Climate for the Cinema in Poland and Hungary," *Cineaste* 14, 4 (1986): 16–22, and the same author's "Hungary: The Magyar on the Bridge," in *Post New Wave Cinema in the Soviet Union and Eastern Europe*, ed. Daniel Goulding, pp. 172–214.

p. 724 Imre Gyöngyössy has said: Gyöngyössy quoted in Seth Mydans, "Hungary's Wartime Anguish Is Relived Through 'The Revolt of Job,' " *New York Times* May 27, 1984, p. 15.

p. 726 variant of Zhdanovian socialist realism: Many members of the Yugoslav cinema's founding generation are also still at work, as evidenced by France Štiglic's *The Merry Marriage* (*Veselo qostivanje*, 1984), Jože Gale's *Wasteland* (*Postota*, 1982), Veljko Bulajić's *High Voltage* (*Visoki napon*, 1981) and *The Promised Land* (*Obecana zemlja*, 1986), and Dušan Vukotić's *Visitors from the Galaxy* (*Gosti iz galaksije*, 1981).

p. 726 Daniel J. Goulding . . . postwar Yugoslav state: See Daniel J. Goulding's essential work, *Liberated Cinema: The Yugoslav Experience* (Bloomington: Indiana University Press, 1985), pp. 11–25.

p. 729 *The City* . . . impounded in *Sarajevo: Comments on*

The City are quoted in Daniel J. Goulding, *Liberated Cinema: The Yugoslav Experience*, p. 70.

p. 730 *I Even Met Happy Gypsies* . . . Grand Prix at Cannes: Petrovic has directed only two features since his *novi film* days: the French–West German coproduction *Gruppenbild mit Dame* (1977), an adaptation of Heinrich Böll's *Group Portrait with Lady*, which employs a largely Yugoslav cast, and the unusual Yugoslav-Soviet-American coproduction *The Wild Wind*, a Partisan epic with a script by Zivojin Paulović.

p. 738 Yugoslav cinema . . . Eastern Europe: Dejan Karaklajic—*Beloved Love/The Love Life of Budimir Traj-cović* (*Lyubavni život Budimira Trajcovića*, 1977), *Erogenous Zones* (*Erogena zona*, 1982); Franci Slak—*Years of Crisis* (*Krizno Razdoblje*, 1981), *Eva* (1983), *The Felons* (*Hudo-delchi*, 1988); Stole Popov—*Australia, Australia* (1976), *The Red Horse* (*Crveni Konj*, 1981), *Happy New Year—1949* (*Srena nova 49*, 1986); Vojko Duletic—*The Tenth Brother* (*Deseti brat*, 1982); Mirza Idrizović—*The Scent of Quince* (*Miris dunja*, 1982), *The Doctor* (*Doktor*, 1986); Janez Drozg—*The Battle at Poziralnik* (*Boj na poziralniku*, 1982); Karpo Godina—*Red Boogie* (*Kaj ti je deklica*, 1983); Predrag Antonijević—*Nothing But Words of Praise for the Deceased* (*O pokojniku sve najlepse*, 1984); Zare Luznik, Boris Jurja-sević, and Mitja Milaveć—*Three Sorts of Slovene Madness* (*Trije prispevki k slovenski blaznosti*, 1984); Branko Baletić—*Plum Juice* (*Sok od Sljiva*, 1982), *Balkan Express* (*Balkan Ekspres*, 1983), *Woman's Day* (*Uvek spremne zene*, 1987); Jovan Acin—*Hey Babu Riba* (1986), *Dancing on Water* (*Bal na vodi*, 1986); Zoran Tadic—*The Dream of a Rose* (*San o ruzi*, 1986); and Goran Marković's *Meeting Place* (*Sabrini centar*, 1989); Zivko Nickolic—*The Beauty of Vice* (*Lepota poroká*, 1986), *In the Name of the People* (*Uime naroda*, 1987); Zlatko Lavanic—*The Magpie's Strategy* (*Stategiia svrake*, 1987); Miroslav Mandic—*A Worker's Life* (*Zivot radnika*, 1987); Damjan Kozole—*The Fatal Telephone* (*Usodni telefon*, 1987); Vladmir Blazevski—*HiFi* (1987); Dragan Kresoja—*Oktoberfest* (1987); Slobodan Stojicic-Lesli—*The Harms Case* (*Slucaj Harms*, 1988). See Andrew Horton, "The New Serbo-Creationism," *American Film* 11, 4 (January-February 1986): 24–30; Daniel Goulding, "Yugoslav Film in the Post-Tito Era," in *Post New Wave Cinema in the Soviet Union*, ed. Daniel Goulding, pp. 248, 284.

p. 738 Josip Tito . . . avid film buff: Tito is quoted in Andrew Horton, "Satire and Sympathy: A New Wave of Yugoslavian Filmmakers," *Cineaste* 11, 2 (1981): 22.

p. 750 during the Stalinist 1950s: Other notable works of the New Bulgarian Cinema include: in 1979—Liudmil Kirkov's *Short Sun* (*Kratko Sluntse*), Ivan Nichev's *Boomerang* (*Bumerang*), Margarit Nikolov's *On the Tracks of the Missing* (*Po diriata na bezsledno izcheznalite*), Ivan Andonov's *The Cherry Orchard* (*Chereshova gradina*), Ivanka Grubcheva's *The Porcupine's War* (*Voinata na taralezhite*), Borislav Sharaliev's *All Is Love* (*Vischko e liubov*), and Marianna Evstatieva's *Moments in a Matchbox* (*Migove v kibritina kutika*); in 1980—Eduard Zahariev's *Almost a Love Story* (*Pochti liubovna istoria*), Nikolai Volev's *The Double* (*Dvoinikut*), Kiran Kolarov's *The Airman* (*Vuzdushniiat chovek*), Iskra Yosifova's *The Journey* (*Puteshestviieto*), Georgi Stoianov's *The Window* (*Prozoretsat*), Ivan Andonov's *Ladies' Choice* (*Dami kaniat*), and Ianush Vazov's *Love Game* (*Igra na liubov*): in 1981—Evgeni Mihailov's *Home for Lonely Souls* (*Dom za nezhni dushi*), Ognian Gelinov's

The Flying Machine (*Letaloto*), Marianna Evstatieva's *Crime in Yellow* (*Poshishtenie zhalto*), and Zako Heskia's *Yo-Ho-Ho*; in 1982—Liudmil Kirkov's *A Nameless Band* (*Orkestur bez ime*), Irina Aktasheva's *Avalanche* (*Lavina*), Nikola Rudarov's *The Racket* (*Kombina*), Dimiter Petrov's *A Dog in the Drawer* (*Kuche v chekmedzhe*), and Vladislav Konomov's *Twenty-four Hours of Rain* (*24 chasa duzhd*); in 1983—Peter Donev's *Bonne Chance, Inspector!* (*Bon Shans, Inspektore!*), Maia Vaptsarova's *Preventive Detention* (*Miarka za neotklonie*), Stefan Dimitrov's *The Return Journey* (*Zavrashtane*), and Kosta Kikov's *A Surge of Tenderness* (*Prilev na nezhnost*); in 1984—Todor Stoianov's *Vibration* (*Vibratsia*), Marianna Evstatieva's *Up in the Cherry Tree* (*Gore na chereshata*), Ivan Dobchev's *For a Young Lady and Her Male Companion* (*Na gospozhitsata i neinata muzhka kompania*), Ivan Rosenov's *The Poet and the Devil* (*Poetut i diavolut*), Borislav Punchev's *The Rescue* (*Spasenieto*), Ivan Nichev's *The Black Swans* (*Chernite lebedi*), Krasimir Spasov's *Just Forget That Case* (*Zabravete tozi sluchai*), Plamen Maslarov's *Green Fields*, Igor Kiuliumov's *Traveling Musicians* (*Putiat na musikantite*), and Sergei Ghiaurov's *Blood That Had to Be Shed* (*Tazi kruv triabvashe da se prolee*); in 1985—Marianna Evstatieva's *A Husband for Mom* (*Muzh za Mama*), Milen Nikolov's *Romantic Story* (*Romantichna istoria*), Evgeni Mihailov's *Death Can Wait Awhile* (*Smurtta mozhe da pochaka*), Nikolai Volev's *Let's Love Each Other Out of Spite* (*Da se liubim na inat*), Nikola Rudarov's *A Cry for Help* (*Vik za pomosht*), Eduard Zahariev's *My Darling, My Darling* (*Skupi moi, skupi moi*), Peter Vassilev's *Maneuvers on the Fifth Floor* (*Manevri no petia etzah*), and Rangel Vulchanov's *Where Are You Going?* (*Za kude putovate?*); in 1986—Nikolai Volev's *All for Love* (*Da ebichash na inat*) and Nicolae Corjos' *Declaration of Love* (*Declaratie de dragoste*); in 1987—Ivanka Grubcheva's *The Thirteenth Bride of the Prince* (*Trinajstata godenica na princa*), Ivan Nitchev's *Black Swans* (*Cernite lebedi*), Roumiana Petrova's *Return to Earth* (*Prizemyavane*); in 1988—Liudmil Staikov's *Time of Violence* (*Vréme razdelno*), Rangel Vulchanov's *Where Do We Go from Here?* (*A sega nakude*).

See Ronald Holloway, "Bulgaria: The Cinema of Poetics," in Daniel J. Goulding, ed., *Post New Wave Cinema in the Soviet Union and Eastern Europe*, pp. 215–47.

p. 752 Romania . . . world center for animated film: Among Popescu-Gopo's best-known features using animation are *Steps to the Moon* (*Pasi spre luna*, 1963), *The White Moor* (*Harap Alb*, 1965), *The Story of Love* (*Povestea dragostei*, 1976), and *Galax* (1984). Winner of awards and medals throughout the world, Popescu-Gopo has also recently directed two animated features: the cautionary *Ecce Homo* (1978), and *Quo Vadis Homo Sapiens* (1983), an anthology of his life's work in animation made to celebrate his sixtieth birthday. Both of these films end with the image of an abandoned baby drifting along through the universe, Mother Earth having been destroyed by nuclear war.

p. 756 domestic films . . . high aesthetic and intellectual caliber: Other members of "The Class of the 1970s" in Romania and their films are: Timotei Ursu—*September* (*Septembrie*, 1978); Aleka Visarion—*Before Silence Came* (*Inainte de tacere*, 1979); Stere Gulea—*The Green Grass of Home* (*Iarba verde de acasa*, 1978), *The Bear's Eye's Curse* (*Ochi de urs*, 1983); Nicolae Margineanu—*The Man in the Overcoat* (*Omul în loden*, 1979), *Stefan Luchian* (1982),

Return from Hell (*Intoarcerea din iad*, 1984), *The Maiden of the Woods* (*Padueanca*, 1987); Zoltan Szilagyi (b. 1952)—*The Gordian Knot* (*Nodul gordian*, 1981, a much-awarded animated feature); Dinu Tănăse—*Dr. Poenaru* (1978), *The Standoff* (*Mijlocas la deschidere*, 1979), *The Broadcast Goes On* (*Emisia continua*, 1985); Tudor Mărascu—*Good Evening, Irina* (*Buna Seara, Irina*, 1980), *The Winner* (*Invingatorul*, 1982); Ada Pistiner—*Freeze Frame at Table* (*Stop cadru la masa*, 1981); Iosif Demian—*A Girl's Tears* (*O lacrima de fata*, 1981), *To Kill a Bird of Prey* (*Lovind o pasăre de prada*, 1984); Constantin Vaeni—*Impossible Love* (*Impossibila iubire*, 1984); Francis Munteanu—*A Piece of Sky* (*Un petec de cer*, 1984); and Cristiana Nicolae—*For Your Sake, Anca* (*De dragul tău, Anca*, 1984).

From previous generations: Lucian Bratu (b. 1924)—*Tudor* (1963, the first Romanian widescreen costume epic and the first great domestic box office success, seen by nearly half the population in the year of its release), *The Bride on the Train* (*Mireasa din tren*, 1980, original screenplay by D. R. Popescu); Iulian Mihu (b. 1926)—*Life Doesn't Spare* (*Viaţa nu iartă*, 1961), *Felix and Otilia* (1972), *The Pale Light of Sorrow* (*Lumina palida a durerii*, 1980); Malvina Urşianu (b. 1927)—*The Party* (*Serata*, 1971), *Transient Loves* (*Trecătoarele iubiri*, 1975), *The Return of King Lapusneanu* (*Intoarcerea lui Voda Lapusneanu*, 1979), *A Light on the Tenth Floor* (*O lumină la etajul X*, 1985); Gheorge Vitandis (b. 1929)—*The Moment* (*Clipa*, 1979, a sort of companion piece to Daneliuc's *Fox-Hunting* [1981], by virtue of adapting a Săraru novel on the same subject); Mircea Mureşan (b. 1930)—*Horea* (1985); Sergiu Nicolaescu (b. 1930)—*With Clean Hands* (*Cu mîinile curate*, 1972), *Ipu's Death* (*Moartea lui Ipu*, 1972), *The Last Bullet* (*Ultimul cartus*, 1973), *The Immortals* (*Nemuritorii*, 1975), *Hot Days* (*Zile fierbinti*, 1975), *The Punishment* (*Osînda*, 1977), *Revenge* (*Revansa*, 1981), and *Ciuleandra* (1985); Elisabeta Bostan (b. 1931)—best known for her children's films *Veronica* (1972), *The Return of Veronica* (*Veronica se întoarce*, 1973), *Ma-Ma* (1979), and *The Clowns* (*Saltimancii*, 1982); and Horea Popescu—*The Wasps' Nest* (*Cuibil de viespi*, 1988). See Michael J. Stoil, *Balkan Cinema: Evolution After the Revolution* (Ann Arbor, Mich.: UMI Research Press, 1982).

p. 761 André Bazin . . . Stalin: André Bazin, "The Stalin Myth in Soviet Cinema," with an Introduction by Dudley Andrew, in *Movies and Methods*, vol. 2 (Berkeley: University of California Press, 1985), p. 38.

p. 762 Khrushchev declared . . . Stalin: Nikita Khrushchev, "De-Stalinization Speech, February 24–25, 1956," in Basil Dmytryshyn, *USSR: A Concise History*, 4th ed. (New York: 1984), p. 563.

p. 763 *King Lear*: See Grigori Kozintsev, *King Lear: The Space of Tragedy: The Diary of a Film Director* (Berkeley: University of California Press, 1977), and *The Age and Its Conscience* (Moscow: BPSK, 1981).

p. 764 *I'm Twenty* . . . over the next eighteen months: Also of note during this period, but *sui generis*, were two films directed by Dovzhenko's widow, Iulia Solntseva (b. 1901) from his original screen treatments: *Poem of the Sea* (*Poema o more*, 1958) and *Story of the Flaming Years* (*Povest*

plamennykh let, 1961). Solntseva spent the rest of her career completing her husband's unfinished projects in *The Enchanted Desna* (*Zacharovannaia Desna*, 1964) and *The Golden Gate* (*Zolotye vorota*, 1970).

p. 765 project . . . *Shadows of Forgotten Ancestors*: For a detailed commentary by Parajanov about the making of his film, see Parajanov, "Shadows of Forgotten Ancestors," *Film Comment* 5, 1 (1968): 38–48. See also Anne Williamson, "Prisoner: The Essential Paradjanov," *Film Comment* 25, 3 (May–June 1989): 57–63.

p. 769 Tarkovski's . . . inaccessible film: For a lucid analysis of this difficult film, see Tony Mitchell, "Andrei Tarkovski and Nostalghia," *Film Criticism* 8, 3 (Spring 1984): 2–11. See also Michael Dempsey, "Lost Harmony: Tarkovski's *The Mirror* and *The Stalker*," *Film Quarterly* 35, 1 (Fall 1981): 12–17; Peter Green, "Andrei Tarkovski (1932–1986): Apocalypse and Sacrifice," *Sight and Sound* 56, 2 (Spring 1987): 108–19; Andrei Tarkovski, *Sculpting in Time* (London: The Bodley Head, 1986); Mark Le Fann, *The Cinema of Andrei Tarkovski* (London: BFI, 1987) Vlada Petric, "Tarkovski's Dream Imagery," *Film Quarterly* 43, 2 (Winter 1989–90): 28–34; and Jonathan Rosenbaum, "Inner Space: Exploring Tarkovski's Solaris," *Film Comment* 26, 4 (July–August, 1990): 57–62. The director is also the subject of two excellent 100-minute documentaries: *Andrei Tarkovski* (1984), written, directed, and edited by Donatello Baglivo: and *Directed by Andrei Tarkovski*, written, directed, and edited by Michal Leszczylowski.

p. 770 his brother . . . Nikita Mikhalkov: Konchalovski's father, Sergei Mikhalkov, is a powerful figure within the Union of Soviet Writers and is said to have close connections within the Central Committee of the CPSU. See Carol Flake, "Stranger in a Strange Land," *American Film* 11, 3 (December 1985): 40–46.

p. 770–71 Filip Yermash . . . personal aim of his existence: Filip Yermash quoted in Mira and Antonín Liehm, *The Most Important Art: Eastern European Film After 1945* (Berkeley: University of California Press, 1977), p. 336.

p. 771 Georgian pioneer . . . Nikolai Shengelaia: The Shengelaias' father, Nikolai (1903–43), was one of the pioneer directors of Soviet Georgian cinema. See Don Willis, "A Singing Blackbird and Georgian Cinema," *Film Quarterly* 31, 3 (Spring 1978): 11–15.

p. 774 Ryazanov's . . . *Station for Two*: Ryazanov and his co-writer, Emile Braginsky, can lay some claim to having pioneered the *bytovye* in a series of extremely popular films about ordinary people caught up in comic circumstances. These include, in addition to those mentioned in the text, *Irony of Fate*, or, *Have a Good Sauna* (*Ironiia sub'by, ili S legkim parom*, 1975), *An Office Romance* (*Sluzhebnyi romans*, 1978), and *A Ruthless Romance* (*Zhestokii romans*, 1984), all smash hits in the Soviet Union. See Anna Lawton, "Towards a New Openness in Soviet Cinema, 1976–1987," in *Post New Wave Cinema in the Soviet Union and Eastern Europe*, ed. Daniel J. Goulding, pp. 1–50; Neya Zorkaya, *The Illustrated History of Soviet Cinema* (New York: Hippocrene Books, 1989), pp. 195–308; and Andrei Plakhov, "Soviet Cinema:

Wind from the East:
Japan, India, and China

p. 778–79 Donald Kirihara . . . *benshi*: Donald Kirihara, "A Reconsideration of the Institution of the Benshi," in *The Reader for Film and Television #6*, ed. William Lafferty and Greg S. Faller (Chicago, 1985). See also Hiroshi Komatsu and Charles Musser, "Benshi Search," *Wide Angle* 19, 2 (1987): 72–90.

p. 779 *benshi* . . . stars in their own right: Technically, *katsuben*. According to Joseph L. Anderson, *benshi* is a broad term meaning speaker or orator, while *katsuben* specifically denotes a person who narrates motion pictures. See his "Spoken Silents in the Japanese Cinema, Essay on the Necessity of Katsuben," *Journal of Film and Video* 40, 1 (Winter 1988): 13–33. See also Peter B. High, "The Dawn of Cinema in Japan," *Journal of Contemporary History* 19 (1984): 23–57. The Performance skills required of the *benshi*, or *katsuben*, were so exhausting that it was common for a single feature to employ several of them in rotation.

p. 780 Heinosuke Gosho . . . Mikio Naruse: On Gosho's and Naruse's later work, see Mark Le Fanu, "To Love Is to Suffer: Reflections on the Later Films of Heinosuke Gosho," *Sight and Sound* 55, 3 (Summer 1986): 198–202; and Phillip Lopate, "a Taste for Naruse," *Film Quarterly* 39, 4 (Summer 1986): 11–21.

p. 784 Venice . . . postwar renaissance: For an extremely sophisticated argument that there was no postwar renaissance but rather a "regression," and that the "golden age" of Japanese film was the period from 1930 to 1945, see Noël Burch's dialectical analysis of Japanese film discourse, *To the Distant Observer: Form and Meaning in Japanese Cinema*, rev. and ed. Annette Michelson (Berkeley: California University Press, 1979). See also, David Bordwell, "Our Dream-Cinema: Western Historiography and the Japanese Film," in *Film Reader* 4, ed. Blaine Allan et al. (Evanston, Ill.: Northwestern University Press, 1979); 45–62; Noel Burch, "Approaching Japanese Film," *Cinema and Language*, ed. Stephen Heath (Frederick, Md.: 1983), pp. 79–96; Donald Richie, "Viewing Japanese Film: Some Considerations," *East-West Film Journal* 1, 1 (December 1986): 23–35; *Journal of Film and Video*, 39, 1 (Winter 1987), Japanese Cinema special issue, ed. Peter Lehman.

p. 793 Kurosawa . . . Mizoguchi: Kurosawa quoted in Richard Tucker, *Japan: Film Image* (London: Studio Vista, 1973), p. 64.

p. 793–94 Jacques Rivette . . . Mizoguchi: Rivette quoted in David Thomson, *A Biographical Dictionary of Film* (New York: William Morrow, 1976) p. 390.

p. 794 Barbara Wolf has put it: Barbara Wolf, *The Japanese Film* (New York: 1976), p. 38.

p. 794 Ozu's films . . . throughout his career: See Kathe Geist, "Yasujiro Ozu: Notes on a Retrospective," *Film*

Quarterly 37, 1 (Fall 1983); 2–9; "Narrative Style in Ozu's Silent Films," *Film Quarterly* 40, 2 (Winter 1986–87): 28–35; and "The Role of Marriage in the Films of Yasujiro Ozu," *East-West Film Journal* 4, 1 (December 1989): 44–52. See also David Bordwell, *Ozu and the Poetics of Cinema* (Princeton: Princeton University Press, 1988).

p. 795–96 Zen doctrine . . . work: For more on the relationship between the Zen aesthetic of discontinuity and the formal qualities of Japanese cinema, see Noël Burch's *To the Distant Observer: Form and Meaning in Japanese Cinema* (cited above). Burch goes so far as to suggest that Japanese audiences found the flicker effect of early projections far less irritating than their Western counterparts, since their traditional aesthetic did not require the illusion of seamless continuity as does the traditional aesthetic of the West. Interestingly enough, the flicker effect in Japan was more pronounced than it was in Western films, since until the twenties Japanese cameras and projectors operated at the rate of twelve frames per second rather than the sixteen to twenty frames common in the West.

p. 796 Will Peeterson has put it: Peeterson quoted in Paul Schrader, *Transcendental Style in Film* (Berkeley: University of California Press, 1972), p. 27.

p. 798 Donald Richie has pointed out: Donald Richie, *Ozu* (Berkeley: University of California Press, 1974), p. 64.

p. 802 *bunraku* puppet theater tradition: In *bunraku* puppet theater, developed during the Tokugawa period (1616–1868), white-faced dolls, expressionless except for mobile eyelids, are manipulated by as many as three black-robed, masked, but fully visible puppeteers (*kuroko*); the musical narrative (*joruri*) is chanted by a a reciter (*gidayu*) to the accompaniment of instruments. Many *bunraku* plays revolved around the theme of *shinju*, or lovers' suicide, motivated by the tension between *giri* (duty) and *ninjo* (human desires). Monzaemon Chikamatsu (1653–1725) was the greatest literary master of the form, and his work forms the basis of many significant Japanese films (e.g., Mizoguchi's *The Crucified Lovers* [*Chikamatsu monogatari*, 1954]). *The Love Suicides at Sonezaki* was filmed again in 1982 by Midori Kurisaki as an actual *bunraku* play, photographed by Kazuo Miyagawa.

p. 803 *Eros plus Massacre*: So central is this work to the New Wave canon that David Desser' pioneering English-language study—*Eros plus Massacre: An Introduction to the Japanese New Wave Cinema* (Bloomington: Indiana University Press, 1988)—is named after it.

p. 803 abortive coup d'état of February 26, 1936: This same coup d'état, known to the Japanese as the *ni-ni-roku* (2–26, or February 26) incident provides the context for Yukio Mishima's 30-minute *Patriotism* (*Yukoku*, 1967), distributed in the United States as *The Rite of Love and Death*, in which a young army officer and his bride make love and then graphically commit *seppuku* in the wake of the revolt's failure. Adopting it from his own short story, Mishima also produced, directed, and starred in this film, which prefigured his own ritual suicide in 1970.

p. 806 Hideo Osabe puts it: Osabe quoted in Joan Mellen, *Voices from the Japanese Cinema* (New York: Liveright, 1975), p. 255.

p. 809 Tadao Sato . . . pornographic: Sato: in Dave Kehr,

"The Last Rising Sun," *Film Comment* 19, 5 (September–October 1983): 31.

p. 810 Sato wrote of such directors: Tadao Sato, "Rising Sons," *American Film* 11, 3 (December 1985): 78. See also Scott L. Malcomson, "Mitsuo Yanagimachi," *Film Criticism* 8, 1: 12–19; Alan Stanbrook, "Tokyo's New Satirists," *Sight and Sound* 57, 1 (Winter 1987–88): 54–57; Keiko I. McDonald, "Family, Education, and Postmodern Society: Yoshimitsu Morita's *The Family Game*," *East-West Film Journal* 4, 1 (December 1989): 53–68; and Jeffrey Sipe, "Death and Taxes: A Profile of Juzo Itami," *Sight and Sound* 58, 3 (Summer 1989); 186–89.

p. 810 television . . . mass medium in India: Introduced experimentally in 1959 but not significantly developed until the mid-seventies, Indian television was initially the province of the ruling elite, with less than one receiver available for every seven hundred people in 1980, for example, and signals covering only 23 percent of the nation. (Color wasn't introduced until 1982, when the INSAT satellite was launched to make truly national programming possible for the first time.) But in July of 1984, the government of Prime Minister Indira Ghandi—in preparation for its fall election campaign—ordered an extension of coverage to 70 percent of the population through the massive setting up of relay transmitters, which it financed by opening up the state-controlled medium to commercial advertising (chiefly by multinationals). Except for instructional programming brought to about one-fifth of the country's 550,000 villages by direct-broadcast satellite, however, Indian television remains urban-oriented and consumerist—which is to say, basically irrelevant to the vast majority of Indians. There were still only 3 million sets in use as the population approached 800 million in the late eighties, although that number should jump to 8 million in the early nineties when an expected increase in production is supposed to lower the cost of color receivers from 1,200 dollars to 600 dollars apiece.

p. 810 weekly audience . . . India: For more on Indian film audiences, see the affectionate docudrama *Cinema Cinema* (1979) by the Indian director Krishna Shah; and Elliot Stein, "Bangalore, Mon Amour: A Voyage to India," *Film Comment* 16, 3 (May–June 1980): 61–71. See also, Chicananda Das Gupta, "New Directions in Indian Cinema." *Film Quarterly* 34, 1 (Fall 1980): 32–42; and Stephen Haggard, "Indian Film Posters," *Sight and Sound* 57, 1 (Winter 1987–88): 62–63.

p. 810 fn. songs . . . songs: Formula for Indian films: Erik Barnouw and Subramanyam Krishnaswamy, *The Indian Film*, 2nd ed. (New York: Oxford University Press, 1980), p. 155.

p. 813 other Bengali filmmakers: Ray also inspired the American director James Ivory (b. 1928) and assisted him in the making of his first feature, *The Householder* (1963), shot on location in Bombay by several members of Ray's regular crew, including his longtime cameraman Subrata Mitra, the film was released simultaneously in English and Bengali. A domestic satire produced by Bombay native Ismail Merchant (1936) and adapted from her own novel by Ruth Prawer Jhabvala (b. 1927), *The Householder* inaugurated the enormously successful artistic collaboration that underwrites Merchant-Ivory Productions. Although India herself has remained the central focus of this team's work in such subsequent features as *Shakespeare Wallah* (1965), *The Guru* (1968), *Bombay Talkie* (1970), *The Autobiography of a*

Princess (1975), *Hullabaloo over Georgie and Bonnie's Pictures* (1978), *Heat and Dust* (1983), and *The Courtesans of Bombay* (1983), Merchant-Ivory has produced eclectic work like *Savages* ((1972; U.K.), *Roseland* (1970; U.S.A.), *The Wild Party* (1974; U.S.A.), *Jane Austen in Manhattan* (1980; U.S.A) and *Quartet* (1981; France), as well as award-winning literary adaptations from Henry James (*The Europeans* [1979]; *The Bostonians* [1984]) and E. M. Forster (*A Room With a View* [1986]; *Maurice* [1987]). See John Pym, *The Wandering Company: Twenty-one Years of Merchant Ivory Films* (London and New York: BFI and MoMa, 1983); and Ben Nyce, *Satyajit Ray: A Study of His Films* (New York: Praeger, 1988).

p. 816 *A Touch of Spice*: The International Film Festival of India (est. 1952) is held annually every other year at Delhi and on alternate years at Bombay, Calcutta, Madras, or Bangalore; *Cinema Vision India* is the industry's professional journal, published quarterly at Bombay.

Two relatively new republics within the Indian sphere of influence also produce films. Sri Lanka (formerly Ceylon), an island nation of 17 million people about 20 miles off of India's southeastern coast, has a government-sponsored Sinhala-language industry that was pioneered nearly single-handedly by the director James Lester Peries (b. 1919). There have been more than a dozen features since 1956, including most recently *Village in the Jungle* (*Baddegama*, 1981), *The Friends* (*Yahalu yeheli*, 1982), *The Time of Kali* (*Kaliyugaya* 1982), *The End of an Era* (*Yuganthaya*, 1985), and *Simion of Maldeniye* (*Maldeniye Simion*, 1987). Bangladesh, a nation of 100 million people created out of East Pakistan in 1971 after the Pakistani Civil War, produces several films each year by direct government grant (e.g., *The Ominous House* [*Suria dighal bari*, Massiouddin Shaker, 1980]; *Affliction* [*Dahan*, Sheikh Niamat Ali, 1986]).

As for Pakistan itself, its cinema was totally dominated by the Indian industry until 1965, when Indian films were banned in the wake of the border war over Kashmir. Pakistani films were mainly poor imitations of the popular Bombay musical, although some interesting films began to be produced during the presidency of Ali Bhutto, 1972–78 (e.g., Jamil Dehlavi's *The Blood of Hussein* [1979]—banned in its own country but widely seen in the West). An occasional original film also surfaced under the military regime of General Zia (e.g., Javed Fazil's *Threshold* [*Dehleez*, 1985], a technically polished adaptation of *Wuthering Heights*). Furthermore, Indian films became widely available once more—often within a week of their release—on smuggled videocassettes, in which a large and apparently unstoppable Pakistani trade developed.

See Firoze Rangoonwalla, *A Pictorial History of Indian Cinema* (London: Hamlyn, 1979); *Satyajit Ray's Art* (New Delhi: Clarion, 1980); Erik Barnouw and S. Krishnaswamy, *Indian Film*, 2nd ed. (New York: Oxford University Press, 1980); Chidananda Das Gupta, *The Cinema of Satyajit Ray* (New Delhi; Vikas, 1980); "New Directions in Indian Cinema," *Film Quarterly* 34, 1 (Fall 1980): 32–41; "A Passage from India," *American Film* 11, 1 (October 1985): 33–38; Derek Malcolm, "Mrinal Sen," *Sight and Sound* 50, 4 (Autumn 1981): 263–65; "Tiger: The Films of Ritwik Ghatak," *Sight and Sound* 51, 3 (Autumn 1982): 184–87; "India's Middle Cinema," *Sight and Sound* 55, 3 (Summer 1986): 172–74; Elliot Stein, "Film India," *Film Comment* 17, 4 (July–August 1981): 60–65; "India, Inc.," *Film Comment*

18, 4 (July–August 1982): 69–75; "The Other India," *Film Comment* 19, 3 (June 1983): 28–32; Aruna Vasudev and Phillipe Lenglet, eds., *Indian Cinema Superbazaar* (New Delhi: Vikas, 1983); Mira Reym Binford, "The New Cinema of India," *Quarterly Review of Film Studies* 8, 4 (Fall 1983): 47–67; *70 Years of Indian Cinema, 1913–1983*, ed. T. M. Ramachandran (Bombay: Cinema India-International, 1985); Aruna Vasudev, *The New Indian Cinema* (Dehli: Macmillan India Limited, 1986); Wimal Dissanayake, "Self and Modernization in Malayam Cinema," *East-West Film Journal* 1, 2 (June 1987): and "Questions of Female Subjectivity and Patriarchy: A Reading of Three Indian Women Film Directors," *East-West Film Journal* 3, 2 (June 1989): 74–90; 60–77; Malti Sahai, "Raj Kapoor and the Indianization of Charlie Chaplin," *East-West Film Journal* 2, 1 (December 1987): 62–76; Sara Dickey, "Accommodation and Resistance: Expression of Working-Class Values Through Tamil Cinema," *Wide Angle* 11, 3 (1989): 26–32; Shampa Banerjee and Anil Srivastava, *One Hundred Indian Feature Films: An Annotated Filmography* (New York: Garland, 1988); Kishore Valicha, *The Moving Image: A Study of Indian Cinema* (Bombay: Orient Longman, 1988); Chidananda Das Gupta, "Seeing and Believing, Science and Mythology: Notes on the 'Mythological' Genre," *Film Quarterly* 42, 4 (Summer 1989): 12–18; *Quarterly Review of Film and Video*, 11, 3 (1989), Indian Cinema special issue, ed. Mira Reym Binford; Andrew Robinson, *Satyajit Ray: The Inner Eye* (London: André Deutsch, 1989).

p. 817 constructive criticism . . . dissident films: From the ancient Chinese proverb "Let a hundred flowers bloom, let a hundred schools contend."

p. 819 Flaherty-like studies of Mongolian . . . life: Inner Mongolia is a remote border Province in northwestern China containing about 8 million people. The adjacent People's Republic of Mongolia is an independent Communist country with a population of about 2 million that has been allied with the USSR since 1946. It has a state film trust, Mongolkino, organized on the Soviet model, which produces a few films each year (e.g., B. Baljinnyam's *I Adore You* [*Bi chamd khayrtay*, 1986]).

p. 819 China Film Corporation . . . most of the eighties: See Jay Leyda, *Dianying: Electric Shadows: An Account of Films and the Film Audience in China* (Cambridge: MIT Press, 1972); John Howkins, *Mass Communication in China* (New York: Longman, 1982); John Ellis, "Electric Shadows in Italy," *Screen* 23, 2 (July–August 1982): 79–83; Mark L. Pinsky, "A Small Leap Forward," *American Film* 9, 6 (April 1984): 52–54; Chris Berry, ed, *Perspectives on Chinese Cinema* (Ithaca, N.Y.: Cornell University Press, 1985); Shao Mujun, "Chinese Film Amidst the Tide of Reform," *East-West Film Journal* 1, 1 (December 1986): 59–68; Alan Stanbrook, "The Flowers in China's Courtyard," *Sight and Sound* 56, 3 (Summer 1987); George Stephen Semsel, ed., *Chinese Film: The State of the Art in the People's Republic* (New York: Praeger, 1987); Paul Clark, "Ethnic Minorities in Chinese Films," *East-West Film Journal* 1, 2 (June 1987): 15–31; Tony Rayns, "The Position of Women in New Chinese Cinema," *East-West Film Journal* 1, 2 (June 1987): 32–44; Esther Yau, "China," in *World Cinema Since 1945* (New York: Ungar, 1987); and "*Yellow Earth*; Western Analysis and a Non-western Text," *Film Quarterly* 61, 2 (Winter 1987–88): 22–33; Paul Clark, *Chinese Cinema: Culture & Politics Since*

1949 (Cambridge: Cambridge University Press, 1987); Ma Ning, "Satisfied or Not: Desire and Discourse in the Chinese Comedy of the 1960s," *East-West Film Journal* 2, 1 (December 1987): 32–49; Chris Berry, "Chinese Urban Cinema: Hyper-realism Versus Absurdism," *East-West Film Journal* 3, 1 (December 1988); 76–96; *Wide Angle* 11, 2 (1989), Chinese Film special issue; Jenny Kwok Wah Lau, "Towards a Cultural Understanding of Cinema: A Comparison of Contemporary Films From the People's Republic of China and Hong Kong," *Wide Angle* 11, 3 (1989): 42–49; Ma Ning, "Symbolic Representation and Symbolic Violence: Chinese Family Melodrama of the Early 1980s," *East-West Film Journal* 4, 1 (December 1989); *Jump Cut* no. 24 (1989): 85–121, special section on the People's Republic of China, ed. Gina Marchetti; Ma Ning, "New Chinese Cinema: A Critical Account of the Fifth Generation," *Cineaste* 17, 3 (1990): 32–35 and "Leftist Chinese Cinema of the Thirties," *Cineaste* 17, 3 (1990), 36–37; Chen Kaige, "Breaking the Circle: The Cinema and Cultural Change in China," *Cineaste* 17, 3 (1990): 28–31; George Semsel, *Chinese Film Theory* (New York: Praeger, 1990); *Perspectives on Chinese Cinema*, ed. Chris Berry (London: BFI, 1990).

p. 820 Li Hanxiang: In 1986, Hanxiang directed *The Last Emperor* (also known as *Pu Yi's Latter Life*), a stately film about the last years of the Emperor Pu Yi, which compares very well indeed with Bertolucci's spectacle of the same title and theme.

p. 821 Hong Kong's film industry: Also worth noting here are the Chinese-American films of Hong Kong native Wayne Wang (b. 1949), which received a good deal of critical attention during the eighties—*Chan Is Missing* (1982), *Dim Sum* (1985), *Slam Dance* (1987), and *Eat a Bowl of Tea* (1989). See Verina Glaessner, *Kung Fu: Cinema of Vengeance* (New York: Bounty Books, 1974); I. C. Jarvie, *Window on Hong Kong: A Sociological Study of the Hong Kong Film Industry and Its Audience* (Hong Kong: University of Hong Kong, 1977); Harlan Kennedy, "Boat People," *Film Comment* 19, 5 (September–October 1983); John A. Lent, "Asian Cinema: A Selected International Bibliography," *Journal of Film and Video* 36, 3 (Summer 1984): 75–84; Tony Rayns, "Chinese Changes," *Sight and Sound* 54, 1 (Winter 1984/85): 24–29; Richard Meyers, Amy Harlib, III, and Karen Palmer, *Martial Arts Movies: From Bruce Lee to the Ninjas* (Secaucus, N.J.: Citadel Press, 1985); Chris Berry, "Chinese Cinema: A New Synthesis" in *Third World Affairs 1985*, ed. Raana Gauhar (London: Third World Foundation, 1986), pp. 412–18; David Chute, ed., "Midsection: Made in Hong Kong," *Film Comment* 24, 3 (May–June 1988), 33–56; Alan Stanbrook, "The Worlds of Hou Hsiao-Hsien," *Sight and Sound* 59, 2 (Spring 1990): 120–24.

p. 821 Hong Kong's 129: Other cinemas of the Pacific rim are those of Thailand, Vietnam, Indonesia, Malaysia, North and South Korea, and the Philippines. The Thai industry is star-and genre-based, producing about eighty films per year for a domestic population of 56 million. Most Thai films are unremarkable, except for the work of several serious directors such as Permphol Cheuriaroon (*Red Bamboo* [*Pai Daeng*, 1979]), Suchart Vuthivichai (*The Last Dewdrop* [1978]), Suwat Sichue (*Khun-Sa the Opium Emperor* [1982]), Vichit Kounavudhi (*Mountain People* [*Khon poo khao*, 1982]), Cherd Songsri (*Puen-Paeng* [1983]), Euthana Mukdasnit

Butterfly and Flower [1985]), and Chart Kopjitti (*House* [1987]). Neighboring Vietnam has a small industry with studios located in Hanoi and Ho Chi Minh City (formerly Saigon), and all films are produced with the assistance of the Ministry of Culture, according to the Soviet model. Even in this context, however, a handful of interesting films have appeared—e.g., Nguyen Ngoc Trung's *Orange-Colored Bells* (*Hoi duiong mau da cam*, 1984), Dang Nhat Minh's *October Won't Return* (*Bao qio cho den thang muoi*, 1984), and Ho Quong Minh's *Karma* (1986), produced in Vietnam with Swiss backing.

With a population of 300 million, 10 million living in Jakarta alone, Indonesia produces about eighty features per year, most of them imitations of American action films. As in Thailand, there are a handful of serious directors—e.g., Ami Priyono, known for his lavish period films (*Roro Mendut* [1985]) and comedies (*Dearest* [Yang, 1985]) and the prolific Teguh Karya, whose work has been lauded at several international festivals (e.g., *Under the Mosquito Net* [*Dibalik kelambu*, 1983]; *Bitter Coffee* [*Secangkir kope pahit*, 1986]; *Mementos* [*Doea tanda mata*, 1986]; *Mother* [*Ibunda*, 1987]).

Malaysian cinema, which inherited an old-style studio system from the thirties, was virtually monopolized by Shaw Brothers until the Nation Film Development Corporation (FINAS) was established in 1981 to upgrade the aesthetic quality of domestic cinema and film culture generally among its population of 17 million. Since that time a number of young independent directors have emerged—Jins Shamsuddin, whose politically themed *Bukit kepong* (1982) broke domestic box office records, Jamil Sulong (*No Harvest but a Thorn* [*Ranjau sepanjang jalan*, 1985]), Rahim Razari (*Death of a Patriot* [*Matinya seorang patriot*, 1985]), and Stephen Teo (*To Go on a Journey* [*Bejalai*, 1987]).

The industry of South Korea (Republic of Korea, population 43 million) currently produces eighty to ninety features per year and has a history going back to the twenties, much of quite distinguished if little known outside the country. During the sixties, in fact, South Korea became the largest film producers in the world, averaging 200 annually throughout the decade; but it experienced a severe slump following the mass diffusion of television in 1969. By late seventies, Korean films had begun to appear on the international festival circuit, and in the eighties, despite some of the strictest censorship laws in any non-communist nation, a so-called cinema of quality emerged, which featured subject matter from the country's ancient mystic culture and some of the best cinematography and lighting available in Asia. Among important contemporary South Korean directors are Kim Soo-Yong (b. 1929—*Gat-Mah-Eul* [1980]; *Late Autumn* [*Man Chu*, 1983]); Chung Jin-Woo (b. 1938—*Shall the Cuckoo Sing at Night?* [*Pocukido bame un-nka*, 1983]; *The Noblewoman* [*Janyo-nok*, 1985]); Lee Doo-Yong (b. 1942—*Pee-Mak* [*House of Death*, 1982]; *The Wheel* (*Yoin-chanhoksa: mulleya mulleya*, 1984]; *First Son* (*Jangnam*, 1985); *Pong* [*The Mulberry Tree*, 1986]; *Eunuch* [1986]; Im Kwon-taek (b. 1936—*Mandala* [1981]; *Village in the Mist* [*Ankaemaul*, 1984]; *Gilsoddeum* [*Gilsodom*, 1986]; *Contract Mother* [*Sibaji*, 1986]); Lee Jang-ho (*Fool's Manifesto* [*Pabo sunon*, 1983]; *The Entertainer* [*Er woo dong*, 1986]); Bae Chang-Ho (*Deep Blue Night* [*Gipgo pureun bam*, 1985]; *Hwang Chinee* [1986]; *Sweet Days of Youth* [1987]); and Myung-Joong Ha (*The Blazing Sun* [*Deng-Pyot*, 1985]).

North Korean film history began in 1945 when Kim Il-

Sung proclaimed the Democratic People's Republic. It initially concentrated on the production of documentaries and, especially during the Korean War of 1950–53, propaganda. A feature cinema began to develop slowly during the sixties and seventies, and in 1987 the first international North Korean film festival was held at Pyongyang, home of the state University of Cinematography since 1953. The most important directors practicing in North Korea (population 22 million) today are Rim Chang Bom (*Thaw* [*Pomnaiui nunsogi*, 1986]; winner of the main prize at the twenty-fifth Karlovy Vary Festival) and Yun Ryong Gyu (the widescreen historical epic *Talmae and Pomdari*, 1987); in 1986 the country's best-known director, Shin Sang-ok, and his actress wife, missing since the late seventies, surfaced in Vienna and asked for American political asylum.

The film industry of the Philippines (population 58 million) was large, exploitative, and studio-based until the sixties. Then the system began to collapse and its major stars established their own production companies, churning out a decade's worth of *batya*, or films for low-brow tastes. During the seventies, however, several Philippine directors garnered international profiles and earned new respect for the domestic industry, most prominently, Lino Brocka, whose *Manila in the Claws of Neon Signs* (*Maynila sa kuko ng liwanag*, 1975) is thought to be the most important Filipino film of the dec-

ade, and whose *Insiang* (1976) captured attention at Cannes in 1978. Brocka's success started a Philippine new wave, in which the collaboration of stylistically experimental directors with adventurous young writers produced such work as the French-trained Ishmael Bernal's *Speck in the Water* (*Nunal sa tubig*, 1976), Eddie Romero's *As We Were* (*Ganito kami noo*, 1976), and Mike de Leon's *Itim* (1976). When Brocka's *Jaguar* (1980) became the first Filipino film ever to compete at Cannes and Bernal's *City After Dark* (1980) the first Filipino film to succeed in the international marketplace, then First Lady Imelda Marcos organized the Manila International Film Festival, which ran for two years, in 1982 and 1983. In that short period, the Philippine new wave gained an international reputation in the continuing work of Brocka (*Lamentations* [*Dung-aw*, 1981]; *Bona* [1981]; *P. X.* [1982]; *My Country* [*Bayan ko*, 1984], *L'Insoumis* [*Fight for Us*, 1989], Bernal (*City After Dark* [1981]; *Himala* [1983]; *The Affair* [*Relayson*, 1985], de Leon (*In the Twinkling of an Eye* [*Kisapmata*, 1981]; *Batch '81* [1982], and Romero (*Desire* [1983], and the work of such relative newcomers as Kidlat Tahimik (*The Perfumed Nightmare* [1979]; *Turumba* [1983]), Laurice Guillen (*Salome* [1981]), Peque Gallaga (*Gold, Silver, Death* [*Oro, plata, mata*, 1983]), and Marilou Diaz-Abaya (*Moral* [1983]; *Of the Flesh* [*Karnal*, 1984]).

The Seventies and the Eighties:
Colonies of the Mind and Heart

p. 822 Third World cinema . . . significant historically: On Third World film, see Roy Armes, *Third World Film Making and the West* (Berkeley: University of California Press, 1987), Part 1: "The Social, Cultural, and Economic Context," pp. 5–49. See also Helen W. Cyr, *A Filmography of the Third World: An Annotated List of 16mm Films* (Metuchen, N.J.: Scarecrow, 1976), and *A Filmography of the Third World, 1976–1983: An Annotated List of 16mm Films* (Metuchen, N.J.: Scarecrow, 1985); Teshome H. Gabriel, *Third Cinema in the Third World: The Aesthetics of Liberation* (Ann Arbor, Mich.: UMI Research Press, 1982); John D. H. Downing, ed., *Film and Politics in the Third World* (New York: Praeger, 1987); Graeme Turner, *Film as Social Practice* (New York: Routledge, 1988); Jim Pines and Paul Willemen, *Questions of Third Cinema* (London: BFI, 1989).

p. 823 Fernando Solanas and Octavio Getino . . . to counter: Solanas and Getino quoted in Julianne Burton, "The Camera as a Gun," *Latin American Perspectives* 5, 1 (Winter 1978): 50.

p. 827 *Vidas errantes* (*Wandering Lives*, 1984): On Mexican film, see Beatriz Reyes Nevares, *The Mexican Cinema: Interviews with Thirteen Directors* (Albuquerque: University of New Mexico Press, 1976); Jesus Salvador Trevino, "The New Mexican Cinema," *Film Quarterly* 32, 3 (Spring 1979): 26–37; Carl J. Mora, *Mexican Cinema: Reflections of a Society, 1896–1980* (Berkeley: University of California Press,

1982); Leonardo Garcia Tsao, "Mexico Tinderbox," *Film Comment* (May–June 1985): 36–38; Elliott Stein, "Don Hermosillo and the Sun," *Film Comment* (June 1986): 53–57.

p. 831 films . . . continue to be made: On Brazilian film, see Randal Johnson and Robert Stam, *Brazilian Cinema* (Rutherford, N.J.: Fairleigh Dickinson University Press, 1982; repr. Austin: University of Texas Press, 1988); Robert Stam, "Slow Fade to Afro: The Black Presence in Brazilian Cinema," *Film Quarterly* 36, 2 (Winter 1982–83); Pat Aufderheide, "Will Success Spoil Brazilian Cinema?" *American Film* 8, 5 (March 1983): 65–70; Judy Stone, "On the Edge," *American Film* 10, 1 (October 1984): 68–71, 80; Dan Yakir, "Braziliant," *Film Comment* 20, 3 (May–June 1984), 56–59; Mark Osiel, "Bye Bye Boredom: Brazilian Cinema Comes of Age," *Cineaste* 24, 1 (1985): 30–35; *Framework* 28 (1985): Special Issue: "Brazil—Post Cinema Novo"; Randal Johnson, *Cinema Novo x Five: Masters of Contemporary Brazilian Film* (Austin: University of Texas Press, 1984) and *The Film Industry in Brazil: Culture and the State* (Pittsburgh: University of Pittsburgh Press, 1987); Robert Stam and Ismail Xavier, "Recent Brazilian Cinema: Allegory/Metacinema/Carnival," *Film Quarterly* 41, 3 (Spring 1988): 15–30.

p. 834 [*Love Is a Fat Woman*, 1987]: On Argentine film, see Tim Barnard, ed., *Argentine Cinema* (Toronto: Nightwood Editions, 1986); Pat Aufderheide, "Awake, Argentine," *Film Comment* (April 1986): 51–55; Silvia Kolbowski, "Out of

Cold Blood: New Argentine Cinema," *Afterimage* (Summer 1986): 5–7.

p. 838 Latin America's most . . . vibrant film culture: On Chilean film, see Michael Chanan, ed., *Chilean Cinema* (London: BFI, 1976); Zuzana M. Pick, "A Special Section on Chilean Cinema," *Cine-tracts* 3–1 (Winter 1980): 17–28, and "Chilean Cinema: Ten Years of Exile: 1973–1983," *Jump Cut* 32 (1987): 66–70; David Ehrenstein, "Raul Ruiz at the Holiday Inn," *Film Quarterly* 40, 1 (Fall 1986): 1–7; Ian Christie, "Raul Ruiz and the House of Culture," *Sight and Sound* (Spring 1987): 96–100; Julianne Burton, "Latin America: On the Periphery of the Periphery," in *World Cinema Since 1945*, ed. William Luhr (New York: Ungar, 1987), pp. 424–46; Gabriel García Márquez, *Clandestine in Chile: The Adventures of Miguel Littin*, trans. Asa Zatz (New York: Henry Holt, 1987); and Mark Falcoff, *Modern Chile 1979–1989: A Critical History* (New Brunswick, N.J.: Transaction Publishers, 1989). Recent films and videos from Chile are available in the "Internal Exile" program from Third World Newsreel (see Part IV). On South American cinema at large, see Luis Trelles Plazaola, *South American Cinema: Dictionary of Filmmakers*, trans. Yudit de Ferdinandy (Puerto Rico: Editorial de la Universidad de Puerto Rico, 1989), which covers the continent proper; and Jorge Sanjines and the Ukamau Group, *Theory and Practice of a Cinema with the People*, trans. Richard Schaaf (Willimantic, Conn.: Curbstone Press, 1989).

p. 840 *When the Mountains Tremble*: For Central American film, see Julia Lesage, "For Our Urgent Use: Films on Central America," *Jump Cut* 27, 1982; repr. *Jump Cut: Hollywood, Politics and Counter Cinema*, ed. Peter Steven (New York: Praeger, 1985), pp. 375–89; Dennis West, "Revolution in Central America: A Survey of Recent Documentaries," *Cineaste* 12, 1 (1982): 18–23; "Revolution in Central America: A Survey of New Documentaries," *Cineaste* 14, 3 (1986); Pat Aufderheide, "El Salvador: Bringing the War Home," *American Film* (June 1983): 50–54; Susan Ryan, "Behind Rebel Lines: Filmmaking in Revolutionary El Salvador," *Cineaste* 14, 1 (1985): 16–21; Alan Rosenthal, "*When the Mountains Tremble*: An Interview with Pamela Yates," *Film Quarterly* 39, 1 (Fall 1985): 2–10; Carol Cooper, "Central America: The Domino Next Door," *Film Comment* (May–June 1986): 39–42; Howard Dratch and Barbara Margolis, "Film and Revolution in Nicaragua: An Interview with INCINE Filmmakers," *Cineaste* 15, 3 (1987): 27–31; Louis Mathews, Hollywood Invades Nicaragua," *Mother Jones* 12, 9 (December 1987): 28–33; Coco Fusco, "Flipped Out in Nicaragua: An Interview with Alex Cox," *Cineaste* 16, 3 (1988): 12–16; Daniel M. Marranghello *El cine en Costa Rica, 1903–1920* (Costa Rica: Coleccion Cultura Cinematografica, 1988), and *Cine y Censura en Costa Rica* (Costa Rica: Coleccion Cultura Cinematografica, 1989); and Catherine Benamou, "Redefining Documentary in the Revolution: An Interview with Paolo Martin of the El Salvador Film and Television Unit," *Cineaste* 17, 3 (1990): 11–17.

p. 845 Cuba's existing apprenticeship system: For Cuban cinema, see Pierre Sauvage, "Cine Cubano," *Film Comment* 8, 1 (Spring 1972): 24–31; Anna Marie Taylor, "Lucia," *Film Quarterly* 27, 2 (Winter 1974–75): 53–58; Margot Kernan, "Cuban Cinema: Tomas Gutierrez Alea," *Film Quarterly* 29,

2 (Winter 1975–76): 45–52; Robert N. Pierce, *Keeping the Flame: Media and Government in Latin America* (New York: Hastings House, 1979); the writings of Julianne Burton, including "Portrait of Teresa," *Film Quarterly* 34, 3 (Spring 1981): 51–58, "Theory and Practice of Film and Popular Culture in Cuba: A Conversation with Julio Garcia Espinosa," *Quarterly Review of Film Studies* 7, 4 (Fall 1982): 341–51, *The New Latin American* (Smyrna Press, 1983), "Film and Revolution in Cuba: The First 25 Years," in Peter Steven, ed., *Jump Cut: Hollywood, Politics, and Counter-Cinema* (New York: Praeger, 1985), pp. 344–59, and *Cinema and Social Change in Latin America: Conversations with Filmmakers*, ed. Burton (Austin: University of Texas Press, 1986); Gaizka S. de Usabel, *The High Noon of American Films in Latin America* (Ann Arbor: UMI Research Press, 1982); Dan Georgakas and Lenny Rubenstein, eds., *The Cineaste Interviews: On the Art and Politics of the Cinema* (Chicago: Lake View Press, 1983); *20 Años de cine Cubano* (Havana: Ministerio de Cultura, Centro de Información Cinematografica, 1983); Jorge A. Schnitman, *Film Industries in Latin America: Dependency and Development* (Norwood, N.J.: Ablex, 1984); *Jump Cut: A Review of Contemporary Media* 30 (1984): special section on "Latin American Film," 44–62; Pat Aufderheide, "Red Harvest," *American Film* 9, 5 (March 1984): 28–34, "On Castro's Convertible," *Film Comment* 21, 3 (May–June, 1985): 49–52, and "Se Permuta," *Film Quarterly* 39, 3 (Spring 1986): 59–60; Tomas Gutierrez Alea, "I Wasn't Always a Filmmaker," *Cineaste* 14, 1 (1985), 36–38; James Roy Macbean, "A Dialogue with Tomas Gutierrez Alea on the Dialectics of *Hasta cierta punta*," *Film Quarterly* (Spring 1985): 22–29; Gary Crowdus, "Up to a Point: An Interview with Tomas Gutierrez Alea and Mirta Ibarra," *Cineaste* 14, 2 (1985): 26–30; Michael Chanan, *The Cuban Image: Cinema and Cultural Politics in Cuba* (London: BFI, 1985); Ana M. Lopez, "Towards a 'Third' and 'Imperfect' Cinema: A Theoretical and Historical Study of Filmmaking in Latin America," unpublished dissertation, University of Iowa, 1986, and "The Melodrama in Latin America: Films, Telenovelas, and the Currency of a Popular Form," *Wide Angle* 7, 3 (1986): 5–13; Thomas E. Skidmore and Peter H. Smith, *Modern Latin America*, 2nd ed. (New York: Oxford University Press, 1989); the two-part documentary feature *New Cinema of Latin America*, written, produced, and directed by Michael Chanan (1986) co-produced with ICAIC, INCINE., Dpto. de Cine, ULA [Venezuela]; GECU [Panama]; Zafra AC [Mexico]; and Tatu Films, Ltda. [Brazil]); *Part I: Cinema of the Humble*, 83 minutes; *Part II: The Long Road*, 85 minutes; New York: a Cinema Guild release.

p. 845 Clyde Taylor, . . . small by Western standards: Clyde Taylor, "Africa: The Last Cinema," in *World Cinema Since 1945*, ed. William Luhr, pp.. 1–3.

p. 847 (*Wife of an Important Man*, 1987): Other Arabic-speaking film-producing countries in the adjacent Middle East include Lebanon, which once had the best studios and laboratories in the Arab world and which is still making films despite its fifteen years of war. Some Lebanese films are Rafiq Hadjjar's *Explosion* (*Al-infigar*, 1983); Heini Srour's *Leila and the Wolves* (*Leila wal dhiab*, 1984); Jean Chamoun's *Women from South Lebanon*; Jocelyne Saab's *The Adolescent Sugar of Love* (*Gazi el banat*, 1975). Syria's recent films, funded through the National Film Organization (NFO), include Mohamed Malass' *Dreams of the City* (*Ahlam al madina*, 1984), and Mohamed Chanin's *The Sun on a Hazy Day*, 1986. In Kuwait, there has been *The Wedding of Zein* (*Urs Zayn*, Khalid Siddik, 1976); in Libya, *Shrapnel* (*Alshazhia*, Mohamed Abdul Salam, 1987), and in the Sudan, *Paradise Slum* (*Deim dar el-naemi*, Cornelia Schlede, 1986). Works by Palestinian filmmakers include *Fertile Memory* (*Al-dahkira al-khasba*, Michel Khleifi, 1980) and *Return to Haifa* (*Kassem Hawal*, 1982). Of the other Muslim cultures of the Middle East, Iran (population 47 million) and Iraq (population 17 million) both produce films. Iraqi cinema, which has been in existence since 1945, is state controlled through the General Organization for Cinema and Theater. It produced its first epic in 1982, the 15-million-dollar *Al-gaadisiyya*, directed by the Egyptian Salah Abu Sief, based on an historical episode from 636 A.D. in which outnumbered Arab forces repulse an army of invading infidels. Like most Iraqi films made since the bloody war with Iran began in 1980 (e.g., Mohammed Shukri Jameel's *Clashing Loyalties* [*Al mas a la al kubra*, 1983]; Mohamed Moumir Fanari's *The Lover* [*Al asheke*, 1986]; Sahib Haddad's *Flaming Borders* [*Al hudud al multahiba*, 1986]), this one is redolent with militant nationalism. From the coming of sound through the revolution of 1979, the media of Iran—like those of Latin America—were dominated by America, through the powerful lobby of the Motion Picture Export Association and, after 1960, the Television Program Export Association. A domestic feature-film industry therefore developed in Iran along America-oriented, escapist lines; between 1931 and the revolution Iran produced over 1,100 motion pictures. Between 1966 and 1976, a progressive national film movement came into being, as foreign-trained directors such as Fereydoun Rahnama (*Siavash in Persepolis* [*Siavash-e-takhte ajmshid*, 1965), Davood Molapour (*Ahoo's Husband*, 1966), and Assoud Kimaee (*Gheysar*, 1966) made their first features. Various film festivals—particularly the Tehran International Festival, inaugurated in 1972—were established with the support of the Ministry of Art and Culture to showcase the new work. The breakthrough film for this Iranian New Wave or New Cinema (*cinema motefavet*) was Darius Mehrjui's (b. 1939) second feature *The Cow* (*Gav*, 1969). This starkly realistic account of peasant life adapted from a short story by the leftist writer Gholam-Hossein Saedi was banned in Iran for more than a year but won prizes at the Chicago and Venice festivals in 1971. It was immediately followed by such other independently produced features as Bahram Beizaee's *Downpour* (1970), Arbi Avanesian's *The Spring* (1970), Nasser Taghvaee's *Tranquility in the Presence of Others* (1971) and *Sadegh the Kurd* (1972), Hajir Daryoush's *Bita* (1972), and Mehrjui's own *The Postman* (*Postchi*, 1970, released 1972). In 1974 the New Wave directors created a film cooperative known as the New Film Group (NFG), which produced Sohrab Shahid Saless's *Still Life* (*Tabi at-e-bijan*, 1974), Mehrjui's *The Cycle* (*Dayerh-e-Mina*, 1974; one of the few Iranian films to be distributed in the United States, in 1979), and Parviz Kimiavi's *Stone Garden* (*Bagh-e-sanghi*, 1975), winner of the Silver Bear at Berlin in 1976. An economic squeeze encouraged by American distributors brought a halt to independent production in Iran, and during 1977 and 1978 no feature or documentary of any worth was released. The Khomeni government imposed strict theocratic (that is, Muslim fundamentalist) censorship after the revolution and many filmmakers fled the country (Saless, e.g., went to West Germany; Mehrjui, to Paris): by 1983, only forty films had been made in the four years since the revolution and twenty three had been banned. In 1987, however, the government's new Farabi Cinema Foundation (FCF) adopted a more liberal policy, and many former New Wave directors—Mehrjui (*The Tenants*, 1987), Taghvai (*Captain Khorsheed*, 1987), for example—returned to work. See *Arab Cinema and Culture* (Beirut, Lebanon: UNESCO, 1963); Hamid Nacify, "Iranian Feature Film: A Brief Critical History," *Quarterly Review of Film Studies* 4, 4 (Fall 1979): 443–64, and *Iran Media Index* (Westport, Conn.: Greenwood Press, 1984); John Motavalli, "Exiles," *Film Comment* 19, 4 (July–August 1983), 56–59; *Dreams Betrayed: A Study of Political Cinema in Iran, 1969–1979* (1985), a film by Jamsheed Akrami (118 minutes); and M. Ali Issari, *Cinema in Iran, 1900–1979* (Metuchen, N.J.: Scarecrow, 1989).

p. 850 *Sambizanga . . . many international awards:* On North African cinema, see Mohamed Khan, *An Introduction to Egyptian Cinema* (London: Infomatics, 1969); Lyle Pearson, "Four Years of North African Film," *Film Quarterly* 26, 4 (Summer 1973): 18–26; *Algerian Cinema*, ed. Hala Salmana et al. (London: BFI, 1976); Lizbeth Malkmus, "The 'New' Egyptian Cinema: Adopting Genre Conventions to a Changing Society," *Cineaste* 16, 3 (1988): 30–33. On sub-Saharan cinema, see *Black Cinema Aesthetic: Issues in Independent Black Filmmaking*, ed. Gladstone L. Yearwood (Athens, Oh.: Center for Afro-American Studies, 1982); and *Twenty-five Black African Filmmakers: A Critical Study, with Filmography and Bio-Bibliography* (Westport, Conn.: Greenwood Press, 1988); Tony Safford and William Triplett, "Haile Gerima: Radical Departures to a New Black Cinema," *Journal of the University and Television Association* 35, 2 (Spring 1983); 59–65; Louise Spence and Robert Stam, "Colonization, Racism and Representation," *Screen* 24, 2 (March–April 1983): 2–20; Homi K. Bhabha, "The Other Question: The Stereotype and Colonial Discourse," *Screen* 24, 6 (November–December 1983): 18–36; Françoise Pfaff, *The Cinema of Ousmane Sembene: A Pioneer of African Film* (Westport, Conn.: Greenwood, 1984), Marcia Landy, "Political Allegory and 'Engaged Cinema': Sembene's *Xala*," *Cinema Journal* 23, 3 (Spring 1984): 31–46; Maryann Oshana, *Women of Color: A Filmography of Minority and Third World Women* (New York: Garland, 1985); Steve Howard, "A Cinema of Transformation: The Films of Haile Gerima," *Cineaste* 14, 1 (1985): 28–29, 30; Sanford J. Ungar, *Africa: The People and the Politics of an Emerging Continent* (New York: Simon & Schuster, 1985); *Jump Cut: A Review of Contemporary Media* 31 (1986): special section on "African Film," 44–50; Manthia Diawara, "Sub-Saharan African Film Production: Technological Paternalism," *Jump Cut* 32 (1987): 61–65, "New Perspectives in African Cinema: An Interview with Cheick Oumar Sissoko," (with Elizabeth Robinson), *Film Quarterly* 41, 2 (Winter 1987–88): 43–48, "Popular Culture and Oral Traditions in African Films," *Film Quarterly* 41, 3 (Spring 1988): 6–14; Nancy Schmidt, *Sub-Saharan African Films and Filmmakers: An Annotated Bibliography* (London: Hans Zell Publishers, 1988); William Fisher, "Ouagadougou," *Sight and Sound* 58, 3 (Summer 1989): 170–73; and *Black Cinema*, ed. Manthia Diawara, (London: Routledge, 1990).

p. 850 German Film Company, or DEFA: East German production is still controlled by DEFA, which devotes up to 50 percent of its output to films dealing with contemporary domestic issues. Popular genres include the literary adaptation, the children's film, and the anti-Nazi film. Owing to a liberalization of cultural policies under Erich Honecker, who succeeded the hard-line Stalinist Walter Ulbricht as party secretary in 1971, several distinguished features in the latter category reached the West during the seventies, including Frank Beyer's film about the Warsaw Ghetto, *Jakob der Lügner* (*Jacob the Liar*, 1976), Konrad Wolf's *Mama, ich lebe* (*Mum, I'm Alive*, 1977), and Evelyn Schmidt's *Seitensprung* (*Escapade*, 1980). Wolf (1925–82), president of the GDR's Academy of Fine Arts, who had brought the nation's fledgling industry to world attention in 1959 when his East German–Bulgarian coproduction *Sterne* (*Stars*) won the Special Jury Prize at Cannes and who had made its first 70mm spectacle in *Goya* (1971, coproduced with the USSR), won the Silver Bear at Berlin in 1978 for his last feature *Solo Sunny*. This film about a singer who is discontented with the drab socialist world around her was a path-breaking work in the GDR, and it was followed by a number of other works that implicitly criticized the status quo, among them Heiner Carow's *Bis dass der Tod euch scheidet* (*Until Death Do Us Part*, 1980), Ulrich Thein's *Romanze mit Amelie* (*Romance with Amelie*, 1982) and *Buergschaft fuer ein Jahr* (*On Probation*, 1983), Frank Beyer's *Der Aufenthalt* (*Held for Questioning*, 1983), Evelyn Schmidt's *Der Fahrrad* (*The Bicycle*, 1982), Hermann Zochoche's *Und naechstes Jahr am Balaton* (*And Next Year at Balaton*, 1982), Roland Graf's *Märkische Forschungen* (*Research in Mark Brandenburg*, 1983), and Lothar Warneke's *Die Beunruhigung* (*Apprehension*, 1982) and *Eine sonderbare Liebe* (*A Strange Love Affair*, 1984). Also of note are Winifred Junge's *Lebensläufe* (*Paths of Life*, 1982), a remarkable documentary from the highly respected DEFA Dokumentarfilm Studios tracing the lives of schoolchildren from 1961–79; the first West German–East German coproduction, *Früehlingssinfonie* (*Spring Symphony*, Peter Schamoni, 1983), a biography of composer Robert Schumann; Rainer Simon's World War I drama *Die Frau und der Fremde* (*The Woman and the Stranger*, 1985), co-winner of the Golden Bear at Berlin; Helmut Hzuiba's children's film *Sabine Kleist, 7 Jahre* (*Sabine Kleist, 7 Years Old*, 1983); the West German films of expatriate director Egon Gunther (e.g., *Morenga*, 1985); and the recent work of Herrmann Zshoche—*Halfte des Lebens* (*A Half of Life*, 1985); *Die Alleinseglerin* (*The Solo Sailor*, 1988); Roland Graf—*Das Haus am Fluss* (*The House on the River*, 1986); Lothar Warneke—*Einer Trage des anderd Last* (*Bear Ye One Another's Burdens*, 1988; and Frank Beyer—*Der Bruch* (*The Break*, 1989). For more, see the sections on the German Democratic Republic in Mira and Antonin Liehm, *The Most Important Art: East European Film After 1945* (Berkeley: University of California Press, 1977), Elaine and Harry Mensh, *Behind the Scenes in Two Worlds* (New York: International Publishers,1978); and Sigrun D. Leonhard, "Testing the Borders: East German Film between Individualism and Social Commitment," *Post New Wave Cinema in the Soviet Union and Eastern Europe*, ed. Daniel J. Goulding (Bloomington: Indiana University Press, 1989), pp. 51–101.

p. 851 DEFA . . . new socialist state: See Thomas Guback, "Shaping the Film Business in Postwar Germany: The Role of the U.S. Film Industry and the U.S. State," in *The Hollywood Film Industry*, ed. Paul Kerr (London: BFI, 1986). The rabid anti-Nazism of the East German government made it appear that East Germans had "forgotten" less about the past than their former countrymen. For example, whereas only one concentration camp (Dachau) was left standing in West Germany, East Germany memorialized over thirty of them and required that all schoolchildren visit at least one in the course of their education. Yet East German camps memorialized not the history of what happened there but the myth of the heroic Communist resistance to it. So if West Germany behaved as if the Holocaust never happened, East Germany convinced itself that it happened to somebody else; and reunification should disturb both allusions profoundly.

p. 852 a manifesto that concluded as follows: Manifesto quoted in *Fassbinder*, ed. Tony Raynes (London, 1976), p. 4.

p. 852 1971 . . . *New York Times*: *New York Times* 1971 quoted in *Time*, March 20, 1978, p. 51.

p. 853 FFA . . . 1978: For film subsidies in West Germany, see Charles Eidsvik, "The State as Movie Mogul," *Film Comment* 15, 2 (March–April 1979): 60–66; Andrea Strout, "West Germany's Film Miracle," *American Film* 5, 7 (May 1980): 37–39; Hans-Bernhard Moeller, "New German Cinema and Its Precarious Subsidy and Finance System," *Quarterly Review of Film Studies* 5, 2 (Spring 1980): 157–68; Jan Dawson, "A Labyrinth of Subsidies: The Origins of the New German Cinema," *Sight and Sound* 50, 2 (Winter 1980–81): 14–20; and William Fisher, "Germany: A Neverending Story," *Sight and Sound* 54, 3 (Summer 1985): 174–79.

p. 853 Thomas Elsaesser writes: Elsaesser in *Fassbinder*, p. 13.

p. 854 cultural dislocation . . . Michael Covino: Michael Covino, "A Worldwide Homesickness: The Films of Wim Wenders," *Film Quarterly* 30, 2 (Winter 1976–77): 16.

p. 858 Fassbinder's . . . melodrama: Fassbinder quoted in Paul Thomas, "Fassbinder: Poetry of the Inarticulate," *Film Quarterly* 30, 2 (Winter 1976–77): 6.

p. 858 Fassbinder . . . Sirk: Fassbinder quoted in Thomas, p. 5.

p. 859 Vincent Canby . . . end of capitalism: Canby quoted in "Rainer Fassbinder—the Most Original Talent Since Godard," *New York Times*, March 6, 1977, sec. 2, p. 13.

p. 860 Fassbinder's comments on Sirk: Fassbinder quoted regarding Sirk in Thomas, pp. 4–5.

p. 861 Of his true ends, he said this: Fassbinder on "realism": Thomas, p. 6.

p. 861 international cinema since Godard: Since his death, Fassbinder has been the subject of two feature-length documentaries—*Der Bauer von Babylon* (*The Wizard of Babylon*, 1982) directed by Dieter Schider, the producer of *Querelle*, and *Das letzte Jahre* (*The Last Year*, 1983) directed by Wolf Gremm, who also directed Fassbinder's last performance as an actor in the police thriller *Kamikaze '89* (1982)—and one dramatic feature à clef, *Ein Mann Wie EVA* (*A Man Like EVA*, Radu Gabrea, 1984). There are also a number of critical books (e.g., Peter Iden et al., *Fassbinder* [Tanam Press, 1981]), monographs (e.g., Richard Collins and Vincent Porter, *WDR and the Arbeiterfilm, Fassbinder, Ziewer, and Others* [London: BFI. 1985]), special journal issues (e.g., *October* 21 [Summer 1982]: "Rainer Werner Fassbinder"), published screenplays (e.g., *The Marriage of Maria Braun*, ed. Joyce Rheuban [New Brunswick, N.J.: Rutgers University Press, 1986]), numerous critical articles, and biographies of varying worth (e.g., Ronald Heyman, *Fassbinder: Filmmaker* [New York: Simon and Schuster, 1984] and Robert Katz, *Love Is Colder Than Death; The Life and Times of Rainer Werner Fassbinder* [New York: Random House, 1987]).

p. 861 Amos Vogel writes: Random House, Amos Vogel, *Film as a Subversive Art* (New York, 1974), p. 314.

p. 864 *Herz aus Glas* . . . Middle Ages: Werner Herzog quoted in Gideon Bachmann, "The Man on the Volcano: A Portrait of Werner Herzog," *Film Quarterly* 31, 3 (Fall 1977): 5.

p. 864 Les Blank's . . . *Burden of Dreams*: Published in book form as *Burden of Dreams: Screenplay, Journals, Reviews, Photographs*, Les Blank and James Bogan, eds, (Berkeley, Cal.: North Atlantic Books, 1984). Earlier, the New German Cinema directors Christian Weisenborn and Edwin Keusch compiled a feature-length portrait of Herzog and his work entitled *Was ich bin, sind meine Filme* (*I Am My Films*, 1979).

p. 865 Amos Vogel has . . . written: Amos Vogel, "Herzog in Berlin," *Film Comment* 13, 5 (September–October 1978): 38.

p. 865 Herzog himself remarked: Herzog in Bachmann, *Film Quarterly* 31: 10.

p. 865 *Ballad of the Little Soldiers* . . . Sandinista government: See George Paul Csiscery, "*Ballad of the Little Soldiers*: Werner Herzog in a Political Hall of Mirrors," *Film Quarterly* (Winter 1985–86): 7–15. See also Timothy Corrigan, ed., *The Films of Werner Herzog Between Mirage and History* (New York: Methuen, 1986).

p. 866 dislocation . . . living in the modern world: For description of Wenders, see Covino, *Film Quarterly*, p. 9.

p. 867 Wenders . . . film language: Wenders quoted in Covino, p. 17.

p. 867 Wenders . . . terms of his art: See Timothy Corrigan, *New German Cinema: The Displaced Image* (Austin: University of Texas Press, 1983), and "Cinematic Snuff: German Friends and Narrative Murders," *Cinema Journal* 14, 2 (Winter 1985), 9–18; and Kathe Geist, *The Cinema of Wim Wenders: From Paris, France, to "Paris, Texas"* (Ann Arbor, Mich.: UMI Research Press, 1988).

p. 871 primary experiences . . . vicarious ones: See *The Brechtian Aspect of Radical Cinema: Essays by Martin Walsh*, ed. Keith M. Griffiths (London: BFI, 1981).

p. 872 J. Dudley Andrew summarizes: J. Dudley Andrew, *The Major Film Theories* (New York: Oxford University Press, 1976), pp. 238–39.

p. 873 aspiring new talents in West Germany: Other important figures of *das neue Kino* whose work has been subsidized by the FFA are Johannes Schaaf (b. 1933)—*Trotta*, 1972; *Dreamtown*, 1974; *Momo*, 1987; Hark Bohm (b. 1939)—*Nordsee ist Mordsee* (*North Sea's the Dead Sea*, 1976); *Moritz, lieber Moritz* (*Moritz, Dear Moritz*, 1978); *Der Fall Bachmeier* (*The Bachmeier Case*, 1983); *Der kleine*

Staatsnwaltk (*The Little Prosecutor*, 1987); Ottokar Runze (b. 1925)—*Im Namen des Volkes* (*In the Name of the People*, 1975); *Verlorene Liebe* (*Lost Love*, 1976); *Stern ohne Himmel* (*Star without a Sky*, 1981); *Feine Gesellschaft, Beschraenkte haftung* (English title: *Society Limited*, 1982); *Der Schnuffler* (*Sniffing Around*, 1984); Ulli Lommel (b. 1944)—*The Tenderness of Wolves* (1975, a stylized remake of Fritz Lang's 1931 film, *M*; *Blank Generation* (1979); *Cocaine Cowboys* (1980); Bernhard Sinkel (b. 1940) and Alf Brustellin (b. 1940)—*Lina Braake* (1975); *Berlinger* (1976); *Madchenkrieg* (*Three Daughters/The Maiden's War*, 1977); *Taugenichts* (*Good-for-Nothings*, 1978); *Kaltgestellt* (*Put on Ice*, 1980); Uwe Brandner—*Halbe-Halbe* (*Fifty-Fifty*, 1979); Klaus Emmerich (b. 1943)—*Die erste Polka* (*The First Polka*); *Geheime Reichssache* (*State Secrets*, 1979); Theodor Kotulla (b. 1928)—*Aus einem deutsche Leben* (*Out of a German Life*, 1978, a biography of the commandant of Auschwitz); the Iranian-born Sohrab Shahid Saless—*Tagebuch aines Liebende* (*Diary of a Man in Love*, 1977); *Die langen Ferien der Lotte H. Eisner* (*The Long Vacation of Lotte H. Eisner*, 1979); *Ordnung* (*Order*, 1980); *Utopia* (1983); *Empfaenger Unbekannt* (*Addressee Unknown*, 1983); Klaus Lemke (b. 1940)—*Ein komischer Heiliger* (*Some Kind of Saint*, 1979); Eberhard Schubert—*Flamme empor* (*Torch High*, 1979); Adolf Winkelmann—*Die Abfahrer* (*On the Move*, 1979); Helmut Dietl—*Der Durchdreher* (*It Can Only Get Worse*, 1979); Norbert Kückelmann (b. 1930)—*Die letzten Jahre der Kindheit* (*The Last Years of Childhood*, 1979); *Morgen in Alabama* (*Tomorrow in Alabama/A German Lawyer*, 1984); Christian Rischert (b. 1935)—*Lena Rais* (1980); Rainer Erler—*Fleisch* (*Meat*, 1979); Hellmuth Costard (b. 1940)—*Der kleine Godard* (*The Little Godard*, 1979); *Echtzeit* (*Realtime*, 1983, co-directed with Juergen Ebert); Peter Stein—*Trilogie des Wiedersehens* (*Trilogy of Reunions*, 1979); Michael Verhoeven (b. 1938)—*Sonntagskinder* (*Sunday's Children*, 1980); *Die weisse Rose* (*The White Rose*, 1982); Wolf Gremm (b. 1942)—*Kamikaze '89* (1982); *Das letzte Jahr* (*The Last Year*, 1983, a documentary on Fassbinder); Percy Adlon—*Celeste* (1981); *Die Schaukel* (*The Swing*, 1983); *Zuckerbaby* (*Sugar Baby*, 1984); children's director Dieter Koester—*Drippel-Droppel* (1981); *Schoene lahme Ferien* (*Pretty Dull Vacation*, 1981); *Der Mauerbande* (*The Berlin Wall Gang*, 1981); *Wilde Clique* (*Wild Bunch*, 1983); *Wohin mit Willfried* (*What to do with Willfried*, 1986); Detlef Gumm and Hans-George Ullrich—*Zivile Knote* (*Fun Raising*, 1985); Harun Farocki (b. 1944)—*Betrogen* (*Betrayed*, 1985); Rolf Schubel—*Nachruf auf eine Bestie* (*Obituary for a Beast*, 1985); Manfred Korytowski—*Die Wannseekonferenz* (*The Wannsee Conference*, 1987); Rudolph Thome (b. 1939)—*Das Mikroscop* (*The Microscope*, 1988). See Charles Eidsvik, "Behind the Crest of the Wave: An Overview of the New German Cinema," *Literature/Film Quarterly* 7, 3 (Summer 1979): 167–81; "West German Film in the 1970s," *Quarterly Review of Film Studies* 5, 2 (Spring 1980 [special issue]); John Sandford, *The New German Cinema* (New York: Da Capo Press, 1980); James Franklin, *New German Cinema: From Oberhausen to Hamburg* (Boston: Twayne Publishers, 1983); Hans Gunther Pflaum and Hans Helmut Prizler, *Cinema in the Federal Republic of*

Germany: The New German Film: Origins and Present Situation (Bonn: Inter Nationes, 1983); Timothy Corrigan, *New German Film: The Displaced Image* (Austin: University of Texas Press, 1983): Klaus Phillips, ed., *New German Filmmakers: From Oberhausen Through the 1970s* (New York: Frederick Ungar, 1984); Erich Rentschler, *West German Film in the Course of Time: Reflections on the Twenty Years since Oberhausen* (Bedford Hills, N.Y.: Redgrave Publishing Company, 1984) and Eric Rentschler, ed., *West German Filmmakers on Film* (New York: Holmes & Meier, 1988); "New German Cinema," *Persistence of Vision* 2 (Fall 1985 [special issue]); Manfred K. Wolfram, "Film in the Federal Republic of Germany," in *Contemporary Germany: Politics and Culture*, Charles Burdick et al., eds. (Boulder, Colo., and London: Westview Press, 1986), pp. 371-94; Richard C. Helt and Marie E. Helt, *West German Cinema since 1945: A Reference Handbook* (Metuchen, N.J.: Scarecrow Press, 1987); Erich Rentschler, ed., *German Film and Literature: Adaptations and Transformations* (New York: Holmes & Meier, 1988); and Thomas Elsaesser, *New German Cinema: A History* (New Brunswick, N.J.: Rutgers University Press, 1989). See also the quarterly journal *Kino: German Film*, published since 1980 by Dorothea and Ronald Holloway in Berlin.

p. 874 Jan Dawson remarked: Jan Dawson, *Wim Wenders* (New York: New York Zoetrope, 1976), p. 3.

p. 874 *das neue Kino . . . for some time to come:* Other German-language film industries are located in Switzerland (discussed in Chapter 13) and Austria; domestic cinema is also produced by the Germanic peoples of the Netherlands, where Dutch is spoken, With a population of only 7 million, Austria produces about thirty films a year, virtually all of them on individual initiative and until recently, at least, virtually all for domestic consumption. During the eighties, however, the overall quality of Austrian films increased, and a few even won festival prizes. Notable among them are *Der Bockerer* (Franz Antel, 1981); *Zechmeister* (Angela Summereder, 1981); *Ein Wenig sterben* (*To Die a Little*, 1981) and *Dicht hinter der Tur* (*Close Behind the Door*, 1984), both made by Iranian-born Mansur Madhavi; *Gehversuche* (*Trying to Walk* [Edwin Zbonek, 1982]); Valie Export's *Praxis der Liebe* (*The Practice of Love*, 1984); Axel Corti's *Eine blaßblaue Frauenschrift* (*A Pale Blue Woman's Handwriting*, 1984); Xaver Schwarzenverger's *Donauwalzer* (*Danube Waltz*, 1984; Grand Prize, Monte Carlo); Käthe Kratz's *Atemnot* (*Fighting for Breath*, 1984); *Die Erben* (*The Inheritors*, 1982); *Was Kostet der Sieg?* (*What Price Victory?*, 1980), both by Walter Bannert; *Malambo* (Milan Dor, 1984, winner of the Grand Prix at Mannheim); *Echo Park* (Robert Dornhelm, 1985, shot on location in Los Angeles with a largely American cast); *Merken sie sich dieses Gesicht* (*Make a Note of This Face* [Gerhard Meseck, 1986]); and *Die nachtmeerfahrt* (*The Nocturnal Voyage* [Kitty Kino, 1986]); but it is generally agreed that the highest level of directorial talent in Austria is in television, a more truly national medium than cinema.

The patron saint of Dutch cinema was the documentarist Joris Ivens (1898-1989), who began his career by founding one of the earliest film societies (Filmliga, 1926) and making such notable experimental shorts as *De brug* (*The Bridge*, 1928) and *Regen* (*Rain*, 1929), before turning to the socially committed work of Burinage (1933; co-directed with the Belgian Henri Storck, *Nieuwe gronden* (*New Earth*, 1933), and *Spanish Earth* (1937), filmed during the height of the Spanish Civil War, with a commentary written and narrated by Ernest Hemingway. Other projects in China (*The 400 Million*, 1939; the United States (*The Power and the Land*, 1940), and Indonesia (*Indonesia Calling*, 1945) kept Ivens away from the Netherlands until after World War II. Then his left-wing politics took him increasingly to Eastern Europe (*Song of the Rivers*, 1954–55), Cuba (where he lectured at ICAIC in the early sixties), North Vietnam (*17th Parallel*, 1967), and the People's Republic of China (*How Yukong Moved the Mountain*, 1973–75; *A History of the Wind* (1988). In his absence, Bert Haanstra (b. 1916) emerged as the leading figure of postwar Dutch cinema with such documentaries as *Spiegel van Holland* (*Mirror of Holland*, 1950), which won the Grand Prix for shorts at Cannes in 1951. In fact, by 1970 Haanstra had amassed more than fifty international awards for his films— twenty for the short *Glas* (*Glass*, 1960) alone—and the Dutch documentary tradition was thriving in the work of such near contemporaries as Herman van der Horst (1911–76), John Ferno (b. 1918), Hattum Hoving (1918–76), Theo van Haren Noman (b. 1917), Jan Vrijman (b. 1925), and many more. In the area of dramatic film, however, the only director who was able to work consistently during this period was Fons Rademakers (b. 1920), whose *Dorp aan de rivier* (*Village on the River*, 1958), *De dans van de reiger* (*The Dance of the Heron*, 1966), *Mira* (1971), and *Max Havelaar* (1976) all earned marks of distinction for Dutch cinema at a time when a theatrical feature industry was virtually nonexistent. In recognition of this lack, the government established the Netherlands Film Academy (NFA) in 1958 to train directors for work in a national cinema, although the state did not establish a system of production subsidies for another twenty years.

Until the eighties, in fact, feature production was carried out by independents like Adriaan Ditvoorst (b. 1940), whose first film was the much acclaimed low-budget *Paranoia* (1967), a hermetic study of a paranoid youth driven to murder in Amsterdam. Ditvoorst continued his excursions into surrealism through three more films—*Antenna* (1969), *De blinde fotograaf* (*The Blind Photographer*, 1972), and *Der mantel der liefte* (*The Cloak of Charity*, 1978)—and became the most highly regarded director in Holland until the money ran out, and he quit filmmaking for six years, returning only with the hallucinatory *De witte waan* (*The White Delusion*, 1984). Other young Dutch filmmakers such as Jos Stelling (b. 1945)—*De pretenders* (*The Pretenders*, 1981); *De illusionist* (*The Illusionist*, 1983); *De wisselwachter* (*The Pointsman*, 1986); Eric de Kuyper—*Casta Diva*, 1981; *Naughty Boys*, 1984; Marleen Gorris—*De stilte rond Christina M.* (*The Silence Around Christine M.*, 1982); *Gebroken spiegels* (*Broken Mirrors*, 1984); and Theo van Gogh—*Een dagje naar het strand* (*A Day at the Beach*, 1984); *Terug naar Oegstgeest* (*Return to Oegstgeest*, 1987)—have been forced to work in the same off-again on-again fashion. But the worldwide success of producer Rob Houwer (b. 1937) and director Paul Verhoeven (b. 1938) with *Soldaat van Oranje* (*Soldier of Orange*, 1977), *Spetters* (1980), and *De vierde man* (*The Fourth Man*, 1983) sparked a resurgence in domestic production that, combined with new state subsidies, resulted in a brief moment of commercial glory for the Dutch feature film.

Not only did Verhoeven himself move on to international production in the French medieval adventure *Flesh and Blood* (1985) and the visceral American science fiction thrillers *Robocop* (1987) and *Total Recall* (1990), but a large number of new directors made debut features that were commercial successes both inside and outside of the country. These included Pieter Verhoff—*Mark of the Beast*, 1981; *The Dream*, 1985; *Van geluk gesproken* (*Count Your Blessings*, 1987); Orlow Seunke—*De smaak van water* (*A Taste of Water*, 1982, Golden Lion, Venice); *Pervola* (*Tracks in the Snow*, 1985); Vivian Pieters—*De prooi* (*The Prey*, 1985); Gerrard Verhage—*Afzien* (*Abandon*, 1986); and Jurrien Rood—*De Orionevel* (*Orion Nebula*, 1987). Perhaps the most striking debut of the era was that of Dick Maas, whose witty horror film *De lift* (*The Elevator*, 1983) won several international awards, broke domestic box office records, and was picked up by Warners for worldwide distribution; Maas' second feature, the sensationalistic comedy *Flodder* (1987), became an even bigger hit. Additionally, filmmakers already at work were able to restore some continuity to their careers: Nouchka van Brakel (b. 1940) made *Van de koele meren des doods* (*Cool Lakes of Death*, 1982) and *Een maand later* (*A Month Later*, 1987) (the latter is the first Dutch film to be bought during production by a major American firm for international distribution, including in the Netherlands) and Ate de Jong made *Een vlucht regenwulpen* (*A Flight of Whimbrels*, 1982), *Brandende Liebe* (*Burning Love*, 1983), and *In de schaduw van de overwinning* (*In the Shadow of Victory*, 1986). Into this environment came such relatively big-budget commercial items as Guido Pieter's *Ciske de Rat* (1984) and *Op hoop van zegen* (*The Good Hope*, 1986), and Rund van Hemerts' *Schatjes!* (*Darlings!*, 1984) and *Mama is boos!* (*Mama is Mad!*, 1986), as well as superbly made entertainment from such veterans as Fons Rademakers (*De aanslag* [*The Assault*, 1986]). Unfortunately, the situation cannot continue, owing to a startling plunge in domestic film attendance (a 26 percent decline between 1982 and 1985 alone)—related, as it is elsewhere, to the diffusion of video— that shows no signs of abating. With its population of less than 15 million, the Netherlands cannot long sustain a feature industry at the present rate of decline in audience. See Rosalind Delmar, *Joris Ivens: 50 Years of Film-making* (London: BFI, 1979), and Peter Cowie, *Dutch Cinema: An Illustrated History* (London: A. S. Barnes, 1979).

p. 881 Kubrick himself has pointed out: Stanley Kubrick quoted in Georges Sadoul, *Dictionary of Films*, trans. and ed. Peter Morris (Berkeley: University of California Press, 1972), p. 387.

p. 882 Fred Silva . . . emptiness of technology: Fred Silva, et al., eds., *Film Literature Index*, vols. 1–5, 1973–77 (New York: R. R. Bowker, 1975–79), p. 15.

p. 882 fn. Kubrick's . . . rides: On Kubrick, see Norman Kagan, *The Cinema of Stanley Kubrick* (New York: Grove Press, 1975); Thomas Allen Nelson, *Kubrick: Inside a Film Artist's Maze* (Bloomington: Indiana University Press, 1982); Michel Ciment, *Kubrick*, trans. Gilbert Adair (New York: Holt, Rinehart and Winston, 1982); and David A. Cook, "American Horror: *The Shining*," *Literature/Film Quarterly* 12, 1 (Spring/Summer 1984): 1–4.

p. 884 fn. In 1969 . . . on videocassette: See Doug McKinney, *Sam Peckinpah* (Boston, 1979), pp. 88–91; Paul Seydor, *Peckinpah: The Western Films* (Urbana, Ill: University of Illinois Press, 1980), pp. 78–84; and David A.

Cook, "*The Wild Bunch* Fifteen Years After," *North Dakota Quarterly* 51, 3 (Summer 1984): 123–30, and "*The Wild Bunch*," *International Dictionary of Films and Filmmakers*, vol. 1, ed. Christopher Lyons (New York: Putnam's 1985), 521–25.

p. 889 fn. More and more . . . "pre-sell" it: See, for example, Thomas Simonet, "Market Research: Beyond the Fanny of the Cohn," *Film Comment* 16, 1 (January–February 1980): 66–69.

p. 889 Leo Janos writes: Janos quoted in "The Hollywood Game Grows Rich—and Desperate," *New York Times*, February 12, 1978, sec. 2, p. 9.

p. 889 Anthony Hoffman . . . has remarked: Hoffman quoted in "After the Moguls, a New Breed Rules Hollywood," *Washington Post*, February 5, 1978, p. M6.

p. 892 Brian De Palma . . . scientific point of view: De Palma quoted in Gary Arnold, "De Palma's Spectacular Sleeper," *Washington Post*, November 21, 1976, p. G5.

p. 892 Vincent Canby . . . save mankind: See Richard Corliss, "We Lost It at the Movies: The Generation That Grew Up on *The Graduate*, Took Over Hollywood—and Went into Plastics," *Film Comment* 16, 1 (January–February 1980): 34–38. Vincent Canby, *New York Times*, July 4, 1976, sec. 10, p. 11. See Also Robert Phillip Kolker, *A Cinema of Loneliness: Penn, Kubrick, Scorsese, Spielberg, Altman*, 2nd ed. (New York: Oxford University Press, 1988).

p. 892 Brewster McCloud . . . Andrew Sarris: Sarris quoted in Diane Jacobs, *Hollywood Renaissance* (New York: 1977), p. 73.

p. 894 Pauline Kael . . . *Nashville*: Pauline Kael, *Reeling* (New York: 1976), p. 447.

p. 895 Altman . . . Golden Age: Gary Arnold, *Washington Post*, July 4, 1976, p. H3. See Judith M. Kast, *Robert Altman: American Innovator* (New York: Popular Library, 1978); Alan Karp, *The Films of Robert Altman* (Metuchen: Scarecrow, 1981); Norman Kagan, *American Skeptic: Robert Altman's Genre-Commentary Films* (Ann Arbor: Pierian Press, 1982); Virginia Wright Wexman and Gretchen Bisplinghoff, *Robert Altman: A Guide to Reference and Research* (Boston: G. K. Hall, 1984); Gerard Plecki, *Robert Altman* (Boston: Twayne, 1985); and Patrick McGilligan, *Robert Altman: Jumping Off the Cliff* (New York: St. Martin's 1989).

p. 902 despite their enormous budgets: Other contemporary American directors of note who are not discussed in the text are, in alphabetical order (with some examples of their recent and/or most important work given in parentheses): Hal Ashby (1929–88—*Harold and Maude*, 1971; *The Last Detail*, 1973; *Shampoo*, 1975; *Bound for Glory*, 1976; *Coming Home*, 1978; *Being There*, 1979; *Second-Hand Hearts*, 1980; *Let's Spend the Night Together*, 1982; *Lookin' to Get Out*, 1982; *The Slugger's Wife*, 1984; *8 Million Ways to Die*, 1985); John Avildsen (b. 1937—*Save the Tiger*, 1972; *Rocky*, 1976; *Slow Dancing in the Big City*, 1978; *The Formula*, 1980; *Neighbors*, 1982; *The Karate Kid*, 1984; *The Karate Kid, Part II*, 1986; *Lean on Me*, 1989; *The Karate Kid, Part III*, 1989; John Badham (b. 1939—*Saturday Night Fever*, 1977; *Dracula*, 1979; *Whose Life Is It, Anyway?* 1981; *Blue Thunder*, 1982; *American Flyers*, 1984; *Short Circuit*, 1985); Ralph Bakshi (b. 1938—*Fritz the Cat*, 1972; *Wizards*, 1977; *The Lord of the Rings*, 1978; *American Pop*, 1981; *Hey, Good Lookin'*, 1982; *Fire and Ice*, 1983); Carroll Ballard (b. 1937—*The Black*

Stallion, 1979; *Never Cry Wolf*, 1983; *Nutcracker: The Motion Picture*, 1986); Paul Bartel (b 1938—*Eating Raoul*, 1981; *Lust in the Dust*, 1984; *Not for Publication*, 1984; *The Long Shot*, 1985; *Scenes from the Class War in Beverly Hills*, 1989); Robert Benton (b. 1932—*Bad Company*, 1972; *The Late Show*, 1977; *Kramer vs. Kramer*, 1979; *Still of the Night*, 1982; *Places in the Heart*, 1984; *Nadine*, 1987); Noel Black (b. 1937—*Pretty Poison*, 1969; *A Man, a Woman, and a Bank*, 1979; *Promises to Keep*, 1985); Don Bluth (*The Secret of Nihm*, 1982; *An American Tail*, 1986; *The Land Before Time*, 1988); Peter Bogdanovich (b. 1939—*Targets*, 1968; *The Last Picture Show*, 1971; *What's Up Doc?*, 1972; *Daisy Miller*, 1974; *Nickelodeon*, 1976; *St. Jack*, 1979; *They All Laughed*, 1981; *Mask*, 1984; *Illegally Yours*, 1988); James L. Brooks (b. 1940—*Terms of Endearment*, 1983; *Broadcast News*, 1987).

Wes Craven (b. 1949—*The Last House on the Left*, 1973; *The Hills Have Eyes*, 1977; *Deadly Blessing*, 1981; *Swamp Thing*, 1981; *The Hills Have Eyes, Part II*, 1983; *A Nightmare on Elm Street*, 1984; *Deadly Friend*, 1986; *The Serpent and the Rainbow*, 1988); Lewis John Carlino (b. 1932—*The Sailor Who Fell from Grace with the Sea*, 1976; *The Great Santini*, 1979, *Class*, 1983); John Carpenter (b. 1948—*Halloween*, 1978; *The Fog*, 1979; *Escape from New York*, 1981; *The Thing*, 1982; *Christine*, 1983; *Starman*, 1984; *Big Trouble in Little China*, 1986; *Prince of Darkness*, 1987; *They Live*, 1988); Michael Cimino (b. 1943—*Thunderbolt and Lightfoot*, 1974; *The Deer Hunter*, 1978; *Heaven's Gate*, 1980; *Year of the Dragon*, 1985; *The Sicilian*, 1987); Martha Coolidge (b. 1946—*Not a Pretty Picture*, 1975; *City Girl*, 1982; *Valley Girl/Foxes*, 1982; *Joy of Sex*, 1984; *Real Genius*, 1985; *Plain Clothes*, 1988); Joe Dante (*Piranha*, 1978; *The Howling*, 1980; *Twilight Zone—The Movie*, 1983; *Gremlins*, 1984; *Explorers*, 1985; *The Burbs*, 1989; *Gremlins 2: The New Batch*, 1990); Andrew Davis (*Stony Island*, 1978; *The Final Terror*, 1981; *Code of Silence*, 1985; *The Package*, 1989); Peter Davis (*Hearts and Minds*, 1974; *Rise and Fall of the Borscht Belt*, 1985; *Winnie/Nelson*, 1986); Jonathan Demme (b. 1944—*Caged Heat*, 1974; *Citizens Band*, 1977; *Last Embrace*, 1978; *Melvin and Howard*, 1980; *Stop Making Sense*, 1983; *Swing Shift*, 1983; *Something Wild*, 1986; *Married to the Mob*, 1988); Richard Donner (*The Omen*, 1975; *Superman*, 1978; *Inside Moves*, 1980; *The Toy*, 1982; *The Goonies*, 1984; *Ladyhawke*, 1984; *Scrooged*, 1988; *Lethal Weapon 2*, 1989); Bob Fosse (1927–87—*Cabaret*, 1972; *Lennie*, 1974; *All That Jazz*, 1979; *Star 80*, 1982); Taylor Hackford (b. 1945—*The Idolmaker*, 1980; *An Officer and a Gentleman*. 1981; *Against All Odds*, 1983; *White Nights*, 1985; *Everybody's All-American*, 1988).

Stuart Gordon (*Re-Animator*, 1985; *From Beyond*, 1986; *Dolls*, 1987; *Robojax*, 1989); Ulu Grosbard (b. 1929—*Straight Time*, 1977; *True Confessions*, 1981; *Falling in Love*, 1984); John Hancock (b. 1939—*Bang the Drum Slowly*, 1973; *Baby Blue Marine*, 1976; *California Dreaming*, 1979; *Prancer*, 1989); John Hanson (b. 1942—*Northern Lights*, 1979; *Wildrose*, 1984; *Smart Money*, 1988); Amy Heckerling (b. 1954—*Fast Times at Ridgemont High*, 1982; *Johnny Dangerously*, 1984; *National Lampoon's European Vacation*, 1985; *Look Who's Talking*, 1989); Monte Hellman (b. 1932—*The Shooting*, 1966; *Ride in the Whirlwind*, 1966; *Two-Lane Blacktop*, 1971; *Cockfighter*, 1974; *China 9 Liberty 37*, 1978; *Iguana*, 1988); George Roy Hill (b. 1922—*Butch Cassidy and the Sundance Kid*, 1969;

Slaughterhouse Five, 1972; *The Sting*, 1973; *Slapshot*, 1977; *A Little Romance*, 1979; *The World According to Garp*, 1982; *The Little Drummer Girl*, 1984; *Funny Farm*, 1988); Walter Hill (b. 1942—*The Driver*, 1978; *The Warriors*, 1979; *The Long Riders*, 1980; *Southern Comfort*, 1981; *48 Hours*, 1982; *Streets of Fire*, 1984; *Brewster's Millions*, 1985; *Crossroads*, 1986; *Extreme Prejudice*, 1987 *Red Heat*, 1987; *Johnny Handsome*, 1989); Tobe Hooper (b. 1943—*The Texas Chainsaw Massacre*, 1974; *The Funhouse*, 1980; *Poltergeist*, 1982; *Lifeforce*, 1984, *Invaders from Mars*, 1986; *The Texas Chainsaw Massacre 2*, 1986); Peter Hyams (b. 1943—*Capricorn One*, 1978; *Han-over Street*, 1979; *Outland*, 1981; *The Star Chamber*, 1983; *2010*, 1984; *Running Scared*, 1985; *The Presidio*, 1988).

Lawrence Kasdan (*Body Heat*, 1981; *The Big Chill*, 1983; *Silverado*, 1985; *The Accidental Tourist*, 1988); Philip Kaufman (b. 1936—*The Great Northfield Minnesota Raid*, 1971; *The White Dawn*, 1974; *Invasion of the Body Snatchers*, 1978; *The Wanderers*, 1979; *The Right Stuff*, 1983; *The Unbearable Lightness of Being*, 1988); Barbara Kopple (*Harlan County, U.S.A.*, 1976; *Keeping On*, 1983); Ted Kotcheff (b. 1931—*The Apprenticeship of Duddy Kravitz*, 1974; *Fun with Dick and Jane*, 1977; *Who Is Killing the Great Chefs of Europe?*, 1978; *North Dallas Forty*, 1979; *Split Image*, 1982; *First Blood*, 1982; *Uncommon Valor*, 1985; *Joshua Then and Now*, 1986; *Switching Channels*, 1988; *Winter People*, 1989; *Hot and Cold*, 1989). John Landis (b. 1951—*The Kentucky Fried Movie*, 1977; *National Lampoon's Animal House*, 1978; *The Blues Brothers*, 1980; *Trading Places*, 1983; *Twilight Zone—the Movie*, 1983; *Spies Like Us*, 1985; *Three Amigos!*, 1986; *Coming to America*, 1988); Spike Lee (*She's Gotta have It*, 1986; *School Daze*, 1987; *Do the Right Thing*, 1989); Barbara Loden (1932–80—*Wanda*, 1970); Tony Luraschi (*The Outsider*, U.K., 1979); David Lynch (b. 1946—*Eraserhead*, 1976; *The Elephant Man*, 1980; *Dune*, 1984; *Blue Velvet*, 1986; *Twin Peaks* [TUM], 1990; *Wild at Heart*, 1990); Terrence Malick (b. 1945—*Badlands*, 1973; *Days of Heaven*, 1978); David Mamet (b. 1947—*House of Games*, 1987; *Things Change*, 1988); Richard Marquand (*Eye of the Needle*, 1981; *Return of the Jedi*, 1984; *Until September*, 1984; *Jagged Edge*, 1985); Garry Marshall (b. 1934—*Young Doctors in Love*, 1982; *The Flamingo Kid*, 1984; *Nothing in Common*, 1986; *Overboard*, 1987; *Beaches*, 1988); Elaine May (b. 1932—*A New Leaf*, 1971; *The Heartbreak Kid*, 1972; *Mikey and Nicky*, 1976; *Ishtar*, 1988); Paul Mazursky (b. 1930—*Bob & Carol & Ted & Alice*, 1969; *Alex in Wonderland*, 1970; *Blume In Love*, 1973; *Harry and Tonto*, 1974; *Next Stop: Greenwich Village*, 1976; *An Unmarried Woman*, 1978; *Willie and Phil*, 1980; *Tempest*, 1982; *Moscow on the Hudson*, 1984; *Down and Out in Beverly Hills*, 1986; *Moon Over Parador*, 1988); John Milius (b. 1944—*Dillinger*, 1973; *The Wind and the Lion*, 1975; *Big Wednesday*, 1978; *Conan the Barbarian*, 1982; *Red Dawn*, 1985; *Farewell to the King*, 1989); Paul Morrissey (b. 1939—*Trash*, 1970; *Heat*, 1972; *Andy Warhol's Frankenstein*, 1973; *Andy Warhol's Dracula*, 1974; *The Hound of the Baskervilles*, 1977; *Madame Wang's*, 1981; *Beethoven's Nephew*, 1985; *Spike of Bensonhurst*, 1988); Robert Mulligan (b. 1925—*To Kill a Mockingbird*, 1962; *Up the Down Staircase*, 1967; *The Summer of '42*, 1971; *The Other*, 1972; *The Nickel Ride*, 1974; *Same Time Next Year*, 1978; *Kiss Me Goodbye*, 1982; *Clara's Heart*, 1988); Floyd Mutrux (*Aloha Bobby and Rose*, 1975; *American Hot Wax*, 1978).

Mike Nichols (b. 1931—*The Graduate*, 1967; *Catch-22*, 1970; *Carnal Knowledge*, 1971; *The Day of the Dolphin*, 1973; *The Fortune*, 1975; *Gilda Live*, 1980; *Silkwood*, 1983; *Heartburn*, 1986; *Working Girl*, 1988; Victor Nunez (*Gal Young Un*, 1979; *A Flash of Green*, 1982); Alan J. Pakula (b. 1928—*Klute*, 1971; *The Parallax View*, 1974; *All the President's Men*, 1976; *Comes a Horseman*, 1978; *Starting Over*, 1979; *Rollover*, 1981; *Sophie's Choice*, 1982; *Dream Lover*, 1985; *See You in the Morning*, 1988); Richard Pearce (*Heartland*, 1980; *Country*, 1984; *No Mercy*, 1987; *Dead Man Out*, 1988); Frank Perry (b. 1930—*The Swimmer*, 1968; *Last Summer*, 1969; *Diary of a Mad Housewife*, 1970; *Play It as It Lays*, 1972; *Rancho Deluxe*, 1974; *Mommie Dearest*, 1981; *Monsignor*, 1982; *Compromising Positions*, 1985; *Hello Again*, 1987); Sidney Pollack (b. 1934—*They Shoot Horses, Don't They?*, 1969; *Jeremiah Johnson*, 1972; *Three Days of the Condor*, 1975; *Bobby Deerfield*, 1977; *The Electric Horseman*, 1979; *Absence of Malice*, 1981; *Tootsie*, 1982; *Out of Africa*, 1985).

Bob Rafelson (b. 1935—*Five Easy Pieces*, 1970; *The King of Marvin Gardens*, 1972; *Stay Hungry*, 1976; *The Postman Always Rings Twice*, 1981; *Black Widow*, 1987; *Mountains of the Moon*, 1989); Steve Rash (*The Buddy Holly Story*, 1978; *Can't Buy Me Love*, 1987); Dick Richards (b. 1936—*The Culpepper Cattle Company*, 1972; *Farewell, My Lovely*, 1975; *Double Exposure*, 1978; *Man, Woman and Child*, 1983; *Heat*, 1987); William Richert (*Winter Kills*, 1979; *The American Success Company*, 1979; *A Night in the Life of Jimmy Reardon*, 1988); Michael Ritchie (b. 1939—*Downhill Racer*, 1969; *The Candidate*, 1972; *Prime Cut*, 1972; *Smile*, 1975; *The Bad News Bears*, 1976; *Semi-Tough*, 1977; *An Almost Perfect Affair*, 1979; *The Island*, 1980; *Divine Madness*, 1980; *The Survivors*, 1983; *Fletch*, 1984; *Wildcats*, 1985; *The Golden Child*, 1986; *The Couch Trip*, 1988; *Fletch Lives*, 1989), Martin Ritt (b. 1920—*The Brotherhood*, 1968; *Sounder*, 1972; *The Front*, 1977; *Norma Rae*, 1979; *Back Roads*, 1980; *Cross Creek*, 1983; *Murphy's Romance*, 1985; *Nuts*, 1987; *Letters*, 1989); Herbert Ross (b. 1926—*Play It Again, Sam*, 1972; *The Last of Sheila*, 1973; *The Seven Per Cent Solution*, 1976; *The Turning Point*, 1977; *The Good-bye Girl*, 1978; *California Suite*, 1978; *Nijinsky*, 1980; *I Ought to Be in Pictures*, 1981; *Pennies from Heaven*, 1981; *Max Dugan Returns*, 1982; *Footloose*, 1984; *Protocol*, 1984; *The Secret of My Success*, 1987; *Dancers*, 1987; *Steel Magnolias*, 1989); Alan Rudolph (b. 1943—*Welcome to L.A.*, 1977; *Remember My Name*, 1978; *Roadie*, 1980; *Endangered Species*, 1982; *Return Engagement*, 1982; *Choose Me*, 1984; *Songwriter*, 1984; *Trouble in Mind*, 1986; *The Moderns*, 1988; *Love at Large*, 1989); Richard Rush (b. 1930—*The Stunt Man*, 1979).

Joseph Sargent (b. 1925—*The Forbin Project*, 1969; *The Taking of Pelham 1-2-3*, 1974; *MacArthur*, 1977; *Goldengirl*, 1979; *Coast to Coast*, 1980; *Nightmares*, 1983); *Jaws: The Revenge*, 1987; John Sayles (b. 1950—*Return of the Secaucus Seven*, 1980; *Baby, It's You*, 1983; *Lianna*, 1983; *Brother from Another Planet*, 1984; *Matewan*, 1987; *Eight Men Out*, 1988); Franklin J. Schaffner 1922-89—*Planet of the Apes*, 1968; *Patton*, 1970; *Papillon*, 1973; *Islands in the Stream*, 1977; *The Boys from Brazil*, 1978; *Sphinx*, 1980; *Yes, Giorgio*, 1982; *Lionheart*, 1987); Jerry Schatzberg (*The Panic in Needle Park*, 1971; *Scarecrow*, 1973; *The Seduction of Joe Tynan*, 1979; *Honeysuckle Rose*, 1980; *Misunderstood*, 1983; *No Small Affair*, 1984; *Street Smart*, 1987; *Reunion*, 1988); Paul Schrader (b. 1946—*Blue Collar*, 1978; *Hard Core*, 1979; *American Gigolo*, 1980; *Cat People*, 1982; *Mishima: A Life in Four Chapters*, 1984; *Patty Hearst*, 1986); Susan Seidelman (*Smithereens*, 1982; *Desperately Seeking Susan*, 1985; *Making Mr. Right*, 1986; *Cookie*, 1989): Joan Micklin Silver (b. 1935—*Hester Street*, 1974; *Bernice Bobs Her Hair*, 1976, for PBS; *Between the Lines*, 1977; *Head over Heels/Chilly Scenes of Winter*, 1979; *Finnegan Begin Again*, 1985, for HBO; *Crossing Delancey*, 1988; *Lover Boy*, 1989); Bob Swaim (b. 1943—*Night of Saint-Germain des Pres*, 1977; *La Balance*, 1982; *Half Moon Street*, 1986; *Masquerade*, 1988); Peter Wang (*A Great Wall*, 1986; *The Laserman*, 1988); Wayne Wang (b. 1949—*Chan Is Missing*, 1981; *Dim Sum: A Little Bit of Heart*, 1986; *Eat a Bowl of Tea*, 1989); John Waters (b. 1946—*Pink Flamingos*, 1974; *Female Trouble*, 1975; *Desperate Living*, 1977; *Polyester*, 1981; *Hairspray*, 1987); Claudia Weill (b. 1947—*Girlfriends*, 1978; *It's My Turn*, 1980; *Johnny Bull*, 1987); Ira Wohl (b. 1944—*Best Boy*, 1979); Robert M. Young (b. 1924—*Alambrista!*, 1977; *Short Eyes*, 1978; *Rich Kids*, 1979; *One-Trick Pony*, 1980; *The Ballad of Gregorio Cortez*, 1983; *Extremities*, 1986; *Saving Grace*, 1986; *Dominick and Eugene*, 1988; *Triumph of the Spirit*, 1989); Robert Zemeckis (b. 1952—*I Wanna Hold Your Hand*, 1979; *Used Cars*, 1980; *Romancing the Stone*, 1983; *Back to the Future*, 1985; *Who Framed Roger Rabbit?*, 1988; *Back to the Future 2*, 1989; *Back to the Future 3*, 1990); Howard Zieff (b. 1943—*Hearts of the West*, 1975; *Housecalls*, 1978; *The Main Event*, 1979; *Private Benjamin*, 1980; *Unfaithfully Yours*, 1983; *The Dream Team*, 1989).

p. 904 *A Primer for Film-Making*: Kenneth H. Roberts and Win Sharples, Jr., *A Primer for Film-Making* (New York: Pegasus, 1971).

Part III

Sample Syllabi, Screening Schedules,
Tests, and Exams

The syllabi, screening schedules, tests, and noncumulative exams in this section are intended as suggestions only; they assume a two-semester sequential course in film history using *A History of Narrative Film*, Second Edition, as the main text. The tests are composed mainly of multiple choice questions keyed to specific chapters of the book, and each is calculated here to yield a full point value of 100. These kinds of questions seem to work best in large classes, but they can and should be supplemented with identifications and essay questions whenever possible. Ideally, of course, students should also write at least one critical and/or historically oriented research paper per semester, but experience has taught me that this ideal is difficult to realize in classes of more than 30–40 students without some kind of grading assistance.

Please note that some of the tests have separate answer sheets (a hedge against page-turner's elbow) and some do not. If you want to assign short essays and/or identifications, you can leave a designated space for these on the answer sheet that will automatically limit the length of the response.

Film Studies 371
History of Film to 1938
Fall Semester 1989
White Hall 101
2:30–4:00 PM

Texts: David A. Cook. *A History of Narrative Film*, Second Edition (W. W. Norton, 1990)—*HNF*
All films on the screening schedule; all films shown in class.

Please note: All technical terms used in *HNF* are cross-referenced and defined at length in the glossary. The book also contains an elaborate system of footnotes clarifying points made in the text. You should check both glossary and notes before posing questions about technical matters in class.

August 31	Chapter 1, "Origins."
September 5–7	Chapter 2, "International Expansion, 1907–1918."
September 12–14	Chapter 3, "D.W. Griffith and the Consummation of Narrative Form," pp. 61–82.
September 19–21	Chapter 3, pp. 82–109.
September 26–28	Chapter 4, "German Cinema of the Weimar Period, 1919–1929," pp. 110–31.
October 3–5	HOUR TEST I, Tues., October 3. (Covers Chapters 1–3)
	Chapter 4, pp. 131–38.
October 12 (10—Fall Break)	Chapter 5, "Soviet Silent Cinema and the Theory of Montage, 1917–1931," pp. 139–92.
October 17–19	Chapter 5, pp. 192–206
October 24–26	Chapter 6, "Hollywood in the Twenties."
October 31– November 2	HOUR TEST II, Tues., October 31. (Covers Chapters 4–6) Chapter 7, "The Coming of Sound, 1926–1932."
November 7–9	Chapter 8, "The Sound Film and the American Studio System," pp. 290–319.
November 14–16	Chapter 8, pp. 319–60.
November 21 (23—Thanksgiving)	Chapter 9, "Europe in the Thirties," pp. 361–77.
November 28–30	HOUR TEST III, Tues., November 28. (Covers Chapters 7–8) Chapter 9, pp. 377–406.
December 5–7	Chapter 9, cont.
December 12	Summation
FINAL EXAM:	Fri., Dec. 15, 12:30 P.M.–3:00 P.M.

In-Class Screenings in White Hall 101
(3:00 PM except as noted below)

Date	Title	Running Time*
August 31	*Origins of the Motion Picture Camera*	21
	The Man Called Edison	28
September 5	*Before the Nickelodeon* (Musser, 1982)	53
September 7	*Lumières' First Picture Shows* (ca. 1895–1900)	14
	A Trip to the Moon (*Le Voyage dans la lune*) (Méliès, 1902)	13
	The Great Train Robbery (Porter, 1903)	16
September 12	*A Nickel for the Movies*	
	A Trio of Edison Comedies (Porter, 1906)	20
September 14	*Fantasy of Méliès* (1903)	10
	Baron Munchausen's Dream (Méliès, 1912)	11
	The Conquest of the Pole (Méliès, 1912)	14
September 19	*The Adventures of Dollie* (Griffith, 1908)	10
	Pippa Passes (Griffith, 1909)	9
	The Lonely Villa (Griffith, 1909)	12
September 21	*A Corner in Wheat* (Griffith, 1909)	13
	The Battle (Griffith, 1911)	10
	The Lonedale Operator (Griffith, 1911)	12
September 26	*The Musketeers of Pig Alley* (Griffith, 1912)	13
	Judith of Bethulia (Griffith, 1913) first reel	48
September 28	*Intolerance* (Griffith, 1916) final reel	30
	D.W. Griffith Interview (1930)	20
October 3	*Broken Blossoms* (Griffith, 1919) first reel	30
		(starts at 3:30)
October 5	*The Cabinet of Dr. Caligari* (*Das Kabinett des Dr. Caligari*) (Weine, 1919) final reel	30
October 12	*Nosferatu* (Murnau, 1922) first reel	30
October 17	*Faust* (Murnau, 1926) first reel	30
October 19	*Berlin: Symphony of a Great City* (*Berlin, die Symphonie einer Großstadt*) (Ruttmann, 1927) first reel	30
October 24	*Battleship Potemkin* (Eisenstein, 1925), final reel, Odessa steps sequence	30
October 26	*October* (*Ten Days that Shook the World*) (Eisenstein, 1928) first reel	30
October 31	*The Man with a Movie Camera* (Vertov, 1929)	30
		(starts at 3:30
November 2	*Sherlock Jr.* (Keaton, 1924) **	43
		(starts at 3:30)
November 7	*Underworld* (von Sternberg, 1927) **	30
November 9	*Fox Movietone News #2* (October 1928–August 1929)	30
November 14	*Blackmail* (Hitchcock, 1929) first reel	30
November 16	*Murder* (Hitchcock, 1930) first reel	30
November 21	*The Man Who Knew Too Much* (Hitchcock, 1934)	90
		(starts at 3:30)
November 28	*The Front Page* (Milestone, 1931) first reel	30

In-Class Screenings (cont.)

November 30	*M* (Lang, 1931) first reel	30
		(starts at 3:30)
December 5	*Triumph of the Will* (*Triumph des Willens*)	
	(Riefenstahl, 1935)	30
December 7	*Alexander Nevski* (Eisenstein, 1938)	
	reel 2, Battle on the Ice	60
December 12	*Made for Each Other* (Cromwell, 1938)	

* In minutes. Running times are for full films on reels. In most cases, only selected portions will be used in class.

** Indicates Film Studies print; instructor will provide.

Film Studies 371
Fall Semester 1989

Screening Schedule

Please note: All of the films to be screened are *texts* in the course(s). Most of them are rented from commercial distributors and cannot be shown more than once. Therefore, your attendance at the regularly scheduled screening sessions is vital to your performance in the course. Don't miss the films. Don't take the course if you can't come to them.

All film programs will begin on Thursday evenings at 8:00 PM sharp in White Hall 101.

Please be on time. No smoking. No pets. No unauthorized guests.

Date	Title	Running Time*
September 7	*Lumières' First Picture Shows* (ca. 1895)	14
	A Trip to the Moon (*Le Voyage dans la lune*) (Méliès, 1902)	13
	Before the Nickelodeon (Musser, 1982)	52
	The Great Train Robbery (Porter, 1903)	16
	Comedy and Magic of Méliès (1903)	8
	Magic of Méliès	13
September 14	*Gertie the Dinosaur* (1909)	8
	Surrealism of Méliès (1903)	13
	Fantasy of Méliès (1903)	10
	Baron Munchausen's Dream (Méliès, 1911)	11
	The Conquest of the Pole (Méliès, 1912)	14
September 21	*Enoch Arden* (Griffith, 1911)	22
	The New York Hat (Griffith, 1912)	17
	The Massacre (Griffith, 1912)	25
	The Battle at Elderbush Gulch (Griffith, 1913)	23
September 28	*The Birth of a Nation* (Griffith, 1915) Tinted version	100
October 5	*The Last Laugh* (*Der letzte Mann*) (Murnau, 1924)	96
October 12	*Metropolis* (Lang, 1926)	120
October 19	*Battleship Potemkin* (Eisenstein, 1925)	67
	Mother (Pudovkin, 1926)	88
October 26	*Storm Over Asia* (*Heir to Ghengis Khan*) (Pudovkin, 1928)	120
November 2	*Blind Husbands* (von Stroheim, 1918)	70
	The Marriage Circle (Lubitsch, 1924)	96
November 9	*Shanghai Express* (von Sternberg, 1932)	80 **
	The Blue Angel (*Der blaue Engel*) (von Sternberg, 1930)	90
November 16	*The 39 Steps* (Hitchcock, 1935)	87
November 30	*Rules of the Game* (*La Règle du jeu*) (Renoir, 1939)	110
December 7	*Stagecoach* (John Ford, 1939)	97 **

* In minutes
** Indicates Film Studies print, to be provided by instructor

Film Studies 372
History of Film since 1938
Spring Semester 1990
Classroom: White Hall 101; TT 2:30–4:00 PM
Screening Room: White Hall 101; Th. 8:00–10:00 PM

Texts: David A. Cook. *A History of Narrative Film*, Second Edition (W. W. Norton, 1991), pp. 262–75.

All films on the screening schedule; all films shown in class.

Please note: All technical terms used in *HNF* are cross-referenced and defined at length in the glossary. The book also contains an elaborate system of footnotes clarifying points made in the text. You should check both glossary and notes before posing questions about technical matters in class.

Jan. 18; 23–25	The Cinema c. 1938. (Background reading for *students who have not taken FS371 or equivalent*): Chapter 7, pp. 262–66; Chapter 8; Chapter 9, pp. 361–77; 388–406.
	Chapter 10, "Orson Welles and the Modern Sound Film," pp. 347–67.
Jan. 30–Feb. 1	Chapter 10, cont., pp. 367–75.
Feb. 6–8	Chapter 11, "War-Time and Post-War Cinema: Italy," pp. 437–56.
	Chapter 11, "War-Time and Post-War Cinema: America," pp. 456–79.
Feb. 13–15	Chapter 12, "Hollywood, 1952–65," pp. 480–506.
	Chapter 12, pp. 506–37.
Feb. 20–22	HOUR TEST I, Tues., February 20, on Chapters 10, 11, and 12.
	Chapter 13, "The French New Wave and Its Native Context," pp. 538–57.
Feb. 27–Mar. 1	Chapter 13, cont., pp. 557–88.
Mar. 6–8	Chapter 16, "European Renaissance: East," pp. 666–724.
Mar. 13–15	

Spring Break

Mar. 22–23	Chapter 16, pp. 724–777.
	HOUR TEST II, Thurs., March 22, on Chapters 13 and 16.
Mar. 27–29	Chapter 17, "Wind from the East," pp. 778–821.
Apr. 3–5	Chapter 14, "New Cinemas in Britain, etc.," pp. 589–621.
Apr. 10–12	Chapter 15, "European Renaissance: West," pp. 622–65.
Apr. 17–19	Chapter 18, "The Seventies and the Eighties," Third World Cinema, pp. 822–850.
	HOUR TEST III, Tues., April 17, on Chapters 14, 15, and 17.
Apr. 24–26	Chapter 18, New German Cinema/Hollywood, pp. 850–905.
	FINAL EXAM: Fri., May 4, 12:30 PM–3:00 PM

In–Class Screenings in White Hall 101—3:00 PM

Thurs., Jan 25	Slides. "Orson Welles: Films, 1941–1969", Videotape (1/2-inch): excerpts from *The Magnificent Ambersons* (Welles, 1942), *The Stranger* (Welles, 1946)—Reel 1
Tues., Jan. 30	*His Girl Friday* (Howard Hawks, 1940)*, *Macbeth* (Welles, 1948)—Reel 1 The Third Man (Reed, 1949)
Thurs., Feb. 1	*The Trial* (Welles, 1962)—Reel 1, Videotape (1/2–inch): excerpts from the films of Welles, 1947–57
Tues., Feb. 6	*Paisa* (Rossellini, 1945), *Casablanca* (Michael Curtiz, 1942)*
Thurs., Feb. 8	*Know Your Enemy: Japan* (Capra, 1944)
Tues., Feb. 13	*Meet John Doe* (Capra, 1941)—Reel 1, Videotape (1/2–inch) Excerpts: *Since You Went Away* (Cromwell, 1944); *Edge of Darkness* (Milestone, 1943); selected *films noirs.*
Thurs., Feb. 15	Videotape (1/2–inch) excerpts: Academy frame vs. widescreen; selected "blockbusters" (e.g. *South Pacific*)
Tues., Feb. 20	*No Place to Hide* (3:30 PM; following test)
Thurs., Feb. 22	*Nuit et brouillard* (Resnais, 1955)
Tues., Feb. 27	*Hiroshima, mon amour* (Resnais, 1959)—Reel 1
Thurs., March 1	*Le Souffle au coeur* (*Murmur of the Heart*, Malle, 1971). *Masculine/féminin* (Godard, 1965)*
Tues., March 6	*Two Men and a Wardrobe* (Polanski, 1958) *Ashes and Diamonds* (Wajda, 1958)—Reel 1 *Knife in the Water* (Polanski, 1962)—Reel 1*
Thurs., March 8	*Knife in the Water,** conclusion *Closely Watched Trains* (Menzel, 1966)–Reel 1*
Tues., March 20	*Rite of Love & Death* (Mishima, 1967) Videotape (1/2–inch) excerpts: *Rashomon* (Kurosawa, 1950)
Thurs., March 22	*Ugetsu* (Mizoguchi, 1953)—Reel 1 (3:30 PM; following test)
Tues., March 27	*Woman in the Dunes* (Teshigahara, 1964)—Reel 1 Videotape (1/2–inch) excerpts: Mizoguchi, Kurosawa, Ichikawa, Ozu
Thurs., March 29	*Henry V* (Olivier, 1944)—Reel 1 *Great Expectations* (Lean, 1946)—Reel 1
Tues., April 3	*Saturday Night and Sunday Morning* (Reisz, 1960)—complete film
Thurs., April 5	Videotape (1/2–inch) excerpts: selected Commonwealth cinema; *L'avventura* (Antonioni, 1959)—Reel 1
Tues., April 10	Videotape (1/2–inch) excerpts: selected Antonioni, Fellini, and Bergman features; selected zoom-lens footage.
Thurs., April 12	New Cinema of Latin America, Pt. 1: "The Cinema of the Humble"
Tues., April 17	*Lucía* (Solás, 1968)—Reel 1 (3:30 PM; following the test)
Thurs., April 19	New Cinema of Latin America, Pt. 2: "The Long Road"
Tues., April 24	Videotape (1/2–inch) excerpts: *Berlin Alexanderplatz* (1980)—Selected New German Cinema; late '60s American cinema: *Bonnie & Clyde*; *The Wild Bunch*; *2001*
Thurs., April 26	Videotape (1/2–inch) excerpts: contemporary American cinema and styles: *Apocalypse Now*; *The Shining*; *Dressed to Kill*; *Blade Runner*; *Scarface*; *Runaway Train*; *Manhunter*

*Indicate Film Studies print; instructor will provide.

Film Studies 372
Spring Semester 1990
White Hall 101, 8:00PM–10:00PM

Screening Schedule

Please note: All of the films to be screened are *texts* in the course. Most of them are rented from commercial distributors and cannot be shown more than once. Therefore, your attendance at the regularly scheduled screening sessions is vital to your performance in the course. Don't miss the films. Don't take the course if you can't come to them.

.

All films will be shown on Thursday evenings at 8:00 PM in White Hall 101.

.

Please be on time.   No smoking.   No pets.   No unauthorized guests.

Date	Title	Running Time*
Jan. 25	*Andy Panda cartoons* (1948)	8
	Made for Each Other (Cromwell, 1938)	85
	Prison Train (Wiles, 1938)	54
Feb. 1	*Citizen Kane* (Welles, 1941)*	119
Feb. 8	*Roma, città aperta* (*Open City*, Rossellini, 1945)	103
	Stagedoor Canteen (Borzage, 1943)	80
Feb. 15	*Kiss Me Deadly* (Aldrich, 1955)*	105
Feb. 22	*Vertigo* (Hitchcock, 1958) Videodisc.	120
March 1	*Breathless* (*A bout de souffle*, 1960, Godard)	90
	Shoot the Piano Player (Truffaut, 1959)*	85
March 8	*Shadows of Forgotten Ancestors** (Teni zabytykh Predkov, 1964)	80
	Adrift (Jan Kadár, 1971)	100
March 22	*Kwaidan* (Kobayashi, 1964)	160
March 29	*The Exterminating Angel** (Buñuel, 1962)	95
April 5	*The Red Desert* (Antonioni,* 1964)	116
April 12	*Teorèma* (Pasolini, 1968)	96
	Persona (Bergman, 1966)	83
April 19	*The Wild Bunch* (Peckinpah, 1969)* Widescreen ratio	135
April 26	*The Last Wave* (Peter Weir, 1977)*	106

*in minutes

*Indicate Film Studies print, instructor will provide.

Film Studies 371
Fall 1989
David A. Cook

Hour Test I

I. Matching. Match the proper dates with the films and/or phenomena. *One point each.*

___ 1877

___ 1882

___ 1901

___ 1915

___ 1909

___ 1903

___ 1839

___ 1895

___ 1824

___ 1891

A) *The Birth of a Nation*

B) *Cinématographe*

C) daguerreotypy (photography, positive process)

D) Marey's chronophotographic gun

E) *A Trip to the Moon*

F) persistence of vision

G) *The Lonely Villa*

H) Kinetograph

I) *The Great Train Robbery*

J) Muybridge's first successful galloping horse photography (series photography)

II. Multiple Choice. *Two points each.*

___ 1. Color in films was

A) introduced with the coming of sound.

B) a normal part of the film viewing experience from nearly the beginning of things.

C) used schematically throughout the 'teens and twenties, according to certain naturalistic and/or symbolic conventions.

D) was applied exclusively by hand until the coming of the Technicolor three-strip process in 1933.

E) None of the above

F) B and C

___ 2. All of the following were factors influencing the advent of feature films except

A) the popularity of French *film d'art.*

B) the international success of *Quo vadis?* and *Cabiria.*

C) the distaste of the middle classes for novels and plays.

D) the demise of the MPCC.

E) Griffith's drive for increased film length.

___ 3. A tracking or travelling shot is one in which

A) the camera is static but appears to move through editing.

B) the camera rotates or tilts on a fixed axis, usually its tripod.

C) the camera actively participates in the action by moving with it either sideways or in depth.

D) the camera is static but an object or person is moved toward it on some kind of track.

E) None of the above

___ 4. The Edison Kinetograph

A) used perforated celluloid roll film.

B) wasn't invented by Edison.

C) contained a stop-motion device to insure the intermittent motion of the film strip.

D) was intended for use in combination with the phonograph.

E) All of the above

F) A and C

___ 5. Griffith's "decline" as a film artist can be attributed to

A) his losing touch with the tastes and values of the audience.

B) his being swallowed up by the industrial system he helped to create.

C) his infatuation with his own reputation for greatness.

D) a long string of financially unsuccessful films from *Way Down East* through *The Struggle*.

E) All of the above

___ 6. A long shot is

A) a shot involving the use of special filters to reduce glare.

B) a shot of relatively great spatial length between camera and subject.

C) a shot that is frequently used to establish a scene when cut together with medium and close shots.

D) None of the above

E) B and C

___ 7. In *A Trip to the Moon* all of the following is true except

A) all of the scenery is artificial and there are many "special effects," (i.e., photographic tricks).

B) the camera assumes the fixed position of a theater spectator.

C) the actors, in general, move from left to right and right to left across the frame, which is treated like the proscenium arch of the stage.

D) the film is composed of shots, in the modern sense, rather than theatrical-style scenes.

E) the narrative is sequential, one scene following another in chronological order.

___ 8. The film in which Griffith first used an intercut chase or "last-minute rescue" sequence was

A) *A Corner in Wheat.*

B) *The Massacre.*

C) *The Battle of Elderbush Gulch.*

D) *The Lonely Villa.*

E) None of the above

___ 9. The difference between the Kinetograph and the *Cinématographe* was

A) that the *cinématographe* was lighter and more portable.

B) that the two machines were based on completely different modes of engineering and serial photography.

C) that the *cinématographe* could both take pictures and project them.

D) A and C

E) None of the above

___ 10. The MPPC did all of the following except

A) restrict film length to one or two reels.

B) attempt to monopolize all three sectors of the industry.

C) use screen credits and other forms of publicity to promote its stars.

D) fight the independent producers aggressively, in court and out.

E) provide exhibitors with films of reliable image clarity owing to its tight control of technology patents.

___ 11. After their pioneering work, Méliès and Porter both

A) continued to make bold innovations in cinema's narrative form.

B) died early deaths.

C) went to Hollywood to work for the new studios there.

D) B and C

E) None of the above

___ 12. The "Nickelodeon boom" of 1907–8 was important because

A) it exponentially increased the demand for film from producers.

B) it gave rise to the distribution sector of the industry, since exhibitors could no longer afford to buy their prints outright.

C) it helped to standardize film length at a single reel, until the advent of features.

D) it stimulated the rapid industrialization of the industry.

E) B and C

F) All of the above

___ 13. One of Griffith's earliest uses of dramatic lighting for expressive effect was in

A) *The New York Hat*.
B) *Pippa Passes*.
C) *The Lonedale Operator*.
D) *The Adventures of Dollie*.
E) None of the above

___ 14. In *The Great Train Robbery*, Porter did all of the following except

A) use back projection to simulate movement through windows and doors.
B) shoot many sequences out of doors.
C) tilt and pan his camera to follow significant action.
D) build his film up completely out of moving *tableaux* rather than shots.
E) use an unusual amount of diagonal composition for the period.

___ 15. Generally speaking, Hollywood was able to dominate the international film market between 1914 and 1918

A) through the monopolistic practices of the MPPC.
B) because no other countries had founded domestic industries yet.
C) because most other countries had to direct their resources toward waging World War I rather than expanding their industries.
D) because only American films were popular with world audiences.
E) None of the above

___ 16. The widespread success of *The Birth of a Nation* helped to

A) set the standard for the Hollywood epic film.
B) attract finance capital to feature production.
C) establish film as a powerful mass medium of persuasion.
D) discourage film attendance by the middle class.
E) All but D

___ 17. The major film industries in Europe prior to 1914 were

A) the British.
B) the Italian.
C) the German.
D) the French.
E) B and D
F) None of the above (i.e., there weren't any important ones)

___ 18. Griffith helped to develop and perfect all of the following techniques except

A) parallel editing.
B) expressive lighting.
C) camera movement and placement.
D) jump cutting and multitrack stereophonic sound.
E) dissolves, fades, and iris shots.

___ 19. The so-called "independent" producers moved to Southern California for all of the following reasons except

A) its better climate and lighting conditions.
B) its cheap labor and real estate.
C) its great distance from the MPPC in the East.
D) its proximity to Las Vegas, where money could be efficiently laundered in the casinos.
E) its wide range of topography and scenery.

___ 20. Which of the following does not occur in *The Birth of a Nation*:

A) Ben Cameron leads a heroic charge at Petersburg and is wounded.
B) Silas Lynch lusts after Austin Stoneman's daughter.
C) The "renegade negro" Gus rapes Flora Cameron and murders her.
D) Reconstruction elections are rigged to favor the black vote.
E) The Klan is formed by whites to protect themselves against abuses by blacks.

___ 21. The content of much early film

    A) seems trivial by contemporary standards.

    B) seems to represent the dominant ideology of the class which produced it.

    C) was determined by demands of technology and conventions of film length.

    D) was often the product of the same person who filmed and edited it.

    E) All of the above

    F) None of the above

___ 22. All of the following are true of "storefront" theaters, or nickelodeons, except

    A) they were the first permanent motion picture theaters in the U.S.

    B) they were attended largely by working-class audiences.

    C) they were designed primarily for the exhibition of features.

    D) they were elegantly designed and luxuriously appointed.

    E) C and D

___ 23. Persistence of vision

    A) is the ability of a camera lens to focus on its subject.

    B) is the ability to recall the plot of a narrative film long after it has been viewed.

    C) was first described scientifically by Roget in 1824.

    D) is the perceptual illusion that makes "movement" possible in motion pictures.

    E) A and C

    F) C and D

___ 24. Louis Feuillade is best known as

    A) the father of narrative editing, or "arranged shots."

    B) the business genius who founded and organized the Pathé Studios in France.

    C) the early French director who pioneered composition in depth and *mise en scène* in several popular serial films.

    D) the inventor of the *Cinématographe*.

    E) All of the above

    F) B and D

___ 25. *The Life of an American Fireman*

    A) was one of the first films to mix archival footage of a real event with footage of stage action.

    B) was originally thought to have intercut exterior and interior shots to suggest parallel events.

    C) was D. W. Griffith's first important film for American Biograph.

    D) was constructed as a stage play, like the films of Méliès.

    E) B and C

    F) A and B

III. Short Essay. Using as many examples from the screenings as possible write an essay of several paragraphs on either A) or B):

A) The evolution of continuity editing from the period of the Edison and Lumières shorts through *The Lonely Villa*.

B) D. W. Griffith's specific contributions to narrative film form.

Forty points.

Film Studies 371
Fall 1989
David A. Cook

Hour Test II

I. Matching. Match the proper person with the films/phenomena. *One point each.*

___ Kuleshov

___ F. W. Murnau

___ Eisenstein

___ Robert Weine

___ Pudovkin

___ Fritz Lang

___ G. W. Pabst

___ Dovzhenko

___ Vertov

___ Stalin

A) *Earth*

B) socialist realism

C) *The Man with a Movie Camera*

D) *Das Kabinett des Dr. Caligari*

E) "invisible editing"

F) *Mother*

G) "creative geography"

H) *October*

I) *Metropolis*

J) *Der letzte Mann*

II. Multiple Choice. *Two points each.*

___ 1. In Eisenstein's theory of dialectical montage

A) meaning is generated through the linkage of shots.

B) meaning is generated through the collision of shots.

C) it is possible to communicate ideological and/or intellectual concepts.

D) it is impossible to impose a meter or tempo exclusive of the content of the shots.

E) B and C

F) All of the above

___ 2. All of the following is true of *Das Kabinett des Dr. Caligari* except

A) it was a horror film.

B) it employed bizarre, expressive sets and make up.

C) it contributed vastly to the evolution of continuity editing and camera movement.

D) it helped establish the German cinema as internationally important.

E) it employed a frame story to mitigate its anti-authoritarian theme.

___ 3. The subjective camera technique involves

A) highly stylized color tinting.

B) viewing events from a "third-person" perspective.

C) editing to create violent perceptual impact.

D) editing which conceals itself.

E) None of the above

___ 4. The VGIX

A) was the German state film school.

B) was the site of the Kuleshov Workshop.

C) was founded by Stalin.

D) was founded by Ludendorff.

E) B and C

___ 5. Weimar and Soviet cinema were very much alike in that

A) both were created by their respective governments.

B) both were exclusively cinemas of political propaganda and agitation.

C) both pioneered the introduction of sound long before the U.S.

D) both were subverted by the Nazis.

E) neither achieved distinction.

F) B and C

___ 6. The doctrine of socialist realism dictates that all Soviet art should

A) follow the Communist Party line.

B) appeal to the intellectuals, who are qualified to understand it.

C) concentrate on formal experiments.

D) serve primarily to teach and instruct the masses.

E) A and D

F) None of the above

___ 7. UFA was

A) founded by the German military government.

B) the largest single studio in Europe before WW II.

C) subverted by the Nazis in the 1930s.

D) the producer of the greatest films of the Weimar period.

E) All of the above

___ 8. The montage experiments of the Soviet cinema during the '20s

A) had little influence beyond Soviet borders.

B) greatly influenced German Expressionism.

C) were admired by the U.S. government owing to their association with Bolshevism.

D) were undertaken mainly to discover the "laws" by which film communicates.

E) None of the above

___ 9. All of the following are characteristics of the work of Dovzhenko except

A) an interest in myth and nature.

B) a poetic sensibility.

C) doctrinaire Stalinism.

D) visual beauty.

E) C and D

___ 10. *Berlin, Symphony of a Great City* is like *The Man with a Movie Camera* in that

A) both were made by Germans.

B) both use color sequences.

C) both concern the activities of a major city from dawn to dusk.

D) both use rapid montage sequences.

E) All of the above

F) C and D

___ 11. The theory of the *kino-eye*

A) was developed by Lev Kuleshov.

B) proposed that meaning in cinema is generated by a collision of shots.

C) favored narrative over documentary cinema.

D) was first practiced in Pabst's *The Joyless Street*.

E) All of the above

F) None of the above

___ 12. Ernst Lubitsch

A) helped to subvert UFA for the Nazis by lending it large sums of money.

B) was the first director of the VGIK.

C) became world famous for his historical costume dramas.

D) left Germany for Hollywood, one of the first of a large migration.

E) directed *Caligari*, uncredited

F) C and D

___ 13. Invisible editing involves

A) making a character disappear from a scene.

B) cutting on movement.

C) violent perceptual dislocation.

D) the creation of extremely fluid narrative continuities.

E) B and D

F) None of the above

14. In *contrast* to Eisenstein, Pudovkin

   A) believed that film editing should proceed as a series of explosions.
   B) rejected the personal and lyrical for the epic.
   C) was a committed Marxist.
   D) made a film to commemorate the tenth anniversary of the Bolshevik Revolution.
   E) None of the above

15. Generally speaking, German cinema of the Weimar period was

   A) reconstituted as soon as the Nazis were defeated in 1945.
   B) highly influential on American cinema in the 1920s, '30s, and '40s.
   C) completely state controlled and used for political propaganda.
   D) a cinema of montage rather than *mise en scène*.
   E) basically pornographic

16. The most important type of montage in *October* is

   A) metric.
   B) overtonal.
   C) tonal.
   D) intellectual/ideological.
   E) rhythmic.
   F) narrative.

17. The "unchained camera"

   A) was a technique developed by F. W. Murnau and Karl Freund.
   B) involves the use of a nearly continuously moving camera.
   C) is sometimes used in combination with the "subjective camera."
   D) was first used as a basic structural principle in *The Last Laugh*.
   E) All of the above

18. Soviet theory suggests that

   A) shots cut together represent the sum of their parts.
   B) each shot in a film has the value of what it represents as a photographic image of something in empirical reality.

   C) the Hegelian-Marxist dialectic simply doesn't work.
   D) each shot has the value of what it represents in relation to the shots with which it is intercut.
   E) All of the above
   F) B and D

19. *Kammerspielfilm* was

   A) the technical term for the Expressionist horror genre.
   B) any film employing overtonal montage.
   C) a filmic version of "intimate theater."
   D) a link between Expressionism and "street realism."
   E) None of the above
   F) C and D

20. The Parufamet agreement

   A) caused the emigration of many German film artists to Hollywood.
   B) temporarily kept the UFA from bankruptcy.
   C) gave the Nazi Party control of the German cinema.
   D) gave UFA control of MGM and Paramount.
   E) A and B

21. The "Golden Age" of German cinema ended primarily because

   A) the Nazis destroyed its studios.
   B) American competition destroyed its markets.
   C) the Soviet invasion destroyed its material base.
   D) the deterioration of German society destroyed its meaning and purpose.
   E) None of the above

22. Before 1917 the Soviet cinema was characterized by

   A) foreign domination.
   B) pornography.
   C) lack of a viable middle- or working-class audience.
   D) proCommunist propaganda.
   E) All of the above
   F) A and C

___ 23. German Expressionist cinema had all of the following attributes except

    A) highly stylized decor.

    B) dark psychological themes.

    C) a preoccupation with ideological manipulation and political control.

    D) use of chiaroscuro lighting.

    E) a reliance on directors, writers, and designers from the other arts.

___ 24. In the Odessa steps sequence

    A) Pabst showed his greatest use of invisible editing.

    B) thousands of people are shown to be massacred.

    C) Eisenstein employed his greatest use of "ideological montage," excluding all other types.

    D) three stone lions are cut together at the end to suggest a metaphor for revolutionary outrage.

    E) None of the above

    F) B and D

___ 25. *Metropolis* and *Mother* are alike in that

    A) both were commissioned by Hitler.

    B) both are science fiction films.

    C) both contain early color and sound sequences.

    D) neither attempts to generate sympathy for the Russian people.

    E) All of the above

    F) None of the above

___ 26. The "Kuleshov effect" demonstrates that

    A) camera movement is more important than editing.

    B) raw film stock can be mass produced through the application of electrical technology.

    C) the most important meaning of a shot is that which it acquires when placed into juxtaposition with another shot.

    D) basically, a shot means only what it is a photographic image of.

    E) A and D

___ 27. G. W. Pabst

    A) was associated with "street realism."

    B) was the first great practitioner of Expressionism.

    C) perfected the "motivated point-of-view" shot.

    D) became an important Hollywood director during the '30s and '40s.

    E) All of the above

    F) A and C

___ 28. All of the following is true of *Potemkin* except

    A) it was intended to incite the masses to hatred of their former rulers.

    B) it contains one of the greatest montage sequences in film history.

    C) it is a film of deep psychological introspection.

    D) it brought it director international acclaim.

    E) A and D

___ 29. The two "world class" directors produced by German Expressionism were

    A) Herbert von Karajan and Josef von Sternberg.

    B) Max Steiner and Eric von Stroheim.

    C) Fritz Lang and F. W. Murnau.

    D) G. W. Pabst and Josef von Sternberg.

    E) None of the above

___ 30. Dziga Vertov

    A) invented montage theory.

    B) was the first director of the Soviet state film school.

    C) pioneered the *cinéma vérité* documentary form.

    D) was Eisenstein's cameraman on *Potemkin*.

    E) None of the above

___ 31. *Metropolis*

A) contains two "Maria" figures—a real one and a false one.
B) was Hitler's favorite film.
C) was recently reissued in a tinted version with a Giorgio Moroder score.
D) has numerous special effects using the "Schüfftan process."
E) All of the above
F) B and C

___ 32. In *Mother*, the father

A) is a preBolshevik revolutionary hero.
B) refuses to become a counter-revolutionary spy.
C) dies with his son in his arms at the film's conclusion.
D) eats a smoked sturgeon and gets drunk on cheap vodka near the beginning of the film.
E) All of the above
F) A and B

___ 33. *Faust*

A) was the last film directed by Fritz Lang.
B) is a good example of the kind of big budget, over produced film that drove UFA into debt.
C) was the paradigm for "street realism."
D) was the first German-Soviet co-production.
E) All of the above
F) A and C

___ 34. In *October*

A) there is a famous montage sequence involving the raising of a drawbridge to divide the city of St. Petersburg.
B) Alexander Kerenski is shown to be a hero of the people.
C) the hero is a Mongolian national fighting in a guerrilla war against British imperialism.
D) Trotsky is shown to be shorter than either Lenin or Stalin.
E) None of the above
F) B and D

___ 35. The reason that so many Hollywood films of the late '40s resemble German films of the twenties is that

A) it took American camera technology about twenty years to catch up with that of Germany.
B) Americans learned how to make films like the Germans during the post–World War II occupation.
C) the same creative personnel were making them.
D) All of the above
E) None of the above

___ 36. Eisenstein based his montage theory on

A) an analogy with Japanese character-writing.
B) an analogy with human language or speech.
C) the Marxist dialectic.
D) All of the above
E) None of the above
F) A and C

___ 37. *Dr. Caligari* and *The Last Laugh* are alike in that both

A) used carefully designed studio sets.
B) incorporate newsreel footage from the front.
C) have plots heavily influenced by fate or destiny.
D) are patently political in intent.
E) None of the above
F) A and C

___ 38. The reason(s) that Stalin wanted to subject the Soviet film industry to his personal will was (were) that

A) he was an antiintellectual.
B) he was an antiSemite.
C) he agreed with Lenin about the political importance of the cinema to the Party's goals.
D) he resented the publicity that directors like Eisenstein were gaining at home and abroad.
E) A and B
F) All of the above

___ 39. The reason that filmic influence is different from literary influence is that

    A) it is essentially trivial, because it doesn't embody ideas.

    B) it is very nearly immediate.

    C) it transcends language categories and national boundaries.

    D) it cannot really travel long distances.

    E) All of the above

    F) B and C

___ 40. *Agitki* were

    A) the first kinds of films produced by the Soviet cinema.

    B) the first type of films directed by Vertov.

    C) newsreels edited in such a way as to stir people up.

    D) attractive to the Soviets because much of the footage had already been shot.

    E) All of the above

    F) B and C

III. Write a brief essay describing the Hollywood studio system as it existed from about 1924 to the coming of sound. *Ten points*.

Film Studies 371
Fall 1989
David A. Cook

Hour Test III

I. Matching. Match the 1930s' studio with the appropriate description. *Two points each.*

___ Warners

___ 20th Century-Fox

___ Paramount

___ RKO

___ MGM

A) Smallest of the majors, created to exploit the sound-on-film system of its parent corporation. Produced Astaire-Rogers musicals, *King Kong*, *Citizen Kane*.

B) Most "European" of the studios. Much UFA talent. DeMille, Lubitsch, and von Sternberg were its major directors during the '30s.

C) Biggest, most prosperous, most "American" of the majors, with access to nearly unlimited production capital. Style characterized by high-key lighting and lavish production design. Produced *Wizard of Oz* and (partially) *Gone with the Wind*.

D) Product of a mid-'30s merger. Hard glossy visual style and good special effects. Produced most of Ford's '30s films and Shirley Temple movies.

E) Identified with the working class. Produced films characterized by low-key lighting and maximum economy of means. Associated with gangster cycle, Busby Berkeley films, social realism, and "biopics."

II. Multiple Choice. *Two and a half points each.*

___ 1. Post synchronization is

A) Eisenstein, Pudovkin, and Alexandrov's theory of sound montage.

B) the standard method of synchronizing record and film in sound-on-disk systems.

C) the practice of separating soundtrack and image track and recording them separately.

D) the naive idea that everything *heard* on the soundtrack must also be *seen* on the screen.

E) None of the above

___ 2. All of the following statements are true of Josef von Sternberg except

A) he tried to eliminate the problem of "dead space" in his films.

B) he was fascinated by lush decor.

C) he was an important pioneer of the early sound film.

D) he was a hard-hitting director of action films.

E) A and B

___ 3. The filmmaker(s) most closely associated with the emergence of the musical as major genre is (are)

A) George Cukor.

B) Busby Berkeley.

C) William Wyler.

D) Fred Astaire.

E) Howard Hawks.

F) B and D

___ 4. Howard Hawks

A) was not terribly interested in the visual texture of his films.
B) favored eye-level medium shots.
C) was obsessed by the theme of professionalism.
D) made distinguished films in every major genre.
E) All of the above

___ 5. *The Jazz Singer* was

A) the first 100 percent, all-dialogue film.
B) the first sound film.
C) the first film to use a prerecorded orchestral score.
D) poorly received by the public.
E) All of the above
F) None of the above

___ 6. Three-color Technicolor was used infrequently during the '30s and '40s because

A) it was crude and didn't offer much verisimilitude.
B) the public didn't want color because it was so infatuated with sound.
C) it was expensive and subject to monopoly control.
D) A and B
E) None of the above

___ 7. The theory of asynchronous or contrapuntal sound suggested that

A) sound should be restricted to the camera's point of view.
B) sound should be an extension and refinement of montage.
C) the relationship between sound and image should be conflictive.
D) sound and image should coincide precisely.
E) None of the above
F) B and C

___ 8. The Production Code was enforced by the studios

A) to promote "American" family values.
B) to keep acts of sex and violence off the screen.
C) to placate the Catholic Legion of Decency.
D) to avert external censorship.
E) All of the above

___ 9. All of the following are true of Hitchcock except that

A) he was influenced by German Expressionism.
B) he was a great montage artist in the tradition of Eisenstein.
C) his films frequently concern individuals trapped in paranoid-like nightmares.
D) though he pioneered the creative use of sound, he failed to make the conversion to the wide screen during the 1950s.
E) he was a master of moving camera shots.

___ 10. The single most important American film genre during the 1920s was

A) the musical.
B) the gangster film.
C) the newspaper film.
D) the Western.
E) None of the above

___ 11. The conversion to sound

A) had the effect of consolidating the studio system.
B) forced the studios into the arms of Wall Street.
C) was spearheaded by the major forces in the film industry to beguile the public with "talkies."
D) was originally seen as a means of adding orchestral scores and sound effects to silent films.
E) All of the above except C

____ 12. *Hallelujah!* was all of the following except

A) an important American film of the early sound era.
B) shot on location with an all-black cast.
C) the first American film to employ post-synchronized sound.
D) the first American film shot in the Fox Movietone process.
E) None of the above

____ 13. Vitaphone

A) ushered in the era of sound.
B) was invented by Western Electric.
C) was the first optical system to be used in the U.S.
D) is, in its basic elements, the sound recording system still in use today.
E) A and B
F) All of the above

____ 14. All of the following is true of filmmaking during the early years of sound except

A) the cameras were placed in sound-proof booths.
B) actors and actresses had to speak directly into the microphones.
C) editing became easier because the soundtrack ran 20 frames ahead of the image track.
D) many performers and directors could not make the transition to sound because their talents weren't suited for it.
E) B and D

____ 15. John Ford was

A) closely associated with the western genre.
B) fascinated by the subject of sexual decadence.
C) essentially a director of "women's pictures."

D) an artist without a fixed moral vision.
E) None of the above

____ 16. Thomas H. Ince is important to the history of film because

A) he pioneered the Biblical epic as genre.
B) he encouraged improvisation in the filmmaking process.
C) his mode of production became the prototype for the Hollywood studio system.
D) he founded Famous Players–Lasky (Paramount).
E) None of the above

____ 17. All of the following is true of the Hollywood B-film except

A) it was rented to the exhibitor at a flat rate rather than a percentage of the gross.
B) it offered a training ground for some important novice directors by providing more creative freedom than the studios.
C) it was instituted during the Depression to give audiences more for their money.
D) it was always more cheaply produced than the A-film which accompanied it.
E) None of the above

____ 18. The chief problem with the earliest sound recording system (i.e., those attempted in the earliest years of the cinema itself) was

A) synchronization.
B) the brevity of cylinders and disks relative to motion picture length.
C) amplification.
D) All of the above
E) None of the above

___ 19. The conversion to sound took place because

A) all of the major Hollywood studios wanted it.
B) Paramount was willing to take a chance on an unproven recording technology.
C) the public was fascinated by recorded dialogue.
D) Western Electric and RCA wanted to create large new markets for their products in the U.S. and abroad.
E) None of the above
F) C and D

___ 20. An *unanticipated* effect of the conversion to optical sound was

A) the addition of sound reproduction equipment in the theaters.
B) the need to build sound stages and convert the production process in the studios.
C) the elimination of chemical toning as a regular practice in class-A features.
D) the unemployment of actors and actresses who could not speak English.
E) the elimination of long, elaborate scripts.

___ 21. The introduction of panchromatic film stock in the early sound era

A) was necessitated by a change in lighting systems.
B) reduced photographic depth of field.
C) eliminated the prospects for Technicolor until after World War II.
D) None of the above
E) A and B

___ 22. In *Blackmail*

A) the director contributed one of his last great films of the silent era.
B) there is much use of on-location sound recording.

C) the camera never moves.
D) a silent film and a dialogue film are combined.
E) there is a brief, two-color Technicolor sequence in the first ten minutes.

___ 23. The so-called "natural" color systems

A) register color on the film base during actual photography rather than having it added in processing.
B) are all additive systems.
C) were first introduced by Technicolor in 1933.
D) are no longer used today.
E) were invented by the Nazis during World War II.

___ 24. *The 39 Steps*

A) is regarded as one of its director's major films.
B) uses creative sound montage.
C) contains a murder sequence on a train.
D) is flawed by terrible acting.
E) A and B
F) None of the above

___ 25. Lewis Milestone's *The Front Page*

A) contains many striking moving camera shots.
B) uses overlapping dialogue.
C) is about newspaper journalists covering an execution.
D) All of the above
E) None of the above

___ 26. *The Man Who Knew Too Much*

A) was its director's first film in color.
B) was its director's first film to use dialogue.
C) was remade in the 1950s.
D) visually shows the influence of German Expressionism.
E) C and D
F) None of the above

___ 27. The Fox "Movietone News"

A) was the world's very first newsreel service.

B) used an optical sound-on-film process that Fox had bought from the Germans.

C) mainly filmed radio plays and people reading poetry for an intellectual audience.

D) All of the above

E) None of the above

___ 28. As seen in class, *Murder* contains which of the following:

A) a trial sequence tinted sepia.

B) a shoot-out between police and spies.

C) a 360 degree pan of the faces of jury.

D) a murder sequence in which there is no recorded dialogue.

E) None of the above

___ 29. All of the following are true of *The Blue Angel* except

A) the director resolves the problem of "dead space" through an unusual use of decor.

B) it is about sexual humiliation and domination.

C) it was the first film to use multi-channel recording to modulate its soundtrack.

D) it stars Marlene Dietrich and Emil Jannings.

E) it was shot in black and white.

___ 30. The Motion Picture Producers and Distributors of America (MPPDA) was

A) headed by a former member of the Harding administration.

B) founded to protect the five major studios' monopoly on distribution from the three minors.

C) created to whitewash the dope, sex, and murder scandals of the early '20s.

D) created to recognize excellence in the American motion picture industry through the conferring of Academy Awards.

E) A and C

III. Write a brief essay on the *economic* consequences of the coming of sound to the American film industry. *Fifteen points.*

Film Studies 371
Fall 1989
David A. Cook

Final Exam

I. Matching. *Two points each.*

___ Marcel Carné

___ Luis Buñuel

___ Fritz Lang

___ Leni Riefenstahl

___ Carl-Theodor Dreyer

A) *Un Chien Andalou*

B) *Olympiad*

C) *La Passion de Jeanne d'Arc*

D) *Quai des Brûmes*

E) *M*

II. Multiple Choice. *Two and a half points each.*

___ 1. The most striking feature of *La Grand illusion* is

A) the great montage work of the battle sequences.

B) its impressive use of early Technicolor.

C) its long takes or sequence shots.

D) its realistic recreation of 19th-century Europe.

E) All of the above

___ 2. Composition in depth is

A) only achieved through deep-focus photography.

B) difficult to achieve with panchromatic film stock.

C) an attempt to link foreground, middle ground, and background within the same shot.

D) technically a function of depth of field.

E) All of the above

___ 3. Many of the great films of "poetic realism" were

A) pessimistic about the future.

B) produced by the writer-director team of Jacques Prévert and Marcel Carné.

C) written by Charles Spaak.

D) a blend of lyricism and realism.

E) A and B

F) All of the above

___ 4. *Que viva México!* was

A) financed by socialist writer Upton Sinclair.

B) one of the great lost masterworks of the cinema.

C) René Clair's first important musical.

D) shot mainly on a sound stage to insure fidelity of recording.

E) A and B

___ 5. *La Règle du jeu*

A) is about the collapse of European society between the wars.

B) has a famous montage sequence.

C) stars its own director.

D) was perceived as a political film when it was released.

E) A and C

F) All of the above

___ 6. The Soviet cinema experienced a decline between the wars because

A) Eisenstein made no films after *Alexander Nevski*.

B) Stalin purged Boris Shumiatski.

C) state support for the cinema was withdrawn.

D) the Soviets didn't convert to sound until after the war.

E) All of the above

F) None of the above

___ 7. All of the following is true of the French film industry during the conversion to sound except

A) René Clair pioneered the creative use of sound.
B) an American-style studio system emerged.
C) the film industry was strengthened through its ownership of sound film patents.
D) a number of important films were produced by the German-owned studio Tobis.
E) A and B

___ 8. Monochromatic film stock

A) was introduced shortly after the conversion to sound.
B) has excellent color registry.
C) permits great depth of field.
D) is still used today.
E) None of the above

___ 9. The "*cine club*" movement

A) was begun by Russian dissidents.
B) prevented the Nazis from totally dominating the German cinema.
C) was closely linked to Italian Fascism.
D) enriched the film environment of France during the twenties.
E) None of the above

___ 10. In *M*

A) there is little use of nonnaturalistic sound.
B) the child murderer is never captured.
C) the Nazis are portrayed as villains.
D) there is much graphic violence.
E) None of the above

___ 11. Jean Renoir is an important figure in film history because

A) his films were extremely effective in spreading Nazi doctrine.
B) he was a great humanist.
C) he was the first major director of the sound film to compose his shots in depth.
D) he was the first major director of the sound film to shoot his films exclusively in color.

E) B and C
F) All of the above

___ 12. In *Alexander Nevski*

A) the Teutonic Knights are made to resemble Nazis.
B) there is much use of contrapuntal sound.
C) there is little montage.
D) A and B
E) B and C
F) All of the above

___ 13. All of the following are true of the German film industry during the thirties except

A) it was a leader in early sound film technology and technique.
B) it was totally nationalized by the Nazis.
C) it became heavily ideological.
D) it primarily produced a cinema of entertainment.
E) B and C

___ 14. The British film industry experienced a boom of sorts during the thirties because

A) the British have a natural affinity for visual expression.
B) quotas were set on the importation of foreign films to stimulate domestic production.
C) England did not suffer from the worldwide economic depression.
D) British filmmakers discovered for the first time the scenic potential of their homeland.
E) A and B

___ 15. All of the following statements are true of *Napoléon* except

A) it used an early widescreen process.
B) it contains some of the era's most extraordinary camera-work and editing.
C) it is one of the great eccentric masterpieces of the early sound film.
D) it was cut from 28 to eight reels for distribution.
E) B and D

____ 16. The major films of Leni Riefenstahl were

    A) propaganda–"documentaries."
    B) financed by the Nazi Party.
    C) very expensively made.
    D) among the few truly important films made during the Third Reich.
    E) B and C
    F) All of the above

____ 17. Jean Renoir's film career

    A) ended with the Nazi Occupation of France.
    B) was destroyed by his association with Hollywood.
    C) had little influence outside of France.
    D) was short by all contemporary standards.
    E) All of the above
    F) None of the above

____ 18. A sequence shot is

    A) a very short take.
    B) any shot in a montage sequence.
    C) an unedited shot which generally constitutes an entire dramatic sequence.
    D) a reverse angle shot.
    E) a shot in which there is great focal length between the camera lens and its object.

____ 19. During the twenties, French cinema was

    A) primarily commercial and entertainment oriented.
    B) virtually unknown outside of France.
    C) dominated by the style of George Méliès.
    D) closely associated with modernism and the avant-garde.
    E) B and C

____ 20. In *Triumph of the Will*

    A) Hitler is played by an actor.
    B) the opening sequence is shot from a barge on the Rhine.
    C) a voice-over narration explains the sequence of events.

    D) All of the above
    E) None of the above

____ 21. Polyvision

    A) bears no relationship to Cinerama.
    B) used a single camera.
    C) could produce widescreen images but not multiple images.
    D) was first used by Eisenstein.
    E) All of the above
    F) None of the above

____ 22. Fritz Lang was

    A) propaganda minister for the Nazi Party.
    B) a rabid anti-Expressionist.
    C) a major pioneer of the French sound film.
    D) famous for directing lighthearted musicals.
    E) None of the above

____ 23. Which of the following filmmakers were important to French "poetic realism"?

    A) Abel Gance
    B) Severin-Mars
    C) Marcel L'Herbier
    D) Jacques Feyder
    E) Julien Duvivier
    F) D and E
    G) None of the above

____ 24. *Ivan the Terrible* was

    A) conceived as a three-part film.
    B) Eisenstein's last work.
    C) first admired and then hated by Stalin.
    D) made in two parts.
    E) All of the above
    F) None of the above

____ 25. René Clair

    A) began his career as an experimental avant-gardist.
    B) was an important pioneer of the early sound film.
    C) made several important musicals.
    D) made films in the U.S. as well as France.
    E) All of the above
    F) None of the above

___ 26. *La Passion de Jeanne d'Arc* was

A) a masterwork of the early sound film.
B) made in France by a Dane.
C) the last great work of Dmitri Kirsanoff.
D) ruined by its talky dialogue.
E) None of the above

___ 27. Jean Vigo

A) was a precursor of poetic realism.
B) made only two feature films.
C) pioneered the early sound film.
D) was the son of a famous anarchist.
E) All of the above
F) None of the above

___ 28. Deep-focus photography

A) was not practiced before *Citizen Kane.*
B) was easily achieved before 1918.
C) was difficult to achieve using panchromatic film stock.
D) has little aesthetic or dramatic value.
E) B and C
F) None of the above

___ 29. *Olympiad* (1936) was

A) commissioned by Hitler.
B) a filmed record of the Berlin Olympics.
C) made to denigrate the Nazi myth of the "superman."
D) poorly photographed trash.
E) A and B
F) None of the above

___ 30. *La Règle du jeu* begins with

A) the hunting party at La Colinière.
B) the Nazi occupation of Paris.
C) persons listening to a radio broadcast.
D) an auto wreck.
E) a political riot.
F) a filmed statement by its director.

Extra Credit. *Three points each.*

___ 31. The precise definition of a "B-film" is

A) a film of inferior, low-grade quality.

B) a film made to be distributed as the second half of a double bill.
C) a racy, scandalous entertainment involving a lot of sex.
D) a film made by amateurs.
E) None of the above

___ 32. *Triumph of the Will* and *Alexander Nevski* are alike in that

A) both films were sponsored by their respective governments.
B) both contain color sequences.
C) both were conceived as propaganda.
D) they were both "election" films.
E) A and C
F) None of the above

___ 33. The diffusion of sound in Europe

A) led to American domination of all European markets until well after WW II.
B) was complicated by a patents war between American corporations and German cartels for control of sound film technology.
C) took place more slowly than in the Soviet Union and Japan.
D) completely excluded RCA and ERPI.
E) None of the above

___ 34. At the conclusion of *Ivan the Terrible, Pt. II*

A) Ivan is assassinated in the church.
B) there is an epic full-scale battle sequence.
C) there is an expressionistic color sequence involving dancing.
D) Vladimir the Pole succeeds Ivan as czar.
E) All of the above
F) None of the above

III. Write a short essay discussing at least *two* of the films seen in class since the last test as political propaganda. *Fifteen points.*

Film Studies 372
Spring 1990
David A. Cook

Hour Test I

I. Matching.

   A. Match directors/producers with their films. *One point each.*

___ De Sica	A) *The Lady from Shanghai*
___ Welles	B) *Why We Fight*
___ Rossellini	C) *La terra trema*
___ Frank Capra	D) *Shoeshine*
___ Visconti	E) *Paisà*

   B. Match events/phenomena with dates. *One point each.*

___ postwar boom	A) 1941
___ Cinerama	B) 1948
___ Bureau of Motion Picture Affairs	C) 1952
___ CinemaScope	D) 1946
___ The "Paramount decrees"	E) 1953

II. Multiple Choice. *Two points each.*

___ 1. Some of the problems initially faced by filmmakers in adjusting to the new widescreen aspect ratios in the fifties were

   A) perceptual dislocation produced by montage.

   B) decreased capacity for composition in depth.

   C) inability to use sound directionally on the new monophonic tracks.

   D) optical distortion in close-up.

   E) A and D

   F) All of the above

___ 2. All of the following are true of Hollywood films during WW II except

   A) at first, they were very naive and unrealistic about the true nature of the conflict.

   B) they were not well-attended by the domestic audience.

   C) they tended to represent democratic ideals and situations which did not always coincide with social reality (e.g., racial equality).

   D) they tended to become grimmer and more realistic as the war progressed.

   E) A and D

___ 3. Composition in depth

   A) requires great depth of field.

   B) is an alternative to montage.

   C) was never used by Welles after *Kane.*

   D) is as difficult to achieve today as it was in 1940.

   E) All of the above

   F) A and B

____ 4. Before our entry into W.W. II, American films had little or nothing to say about the rise of Nazism or Nazi aggression in Europe because

A) there was much covert sympathy for fascism in the U.S., especially among business leaders.

B) the same interests which backed the American film industry had corporate ties with German firms.

C) Hollywood didn't want to run the risk of offending audiences in its fascist or pro-fascist overseas markets.

D) All of the above

E) None of the above

____ 5. After leaving Hollywood for personal and professional reasons, Orson Welles moved to Europe where

A) he was able to marshal the technical resources of the great continental studios for his films.

B) he made films on shoestring budgets but enjoyed great creative freedom.

C) he was investigated as a traitor by HUAC.

D) he signed a ten-film contract with British Paramount for adaptations of Shakespeare.

E) None of the above

____ 6. All of the following are important aspects of American cinema of the fifties except

A) the "blockbuster" phenomenon.

B) nearly full color production (i.e., over 50%).

C) experiments with new optical formats.

D) strict adherence to the Production Code.

E) political conservatism

____ 7. F.D.R. was able to get the studios to cooperate with his war aims effort by

A) threatening to have their executives prosecuted for treason.

B) temporarily soft-pedaling the Justice Department's antitrust suit brought in 1938.

C) drafting prominent filmmakers into the Army Signal Corp *en masse*.

D) declaring motion picture production an "essential industry."

E) All of the above

F) B and D

____ 8. The story of *Citizen Kane*

A) is told in flashback by Kane at the end of his life.

B) is based on the life of Time-Life founder Henry Luce.

C) is related by ten separate narrators.

D) contains several vivid dream sequences.

E) All of the above

F) None of the above

____ 9. The new realistic genre(s) of post-war Hollywood was (were)

A) *film noir*.

B) the so-called "woman's picture."

C) the "social consciousness" film.

D) "March of Time" newsreels.

E) semi-documentary melodrama.

F) All of the above

G) A, C, E

____ 10. All of the following were widescreen processes developed in the fifties except

A) Vista Vision.

B) CinemaScope.

C) Stereoscopic 3-D.

D) Panavision-70.

E) Todd-AO.

____ 11. To achieve "deep-focus" for *Citizen Kane*, Welles and Toland used

A) unusually narrow lens apertures.

B) high intensity lighting in combination with plastic-coated lenses.

C) untra-fast film.

D) widescreen Panavision cameras.

E) All of the above

F) A, B, C

12. Neorealism ended so suddenly because

    A) it had little influence outside of Italy.
    B) the Italian government became hostile to its representation of Italian society.
    C) widespread terrorism made on-location shooting increasingly difficult.
    D) Italy's "economic miracle" of the fifties left the movement without any subject matter.
    E) B and D
    F) All of the above

13. Anamorphic widescreen processes

    A) imprint wide-frame images on wide-gauge film.
    B) "squeeze" wide-frame images onto regular-gauge film.
    C) use three 35mm cameras running side-by-side to produce an ultra wide-frame image.
    D) use two overlapping 35mm cameras to produce an image frame in stereoscopic depth.
    E) None of the above

14. Which of the following are used on the sound track of *Kane*?

    A) Overlapping dialogue (also referred to as sound montage)
    B) Four-channel stereo
    C) The "lightning mix"
    D) Directional sound
    E) Orchestral music
    F) All of the above
    G) A, C, D, E
    H) B, C, E

15. Which of the following is *not* a major neo-realist film?

    A) *Bicycle Thieves*
    B) *Ossessione*
    C) *La terra trema*
    D) *The Last Days of Pompei*
    E) *Umberto D.*
    F) *Open City*

16. Widescreen processes were developed in the early fifties in response to

    A) the larger screens installed in recently constructed theaters.
    B) the popularity of *film noir*.
    C) the threat of television.
    D) the critics' demands for increased realism.
    E) All of the above
    F) None of the above

17. In the films Welles made after *Kane*, there is nearly always

    A) deep-focus photography and expressionistic lighting.
    B) a central character destroyed by ambition.
    C) an emphasis on the grotesque in human nature.
    D) an impressive economy of means.
    E) All of the above
    F) None of the above

18. Which of the following genres emerged as distinct American film types during the fifties?

    A) the Western
    B) the science fiction film
    C) the musical
    D) the comedy
    E) the gangster film
    F) All of the above

19. Which of the following is *not* a major characteristic of Italian neorealist film?

    A) an attempt to create the "illusion of the present tense."
    B) on-location shooting in available (i.e., natural) light.
    C) a heavy reliance on plot and well-defined individual characters.
    D) the reconstruction of "contemporary history."
    E) a mixture of professional and non-professional actors.
    F) B and D

___ 20. Cinerama is important because

A) it was cheap, flexible and simple to use, making conversion to wide-screen commercially possible.
B) it was the catalyst for the wide-screen revolution, although its own technology was both clumsy and expensive.
C) it was the first widescreen process ever used in film history.
D) it gave the American cinema some of its greatest epic narratives.
E) None of the above

___ 21. Which of the following is true of *Open City*?

A) It contains a lot of grainy, news-reel-like footage.
B) It connects the past and present by mixing black-and-white with color stock.
C) It was filmed largely on a meticulously detailed studio set Cinnecittà.
D) It depicts events which took place some five years before the film's production.
E) None of the above
F) All of the above

___ 22. All of the following are used in *Kane* except

A) radical camera angles.
B) overlapping dissolves.
C) moving camera shots.
D) conventional narrative structure.
E) a film within a film.
F) C and E

___ 23. Which of the following is *not* associated with the Hollywood blacklist?

A) the "Waldorf Statement"
B) *Red Channels*
C) HUAC
D) the double bill
E) the "Hollywood Ten"

___ 24. Which of the following may be regarded as major contributors to neorealism?

A) Giovanni Pastrone
B) Cesare Zavattini
C) Luchino Visconti
D) Vittorio De Sica
E) Enrico Guazzoni
F) All of the above
G) B, C, D

___ 25. Welles was able to make *Kane* different from the standard Hollywood product of the era because

A) he was given an enormous budget.
B) he was given complete control over all aspects of production.
C) he was able to use RKO established contract-stars for his cast.
D) coming from radio, he had no pre-conceived notions of how a film should be made.
E) with RKO's new Arriflex cameras, "deep-focus" was simple to achieve.
F) All of the above
G) B and D

___ 26. By the end of the decade of the fifties all of the following had occurred except

A) the weakening of the Production Code.
B) the rise of independent production.
C) the divestiture by the studios of their exhibition chains.
D) a significant loss of the movie industry audience to television.
E) the rise of a new fashion for depicting graphic violence.

___ 27. The narrative structure of *Kane* may best be described as

A) a series of flashbacks.
B) circular (i.e., it ends where it begins).
C) four major events plus a "newsreel."
D) relatively complex.
E) All of the above
F) None of the above

___ 28. Which of the following phenomena is *not* associated with post-war Hollywood, 1945–1950?

    A) increased on-location shooting

    B) the "Paramount decrees"

    C) the lowest box office receipts of the decade in 1946

    D) the rise of television

    E) the HUAC hearings

___ 29. Among *Kane*'s themes are

    A) the multisided nature of the truth.

    B) the fraudulence of the mass media.

    C) the way in which wealth and power bring happiness.

    D) the fidelity with which film can represent reality.

    E) All of the above

    F) A and B

___ 30. Which of the following did *not* contribute to the rise of Italian neorealism?

    A) the intense professional training of young filmmakers at the *Centro Sperimentale*

    B) Marxist theory and politics

    C) the desire to resurrect the great Italian costume epics of the 'teens

    D) a rejection of "calligraphism"

    E) the influence of Soviet expressive realism

    F) B and D

III. Answer *one* of the following two questions. *30 points.*

A) Write a short essay comparing *Made for Each Other* and *Citizen Kane* in terms of 1) narrative structure, including editing; 2) lighting and camera style; 3) sound recording. Use specific examples from the films of each.

B) Write a short essay comparing the "realistic" modes of *Open City* and *Kiss Me Deadly* in terms of the three elements listed in A) above, plus 4) ideological orientation and 5) acting style.

Film Studies 372
Spring 1990
David A. Cook

Hour Test II

I. Matching. French New Wave. *Two points each.*

___ Truffaut

___ Godard

___ Resnais

___ Chabrol

___ Malle

A) His major theme is the effect of time upon memory, which is explored by breaking the boundaries of conventional narrative form. Directed films which investigated the relationship of the human mind to states of reality.

B) He was influenced by the American B-film, Hitchcock, Jean Renoir; directed experimental, multi-genre films, Hitchcock-like thrillers and psychological autobiographies. Thought to be the most "romantic" director to emerge from the New Wave.

C) He has produced films with a wide variety of styles and subjects which are characterized by the simultaneous presentation of material from opposing points of view. Has made films on such controversial themes as incest and child prostitution.

D) He was influenced by Hitchcock more than any other New Wave figure; produced films which explore violence, criminality, and their impact upon human relationships.

E) He is the most prolific and stylistically radical of the New Wave directors. Produced "critical essays" which worked out social or political theories and which tended to attack Western capitalism.

F) He produced surreal allegories which attacked the religious and political hypocrisies of bourgeois society and satirized the Franco regime.

II. Multiple Choice. *Two and a half points each.*

___ 1. Before the French New Wave, the French cinema

A) was completely undistinguished.

B) was heavily influenced by literature.

C) had been ruined by the Occupation.

D) experienced an influential documentary movement.

E) None of the above

F) B and D

2. Development of film art impeded in the Eastern European countries by

A) Nazi occupation and/or collaboration.
B) the death of Stalin.
C) the creation of FAMU and the Łódz film school.
D) the contempt of Eastern Europeans generally for film art.
E) All of the above

3. In addition to its five "world-class" major figures, the French New Wave produced which of the following important filmmakers?

A) Agnès Varda
B) Jacques Rivette
C) Eric Rohmer
D) Henri Langlois
E) Alexandre Astruc
F) All of the above
G) A, B, C

4. *Shadows of Forgotten Ancestors* is a film

A) which retells a Ukrainian folk legend about undying love.
B) whose technique is dramatically dependent on unusual sequence shots.
C) in which there is no music, only naturalistic sound.
D) All of the above
E) A and B

5. The ultimate influence of the French New Wave on world cinema was

A) to return the French cinema to its literary roots.
B) to demonstrate that film could be a medium of personal artistic expression on a par with the other arts.
C) to demonstrate that film was basically a collective art form.
D) to prove that film was a form of audio-visual language.
E) All of the above
F) B and D

6. The Czech "New Wave" ended because

A) its films failed at the box office.
B) it was overwhelmed by the French New Wave at international film festivals.
C) it was basically just another form of "socialist realism."
D) it was crushed by the Soviet invasion of August 1968.
E) None of the above

7. Which of the following is true of *Breathless*?

A) It contains both color and black-and-white sequences.
B) It is representative of the documentary movement which influenced the New Wave.
C) It contains both lengthy tracking shots and still photographs.
D) It places the blame for the death camps squarely on the shoulders of the Nazi leaders and no one else.
E) All of the above

8. Which of the following is *not* associated with the theoretical base of the French New Wave?

A) the *caméra-stylo*
B) *mise-en-scène*
C) *la politique des auteurs*
D) *la trahison des clercs*
E) All of the above

9. Generally speaking, cinema in the Eastern European nations is

A) state subsidized.
B) openly critical of government policy and officialdom.
C) extremely subtle and symbolic in conveying its meanings.
D) not widely patronized due to the high recreational value placed on television.
E) All of the above
F) A and C

___ 10. Which of the following is *not* characteristic of French New Wave technique?

   A) elliptical editing
   B) shaky hand-held cameras
   C) improvisation
   D) location settings
   E) studio-recorded Dolby sound
   F) natural lighting

___ 11. The director who best exemplifies the "Polish school's" romantic pessimism, and who achieved international stature doing so, is

   A) Aleksander Ford.
   B) Jerzy Kawalerowicz.
   C) Andrzej Munk.
   D) Andrzej Wajda.
   E) Georg Stolti.
   F) None of the above

___ 12. Which of the following is *not* an important early New Wave film?

   A) *Breathless*
   B) *Hiroshima, mon amour*
   C) *Les Quatre-cents coups* (*The 400 Blows*)
   D) *The Sorrow and the Pity*
   E) *Jules and Jim*
   F) *Last Year at Marienbad*

___ 13. A country that has not yet produced a distinguishable and artistic cinema?

   A) Albania
   B) the Soviet Union
   C) Yugoslavia
   D) Hungary
   E) Czechoslovakia
   F) All of the above

___ 14. A jump cut is

   A) a cut from one dramatic scene to the next.
   B) a cut between an exterior shot and an interior shot.
   C) a cut made to conceal the movement of an actor from one camera set-up to another.
   D) a cut made to convey narrative information.
   E) None of the above

___ 15. The young cinéastes of the New Wave were reacting against

   A) classical Hollywood editing styles.
   B) the French cinema's "tradition of quality."
   C) self-reflexive cinema.
   D) films which call attention to themselves.
   E) All of the above
   F) A and B

___ 16. Which of the following films screened for this class since the last test was in color?

   A) *Hiroshima, mon amour*
   B) *The Rite of Love and Death*
   C) *Breathless*
   D) *Le Souffle au coeur* (*Murmur of the Heart*)
   E) None of the above

___ 17. The Hungarian cinema's most internationally prominent director is

   A) Zoltán Fábri.
   B) Pál Gábor.
   C) Marta Meszaros.
   D) Petér Grothár.
   E) Miklós Jancsó.
   F) István Gaál.

___ 18. Which of the following directors were predecessors of the French New Wave?

   A) Jacques Tati
   B) Max Ophüls
   C) Robert Bresson
   D) André Bazin
   E) Claude Lévi-Strauss
   F) A, B, C

___ 19. Roman Polanski's career

   A) began in his native Poland.
   B) has been hampered by his flight from the United States.
   C) includes many dark and violent films.
   D) has been characterized by personal tragedy.
   E) All of the above
   F) A and C

___ 20. Which of the following institutions were important in forming the direction of the French New Wave?

A) L'Académie Française
B) the Cinémathéque Française
C) *Cahiers du cinéma*
D) *les trains du grande vitesse*
E) B and C

___ 21. As a film, *Vertigo* is

A) very typical of the fifties.
B) notable for its black-and-white sequences.
C) enclosed and claustrophobic because it was filmed entirely on a sound stage.
D) flawed by its upbeat happy ending.
E) All of the above
F) None of the above

___ 22. All of the following are true of *Breathless* except

A) the hero dies at the end.
B) it is filmed in grainy black-and-white.
C) it contains no allusions or references to other films.
D) Michel is betrayed by his girlfriend.
E) there is a long, naturalistic bedroom scene.

___ 23. The movie title "Shadows of Forgotten Ancestors"

A) means something like "memories from the past" or "archetypes of the collective unconscious."
B) was chosen by Parajanov to signal his doctrinaire Marxism.
C) was changed by the filmmakers from the original "Wild Horses of Fire."
D) alludes to the burial practices of the Gulsuls.
E) A and C

___ 24. *Vertigo* contains

A) a dream sequence.
B) several dizzying reverse tracking-zoom shots.
C) no score, only naturalistic sound.
D) two dance sequences.
E) a shoot-out between Scottie and Gavin Elster.
F) A and B

___ 25. Which of the following is (are) true of Soviet cinema since W.W. II?

A) It flourished under Stalin.
B) There was a revival of sorts during the Khrushchev years, 1954–1965.
C) It is no longer subject to state censorship.
D) Filmmakers are trained at the VGIK and, when graduated, sent out to work in various studios in Russia and the autonomous republics.
E) None of the above
F) B and D

___ 26. In *Vertigo*

A) "Madeleine" dies approximately half-way through the film.
B) Scottie thinks that "Madeleine" is married to his old college friend Gavin Elster.
C) Gavin Elster murders his wife.
D) "Madeleine" and Judy are the same person.
E) All of the above
F) None of the above

___ 27. All of the following are true of *Shadows of Forgotten Ancestors* except

A) Ivan dies very much like his father before him.
B) Ivan ultimately joins Marichka in the afterlife.
C) the final shot in the film shows Ivan sailing down a river on a barge.
D) blood appears at one point to stream across the camera lens.
E) Palagna has an evil union with a sorceror.

___ 28. *Breathless* (1959) was unusual for its era because

A) it contained no jump cuts.
B) it used only studio lighting.
C) its camera movements called attention to themselves.
D) its editing followed the classical Hollywood paradigm.
E) it was budgeted at over 20 million dollars.
F) C and D

___ 29. In *Shadows of Forgotten Ancestors*

A) Ivan pushes Marichka off of a tower.
B) Marichka dies mysteriously by falling from a cliff.
C) Parajanov sets up several sequence shots by establishing point-of-view and then violating it.
D) Ivan finds warmth and happiness with his wife Palagna.
E) None of the above
F) B and C

___ 30. All of the following are true of *Vertigo* except

A) the final shot shows Scottie driving back to San Francisco across the Golden Gate Bridge.
B) it contains themes of voyeurism and sexual obsession.
C) it contains a flashback that resolves the mystery for the audience.
D) there are multiple images of spirals and plunging descents.
E) "Madeleine" supposedly believes herself to be possessed by the spirit of her ancestor, Carlotta Valdez.

III. Essay. *Fifteen points.*

Discuss the difficulties of presenting widescreen films in video formats and describe the three different techniques used to do so, explaining why credits are a special problem.

Film Studies 372
Spring 1990
David A. Cook

Hour Test III

I. Matching. *Two points each.*

___ *Persona*

___ *Kwaidan*

___ *Rashomon*

___ *L'avventura*

___ *Teorèma*

A) Four separate versions of the "truth"; introduced modern Japanese cinema to the West.

B) Search for a mysteriously disappeared character which equates film time with real time.

C) Modern-day parable of Christ's return to earth.

D) Anthology film of Japanese ghost stories.

E) A film about identity transference and media representations of reality.

II. Multiple Choice. *Two and a half points each.*

___ 1. Which of the following directors were members of Japan's second post-war generation?

    A) Masaki Kobayashi
    B) Kon Ichikawa
    C) Dasuke Kagemusha
    D) Keiko Matatubi
    E) None of the above
    F) A and B

___ 2. British "social realism" was

    A) a reaction against an excessively literary and traditionally class-bound cinema.
    B) influenced by both Italian neo-realism and the French New Wave.
    C) concerned with the boredom and world-weariness of the wealthy middle classes.
    D) devoted to redeeming the values of empire in the name of Church and state.
    E) All of the above
    F) A and B

___ 3. The zoom lens

    A) is a lens of fixed focal length.
    B) was not perfected until the '60s.
    C) makes possible such techniques as optical tracking.
    D) is little used by contemporary filmmakers.
    E) All of the above
    F) B and C

___ 4. The Australian film industry

    A) was created by government subsidy and tax incentives in the '70s.
    B) has produced many original and striking new films.
    C) has been plundered by non-Australians making large numbers of films on non-Australian themes.
    D) All of the above
    E) A and B

___ 5. The Indian cinema

    A) has the highest annual output of any in the world.
    B) is intended mainly for domestic audiences.
    C) is dominated artistically by Satyajit Ray and his followers.
    D) is the country's most popular form of mass entertainment.
    E) A and B
    F) All of the above

___ 6. Yasujiro Ozu

A) made films devoted mainly to Japanese family life.
B) was a master of off-screen space.
C) was influenced by Zen aesthetics.
D) was fond of low-angle, eye-level camera shots.
E) B and D
F) All of the above

___ 7. The concept of off-screen space

A) treats the outer edges of the screen like the frame of a painting or photograph.
B) treats the screen as a "window on the world," beyond which there is more of the same spatial reality contained within the screen.
C) allows a director to violate the 180 degree rule.
D) demands that there is never an "empty scene" in a film.
E) All of the above
F) B and C

___ 8. Which of the following best describes the work of Luis Buñuel?

A) surrealist
B) anti-Fascist
C) anti-Catholic
D) anti-bourgeois
E) All of the above
F) None of the above

___ 9. Nagisa Oshima

A) is the most prominent director of the Japanese "New Wave."
B) is a radical, sometimes pornographic, critic of Japanese society.
C) employs the classical techniques of Mizoguchi and Ozu.
D) was an important director of *jidai-geki*.
E) C and D
F) A and B

___ 10. Which of the following directors were associated with the "Second Italian Film Renaissance?"

A) Ermanno Olmi
B) Pier Paolo Pasolini

C) Bernardo Bertolucci
D) Alfredo Fetuccini
E) Giovanni Linguini
F) All of the above
G) A, B, C

___ 11. The Japanese studio system

A) was modeled on the American system.
B) declined during the '60s owing to the introduction of color television.
C) has recently taken to the production of exploitation films.
D) All of the above
E) B and C
F) None of the above

___ 12. The films of Ingmar Bergman

A) have mainly been subsidized by the Swedish state.
B) represent a great body of comic art.
C) often comprise a series of trilogies.
D) are technically as innovative as those of Antonioni and Godard.
E) All of the above
F) A and C

___ 13. Kenji Mizoguchi

A) directed only a handful of feature films.
B) favored montage over *mise-en-scène*.
C) founded the "New Wave" of the '60s.
D) exulted in the values of feudalism and believed that women were inferior to men.
E) All of the above
F) None of the above

___ 14. British "social realism" ended because

A) the government so strongly opposed it.
B) like Italian neorealism, it died of its own success.
C) it couldn't compete with the French New Wave.
D) it was unpopular with American audiences.
E) None of the above

___ 15. Akira Kurosawa is

A) a master of the *samurai* film.

B) the most "Western" of the major Japanese directors.

C) a liberal humanist, devoted to the "life of the mind."

D) All of the above

E) A and B

___ 16. The films of Federico Fellini

A) tend to be visually extravagant.

B) often contain autobiographical elements.

C) are militantly neorealistic.

D) are very traditional in narrative terms.

E) None of the above

F) A and B

___ 17. Which of the following terms best describes the era of cinema which followed the French & Italian revolutions of the '60s?

A) documentary realism

B) Eisensteinian montage

C) subjective involvement and *mise-en-scène*

D) widescreen sequence shot

E) All of the above

F) C and D

___ 18. A *jidai-geki* is

A) a film of contemporary life.

B) a children's film.

C) any film set before the Meiji Restoration.

D) any film set before World War II.

E) None of the above

___ 19. Michelangelo Antonioni

A) began as a neorealist.

B) employs the long take, or sequence shot, to render the duration of real time on the screen.

C) is concerned with the effect of his characters' material environment on their inner lives.

D) has decisively influenced the development of modern widescreen cinema.

E) All of the above

F) None of the above

___ 20. Which of the following things are true of Japanese silent films?

A) They had narrators.

B) They used female impersonators.

C) They were modeled on *kabuki* theater.

D) All of the above

E) None of the above

___ 21. *Teorèma*

A) uses sex as a metaphor for religious ecstasy.

B) is shot entirely in black-and-white.

C) begins with a documentary or newsreel sequence.

D) is about a group of 15th-century cannibals.

E) A and C

___ 22. In *Kwaidan*

A) the aerial photography sequences make up for the film's shoestring budget.

B) the flashforwards are uniformly in black and white.

C) there is a spectacularly staged train collision.

D) the role of the Pope is played by Albert Finney.

E) A and B

F) None of the above

___ 23. In *L'avventura*

A) there are long takes equating screen time with "real time."

B) the woman who disappears on the island reappears near the end of the film.

C) only the middle classes seem capable of achieving true happiness.

D) Roman Catholicism plays a central role.

E) All of the above

F) None of the above

___ 24. All of the following are true of *Persona* except

    A) there are many large close-ups.

    B) there is a prologue consisting of images of suffering.

    C) Elisabet marries Alma's fiancee.

    D) Elisabet's husband appears at the villa.

    E) there are several documentary or newsreel images.

    F) A and B

___ 25. All of the following are true of *Kwaidan* except the following

    A) there are four separate stories.

    B) the film is a *jidai-geki*.

    C) the film is shot primarily in black and white.

    D) there is a stylized battle sequence in one of the segments.

    E) one of the characters is tattooed.

    F) B and D

___ 26. Which of the following films—to the extent seen in class—is (are) in color?

    A) *Saturday Night and Sunday Morning*

    B) *Great Expectations*

    C) *Persona*

    D) *Red Desert*

    E) *The Hidden Fortress*

    F) B and D

    G) A and C

___ 27. Which of the following phrases best describes the characteristics of the telephoto lens?

    A) short focal length, great depth of field

    B) long focal length, great depth of field

    C) short focal length, little depth of field

    D) no focal length, little depth of field

    E) no focal length, no depth of field

    F) None of the above

___ 28. The "adventure" in *L'avventura*

    A) is contained in its epic battle sequence.

    B) occurs entirely in the minds of the three protagonists who "disappear."

    C) is never resolved or satisfactorily explained.

    D) is ruined by the film's happy ending.

    E) occurs after the main characters have died.

___ 29. The "theory" of *Teorèma* is

    A) that Marx and Freud were both wrong.

    B) that religion, in its original form, and sex have something in common.

    C) that the Pope is infallible.

    D) that all middle-class housewives are subconscious nymphomaniacs.

    E) that institutional Catholicism will redeem the world.

    F) None of the above

___ 30. A characteristic of most Australian films, 1975–81, is

    A) razor sharp black-and-white cinematography.

    B) pro-British political perspective.

    C) crystal-clear southern light.

    D) stories adapted from the turn-of-the-century Australian literary revival.

    E) None of the above

    F) C and D

III. Short Essay. Choose A *OR* B—*not* both.
Write essay on ANSWER SHEET. *Fifteen points.*

A. Discuss the characteristic elements of British "social realism" as contained in the in-class excerpt from *Saturday Night and Sunday Morning*. Use specific examples from the film.

B. Briefly describe the evolution of Japanese cinema from its *Kabuki* period through the present. Be sure to describe its major genres and to specify main ways in which it is (or has been) formally different from other national cinemas.

Film Studies 372
Spring 1990
David A. Cook

Final Exam

I. Matching. Match the film with its director. *One point each.*

___ Humberto Solás

___ Arthur Penn

___ Sam Peckinpah

___ Werner Herzog

___ Stanley Kubrick

A) *Aguirre, the Wrath of God*

B) *Lucia*

C) *Bonnie and Clyde*

D) *The Wild Bunch*

E) *2001: A Space Odyssey*

II. Multiple Choice. *Three points each.*

___ 1. A hallmark of Third World cinema is

    A) support for the political status quo.

    B) devotion to slick, commercial production values.

    C) an attempt to replace the "false consciousness" of the audience with a true understanding of its culture and history.

    D) high contrast lighting and studio shooting.

    E) use of American professional actors.

    F) None of the above

___ 2. The "new American audience" of the '60s was

    A) composed of the first generation in history which had grown up watching television.

    B) comparatively better educated and more affluent than its predecessor.

    C) predominantly middle class.

    D) relatively young.

    E) All of the above

    F) None of the above

___ 3. Which of the following was instrumental in the rise of New German Cinema?

    A) the Film Subsidies Bill and the Film Subsidies Board (FFA)

    B) the "Oberhausen manifesto"

    C) Volker Schlöndoroff

    D) Alexander Kluge

    E) All of the above

    F) None of the above

___ 4. Which of the following trends are characteristic of Hollywood in the '70s?

    A) low budget productions concentrating on intimate family dramas

    B) a dramatic inflation in production costs

    C) a return to the production of B-films

    D) the absorption of studios by conglomerates

    E) All of the above

    F) B and D

___ 5. Which part of the Third World led the development of a distinct cinematic style in the early sixties?

    A) Africa

    B) Latin America

    C) Indonesia and Malaysia

    D) China

    E) All of the above

___ 6. The best known and most prolific director of *das neue Kino* was

    A) Werner Stipetic

    B) Bernhard Sinkel

    C) Reinhard Hauff

    D) Wim Wenders

    E) Rainer Werner Fassbinder

___ 7. *2001* is an important film historically owing to

A) its pioneering use of special effects.

B) its treatment of the theme of the relationship between humanity and technology.

C) its contemporary rock music sound track.

D) its polemical endorsement of nuclear war in outer space.

E) All of the above

F) A and B

___ 8. The main European practitioner of "minimal" or "materialist" cinema is

A) Werner Herzog.

B) Peter Lilienthal.

C) Hark Bohm.

D) Jean-Marie Straub.

E) Max Nosferatu.

F) None of the above

___ 9. Many new American filmmakers of the '70s

A) made films which were intensely calculated in terms of effect.

B) were trained in formal academic film programs.

C) had little formal education and became directors through the trade union apprenticeship system.

D) made films of great social and political commitment.

E) None of the above

F) A and B

___ 10. The redevelopment of (West) German cinema after World War II took so long because

A) most of the production equipment had fallen under Soviet control in the Eastern zone.

B) the material and industrial base of the country had been destroyed by Allied bombing.

C) Germans suffered a form of collective "cultural amnesia" about the years of Nazi rule which had sapped the nation of its intellectual and artistic strength.

D) American interests controlled the distribution section of the film industry.

E) All of the above

F) None of the above

___ 11. In the '60s, Hollywood fell behind the rest of the world aesthetically and commercially because

A) it failed to identify the changing character of its audiences.

B) of its extravagant search for a winning box office formula.

C) of the increasing cheapness of its productions.

D) of official government censorship.

E) None of the above

F) A and B

___ 12. A crucial feature of the films of Rainer Fassbinder is

A) widescreen composition.

B) black-and-white photography.

C) light comedy.

D) melodrama.

E) high-contrast lighting.

F) All of the above

___ 13. The violence in *The Wild Bunch*

A) is mild compared to that of *Bonnie and Clyde*.

B) aroused a storm of outraged controversy.

C) is more symbolic in its exaggeration than realistic.

D) was intended by its director to evoke the war in Vietnam.

E) All of the above

F) All but A

___ 14. The most visionary, even mystical, director of *das neue Kino*, who has made films on subjects ranging from power-crazed Spanish conquistadores in Brazil to the collective madness of a small medieval German village, is

A) Bertolt Brecht.

B) Wilhelm Furtwangler.

C) Peter Handke.

D) Werner Herzog.

E) Max Snelling.

F) Ulli Lommel.

___ 15. In the 1980s it seems likely that

A) there will be a return to old-style studio production.
B) cable and satellite delivery systems will have little or no effect on the film industry.
C) the technology of film and video will merge.
D) people will turn away from movies and television in favor of books and radio.
E) None of the above

___ 16. The film *Lucía* is

A) a lavish widescreen epic of the American West.
B) about the condition of women in post-revolutionary Hungary.
C) essentially a musical comedy.
D) shot entirely in color and 3–D (Natural Vision).
E) None of the above

___ 17. *Bonnie and Clyde* was an important film historically because

A) it captured the spirit of the times and appealed to the new American audience.
B) it was one of the first American films to borrow freely from the techniques of the French New Wave.
C) it introduced a new aesthetic of violence into the American cinema.
D) All of the above
E) None of the above

___ 18. Generally speaking, New German Cinema is

A) vastly popular with domestic audiences.
B) subsidized by the state.
C) highly conservative in terms of technique.
D) essentially up-beat and optimistic.
E) All of the above
F) None of the above

___ 19. The success of films like *Easy Rider*

A) caused a return to studio production.
B) inspired the production of numer-

ous big budget epics like *The Sound of Music*.
C) produced a spate of low-budget "youth-culture" movies.
D) led to the creation of the gory "psycho-slasher" genre.
E) None of the above

___ 20. Perhaps the most important and serious director working within the American system today is

A) Sydney Lumet.
B) John Frankenheimer.
C) Brian De Palma.
D) Robert Altman.
E) Paul Schrader.
F) None of the above

___ 21. Graphically stylized ballistic violence entered the American cinema in the late '60s as a reflection of

A) the spiralling divorce rate.
B) the representation of the war in Vietnam on television.
C) the assassination of John F. Kennedy and others.
D) the need to compete with cheaply produced European slasher films.
E) All of the above
F) A and B

___ 22. Which of the following statements about Pasolini's *Teorèma* is (are) not accurate?

A) It is a Marxist allegory whose main purpose is to question the materialistic basis of Western culture.
B) It explores and explodes the bourgeois compulsion to accumulate goods and wealth.
C) It shows the intense disruption of a family and its members as individuals, a disruption wrought by the extreme sexual allure of an extra-terrestrial being.
D) It demonstrates that no amount of skillful camera work and editing can compensate for the fact that Pasolini obviously does not believe that films should be or can be allegorical.
E) A and B

___ 23. As a general result of the divestiture following the Paramount decrees,

A) the minor studios lost their exhibition claims.

B) the major studios lost their distributorships.

C) over a period of time, the minors became majors too.

D) the majors all went bankrupt.

E) All of the above

F) None of the above

___ 24. The main tendency in film industry economics today is for

A) decentralization and demonopolization.

B) the rise of many small independent distributorships.

C) the conglomeration of several media interests into large single corporations.

D) exclusively national ownership of exclusively national companies.

E) film companies to shy away from cable and video distribution.

F) None of the above

___ 25. Judging from the works of Alan Sondheim, the contemporary experimental avant-garde movement in American film

A) uses a lot of sexual, even pornographic, images.

B) is interested mainly in telling stories.

C) represents relatively high-budget entertainment.

D) relies heavily on high-tech computer graphics and state-of-the-art special effects.

E) All of the above

F) None of the above

G) C and D

___ 26. *The Wild Bunch*

A) is extremely typical of its genre.

B) has virtually no precedents in the American cinema.

C) influenced many Westerns and other action-genre films that came after it.

D) is a brutal, exploitative film with no redeeming social value or theme.

E) A and B

F) None of the above

III. Write a short essay-style answer on the following topic. *Seventeen points.*

Discuss the use of violence in *The Wild Bunch*, both in terms of (a) its technical representation and (b) its relationship to the film's theme.

EXTRA CREDIT

For a total of *ten extra points*, discuss the use of (a) sound and (b) special visual effects in *The Last Wave*.

Part IV

Film and Video Rental Sources

A. 16mm Rental Sources

Just a few years ago, this section would have been considerably longer, but the incursions of video into the nontheatrical rental market have caused the disappearance of many rental sources and the shrinking of many others. Some of the surviving companies compete with themselves by offering video versions of their own film titles; others have significantly reduced their inventories, so that some titles no longer exist on 16mm or on tape at all. Companies that continue to maintain relatively large collections of instructionally viable and affordable 16mm films, both foreign and domestic, are Films Incorporated—incorporating the Janus Films Classics Collection and the Samuel Goldwyn Classics Collection—(5547 N. Ravensweed Avenue, Chicago, Il 60640–1199); Swank Motion Pictures (201 S. Jefferson Avenue, St. Louis, MO 63166); New Yorker Films (16 West 61st Street, New York, NY 10023); Kino International (333 West 39th Street, Suite 503, New York, NY 10018); New Lane Cinema (853 Broadway, New York, NY 10003); Prestige Film Company—incorporating Almi Pictures, Inc. and Miramax Films—(18 East 48th Street, Suite 1601, New York, NY 10017); Cinecom Entertainment Group (1250 Broadway, New York, NY 10001); and The Cinema Guild (1697 Broadway, New York, NY 10019).

Relatively large collections of classics and documentaries are maintained by the Circulating Film Library of the Museum of Modern Art (11 West 53rd Street, New York, NY 10019); Ivy Films (165 West 46th Street, New York, NY 10036); and the Rohauer Collection of Alan Twyman Presents (592 S. Grant Avenue, Columbus, OH 43205). Budget rental sources offering usually respectable prints are Budget Films (4590 Santa Monica Boulevard, Los Angeles, CA 90029); Kit Parker Films (1245 Tenth Street, Monterey, CA 93940); Festival Films (2841 Irving Avenue South, Minneapolis, MN 55408); and Em Gee Film Library (6924 Canby Avenue, Suite 103, Reseda, CA 91335).

Specialized collections include East-West Classics—mainly Japanese—(1529 Acton Street, Berkeley, CA 94702); Third World Newsreel (335 West 38th Street, 5th Floor, New York, NY 10018); Zipporah Films—Frederick Wiseman's documentaries—(One Richdale Avenue, Unit #4, Cambridge, MA 02140); the Film Program of the American Federation of the Arts—experimental and avant-garde, foreign and domestic—(41 East 65th Street, New York, NY 10021); Film-Makers' Cooperative—New American Cinema—(175 Lexington Avenue, New York, NY 10016); Women Make Movies, Inc.—feminist media arts—(Suite 212, 225 Lafayette Street, New York, NY 10012); and Canyon Cinema—American experimental cinema—(2325 Third Street, Suite 338, San Francisco, CA 94107).

Any of these distributors will send you a catalogue upon request, usually free of charge, and should be happy to accept your institution's purchase order for rental fees. (It should be noted that inexpensive rentals are available from many university film/video archives, often for a simple amortization fee; this is also true of several cultural services attached to foreign consulates—e.g., the French American Cultural Services and Educational Aid [FACSEA], 972 Fifth Avenue, New York, NY 10021.)

B. Video Rental and Purchase

Prerecorded videocassettes and laser discs offer another source of screening materials, almost always of a higher audio-visual quality than available through telecast, although they are certainly not preferable to 16mm prints except in special applications. Prerecorded videocassettes and laser discs can be purchased from a variety of local sources (including, in many communities, grocery stores, discount chains, and filling stations) and both purchased and/or rented from the video stores that have spread across the land like storefront theaters during the "nickelodeon boom" of this century's first decade. Mom-and-pop operations typically compete with such national chains as Blockbuster Video in most parts of the country, but a shakeout in the marketplace is inevitable, and it should ultimately yield lower prices (indeed, "sell-through" prices on new video titles dropped by approximately 65 percent between 1988 and 1990). In the meantime, there are a number of bargain priced mail order sources for prerecorded foreign and domestic titles, including Facets Multimedia, Inc. (1517 West Fullerton Avenue, Chicago, IL 60614); Evergreen Video (228 West Houston Street, New York, NY 10014); Blackhawk Video (5959 Triumph Street, Commerce, CA 90040–1688);

Pendragon Sales—great deals on Beta-format only—(430 West 54th Street, New York, NY 10019); Filmic Archives (The Cinema Center, Botsford, CT 06404–0386); Video Images (495 Monroe Turn-pike, Monroe, CT 06468); Publishers Central Bureau Video (1 Champion Avenue, Avenet, NJ 07001–2301); Barnes & Noble Video (126 Fifth Avenue, New York, NY 10011); and Discount Books and Video (930 North Main Road, Vine-land, NJ 08360).

Specialized video rental sources include Historic Films—mainly World War II documentaries and propaganda films—(P.O. Box 29035, Chicago, Il 60629); War and Peace Video—Soviet war films, fantasy, and science fiction—(P.O. Box 1732, Bellaire, TX 77402); Tamarelle's International Films, Ltd.—foreign classics, emphasizing French cinema—(110 Cohasset Stage Road, Chico, CA 95926); and Sinister Cinema—grade-B horror, science fiction, and exploitation—(P.O. Box 777, Pacifica, CA 94044).

Videotape rentals are also available from many university film/video archives. Some laser disc purchase sources are Sight and Sound Laser Video Discs (1275 Main Street, Waltham, MA 02154); Ztek Co. (P.O. Box 1968, Lexington, KY 40593); and most valuable for film studies usage, the Voyager Company—Criterion Collection—(2139 Manning Avenue, Los Angeles, CA 90025).

Prerecorded videocassettes are usually dubbed at the slowest speed and sometimes feature impressive letterboxing (the films in the Connoisseur Video [8455 Beverly Boulevard., Suite 302, Los Angeles, CA 90048] Japan collection, for example). Laser discs (LV discs) offer more highly resolved sound and image than tape. Especially impressive are the titles in the Voyager Company's Criterion Collection, which are mastered from the best available 35mm prints. The CAV-format editions in the collection—*King Kong*, *Swing Time*, *The Wizard of Oz*, *Citizen Kane*, *The Magnificent Ambersons*, *Singin' in the Rain*, *Scaramouche*, *High Noon*, *Invasion of the Body Snatchers*, *Lola Montes*, *North by Northwest*, *Lawrence of Arabia*, *8 1/2*, *A Hard Day's Night*, *The Graduate*, *2001: A Space Odyssey*, *Taxi Driver*, *Blade Runner*, etc,—also contain supplemental material (e.g., shooting scripts, screenplays, production stills, storyboards, outtakes, trailers, etc.) and, where appropriate, are carefully letterboxed to preserve their original widescreen ratios. Because of their random access feature, discs are especially valuable for classroom lecture/demonstration. For example, in a course I recently taught on Orson Welles, we were able to study textual variations in *Touch of Evil* by comparing the entire long version in LV search mode with Terry Comito's critical edition of the continuity script (New Brunswick, N.J.: Rutgers University Press, 1985).

C. Other Video Sources

As many film teachers are aware, it is now legal in the United States and Canada to use films taped directly form broadcast and cable channels for private, noncommercial use, which includes instructional use in nonprofit institutions. Theatrical features—and, more recently, made-for-TV movies—have been a mainstay of broadcast network and local station programming for decades, and many teachable films are widely available through those sources. But such films are invariably cut for commercial advertising and otherwise altered to fit predetermined schedules and the Academy-frame shape of the cathode ray tube (see the section on pan-and-scan, frame-cutting, and letterboxing in IM, Chapter 12). More valuable are the uninterrupted films shown (usually) at their full length and occasionally letterboxed by the various subscription cable channels. These include the premium services HBO, Cinemax, The Disney Channel, Showtime, and The Movie Channel; such pay-per-view channels as Viewer's Choice and Request; and non-premium channels like Bravo and American Movie Classics. A category unto itself is the 24-hour commercial satellite network, or "superchannel," TNT (Turner Network Television), which shows about 200 movies per month, most of them vintage titles from the 3,500 film library that Turner acquired in 1986. Half of these are features released by MGM before 1982, while the rest are pre-1948 Warner Bros. and RKO releases, many of them B-films, as well as 6,000 cartoons and short subjects. Of special interest to film historians is the large number of hard to find and never televised silent classics (*Greed* [Von Stroheim, 1924]; *Ben Hur* [Fred Niblo, 1926]; *The Wind* [Victor Seastrom, 1928]) and early talkies (*Hell's Highway* [Roland Brown, 1929];

Dynamite [C.B. DeMille, 1930]; *Wild Boys of the Road* [William Wellman, 1933]). Most remarkable, given his notorious commitment to colorization, are Turner's high standards of restoration for these films, which are telecast from one-inch video masters that have been created from archival-quality original negatives and masters, enabling them to be seen to greater advantage than at any time since their original release. (TNT's films do contain commercial interruptions—often, it seems, the maximum permitted by the FCC—but they are invariably shown at full length.)

Program offerings for these services are listed in local cable guides; excluding pay-per-view, they are also listed in *TV Guide* and local newspapers, together with broadcast programming. American Movie Classics and TNT publish their own monthly program guides by subscription, and there is one national monthly guide to all cable services offering classic films—The Paper Channel (McCrary Research Corporation, P.O. Box 700278, Wabasso, FL 32970), which features articles and notes, a daily annotated schedule, and a dated title index.